HENRIETTA MARIA

*After Elizabeth: The Death of Elizabeth and
the Coming of King James*

*The Sisters Who Would Be Queen: The Tragedy of Mary,
Katherine and Lady Jane Grey*

Tudor: The Family Story

White King: Charles I, Traitor, Murderer, Martyr

HENRIETTA MARIA

Conspirator, Warrior, Phoenix Queen

LEANDA de LISLE

Chatto & Windus
LONDON

1 3 5 7 9 10 8 6 4 2

Chatto & Windus, an imprint of Vintage, is part of the Penguin Random House group of
companies whose addresses can be found at global.penguinrandomhouse.com

Penguin
Random House
UK

First published by Chatto & Windus in 2022

penguin.co.uk/vintage

A CIP catalogue record for this book is available from the British Library

HB ISBN 9781784742966
TPB ISBN 9781784742973

Typeset in 11.75/15.5pt Arno Pro by Jouve (UK), Milton Keynes

Printed and bound in Great Britain by Clays Ltd, Elcograf S.p.A.

The authorised representative in the EEA is Penguin Random House Ireland,
Morrison Chambers, 32 Nassau Street, Dublin D02 YH68

Penguin Random House is committed to a sustainable future
for our business, our readers and our planet. This book is made
from Forest Stewardship Council® certified paper.

For Cosima

Cherchez la femme
Alexandre Dumas

Contents

List of Illustrations

First Plate section

Portrait of Henrietta Maria, Daniel Dumonstier, c. 1625, graphite on paper (Photo: © Harry Brejat 2022. RMN-Grand Palais /Dist. Photo SCALA, Florence)

The Medici Cycle: The Triumph of Juliers, 1 September 1610, Peter Paul Rubens, 1622–25, oil on canvas (Photo: © Bridgeman Images)

The Lady with a Fan, thought to be French courtier Marie de Rohan, Duchess of Chevreuse, Diego Velázquez c. 1640 oil on canvas (Photo: © The Print Collector / Alamy)

Double portrait of George Villiers, Marquess (later Duke) of Buckingham and his wife Katherine Manners, as Venus and Adonis, Anthony van Dyck, c. 1620, oil on canvas (Photo: © CC0 1.0)

Proscenium and standing scene, stage design for the play 'Florimène', Inigo Jones, c. 1635, pen and ink on paper (Photo: © Reproduced by permission of Chatsworth Settlement Trustees / Bridgeman Images)

Gold signet ring, the shoulders cast and enamelled with crowns above an HMR monogram. (Photo: Royal Collection Trust / © Her Majesty Queen Elizabeth II 2022)

Charles I and Henrietta Maria, Daniel Mytens, c. 1630–32, oil on canvas (Photo: Royal Collection Trust / © Her Majesty Queen Elizabeth II 2022 / Bridgeman Images)

Cardinal Richelieu, Philippe de Champaigne, 1640, oil on canvas (Photo: ©Universal History Archive / UIG / Bridgeman Images)

The three eldest children of Charles I, Anthony van Dyck, 1635, oil on canvas (Photo: Royal Collection Trust / © Her Majesty Queen Elizabeth II 2022 / Bridgeman Images)

Somerset House, London, Benjamin Cole and Leonard Knyff, 1755, coloured engraving (Photo: © Look and Learn / Peter Jackson Collection / Bridgeman Images)

Opening Mass of Quarant'ore, 12 March 2013, The London Oratory (Photo: © Courtesy of Charles Cole/London Oratory)

A design for a Quarant'ore, Pietro da Cortona, c. 1632–3, pen and ink with wash over black chalk (Photo: Royal Collection Trust / © Her Majesty Queen Elizabeth II 2022)

Equestrian portrait of Elisabeth de France, wife of Philip IV of Spain, Diego Velázquez, c. 1635, oil on canvas (Photo: © Bridgeman Images)

The French Forces: Louis XIII and Gaston d'Orléans, Abraham Bosse, ca. 1630, etching (Photo: © CC0 1.0/courtesy of The Met/ The Elisha Whittelsey Fund, 1956)

Portrait of Queen Henrietta Maria, Studio of Sir Anthony Van Dyck, ca.1632, oil on canvas (Photo: © Private Collection, courtesy of Philip Mould & Company)

William Davenant, English poet and playwright, title page engraving of Davenant from his collected works, after a portrait by John Greenhill, 1673 (Photo: © Pictorial Press Ltd / Alamy)

William Prynne, Wenceslaus Hollar, English Controversialists c. 1637–1640, etching (Photo: ©CC0 1.0/Courtesy The Wenceslaus Hollar Collection/University of Toronto)

Second Plate Section

Christine Marie of France, Duchess of Savoy as Minerva, Charles Dauphin (Delfino), c. 1630, oil on canvas (Photo: © Album / Alamy)

Thomas Wentworth, 1st Earl of Strafford, studio of Anthony van Dyck, 1640, oil on canvas (Photo: © Fine Art Images / Bridgeman Images)

Lucy Percy, Countess of Carlisle, Anthony van Dyck, c. 1637, oil on canvas (Photo: © Bridgeman Images)

Charles I, Henrietta Maria, their children, and Marie de' Medici, with attendants, in St. James's Palace. Illustration from the book, *Histoire de l'entrée de la Reyne Mère dans la Grande Brètaigne*, by Jean Puget de la Serre, London, 1639 (Photo: ©CC0 1.0/Courtesy of The Met/Harris Brisbane Dick Fund, 1917)

Illustration from *Englands Comfort, and Londons Joy: Expressed in the Royall, Triumphant, and Magnificent Entertainment of our Dread Soveraigne Lord King Charles, at his blessed and safe returne from Scotland*, London, 1641 (Photo: © The British Library Board/Bridgeman Images)

Portrait of Queen Henrietta Maria as St Catherine, Anthony van Dyck, c. 1639, oil on canvas (Photo: © Private Collection, courtesy of Philip Mould & Company)

John Suckling, Anthony van Dyck, c. 1638, oil on canvas (Photo: © GL Archive / Alamy)

Mountjoy Blount, 1st Earl of Newport, Lord George Goring and a Page, Anthony van Dyck, 1635–1640, oil on canvas (Photo: © Petworth House/National Trust Images/Derrick E. Witty)

The departure of queen Henrietta Maria of England from Scheveningen in 1643, Paulus Lesire, 1644, oil on canvas (Photo: © The Picture Art Collection / Alamy)

Religious items being burnt during the English Civil War, 1643. "Crucifixes papistorall bookes in Somerset and Jameses ware burnt and Caphuchin friers sent away." From *True Information of the Beginning and Cause of all our troubles [the Civil War], etc.* [A new edition, continued to January 1648-9, of John Vicars's "Sight of ye Trans-actions of these latter Yeares." With engravings, thought to be by W. Hollar. (Photo: © The British Library Board / Bridgeman Images)

An early photograph of the 36 arch medieval Burton bridge that was replaced in 1863 (Photo: © CC0 1.0)

Statue of Henrietta Maria, St John's College, Oxford, Hubert Le Sueur, c. 1635 (Photo: © PjrStatues / Alamy)

Portrait of Henrietta Maria, Daniel Dumonstier, 1645, graphite on paper (Photo: © Private Collection, courtesy of Philip Mould & Company)

Anne of Austria, Peter Paul Rubens, c. 1622–25, oil on canvas (Photo: © Bridgeman Images)

Detail from An Eyewitness Representation of the Execution of King Charles I in 1649, John Weesop, c. 1649 (Photo: © Bridgeman Images)

Henrietta Maria as Mary Magdalen, Schelte Adamsz Bolswert after Peter Paul Rubens, undated engraving 1596–1659 (Photo: © Courtesy of the Rijksmuseum / CC0 1.0)

Mancini Pearls, earrings given by Louis XIV to Marie Mancini, c. mid-17th century, pearls and diamonds (Photo: © Christie's Images / Bridgeman Images)

Charles II dancing at a ball at court, Hieronymus Janssens, 1660, oil on canvas (Photo: Royal Collection / Royal Collection Trust © Her Majesty Queen Elizabeth II, 2022 / Bridgeman Images)

Detail from Louis XIV and the Royal Family, Jean Nocret, 1670, oil on canvas (Photo: © Photo12/Ann Ronan Picture Library/Alamy)

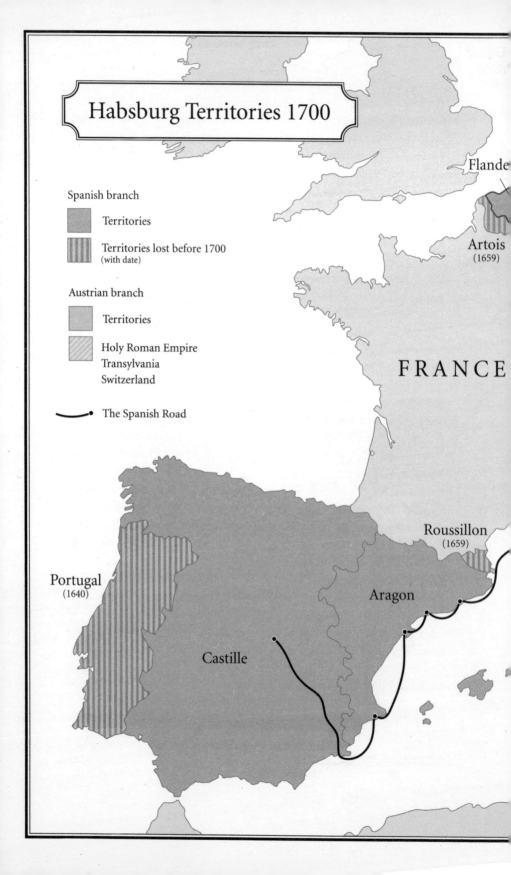

Habsburg Territories 1700

Spanish branch

Territories

Territories lost before 1700
(with date)

Austrian branch

Territories

Holy Roman Empire
Transylvania
Switzerland

The Spanish Road

Flande

Artois
(1659)

FRANCE

Roussillon
(1659)

Portugal
(1640)

Aragon

Castille

United
Provinces
(1648)

POLAND

HOLY ROMAN
EMPIRE
Bohemia

Transylvania

Charolais
(1659)

Switzerland
(1648)

Austria

Hungary

Valtellina
Passes
Mantua

Savoy

Milan

OTTOMAN
EMPIRE

Piedmont

Montferrat

Naples

Sardinia

N

0   100   200 miles

0   200   400 km

Sicily

DESCENDANTS OF FRANCESO I (DE' MEDICI)

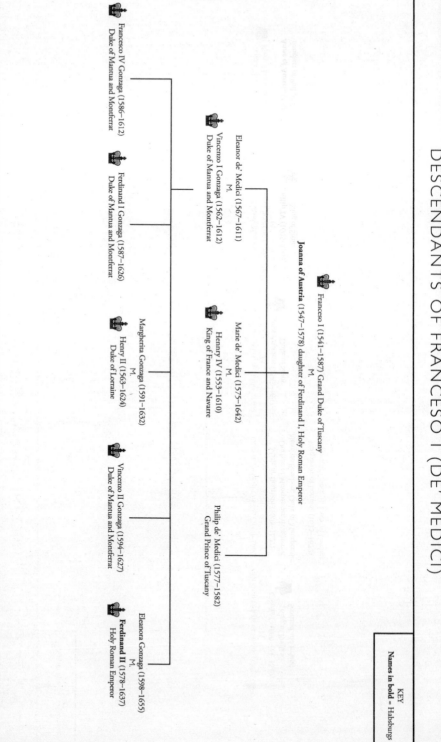

Franceso I (1541–1587) Grand Duke of Tuscany
M.
Joanna of Austria (1547–1578) daughter of Ferdinand I, Holy Roman Emperor

Eleanor de' Medici (1567–1611)
M.
Vincenzo I Gonzaga (1562–1612)
Duke of Mantua and Montferrat

Marie de' Medici (1575–1642)
M.
Henry IV (1553–1610)
King of France and Navarre

Philip de' Medici (1577–1582)
Grand Prince of Tuscany

Francesco IV Gonzaga (1586–1612)
Duke of Mantua and Montferrat

Ferdinand I Gonzaga (1587–1626)
Duke of Mantua and Montferrat

Margherita Gonzaga (1591–1632)
M.
Henry II (1563–1624)
Duke of Loraine

Vincenzo II Gonzaga (1594–1627)
Duke of Mantua and Montferrat

Eleanora Gonzaga (1598–1655)
M.
Ferdinand II (1578–1637)
Holy Roman Emperor

DESCENDANTS OF HENRY IV (BOURBON)

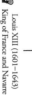

Henry IV 'the Great' (1553–1610)
M.
Marie de' Medici (1575–1642) daughter of Francesco I, Grand Duke of Tuscany

Louis XIII (1601–1643)
King of France and Navarre
M.
Anne of Austria (1601–1666)
daughter of Philip III of Spain

Elisabeth of France
or Isabella of Bourbon (1602–1640)
M.
Philip IV (1605–1665)
King of Spain

Christine of France (1606–1663)
M.
Victor Amadeus (1587–1637)
Duke of Savoy

Gaston, Duke of Orléans (1608–1660)
1ˢᵗ M.
Marie de Bourbon (1605–1627)
Duchess of Montpensier, daughter of
Henri de Bourbon, Duke of Montpensier
2ⁿᵈ M.
Marguerite of Lorraine (1615–1672)
daughter of Francis II, Duke of Lorraine

Henrietta Maria of France (1609–1669)
M.
Charles I (1600 – ex. 1649)
King of England,
Scotland and Ireland

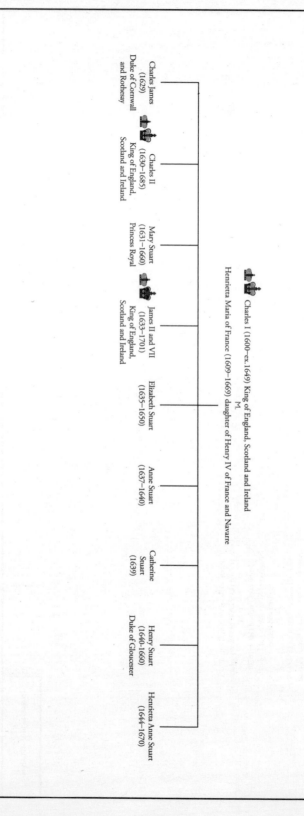

Charles I (1600–ex.1649) King of England, Scotland and Ireland
M.
Henrietta Maria of France (1609–1669) daughter of Henry IV of France and Navarre

Charles James
(1629)
Duke of Cornwall
and Rothesay

Charles II
(1630–1685)
King of England,
Scotland and Ireland

Mary Stuart
(1631–1660)
Princess Royal

James II and VII
(1633–1701)
King of England,
Scotland and Ireland

Elizabeth Stuart
(1635–1650)

Anne Stuart
(1637–1640)

Catherine
Stuart
(1639)

Henry Stuart
(1640–1660)
Duke of Gloucester

Henrietta Anne Stuart
(1644–1670)

DESCENDANTS OF LOUIS XIII (BOURBON)

Louis XIII (1601–1643) King of France and Navarre
M.
Anne of Austria (1601–1666) daughter of Philip III of Spain

Louis XIV (1638–1715)
King of France and Navarre
M.
Maria Theresea of Spain (1638–1683)
daughter of Philip IV, King of Spain

Philippe, Duke of Orléans (1640–1701)
Duke of Anjou later Duke of Orléans 'Monsieur'
1st M.
Henrietta of England (1644–1670)
daughter of King Charles I of England,
Scotland and Ireland
2nd M.
Elizabeth Charlotte of Palatine (1652–1722)
daughter of Charles Louis, Elector Palatine

Preface

Here are some of the things I have often read and heard said about Henrietta Maria: she was 'frivolous', 'extravagant', had bad teeth and skinny arms; she was an adulteress who secretly married Henry Jermyn; she was 'implacably Catholic', she 'made King Charles Catholic' and caused the Civil War; later she proved to be an unloving mother to her son, Henry, Duke of Gloucester, whom she tried to make Catholic because she was a bigot, and finally, at the Restoration she was an irrelevance, nothing more than a shrivelled and miserable old lady. She was, in short, the classic witch-Eve.

Frivolous – so morally weak – Henrietta Maria had been corrupted by the papal Antichrist as Eve was by Satan. Bearing the disfigurement of sin, glimpsed in her bad teeth, she spent extravagantly on clothes and perfumes to project a false beauty which she used to seduce Charles into evil, and so brought sorrow and death to the demi-paradise of England. We not only accept parliamentary propaganda from the past – for example that Henrietta Maria wore the 'breeches' in her marriage – we have promoted new myths to support it. Charles is often described, entirely inaccurately, as a physical weakling and a fop. Nor can she be associated with royalist victory at the Restoration.

This is supported, but only by selective quotation – so we have, for instance, the diarist Samuel Pepys describing Henrietta Maria when he first saw her, still grieving over the death of her son Henry, dressed in black, looking very ordinary, and not his later descriptions of her court as more merry than that of the merry monarch, Charles II.

The familiar tropes connected to Eve predate the Reformation and are still used against women of all kinds. But our attitude to Henrietta Maria is also clearly linked to our confessional history. The term 'popish', much bandied around in the seventeenth century, referred to a form of political and spiritual tyranny which hotter Protestants associated with the Catholic Church, but which was deployed quite broadly, often against anti-Puritans. The Catholic association alone remains embedded in our national psyche.

The belief that Protestantism is responsible for the work ethic that built the empire and the emergence of democracy are amongst our most treasured national myths. The converse of this is that Henrietta Maria, the popish Catholic, must be responsible for Charles's authoritarianism. We have bought into the deep state conspiracy theories of the seventeenth century. We have also forgotten the complexity and contradictions of the past. Many of those who fought hardest for 'liberty' against Charles denied it to the slaves they shipped from Africa to the Americas, and to the Catholic Irish they cleansed from their lands. There was no monopoly on virtue or sin. Henrietta Maria's story would not have interested me, however, had it only allowed me to say what she was not: not frivolous, not a fanatic, not weak, not responsible for the Civil War, not an unloving mother – though I am pleased to do so. The interest is rather in revealing the story of who she was and what drove her.

From popish brat to Phoenix Queen I hope her character will emerge in all its light and shade: capable of great kindness, especially to lowly servants, yet also brutally frank, not least with her husband, she was a warrior and a wit, had an acute sense of the ridiculous but also a spiritual inner life that gave her gravitas. She struggled with the admonition to obey her husband and her son as heads of their households and as kings, yet both loved her, and if she could not win their battles for them, no one could have fought harder to do so.

My biography of Charles I, *White King*, attempted to look at Charles's reign and the Civil War from his point of view. It asked what was the 'divine right of kings' and why did he believe in it? What were his religious beliefs and how did they differ from those of his opponents? Who was the man behind the myths? Why did he behave the way he did? Henrietta Maria was a very important part of his life and I learned that readers enjoyed being introduced to a dynamic queen who was a significant political player. This book tells the story of her life from her point of view.

Although Henrietta spent less than half her life in England with Charles, inevitably there will be a crossover with *White King*. That poses particular difficulties for a writer. I have used a combination of adding new material and trimming old to reshape those sections of the narrative in line with the queen's perspective. Those hoping to meet her great frenemy Lucy Carlisle again will not be disappointed, but there is now a larger cast of women. Indeed another challenge has been the scale of the story. I introduce Henrietta Maria as the Bourbon princess, born into the 'society of princes' who ruled Europe. British history is too often told in isolation, but what happened here cannot be understood without some knowledge of what was happening there. Henrietta Maria's world is one where family quarrels are fought out with armies bringing death to villages, cities, even whole regions. It is also a time when rulers might be killed by their own subjects and co-religionists, if they do not consider them Catholic enough, or Protestant enough.

Henrietta Maria was not yet six months old when her father, the great warrior king Henry IV of France, was assassinated by a Catholic fanatic who disapproved of his alliance with Protestants against the Catholic Habsburgs. She was said to have been very like Henry and she would often invoke her father's name as an example of physical courage and in his friendships to Catholics and Protestants. In this she saw herself very much as his daughter. Her marriage to Charles represented another alliance with a Protestant power aimed against the Catholic

Habsburgs. Her enmity to that dynasty contrasted with the Bourbon–Habsburg friendship her mother wanted.

Yet Henrietta Maria, named after both her parents, was also very much the daughter of Marie de' Medici. As Henry's consort Marie's influence in France set the standard in Europe for centuries to come on court manners, theatre, luxury goods, and the art of haute cuisine – a standard her daughters would seek to follow. As a widow and ruler Marie showed great confidence in what a woman was capable of, exercising power in a man's world, without apology – a crime for which she has yet to be forgiven.

Marie wished to promote the idea that women in the society of princes could play a vital role in the governance of Europe. Kings of this period saw war as the engine of expansion and the valorisation of that process raised them to greatness. Marie de' Medici's vision was a familial rather than a nationalistic model, with women exercising a civilising influence as wives and mothers that would restrain male aggression. She saw glory in peace, and argued women were inspired by love rather than mere ambition.

After Henry IV's death, Marie used her role as regent to push her agenda forward. When Henrietta Maria was almost six she witnessed the double weddings of her sister Elisabeth to the future Philip IV of Spain, and of Philip's sister, Anne of Austria, to her brother Louis XIII. The shared – and contrasting – experiences of Henrietta Maria's sisters and sister-in-law form another important element of this biography, illuminating the complex role of royal consorts.

Although producing male heirs remained a consort's principal task, there was another challenge the sisters faced. Like their mother, they were foreigners in the lands of their husbands. A question mark hung over their fidelity. Would they be true and loyal, or infect their adopted homeland with the influence of the rival dynasty?

Henrietta Maria faced still greater obstacles to success than her sisters. Anglo-French relations were collapsing even before she reached England. It was, furthermore, a kingdom of a different religion and with a king who was an active persecutor of her co-religionists. A year after her arrival in England Henrietta Maria was begging to come home. Yet the mission Marie set for her daughter – to be a good Catholic and a good queen to the Stuart kingdoms while never forgetting her French heritage – was to become a driving force of Henrietta Maria's life. The future was to be an extraordinary adventure as Henrietta Maria fought the odds to overcome many obstacles to achieving her aims. The highs she enjoyed, the friendships she made, the tragedies she suffered, in three countries, in peace and war, are a story of high drama and allow us to see the civil wars from a wider perspective. How far did she succeed in her quest? The verdict of many of her contemporaries in Europe was very different to what we are familiar with in England. She was hailed as a great queen, even a martyr and a saint. Perhaps at the very least, the woman seen as the worst queen consort ever to have worn the crown of the three kingdoms deserves our reconsideration.

Part One

THE SOCIETY OF PRINCES

1

A CARPENTER'S WORKSHOP

SEE THE MIDWIFE. WITH HER CLEFT CHIN, NEATLY PLUCKED eyebrows and bold eyes, Louise Bourgeois liked to dress as the professional she was: starch collars and neat ribbed dresses, adorned with a small, shining crucifix.[1] Today, however, on a summer evening in 1601 she is in a Parisian palace. A group of courtiers are milling about after a dinner hosted by a rich financier. She is watching a small wiry man, with a high nose, standing in the middle of the room. Henry IV, head of the House of Bourbon, is 'retelling feats of valour' – largely his own.[2]

Louise Bourgeois's king had fought and won a civil war that had been fuelled by dynastic uncertainty and religious division. As a Protestant, he had led the forces of the Calvinist minority, the Huguenots. Then, in 1593, Henry had converted to the Catholicism of the French majority. His apocryphal comment on this was that 'Paris is worth a Mass'. The civil wars had ended and under the 1598 Edict of Nantes Henry had granted his former co-religionists widespread privileges as well as religious liberty. Protestants and Catholics could both practise their faith in France. Yet dynastic uncertainty remained. Henry had no legitimate son.

Louise's Europe was not a collection of nation states ruled by politicians, or even individual monarchs. It was a place of regions and dialects dominated by ruling families – a 'society of princes' related by blood and marriage. The greatest of these were the Bourbons in France and their rivals the Habsburgs. Known as the House of Austria, they had long moved beyond their geographical origins and ruled vast swathes of Europe. Indeed, France was surrounded by Habsburg power.

To the west, the head of the senior branch of the Habsburgs, Philip III, ruled Spain and Portugal, along with their worldwide empires. To the south Philip also held the Duchy of Milan, southern Italy and Sicily. To the east and north, Philip's half-sister, Isabella, and her husband, Albert, ruled the Spanish Netherlands which covered most of modern-day Belgium and Luxembourg, as well as parts of what is now northern France and west Germany. These areas would return to the Spanish crown on Isabella's death in 1633.

Meanwhile, the head of the junior branch of the Habsburgs, the Holy Roman Emperor Rudolf II, held the crowns of Hungary and Bohemia as well as the overlordship of more than 200 Protestant and Catholic territories across central Europe. Even the Pope was afraid that the Habsburgs aspired to become a 'universal' monarchy. France, however, had the advantage of a huge and growing population, while Spain's wealth, as well as its people, was being dissipated in holding down territory across the globe. Henry wanted the Bourbons to supersede the Habsburgs as Europe's leading dynasty. War was a means of expansion, but he could not achieve his aim with armies alone.

The society of princes also required fertile queens and efficient midwives. A bride could bring an alliance, a large dowry, further territory – but their most important role was to deliver heirs and secure the future of a dynasty. Consorts who failed in this regard were rejected, their marriages annulled. The most infamous example was that of Henry VIII of England, who made himself head of his own church in 1533, after the Pope had denied him a marriage annulment. Since then, popes had become more understanding of the needs of monarchs who had no sons.

Henry VI's former wife, Margaret, last of the House of Valois, was a brilliant intellect and once a great beauty, but barren. Their marriage was annulled and she had been replaced by Marie de' Medici, a daughter of Francesco I, Grand Duke of Tuscany. 'Whatever else, be pregnant,' Marie's family had warned her when she had left Florence.[3] Less than a year after her wedding she was, and it was Marie that Louise Bourgeois hoped to meet that night.

Louise spotted Marie lounging on a green bed – the colour of fertility. The twenty-six-year-old still wore the stiff Italian fashions of her homeland, which she adorned with a profusion of ornaments and jewels. She had tawny hair and the fair skin of her Habsburg mother, Joanna of Austria, daughter of the Holy Roman Emperor Ferdinand I (who had died in 1564). Marie's natural curves were accentuated by her pregnancy, which was displayed for all to see. Her facial features were small, pretty and as well balanced as those of a well-fed cat.

Henry wanted Marie to use the old midwife who had delivered his many illegitimate children, but on the last occasion his mistress and her baby had died. It had taken days, with the child taken from the mother's womb in pieces, and those around the deathbed had fainted at the horror. Understandably, Marie wanted a different midwife and had asked her ladies-in-waiting to find her someone younger. In Paris most members of the Guild of Midwives did not begin their training until they were past childbearing age, but Louise Bourgeois was still only thirty-eight.

As the dinner guests gossiped and listened to the king's war stories, the midwife was introduced discreetly to the queen's closest friend, a dark-haired young woman with intelligent, deep-set brown eyes called Leonora Concini. She was said to be the daughter of Marie's childhood nurse and a carpenter called Galigai. Yet, despite this modest background and severe bouts of depression, Leonora had been Marie's confidante since they were girls. She had come to France as her hairdresser – a job that allowed them to talk every day – and one at which Leonora excelled.[4] The embarrassment of Leonora's low class had then been solved with a marriage to a Florentine gentleman called Concino Concini.

Leonora questioned Louise thoroughly on her credentials as a midwife. She was impressed and, at 11 p.m., as the royal party began to leave, she spoke to Marie. The queen wanted to see Louise immediately, but without the king finding out; so while Henry and the other senior court figures were settling in their carriages, Marie waited in her sedan chair at the top of the palace steps. Louise saw six pages carrying burning torches and the lackeys who carried the sedan standing by it in their livery of blue, red and white. 'I curtsied to the queen who looked at me for about as long as it takes to say the Our Father.'[5] Nothing was said, but later, at the Louvre, Marie told Henry that she thought this 'somewhat young, tall and lively' woman, recommended to her by Leonora, was exactly the midwife she wanted.

Henry asked for Louise's clients to be interviewed and after this process was compete Louise was summoned to see Marie in the Louvre. Louise was happy to offer the queen the expensive extras her richest clients expected. She would, for example, wrap newly delivered mothers in the freshly flayed skin of a black goat to slow post-partum bleeding. Marie told her she just wanted her to attend to the birth of her children as she would to her poorest clients. 'I was never mistaken in anything I chose,' Marie reassured her, and laughed at Louise's surprise, her cheeks turning scarlet.[6]

On 27 September 1601 Marie de' Medici sat in a birthing chair, face to face with three Princes of the Blood. They were junior descendants of past kings of France and there to witness a state event. Marie tried to keep her dignity by remaining silent as she bore down to deliver her child, while Louise and Henry begged Marie to scream, worried that otherwise her throat would swell. Then, at last, the baby was born. Louise announced it was a boy and tears 'as big as peas' rolled down Henry's face. This was the first dauphin – that is, the undisputed heir of a French king – to be born in eighty years, he said. Marie fainted and she was still lying on the floor when the king ushered in 200 courtiers, to celebrate. 'Don't be angry,' Henry told the horrified midwife, 'this child belongs to everyone.'[7]

The dauphin was named Louis, after the royal saint, Louis IX. Two daughters followed, Elisabeth in 1602 and Christine in 1606. In April 1607, Marie had another son, who died before his christening. A third, Gaston, was born in 1608, prompting an overexcited valet to kiss the first lady of the bedchamber 'so heartily . . . that she was left with only one tooth'. Louise Bourgeois was also embraced, by the Treasurer of France no less, and 'as tightly as a mouse would hold a piece of lard'. [8] The king rewarded Louise with a special cap granted only to highly favoured royal servants: a piece of oblong cloth, folded simply in two, pinned on her upswept hair. No other midwife in France had ever been allowed to wear one. Louise, however, wanted wealth as well as honour. Her husband, although a surgeon, had never earned enough to support his family. She was the principal breadwinner and was determined to demand the maximum salary for her work.

When Marie became pregnant again in 1609, Louise asked her for an annual stipend of 600 ecus. Marie agreed, but Henry had to make the final decision – and so Louise went to the Louvre to see the king. The main royal residence in the winter, the Louvre was a collection of buildings of different periods and styles. The north and east wings, used for government business, were the oldest and remained Gothic in appearance. The western and southern wings were in the modern Renaissance style. These were connected by the beautiful four-storey Pavilion of the King.

In 1601, when Louise had had her first official meeting with Marie de' Medici, the Louvre had still showed the depredations of the years of war. Marie described it as 'half ruined, half built'. Now around 1,500 servants waited on Henry in magnificent rooms laid out by Marie in the Pavilion and it was here, in an apartment facing the river Seine, that Louise Bourgeois had her appointment.

The midwife knew her demand for 600 ecus was extremely steep, but looking after the queen during her confinement made her unavailable to other clients for months at a time. Henry told Louise she could have 300 ecus a year, but that she would receive a bonus of 500 for any boy she delivered, and 300 if the baby was a girl. 'More must be given for sons than for daughters,' Henry reminded her.

Louise knew she had done well, even if she had not got everything she wanted. Her salary now amounted to nine times the salary of the midwives in Paris's main hospital, the Hotel Dieu – and she hoped she was about to earn her bonus by delivering another boy.[9] Instead this determined professional was the first face that Henrietta Maria would ever see.

A large room was required for the theatre of a royal birth. It had to accommodate not only the courtiers that would come to see the queen as soon as the baby was born, but also the furniture. This included a state bed of red velvet embroidered with gold, and a grand pavilion that stretched out like a tent in four directions, with thick ropes. There was a 'bed of travail', where the queen would begin her labour, and a 'chair of travail' where she would deliver her baby. These too were covered in red velvet and had their own canopies – symbols of royal authority.

The most suitable room in Marie de' Medici's apartment was occupied by a carpenter she employed to mass-produce seraphic rosaries.[10] They were popular in Italy and meant a great deal to Marie. Beads marked seven decades of prayers, with each decade dedicated to one of the Seven Joys in the life of Mary, the mother of God. In Lent they were dedicated to the Seven Sorrows. It was after Mary – the redeemed Eve – that Marie had been named, and she was proud of it.

According to the Old Testament myth, Eve, the first woman, had been created from Adam's rib to be his companion, but had proved weak, ambitious and lustful. She was corrupted by the Serpent – the most phallic of beasts – and rebelled against God. She then seduced Adam into following her example and so brought about the Fall, when disease and death entered the world. Men claimed all the daughters of Eve shared her vices. In the words of a leading French lawyer, women were by nature 'imbecilic, inconstant, foolish, savage, ambitious, and deceitful'.[11]

Yet Eve was redeemed in the New Testament story of the Virgin Mary. The first of the Seven Joys celebrated in the seraphic rosary is the Annunciation, when the angel Gabriel tells Mary she is to be the Mother of God. Where Eve brought death Mary will bring eternal life through her son. The last of the Seven Joys is the Assumption when, at the end of Mary's time on earth, God calls her to Him and she is crowned as Queen of Heaven. The story gave women a place of honour, even of power. Eva (Eve) was turned to 'Ave': the salute of the angel Gabriel to Mary.

The room was cleared of the carpentry tools and furnished for the royal birth. An array of the holy relics of St Margaret of Antioch, patron saint of mothers in childbirth, were laid out, including the saint's girdle, which Marie would place on her belly.[12] At five in the evening on 25 November 1609, Marie went into labour. As her ladies-in-waiting left the room Marie handed each of them a newly turned rosary. A few close friends remained, as well as a number of men.

The eight-year-old dauphin, a thickset boy who closely resembled his mother, had been desperate to witness the birth, but Henry had forbidden it. He had, though, allowed his eldest illegitimate son, the fifteen-year-old César, Duke of Vendôme, to do so. The midwife also remembered the monks who knelt in the room praying, their rhythmic chanting of the rosary a pulse of sound: 'Ave Maria, full of grace, the Lord is with thee . . .'

Marie's labour processed rapidly and at 10.30 that night, Henrietta Maria was born. The dauphin was allowed to see his sister straight away. He held her tiny hand, shouting out that she had squeezed his back and that she was laughing at him.[13] His sister was to be named after both of their parents, Henry and Marie – or Maria in Italian.[14] The celebrations for a third daughter were muted. There was no wild kissing and Louise Bourgeois had to accept the lower bonus of 300 ecus. Henrietta Maria's godfather, the papal nuncio Maffeo Barberini, did, however, regard her birth as significant. The time would come, he prophesied, 'when this little princess would be a great queen.'[15]

THE WRONG RELIGION

HENRY FELT UNEASY WHEN HE WOKE ON THE MORNING OF Friday 14 May 1610. He asked for the six-month-old Henrietta Maria to be brought to him along with her two-year-old brother, Gaston, 'to divert his thoughts.'[1] He enjoyed playing with his children, and Henrietta Maria, with her large, laughing mouth, looked just like him, although his own was disfigured by a scar. It had been made by a Catholic fanatic in 1594, who had been aiming for Henry's throat. There had been twenty-three such attempts on his life and he wasn't the only monarch to face such dangers.

After the Reformation a theory had developed that rulers drew their authority from the people, who therefore had the right to depose, or even kill, those of the 'wrong' religion. But what was the 'wrong' religion? For Catholics it was Protestantism, and for Protestants – it was complicated. As the rivalry between the Catholic Bourbons and the Catholic Habsburgs suggested, Catholics were not always on the same side, but their differences had more to do with power politics than faith. They shared the same fundamental beliefs, while Protestants might regard a different brand of Protestant as a heretic or an idolator.

A defining difference between Martin Luther – godfather of the Reformation – and his later rival John Calvin, concerned the Eucharist service. For Catholics the Mass tears away the curtain of time to the very moment of Christ's crucifixion. It is a sacrifice and as such requires a priest and an altar. When the priest consecrates the bread and wine they are immediately substituted with God's body and blood. Luther believed God is present in the Eucharist, although not in every element, while for Calvin Christ was not physically present. For many Lutherans, Calvinists were heretics. For many Calvinists, Lutherans were idolators.

In the Europe of 1610 the kingdoms of Sweden and Denmark were Lutheran. The English and Scottish tradition sprang from Reform Protestantism of which John Calvin was part. The Church of England had, however, never embraced full-blooded Calvinism, and had kept the old Catholic structure of an episcopate, that is government by bishops. The Scottish Kirk, or Church, had a more advanced Calvinism, but their king, James Stuart, although a firm Calvinist, saw bishops as an essential prop of royal rule, as well as ordained by God and dating back to the earliest Christian Church.

James had insisted bishops work alongside the Kirk's Calvinist councils, known as presbyteries, and had outlined his arguments in tracts arguing that God had granted kings a divine right to rule. They were the final human arbiter in their kingdom on what the right religion was, and if a king was wrong, then it was for God alone to punish him. These claims hadn't prevented a kidnap attempt against him in Scotland in 1600, backed by anti-episcopal Presbyterians. Nor had it stopped the Gunpowder Plot of 1605, in which English Catholics had hoped to blow him up in Parliament.

As for Henry Bourbon – he was an apostate to many Protestants while a great number of Catholics did not believe his conversion was genuine. Fortune-tellers regularly assured Henry of his doom. There were said to have been new 'portents' of his murder that very day, but Henry had other concerns. He was preparing to lead a war and had an army of 22,000 ready to deploy against his Habsburg rivals. Several strategically important territories on the Rhine had become the focus of a disputed inheritance. Henry was supporting pro-French claimants. The fact they were Protestant was problematic, but the Pope, anxious to avoid absolute Habsburg hegemony, accepted his argument that this was a dynastic and not a religious matter.[2]

Henry planned to leave Paris for his army in northern France a few days later. Marie de' Medici was to act as regent in his absence. All his children were staying in the Louvre for important ceremonies he had set in place to associate her with his royal authority. The first, and most significant, ceremony was Marie's coronation which had taken place in the Basilica of Saint-Denis the previous day. Henry thought Marie had never looked so beautiful. She had cleverly updated the archaic coronation costume of the past and dressed in a fashionable, bejewelled gown with a twenty-six-foot blue velvet train, embroidered with fleur-de-lys.

Marie's coronation was to be followed by a formal 'entry' to Paris. Henry left the Louvre at 3.45 p.m. to inspect the preparations. Fifteen vast, painted wood structures had been built across the city, depicting Marie as a supportive wife and the mother of princes. It was considered unnatural – and therefore evil – for a woman to rule, but Marie's love as a wife and mother permitted her to do so in Henry's name.[3] As the royal carriage passed through the long archway linking the inner and outer courtyards of the Louvre, a large man with striking red hair saw Henry had pulled back the heavy leather curtain – glass was not used for another two decades. The king was clearly visible.

The man followed the carriage which jolted down streets packed with traffic and rutted with mud and filth, while Henry discussed his war plans with three companions. The man's name was Jean-François Ravaillac. He was thirty-one and had lived through the civil wars, when the Huguenots had desecrated Catholic churches in his home town of Angoulême and had lynched their clergymen. It angered him that Henry was about to make war against the Habsburgs in what Ravaillac believed was a Protestant cause. Like the man who had tried to kill Henry in 1594, he didn't believe Henry was a true Catholic.

In the rue de la Ferronnerie, two wagons, one loaded with hay, another with barrels of wine, blocked the king's path. As his driver pulled to the left, the carriage lurched, then tipped in a low ditch. One of Henry's companions was reading out a dispatch to Henry as Ravaillac climbed, unnoticed, up onto the carriage's raised right wheel. He drew a knife and, bracing himself against a spoke, he struck at Henry three times. Twice he hit Henry's chest. The third blow caught the sleeve of one of the king's companions, as he belatedly raised his arm to defend the king. 'I am wounded,' Henry said, 'it is nothing.' Already, however, he was sinking into unconsciousness, blood gushing from his mouth.

The first moment Marie realised anything was amiss was when she heard the noise of panic and men running in the Louvre. She asked one of her attendants to discover if anything had happened to the dauphin (after all, Henry had left the palace). The woman returned with the news that the king had been injured. Marie dashed to see him. Henry lay on a bed in his dressing room with his doublet open and his exposed shirt soaked in blood. It was evident he was dead. As she staggered in shock, her ladies reached to hold her up.

A witness arriving at the palace shortly afterwards described a scene that 'beggars description. The whole court, shocked and stunned with grief, stood silent and motionless as statues.' The queen was in her chamber, 'very distressed'. Louis was with her, along with a number of princes and lords, 'tears running down their cheeks'.[4]

As the news spread, shops shut and houses were barricaded, while aristocrats galloped through the streets with swords drawn. Law and authority in France had died with Henry. It was a matter of urgency to impose recognition of a new government. Louis was eight years old and weakness at the top would attract predators. As the Old Testament adage ran: 'Woe to the O land where thy king is a child.'[5] Henry's leading adult male royal relatives, the Prince of Condé and the Count of Soissons, were out of Paris. Marie could have waited for them to return and form a government. She did not.

Marie intended to seize power while framing her actions in the context of the permitted feminine roles of wife and mother described in the stations set up for her Grand Entry. Eve was condemned as ambitious for ruling Adam – the first man. Yet what of the Virgin Mary, the second Eve? The thirteenth-century philosopher and theologian Bonaventure, who was associated with the promotion of the seraphic rosary, claimed that God would deny Mary nothing in heaven for she had denied him nothing on earth. Mary held power, so, Marie believed, she could also.

Within two hours Marie had secured recognition from the high court of the Parliament of Paris that she was regent for her son. The following day there was to be a formal ceremony to confirm her role. She was anxious that it also consolidate her right to act with full administrative and guardianship powers. To achieve this Marie needed to win the support of Parliament's delegates. She had been trained by the finest actors in Italy – the best in Europe – in how to move and speak in court theatricals. She planned to project a powerful image of a grieving widow to whom Henry had entrusted his legacy and their son.

When the ceremony opened Marie was standing on Louis's right under a canopied throne. She was dressed in black: henceforth she would almost always dress in black. It associated her with Henry as his widow. This was power dressing. She lifted her veil, to reveal a face etched with misery. The delegates had expected Louis to speak first, but it was Marie who did so, making clear her role as regent was not to be a passive one.

Marie expressed her hope they would respect the young king and asked, as a wretched widow, for their help and support. In her care he would always listen to their good advice, she promised. Periodically she paused to sob. Finally, she burst into tears and descended the platform to leave.[6] It was a tour de force. The regency of Marie de' Medici had begun.

Ravaillac had not attempted to evade arrest and was tortured to discover his motives and accomplices.[7] Links were sought to the so-called devots (literally 'the devout') who disapproved of alliances with heretics such as Henry had made. It transpired, however, that Ravaillac was simply a mentally ill man, who had been vulnerable to the more extreme language used by those who had attacked Henry's foreign policy.[8] It is the kind of story we still see repeated today.

The execution took place on 27 May, in the Place de Grève where Ravaillac was tortured again before being slowly torn apart by horses.[9] Even this didn't satisfy the crowd. The remnants of flesh and bone were stamped on by the Parisians, stabbed at and eaten, then a bonfire was lit beneath Marie's windows in the Louvre to burn the scraps.

Nine days later Henrietta Maria was carried in the lower hall where her father's body lay for the ritual sprinkling with holy water. Louis's younger brothers wept bitterly.[10] Henry was buried at Saint-Denis where Marie had so recently been crowned on 1 July.[11]

Marie would have no more children and, as an act of kindness to the midwife Louise Bourgeois, who had lost her main income with Henry's death, Leonora Concini gave her one of Louis's cloak bags. It was a gift for her son who was delighted to own something that had belonged to the new Louis XIII. Henrietta Maria took part in her brother's coronation in Reims Cathedral on 17 October 1610.[12] Louis found it hard to play the grave part allocated to him in the ceremony. He was so horrified to be kissed by the leading noblemen that he wiped his face and, when he was led to the altar, he had malicious fun trying to catch a nobleman's train with his foot – a reminder of just how young he was.[13]

While Louis remained with Marie de' Medici, Henrietta Maria and her other siblings were returned to the royal nursery at Château Vieux in Saint-Germain-en-Laye. Set on a hill at the edge of a forest, a two-hour coach ride from Paris, Saint-Germain was a demi-paradise of terraced gardens with flower beds planted, 'like a knot of divers ribbons most pleasing and most rare', of grottos and elaborate fountains.[14] Here she spent the next few years in the care of a distant cousin of her father, Madame de Monglat. Henrietta Maria called her Maman Ga, and her daughter, Madame St George, was her Mamie.[15] Henrietta Maria's actual mummy now had a kingdom to rule and considerable dangers to face.

There was civil unrest, especially in the south, where Catholics and Protestants lived in close proximity. Meanwhile, the leading Prince of the Blood, the twenty-one-year-old Henry Condé, claimed that as Louis's senior adult male relative, it was his rightful place to act as protector of the king. Marie deployed all the expertise of the Medici in propaganda to counter his arguments. She commissioned Frans Pourbus the Younger to produce a new kind of portrait for a Queen of France. It showed her wearing her coronation robes, decked in royal symbols. Pamphlets were mass-produced advertising Louis's divine status as king, often with out-sized images of Marie at his side.

Marie used the fashionable trope of the 'strong woman' to explain her exceptional role. These were women who, through strength of character, overcame the violent sexual urges to which women were subject and allowed Marie to extend the ordinary female virtue of caring for her children, to caring for the whole of society.[16] Marie did not, however, forget her own children who looked forward passionately, if also anxiously, to her visits. She was a formidable parent who was proud of the quelling power of her gaze, at whomsoever it was directed, and her children not least.

Marie had not known a mother herself. Joanna of Austria had died when Marie was only three, and, as she commented to Louis, Marie and her son were alike in having 'a natural dryness'.[17] Yet she was not uncaring. Marie insisted she was kept informed of everything about her children, 'even in their private pastimes', and fussed over their health. When Henrietta Maria developed a fever in October 1611, Marie ordered that her daughter 'lack nothing that might afford any remedy or solace in her complaint' and sent a physician to ensure her instructions were carried out.[18] The following month her four-year-old second son fell seriously ill. Marie spent days at his bedside, tending her little boy. Sadly, just over a week short of Henrietta Maria's second birthday, he died, his life marked simply as that of 'N. Duc d'Orleans': N standing for 'non nomme', that is, 'unnamed'.[19]

It says something of Marie that she defended the doctors who had cared for her lost son against criticism, while being in no way compla-cent. Specifically, she pursued the additional services of a Portuguese

Jewish doctor called Elijah Montalto. Five years earlier, in 1606, he had treated Marie's friend Leonora for depressive episodes in which she would weep and shriek with such force witnesses feared she would choke. Montalto's prescription was calm, 'a few ordinary physicks', meditative prayer and some morale-boosting almsgiving.[20] This worked well, but Henry, to emphasise his piety, had refused to have a Jew at court and so Montalto had left to work in Florence. Marie persuaded him to return, promising his family the freedom to practise their faith.[21]

Montalto attended on the royal children in the same down-to-earth manner as he had Leonora. In one surviving letter Montalto sets the queen's mind 'entirely at rest' that, while her second daughter Christine was suffering a 'slight irregularity of the pulse', it was nothing to be worried about and he had ordered that all medicines given to her following a tummy upset should be ceased.[22] This was no small thing during a period when doctors liked to be seen to earn their keep, prescribing medication and even performing surgery with very little idea what they doing. Poor Louis had been a victim of just such overtreatment. When he was two days old, panic had set in that his sucking reflex wasn't strong enough. Cuts were made in his mouth that had left him with a lolling tongue and a severe stammer. He barely spoke.

Henrietta Maria saw Louis at ceremonies like those at Easter and other holy days, when he was brought out to heal the sick: a reminder that he was God's anointed. Dressed in purest white he would touch upwards of 900 scrofulous subjects, stumbling over the phrase, 'The king touches you: God heals you.'[23] He was much happier visiting his siblings at Saint-Germain where they would have supper, play cards and enjoy cooking. Louis's speciality was omelettes.

In January 1612, Henrietta Maria's eldest sister, the nine-year-old Elisabeth, moved out of Saint-Germain to join Louis in the adult world of the Louvre. After Henry had been killed, the disputed provinces in the Rhineland had been divided up amongst the German princes, so avoiding the Habsburg domination over them that he had feared. Marie had seized the opportunity to follow a peace policy and was now to announce a double marriage alliance. Elisabeth – described as 'pretty as an angel' – was to be betrothed to the six-year-old heir to Philip III of Spain, the future Philip IV. The ten-year-old Louis would marry the Infanta Ana, later remembered as Anne of Austria.

Marie's vision for France's future in Europe was familial rather than nationalistic. Women would exercise a civilising influence within the society of princes, using their roles as wives and mothers to restrain male aggression. She claimed her actions built on Henry's legacy in ending the civil wars in France, by extending it across the continent. The leading dynasties would be bound by faith and blood, while France's domination would be cultural rather than militaristic.

The betrothals were celebrated in three days of court entertainments in Paris that would set the standard in Europe for decades to come. On one day a crowd of 10,000 gathered in the Place Royale to see a procession of princes on horses wrapped in cloth of silver and gold, of elephants, and mocked-up dragons that seemed to fly by themselves. At the centre of the parade was a pedestal supporting representations of the monarchies of France and Spain around which little boys, dressed as cupids, threw flowers and trampled on military weapons.[24] The day ended with a sham fortress bursting into flames while 2,000 rockets were sent into the sky, illuminating the night with the letters M for Marie and L for Louis. Modesty was not amongst her greatest virtues.

That June Henrietta Maria saw Elisabeth wearing strange new clothes – a stiff conical Spanish court dress with a closed neck ruff designed to restrict her movement and breathing. They were a gift from Philip III's half-sister, Isabella, Governess of the Netherlands. It marked a hope for change of allegiance. Marie too had changed costume after the birth of Louis, from Italian clothing to French. When Elisabeth married she would be expected by the Spanish to give up the gaiety encouraged in women at the French court, and which was represented in their more free-moving clothes. Instead, she would take on the character of a Spanish royal consort and use the slow, almost imperceptible gestures that their court etiquette demanded.

Elisabeth wore her new dress in August 1612 at the signing of the wedding contract, and the Spanish diplomats reported she looked 'very beautiful'.[25] It must have seemed fun for a little girl to dress up in her costume, like play-acting in fancy dress. Yet it reflected a challenge. Consorts like Elisabeth were valuable gifts, offered by one dynasty to another as future mothers of sons, but for the recipients these outsiders were also objects of suspicion. Concerns about where their true loyalties lay were often reflected in accusations of adultery.

The power to change identities, as Elisabeth would from French to Spanish, was also a power held by witches. And witchcraft was another crime levelled against them.[26] The actual marriage between Elisabeth and Philip was, however, years away and seemed to be nothing more than a distant adventure.

THE WITCH'S SPELL

HENRIETTA MARIA WAS GROWING UP FIERCE AND SELF-WILLED. In one of her earliest surviving letters she apologises to her governess for a 'little sulky fit'. She was sorry for it but, she admitted, 'I cannot be right all of a sudden.' She could only promise Maman Ga that 'I will do all I can to content you; meantime, I beg you will no longer be angry with me.'[1] Marie de' Medici was determined to channel her passionate temperament to good. She kept a close eye on her, writing letters to 'My daughter Henrietta' praising her for doing 'the little exercises' her 'good mother' had asked of her while also offering assurances of her 'immeasurably natural affection'.[2]

The education Marie prescribed was light on academics – Marie had never even learned how to write French properly. The focus was instead courtly and religious, highly influenced by the French notion of '*honnêteté*', a religious fashion that invested women with the Neoplatonic qualities of Beauty, Virtue and Love, and which could be used to improve relations between the sexes and more widely in society. Where in the old tradition of the culture of courtly love, women were static objects of desire, it offered a more active role, and there was another fashion that Henrietta Maria would absorb and that drew from *honnêteté*: a style of thought and expression known as '*préciosité*' which promoted a culture of refinement and wit over macho posturing and thuggery.

As a royal princess Henrietta Maria was expected not only to participate as a member of a cultural elite, she was also expected to perform on
the great stage of national life. To help her, professional Italian actors of
the kind who had trained Marie taught her how to move, sing and
deliver speeches in court theatricals. Marie would often supervise her
children's rehearsals, checking that they knew their lines. It was not
unusual for the girls to perform as Amazonian heroines, even to take
male parts, and they were encouraged to act as producers as well as per-
formers. In time they would understand that plays, ballets and masques
were a useful means of placing and insinuating political messages in the
public consciousness.

Marie also addressed Henrietta Maria's spiritual development. Most
strikingly she introduced her to a powerful female contribution to the
'devot' movement. The decades of civil war had left the French Catholic
Church in a pitiable state, but an educational renewal was now going
hand in hand with a vigorous missionary effort. This was spearheaded
by the devots who were dedicated to regaining ground lost to Protestantism, and the movement had inspired an explosion of new religious
houses for women around Paris. The first of these convents had been
contemplative orders where the nuns lived simple lives growing their
own food, studying and praying. The latest incorporated schools and
programmes for religious retreat in which laywomen were invited into
their secluded world.

Court satires mocked the idea of ladies taking spiritual direction from
other women, but Marie de' Medici played a vital role in encouraging
the fashion, retreating with her daughters to her favourite convents during major feasts and fasts.[3] Many women enjoyed escaping the strains of
a male-dominated society to a female world. Time spent in meditation
and reflection also seems to have helped to bolster the confidence that
allowed Marie to thrive on power politics, from which women were supposed to be excluded.

Although the regency came to a formal end in 1614 when Louis
reached his majority, aged thirteen, Marie continued to rule at the

king's 'pleasure'. Louis was an often sullen teenager, who enjoyed practical and outdoor activities: building miniature forts, or going hunting.
He may not have struck his mother as very intelligent. There were many
powerful men who desired to have the ear of the king. Marie kept them
at bay, surrounding Louis with persons of 'mediocre capacity and little
spirit' in order to protect her position. His favourite was an easy-going,
middle-aged minor nobleman called Charles d'Albert who looked after
his collection of larks and finches. There were, however, other threats.

In the summer of 1615, France was in rebellion. Henry, Prince of
Condé, and other anti-Habsburg grandees believed the planned Franco-
Spanish marriages were against French interests. Condé argued Marie
was being led astray by her advisors and in particular Leonora's husband,
Concino Concini. The fact he was Italian didn't help and there were
rumours that Concini and Marie were having an affair. This damaged
Marie's claims to be the exceptional 'strong woman' France needed.

As the wedding dates approached, Marie deployed an army of 10,000
infantry and 15,000 cavalry to contain the northern rebels. A further
army of 3,000 foot and 1,000 horse accompanied the royal party to Bordeaux where the marriages of Louis to Spanish Infanta Anne of Austria,
and Elisabeth to the Infante Philip of Austria were due to take place. The
future Generalissima, Henrietta Maria, was only five when she rode with
an army for the first time.

The Huguenots in the south-west through which the family passed
were threatening to join Condé and there were stories of atrocities in
rebel-held areas, but the royal family arrived safely at their destination on
7 October 1615.[4] Elisabeth was married in a proxy ceremony eleven days
later. Marie gave her eldest daughter a farewell letter outlining the mission
she wished her daughter to achieve. As the wife of the future Philip IV
Elisabeth was to help maintain peace between Europe's two greatest
dynasties and good relations between the brothers-in-law. It was a grand
project, but cold comfort. At the exchange ceremony Elisabeth and Louis
had sobbed and clung to each other until the Spanish ambassador broke
up the scene demanding of Elisabeth, 'Come away, Princess of Spain!'

Elisabeth was horrified to be losing her family and Louis was distraught at bidding farewell to his closest childhood companion. Elisabeth left for the Spanish frontier on 21 October 1615. Louis's wedding took place just over a month later, on Henrietta Maria's sixth birthday, 25 November, at the Cathedral of Saint-André. The fourteen-year-old bride and groom looked very alike, and Louis may have seen in Anne a family resemblance to Elisabeth. They were, after all, cousins. The bride and groom smiled at each other during the ceremony – but there were no smiles later when the time came to consummate the marriage.

In matters of sex Louis was a damaged boy and in this his father bears a good portion of the blame. As is often the case with successful men, his priapism has been admired, seen as a reflection of his virility, and as part of the same human warmth he showed in playing with his children. The reality is that it had a seamy side. As Henry had grown older, so he had developed a taste for very young girls. Condé's wife had been fourteen when Henry fell 'in love' with her. Henry was, by then, already a father to Louis, and perhaps he saw in the boy his own mortality and fading potency. He obsessed over Louis's ability to sire a future dauphin and so much attention was paid to Louis's penis that, aged three, the confused child would offer his genitals to be kissed instead of his hand.

After Elisabeth was born Henry had used her to further Louis's sexual education, pointing out differences in their anatomy, encouraging them to play bride and groom. Louis was disturbed by the fact she had no precious penis. His father was constantly boasting about his own, even showing off his erect member.[5]

Louis would, in later life, be attracted to both men and women, but sex never seems to have been a source of much pleasure for him. With Anne of Austria his deepest anxieties were at their most evident. Stories circulated that Louis had pissed on Anne instead of inseminating her. Whatever had really happened, Louis would be unable to recover his nerve and perform his kingly duty for a further four years. He would not even share a meal with his wife for the next six months. A witness recalled seeing the unhappy Anne sitting alone in the Louvre on a cushion, in the Spanish manner. She wore a green dress embroidered in silver and gold with a closed ruff, and long trailing sleeves fastened with great diamonds serving as buttons. A green cap, matching the dress, was fixed with a black heron feather that enhanced her golden, curled hair.[6]

Anne shared Henrietta Maria's natural gaiety and warmth, but Henrietta Maria resented the sister-in-law who had replaced her actual sister. Marie encouraged Henrietta Maria in 'those little malicious things which are great ills to those who receive them at certain times.'[7] Keeping Anne isolated made it easier for Marie to stay in control. The fact Elisabeth was clearly miserable in Spain was a further reason for Henrietta Maria to dislike the lonely child-queen residing in the Louvre.

Elisabeth had been spared the kind of ordeal Anne had endured on her wedding night – her marriage was not to be consummated until she was eighteen – but she wrote to her sisters often, describing a drab new life in the palace of the Alcazar, where she was forbidden the ball games and other exercises she was used to. She wished, she wrote, to be a little bird like those owned by Louis, who could escape her cage and fly back to them.

Henrietta Maria dispatched gifts to console Elisabeth who wrote back, delighted with the 'little ornaments that you sent me, they are prettiest that could be seen! They could not be otherwise coming from you.' She mentioned a white and cornelian box, 'which I have with me right now'. Elisabeth was also transfixed by the immediacy of Henrietta Maria's news 'that you were going at that moment to walk with the king'. She asked Henrietta Maria to send her portrait – and to dress as she was in a closed Spanish ruff.[8] If Henrietta Maria was married to another Spaniard, she would be with her sister again.

In an age of personal monarchy, personal relations mattered. In England King James had fallen in love with a beautiful young man called George Villiers whose meteoric rise saw him gather titles and honours and, above all, power. Marie de' Medici could not make Leonora a minister, but she had made Concini a Marshal of France and Leonora wished she had not. By 1617 she had separated from her increasingly arrogant husband, warning Marie 'he will ruin us both'.[9]

Concini had urged the arrest of the Prince of Condé on 1 September 1616 after a peace treaty had been signed, and so insulted the entire French elite. He had then persuaded Marie to dismiss Henry IV's powerful ministers in favour of his own clients. Most foolishly of all he treated Louis like an errant boy rather than as a king who had reached his majority. Leonora's mental health collapsed and there was now no Jewish doctor to help her. Montalto had died of plague nearly a year earlier in February 1616.[10] She made plans to return to Italy, but on 24 April 1617 it was made evident that she had left it too late.

Concini was on his way to see Marie at eleven that morning. Marie was in her apartment on the ground floor of the south wing of the Louvre. Louis was taking the air on a balcony adjoining her bedroom waiting for the news that was soon brought to him. Concini was being shot and stabbed in the courtyard just inside the eastern gates of the Louvre. Louis had been in the apartment as he wanted to ensure that Concini wasn't killed in front of her. With the assassination carried out he left his mother's rooms ordering his guards to replace hers at the door. He then made his way to a second-storey window overlooking the courtyard. A crowd was already cheering Concini's death. Louis raised his sword and cried out to them, 'Now I am king!'[11]

It is not difficult to imagine Henrietta Maria's terror, aged seven, when the news reached Saint-Germain that her mother had been arrested and Concini murdered. It is common for children who have lost a parent to violence to fear losing the other in a similar way. Henrietta Maria, Christine and Gaston all begged to see their mother. Their request was refused. Meanwhile, locked in her apartment, Marie demanded to know, 'Whose counsel?' Who had advised Louis to have her arrested? The answer was, amongst others, Charles d'Albert, the man in charge of Louis's birds. Marie had underestimated him. She had also underestimated her son, whose concern now was to justify his actions to his subjects.

A king who bore the title 'His Most Christian Majesty', as Louis did, could not be tainted by an act of murder. The official version of events was that Concini had been killed while 'resisting arrest'. This begged the question, for what crime? Concini could not be tried, but he could still be judged as an accomplice to Leonora's crimes and if she were executed the huge wealth the Concinis had accumulated would be up for grabs. Other guards were dispatched to arrest Leonora, who had her own rooms in the Louvre.

Leonora was stripped of all her possessions, down to her undershirt, and taken to the fortress of the Bastille. She found she was accused of plotting the king's death and of gaining her influence with Marie by magic. Since she had held no high political office, witchcraft was the simplest way to explain her power. Word spread that Leonora was fantastically ugly. The woman who had done the queen's hair so beautifully was said to have 'the hair of Medusa' as well as 'a nose like an elephant'.[12] Ugliness was associated with the corruption that Eve had brought into Paradise at the Fall. Leonora begged for Louis to be reminded that he had known her all his life and been on good terms. Louis's answer was to have her moved to 'a nasty little cell' in the Conciergerie, a medieval palace with an infamous torture chamber.[13]

Marie de' Medici did not dare plead for her friend's life. The fall of the Concinis was a surrogate attack on herself as regent, and to have asked for mercy for Leonora would suggest the spell Leonora had cast over her still held. That could prolong the banishment to which she was condemned.

On 3 May Henrietta Maria saw her mother at a staged farewell at the Louvre. Marie was to be sent to the Château de Blois in the Loire, 180 kilometres from Paris. Louis, dressed in white, delivered a few prepared words. Marie, in black, kissed Louis and cried so hard that even Louis broke down. He did not stay to watch the nine-year-old Gaston deliver a farewell speech. Henrietta Maria had no idea when – or if – she would see her mother again. Leonora, meanwhile, considered the role Concini had played in Marie's fall. 'Poor woman,' she observed. Yet Marie's punishment was a lighter one than her own.

The charges against Leonora were now piling up. It was said Leonora had acted with her husband to usurp the king's authority and traffic with foreign powers and that she had consorted with sorcerers. The Jewish doctor Montalto was named as chief amongst them. It was usual for those accused of witchcraft to implicate others and it would have been easy for Leonora to heap the blame on a dead Jew as the instigator of her diabolical practices. Leonora refused to do so, only referring to Montalto as 'a very gallant man'. Nevertheless, members of her household gave the judges enough material to convict her, with Montalto named as an accomplice. Even Condé was disgusted. 'It was not she who was guilty of the ills that affected France,' he observed, 'but her husband.'[14]

Leonora's last request before her execution was for her thirteen-year-old son, Henry, who had been named after Henry IV. He had been found wandering the Louvre, hungry and abandoned after her arrest. He had served Louis loyally since early childhood and she asked for him to be allowed to keep some of the wealth his parents had accumulated. Marie's chief servitor, Armand Jean du Plessis, the future Cardinal-Duc de Richelieu, duly intervened for the child. Although the boy was denied the titles and wealth that were to be divided amongst Concini's enemies, he was helped to return to Florence.

On 8 July 1617, Leonora was taken to the same spot where Henry's IV assassin had been torn apart by horses. Parisians had been impressed by Leonora's courage in court and they noted that, while her skin was dark and her face freckled and lined, 'she did not seem so ugly as they had imagined'. Her calm and dignified manner in the face of death excited further respect and pity. With the faggots laid, and the swordsman ready, Leonora cried out her forgiveness of the king. She was beheaded and her body burned as the crowd watched in silence.

Leonora's reputation was to be forever tainted by the accusations of her 'witch-like' appearance and any good that she had ever done was blotted out. In one sad example the midwife Louise Bourgeois edited the second edition of her memoirs, so that no one would know that Leonora had been kind to her after Henry IV had died. There was no mention of Leonora passing on Louis's cloak bag, or how proud Louise Bourgeois's son had been to use it.[15] Such was the fall in reputation of one woman in Henrietta Maria's story.

Christine was married on her thirteenth birthday, 10 February 1619. She was small for her age, so she looked even younger than she was. In Italy they called her the '*sposa bimba*' – the baby bride. It was, however, Henrietta Maria who drew the attention of the great Bishop of Geneva, Francis de Sales. Known for his gentle approach to religious divisions he saw something in her that suggested to him that 'God intended her to be a great support of the glory of the Church.'[16] As for Henrietta Maria, her focus that day was surely Christine who was being served up to a groom nineteen years her senior: Victor Amadeus, Prince of Piedmont, heir to the Duchy of Savoy.

This was not as grand a marriage as that of Elisabeth, but it served a useful purpose in the rivalry between the Bourbons and the Habsburgs. The dukes of Savoy were the gatekeepers of the Alps, which were vital to Louis XIII because they lay next to France's unruly southern provinces and dominated the supply route between Spain and its other European possessions.

Louis, who had recently discovered a brief enthusiasm for sex, accompanied Christine to her bedroom and he remained for some time after her husband arrived.[17] He then went to Anne's bedchamber and made love to her for two hours.[18]

Marie de' Medici, who was still in banishment, was none too pleased to have missed Christine's wedding. Twelve days later she cut her skirts and shinned down a ladder out of a window to flee the Château de Blois. Aged forty-three, and increasingly portly, Marie's escape route proved a struggle, but what Marie lacked in athleticism she made up for in determination. Sixty feet down from her window she reached a terrace. Exhausted, she sank in her skirts like a collapsed soufflé. Her male companions had to use a large cloak to lower the queen mother the rest of the way to the ground.

Marie might have chosen to leave by the front door, which was not heavily guarded – but she wished to make a point. The next day she wrote a letter to Louis telling him that she had been driven to extremity in fear for her liberty and her life, but that the most painful thing to her at Blois had been not being able to see him.[19] She had with her a considerable amount of jewellery which she sold or pawned to fund a propaganda campaign. This began immediately with the publication of a series of pamphlets warning the young king was in the clutches of evil counsellors. At the same time, Marie raised an army. The so-called 'War of Mother and Son' ended after a couple of months without a shot being fired.

Louis hoped to buy Marie off with the governorship of Anjou, and on 1 September 1619 Marie was reunited with her children after a separation of more than two years.[20] The nine-year-old Henrietta Maria could not contain her joy and leapt into her mother's arms. Marie had soon departed for Anjou, but she wrote regularly and on 15 January 1620 she also sent Henrietta Maria a pair of earrings. They are described in a sale in 1979 as weighing fifty carats, white with a faint pink undertone. One has a slight bulge. The other is said to be one of the most perfect drop pearls ever known. Marie instructed Henrietta Maria to 'wear them as a mark of your affection.'[21] What she really meant was as a mark of loyalty.

The governorship of Anjou was not enough for Marie, who was determined that she should be her son's leading counsellor. Come the spring, Marie was in a second war with her son. This time their opposing military forces met in battle. Louis's army proved victorious and in August 1620 Marie accepted defeat. Louis weakly offered her a few crumbs of comfort: amongst them he promised to ask the Pope to make Richelieu a cardinal, but for eighteen long months Marie stewed in frustration that she remained excluded from power. Then on 15 December 1621 Louis's favourite, Charles d'Albert (who had been raised to the title Duke of Luynes) died of scarlet fever. Without him, the twenty-year-old king proved unable to resist his mother's powerful personality. Within six weeks Marie was on Louis's council.

4

A PRINCE ERRANT

HENRIETTA MARIA WAS THE LAST OF LOUIS'S SISTERS TO REMAIN
in France. He would tell her he was 'her best brother', even though
Gaston was closer to her in age, and assured her 'I do not stop thinking
of you and wish I could send you more proof of my love.'[1] Often, in
1621 and 1622, Louis's letters were addressed 'from the field'. The
Huguenots in the south-west and Languedoc were in rebellion.
Although Marie had reissued the Edict of Nantes that guaranteed
Protestants their religious freedoms, the Catholic Revival spearheaded
by the devots was gathering momentum in France and this made them
fearful for the future.[2]

The Huguenots dreamed of turning Protestant France into a
quasi-republic, modelled on the Dutch Netherlands. The Dutch had
overthrown Habsburg rule in the previous century, splitting away
from the Spanish Netherlands. Louis was determined to prevent the
creation of any state within a state in France. He told Henrietta Maria
proudly of 'the conquests I have made', but 'I am never happier', he
observed, 'than when I hear your news and when I know you are
well'.[3] How long was it, however, before Henrietta Maria would leave
France as her sisters had?

Elisabeth was already Queen of Spain, where she was now known as
Isabel.[4] Christine, aged sixteen, had a healthy son, and Henrietta Maria,
who turned thirteen in November 1622, knew the time had come for

her brother and mother to consider her place in the bridal market.[5] She hoped to stay in France and marry one of the Princes of the Blood, the eighteen-year-old Count of Soissons.

Elisabeth teased Henrietta Maria that she had heard about her 'little love games' with Soissons. 'I would love to be able to see them,' she wrote, and she sent Henrietta Maria 'toys' for her play-acting.[6] But the groom Marie de' Medici and Louis XIII had in mind for Henrietta Maria lay further afield: the twenty-two-year-old heir to King James of Britain, Charles, Prince of Wales.

A marriage alliance with the Stuarts offered several possible advantages for France.[7] Just as Savoy held a key role in the balance of power in Europe as a gatekeeper to the Alps, so Britain's navy dominated the Channel. This would help tip the balance of power against the Habsburgs. An alliance would also prevent collusion between the Stuarts and their fellow Protestants in France. There was, however, a complicating factor: King James's enthusiasm for a Spanish match. He had married his daughter – another Elizabeth – to the head of the German military alliance known as the Protestant Union: the Calvinist Frederick V, Prince-Elector of the Palatinate, a region in the Rhineland.

In 1619, Frederick had backed a Protestant-led rebellion against the Holy Roman Emperor, Ferdinand II, and taken the throne of Bohemia. The Habsburgs had sworn Frederick's rule would only last one winter and so it had proved. They had retaken Bohemia and then seized the Palatinate. The so-called Winter King and his Stuart queen were driven into exile in the Dutch Republic. Much of Europe was now engulfed in what would become known as the Thirty Years' War, with the Dutch Republic and the Protestant Union fighting the Habsburgs and a Catholic League under Maximilian of Bavaria.

With the Habsburgs and the Catholic League enjoying a string of victories and with limited military options of his own, James hoped that a match between Charles and the Infanta Maria could see the return of the Palatinate as a gift. In return he dangled the possibility for Philip IV of an Anglo-Spanish alliance aimed at France. His plans were, however, deeply unpopular with those of his subjects who saw the war in apocalyptic terms as a battle between the godly and the forces of the papal Antichrist. These were largely the so-called Puritans. The term had its origins in the Elizabethan period and applied to those who wanted the English Church reformed on more advanced Calvinist lines.

There were shades of opinion, however, even within Puritanism. James's reforms of the Church of England on his accession had kept the more moderate Puritans within the fold. He drew the line at those Puritans who wished to abolish the episcopate. Now, however, with even moderate Puritans opposing the Spanish marriage he had begun favouring members of a new movement who actively opposed Puritanism – the so-called 'Arminians'.

The term 'Arminian', like 'Puritan', was intended to be an insult. It was drawn from the name of a Dutch theologian, Jacobus Arminius, who had attacked the Calvinist theology of predestination. This was that a few people, known as the Elect, were predestined to heaven – whatever they did in life – while everyone else was predestined to hell. In fact, the defining characteristics of the English Arminians had nothing to do with predestination. What interested them was bringing 'order' to Reform Protestantism. They favoured ceremony and ritual in beatified settings, over a focus of sermons and extempore prayers, drawing their inspiration from a phrase in Psalm 96: 'the beauty of holiness'.

To the Arminians the Pope was not a demonic entity, but merely the overpowerful Bishop of Rome, while the Habsburgs were just another dynasty, one with whom Britain could do business, if it was in line with national interests.

The Spanish match was causing huge acrimony in British political life and within the Church of England. Yet the French ambassador believed British and Spanish interests were so different that the marriage negotiations were in any case doomed, and could only end in further animosity between the kingdoms. Then, a most extraordinary thing occurred.

In February 1623, while Henrietta Maria was taking part in a rehearsal for a ballet, Charles turned up in disguise at the Louvre, along with his father's minister favourite, the thirty-year-old George Villiers, Marquess of Buckingham. Charles had had one of the rushes of blood to the head that would afflict him throughout his life. He had decided to woo the Infanta Maria in person and was travelling to Spain via France. He hoped to discover if the Spanish were serious in their negotiations, or simply stringing his father along to prevent the British from giving military support to his brother-in-law, the Winter King.

Buckingham was backing Charles in what James saw rightly as a reckless adventure, largely as a means of gaining favour with the prince. The murder of Concino Concini on the orders of the fifteen-year-old Louis XIII in 1617 had been a wake-up call. It had made him realise it was dangerous to antagonise James's heir and equally important to have his friendship. Since the French opposed the Spanish match, which would be aimed against them, the men had to travel in secret.

Charles and Buckingham had had a wild ride to Paris from the coast. As a young child Charles's legs were weak, but following the death of his elder brother Henry, aged eighteen, when he was eleven, he had worked hard to strengthen them, running and riding, until he had become exceptionally fit and strong.[8] 'He holds [the horses] up by main strength of mastery and cries still on! On!! On!!!', Buckingham wrote to James of their journey.[9] The two men had found rooms at an inn on the rue Saint-Jacques and then gone 'to a periwig maker'.

Buckingham was tall and handsome, 'A man to draw an angel by' was one description.[10] Charles was short but also striking, having, 'a truly royal presence . . . a grave brow, much grace in his eyes and in the movement of his body'.[11] Their appearance was, however, hidden under wigs and false beards before they made their way to the Louvre.[12] There they saw Louis walking in a gallery with his courtiers and Marie de' Medici dine in state, before they arrived for the ballet.

A drawing of Henrietta Maria by Daniel Dumonstier in chalk and coloured pencil depicts her at around this time with an impish face, her hair styled in a bob with a short fringe, like a seventeenth-century Audrey Hepburn. She is smiling at the viewer, her eyes turned, with the slight squint of an excited child, and her mother's pearls hang from her ears. Henrietta Maria performed in the ballet as the goddess Iris, messenger of the gods and personification of the rainbow, while Anne of Austria played Juno, wife of Jupiter, king of the gods.

In a letter to his father that night Charles said he thought Anne was so beautiful it made him all the more enthusiastic to see her sister, the infanta.[13] Henrietta Maria did not even get a mention. The next morning the prince errant and the favourite rode on for Madrid, arriving on 7 March 1623. Yet his brief visit had marked a disturbance in her world, the ripples of which would carry her towards a future she never asked for and could not avoid.

The seventeen-year-old Philip IV teased his sister, the Infanta Maria, that she must be very beautiful to have attracted a prince to come all the way from England. The infanta, 'a very comely lady . . . of a Flemish complexion', was not amused.[14] She declared that the only positive aspect of a marriage to Charles was that she would end up dying a martyr.[15] Did they not kill Catholics for their religion in England? They did. Nevertheless, Philip was enthusiastic. The last Anglo-Spanish match, between Catherine of Aragon and Henry VIII, had ended in England's split from the Catholic Church. Philip hoped a new marriage could heal that rift.

After argument and delay, a meeting was set for Easter Day. Charles set off for the Alcazar palace with a large train of followers and met Philip outside his chapel. Philip was dressed in black and gold, a plain white standing collar framing a pale face with full lips and an undershot jaw. Charles had planned to dress for the occasion in a pair of sky-blue hose that would complement the blue ribbon of his Order of the Garter. Spanish courtiers had, however, persuaded him to wear something dark and plain in accordance with their court etiquette. He added large diamonds and pearls in a show of magnificence.[16]

The king and prince went together to the queen's apartment, where Elisabeth and the Infanta Maria greeted them. Elisabeth was almost unrecognisable from the French princess who had left France and her family in 1615. Aged twenty, elegant and black-eyed, Elisabeth had been described by her father-in-law before he died in 1621 as 'a complete woman'.[17] This was not, however, what the Spanish people were being told. Queen consorts threatened the influence of minister favourites, and Philip's, Gaspar de Guzman, Count of Olivares, was spreading unpleasant rumours to undermine her marriage and reputation. Elisabeth's mission was Franco-Spanish peace; Olivares wanted war and deployed all the old tropes about Eve against her.

Elisabeth was said to be lame. A small deformity was a red flag, a warning that a satanic hag lay behind the mask of beauty. Elisabeth's was hidden beneath her skirts – and what else lay there? Lust. Elisabeth's lover was said to be a courtier poet – an enemy of Olivares – who had been stabbed in his coach the previous year: a death cruelly mimicking the assassination of Henry IV.[18]

Four thrones had been laid out: Philip and Charles sat on the outside, Elisabeth and the Infanta Maria on the inside. The prince had a long, affectionate speech prepared for the infanta and was surely feeling nervous about delivering it. In common with Louis, Charles had been born with a lingual deformity. He had been spared the operation that Louis had endured and he had only a mild stutter, but he preferred to be brief. He now began battling his way through a very long speech.

After about an hour the infanta began to look wearied and Elisabeth impatiently waved Charles down. The infanta then delivered her reply in a few set phrases that had been written for her. Onlookers were impressed that she managed to keep her face entirely expressionless. This humiliating scene was played out in different ways for months as the negotiations lingered on. Olivares disliked Buckingham, whom James raised to a dukedom in May, and he made this plain. According to Venetian diplomatic circles his wife put 'the most diseased woman in Spain into [Buckingham's] bed'.[19] Charles was equally irritated by Philip's efforts to convert him to Catholicism.

The prince had been well educated by his father in matters of theology and believed the Church of England to be 'the best in the world'. It encapsulated the right of kings to rule Church as well as State, having the king and not the Pope, at its head. Charles, who had a highly visual imagination, was also attracted to the new Arminian movement, seeing a theatre of ritual and beauty as a mean of fostering a deferential society suited to the Stuarts' sacramental, divine-right kingship. The formality and grandeur of the Spanish court appealed to Charles, not its religion. In October 1623 Charles left Madrid betrothed to Maria, but only because he feared that otherwise he might be kept in Spain. He was intending to break the engagement as soon as he could.

James's representative, Henry Rich, soon to be Earl of Holland, arrived in Paris on Sunday 24 February 1624.[20] Handsome, beautifully dressed and smooth-talking, the thirty-three-year-old was to be a significant figure in Henrietta Maria's life for a quarter of a century. He was now in Paris to test the waters for a marriage alliance that would regain the Palatinate with the backing of French military might. The waters were warm, but Louis XIII and Marie de' Medici had to be careful. Charles remained betrothed to the infanta. They could not offer up a daughter of France only for her to be rejected.[21] Henrietta Maria was simply to be displayed to the best advantage as a possible bride, with nothing formal declared.

It was helpful that Holland was an enthusiast for a French match. He came from a family allied to the moderate Puritan party and his late uncle, Robert Devereux, 2nd Earl of Essex, had been a great hero of the Elizabethan war with Spain. He saw an alliance with France as a means of weakening the Habsburgs. Even so, Holland could not be relied on to sell Prince Charles a duck as a swan. That night Holland was to see Henrietta Maria dance in a new ballet, *The Dance of the Garden Nymphs*. It was only a year since Henrietta Maria had performed in a ballet in front of Prince Charles and been overlooked.

Holland left his luggage at the Hôtel de Chevreuse and headed straight for the Louvre. The *hôtel* belonged to Claude de Lorraine, Duke of Chevreuse, whose guest Holland was. Holland found the duke and duchess in their rooms at the Louvre changing for the theatre.

Slightly built and curly-haired, the forty-five-year-old Chevreuse was one of the so-called 'foreign princes' (*princes étrangers*) who held French titles, but were also recognised as junior members of dynasties that reigned abroad. The duke came from the House of Guise, a cadet branch of the House of Lorraine, which was then an independent duchy. James's grandmother had been a Guise, so he was a suitable host for James's ambassador. He was also good company, known as both a risk-taker and an extravagant pleasure-seeker, qualities that were united in his choice of a wife.

The twenty-three-year-old Madame de Chevreuse, 'a 'potent beauty' with red-gold hair, was the widow of Louis's late favourite Charles d'Albert and was to be another significant figure in Henrietta Maria's future. She was Anne of Austria's closest friend, 'communicating to her, as much as she could, her own gay and lively humour, which turned the most serious things of the greatest consequence, into matters for jest and laughter'.[22] Holland was stunned by the 'extraordinary' amount of diamonds she was wearing.[23]

The couple assured Holland that he would soon meet Henrietta Maria and that she 'had seldom put on a more cheerful countenance' than at the prospect of being wooed by Charles. Henrietta arrived shortly afterwards, accompanied by Anne, and behaved as she had surely been instructed to, wreathed in smiles. Holland was impressed by the sparkling figure before him. 'I swear to God, she is a lovely Sweet young creature,' he dispatched to Buckingham. She was small for her age, 'but her shape is perfect', and he had heard that her sister Christine (who looked very like her) had also been small and was 'now grown a tall and a goodly lady'. One word of caution was struck. Holland was warned that Charles had a rival in Henrietta Maria's French beau, Soissons. If Holland were not negotiating for a marriage on behalf of 'so great a prince', Soissons said he would have 'cut his throat'.[24]

The subject of the ballet Holland now attended was the arrival of the

Gods of the Garden after a long winter. Flora's divine nymphs danced with the arrival of spring, each nymph representing a different flower. Henrietta Maria was dressed as a sunflower. Light was associated with God and the sunflower reflected the sun queen, Marie de' Medici, who was watching the performance. 'Today when I appear so beautiful / Shining in a splendour without equal', Henrietta Maria declared, 'I turn . . . Towards your celestial beauty / Great sun who gave birth to me.'[25]

Two days later Holland wrote to Prince Charles declaring Henrietta Maria 'the sweetest creature in France' and 'a Lady of as much loveliness . . . as any creature under heaven'. 'She dances (the which I am witness of) as well as ever I saw any.' She had a voice that was beautiful 'beyond imagination'. He had seen her since the ballet, and noted her conversations with her mother showed intelligence with 'an extraordinary discretion and quickness'. Yes, she was small for her age, but 'her wisdom' was 'infinitely beyond it'.[26]

By the end of March, with Philip IV refusing to give written guarantees on the return of the Palatinate, James had agreed to end negotiations for the Spanish match, and those for a marriage between Prince Charles and Henrietta Maria had begun.[27]

In May 1624 King James was already writing to Henrietta Maria as 'my dearest daughter'. Prince Charles claimed in his letters he recalled seeing her in the ballet the previous year 'although unknown to you', and thought her beauty matched 'the lustre' of her 'virtues'.[28] She made a public gesture of placing his letters in her bosom and they exchanged pocket portraits. Both were pleased with what they saw. Henrietta Maria kept a miniature of Charles as Prince of Wales with her for the rest of her life. Charles, meanwhile, sat in his private study with her image and 'fed his eyes many times with the sight and contemplation of it'.[29] James told Henrietta Maria that Charles had 'no repose of spirit' as he waited her letters.[30] This may even have been true.

The image of regal dignity that Charles liked to project has, with the passage of time, obscured the earthlier side of his personality. James had convinced him that royal bastards were dangerous to legitimate off-spring. There had been mistresses, although their names had been kept from James with Buckingham's help.[31] Charles would never, however, have a public mistress and he looked forward to the physical side of marriage. In this he was encouraged by a baby-faced favourite of Buckingham, the ambitious, charming, twenty-two-year-old Wat Montagu, who was part of the negotiating team.

Wat boasted that his stories about Henrietta Maria had made Charles fall in love with 'every hair on Madam's head'.[32] Indeed Charles had sworn lewdly to him that he was determined 'she shall have no more powder till he powder her and blow her up himself'. [33] There was, however, another reason than sexual desire for Charles to push for the negotiations to move forward. He was fearful that his father would slide back towards a Spanish alliance. Certainly, James feared the French match would not achieve all Charles hoped. His son was an idealist. James was a hard-nosed realist.

James knew the British desire to 'do' something about the Palatinate would not necessarily translate into their being prepared to accept the higher taxes necessary to pay for the long, hard war against the Habsburgs that Charles now sought. Nor would they welcome an alliance with France if the price proved to be a relaxation of the penal laws against British Catholics. There was a deep neurosis about the security of Protestantism in the kingdoms of Scotland, England and England's colony in Ireland. Protestantism was already losing ground across Europe, and not just to Habsburg armies.

The reforms of the Council of Trent in the mid-sixteenth century had re-energised the Catholic Church, which had been gathering converts, not least in France. Persecuting Catholics was seen as necessary to prevent them seducing the godly from the path of righteousness. Catholics were fined heavily for non-attendance of Church of England services and blocked from attending any Mass, the central act of Catholic worship, by being denied access to priests. At its worst the persecution saw

Catholic clergy executed for the crime of simply exercising their office in England.

James was certain that Pope Urban VIII, the former nuncio Maffeo Barberini, would never grant a dispensation to allow his god-daughter to marry an active persecutor. Henry Holland was nevertheless optimistic that Louis would be pragmatic. Louis had proved as willing as his father Henry IV to ally with Protestants against the Habsburgs. The two dynasties were currently quarrelling over the Val Tellina passes in northern Italy. These were vital for communications between the Spanish and Austrian Habsburgs. Louis was backing the Protestant rulers, known as the Grey League, against the papal army, which was protecting the Catholic, pro-Habsburg population.

On the matter of the persecution, James merely offered to grant Catholics 'favour', if they kept 'their consciences to themselves'.[34] The chief French negotiator, the Marquis of Vieuville, accepted these modest assurances, in addition to vital guarantees that Henrietta Maria and her train would be able to practise their religion. James's negotiators were even led to believe that the French were more concerned about the form of the treaty than whatever happened to British Catholics after it was signed. Then, in June 1624, word arrived in Paris that an old and ailing English priest had been imprisoned, putting his life at risk for failing to comply with the latest expulsion of Catholic clerics from England. Those already in exile in Paris were not slow to point out that His Most Christian Majesty was about to be dishonoured by marrying his sister to a man who martyred priests. Louis and Marie were appalled.

For Marie the hopes of ameliorating the persecution of Catholics in Britain was one of the most attractive possible benefits of the match. In August Vieuville was sacked. In his place came Marie's former chief servitor, the thirty-nine-year-old Cardinal Richelieu. A brilliant mind in a fragile body, Richelieu had been raised to the king's council four months earlier, with Marie's backing. He set about his task with ruthlessness. Buckingham had foolishly let slip that he had acted as guarantor to James of the benefits of a French alliance. His future was entirely dependent on the success of the treaty and this was something Richelieu now exploited.[35]

The cardinal began by demanding that James's secret and verbal promises to allow Catholics to hear the Mass in their homes be signed and sworn to on his honour as king. James dug in his heels and agreed only to sign a secret memorandum that would allow Catholics some liberty to practise their religion without being disturbed in their property or persons. As a mark of goodwill he then instructed his judges to release Catholics imprisoned because of their religion.[36] That, however, was as far as he would go.

Urban was disappointed but Marie de' Medici's confessor, Pierre Berulle, assured the Pope that Henrietta Maria's marriage could still kick-start the reconversion of the Stuart kingdoms.

The leading cleric of the devot movement, and founder of the famous French School of Spirituality, Berulle offered to travel with Henrietta Maria to England to guide her in her work. Louis assured the Pope his sister would raise her children as Catholics while they were under her care and instructed Henrietta Maria to swear to this in writing. She was also obliged to promise to act as a protector of her co-religionists and to try and bring about the reconversion of Britain.

Charles proved willing to agree to French demands that his children be raised by their mother (and therefore as Catholics) while they were still young, as he was anxious for the marriage to go ahead as soon as possible. Parliament had paid for an army of mercenaries and pressed men who Charles wished to deploy to raise the Habsburg siege on the Dutch city of Breda. James was showing signs of cold feet. With the assurances made, the Pope duly granted the dispensation. The French promised that negotiations for a military alliance could go ahead as soon as the wedding had taken place.

On 23 March 1625 Wat Montagu predicted that Henrietta Maria would be delivered to Charles in a month. His promises were disappointed when, four days later, King James died. Aged fifty-eight and a heavy drinker, James had been in poor health for some time. He had been finished off by a tertian ague – a form of malaria. It was convenient timing for Charles and Buckingham since James was still reluctant to go to war. Indeed the Habsburgs later spread a rumour that Buckingham had killed James with a poisoned cordial to prevent him reopening their negotiations over the Palatinate.

With that danger now passed Charles immediately ordered that his army relieve Breda. A new date was also set for the wedding. It would go ahead on May Day, according to the English calendar. Charles's kinsman, the Duke of Chevreuse, would stand in as his proxy.[37] Organising and attending James's funeral meant that he would not be free to attend, but such proxy marriages were not unusual. Elisabeth had undergone one before she left for Spain.

Henrietta Maria's other sister Christine responded joyfully to the news of the impending nuptials. Savoy had allied with France and Venice against the Habsburg bid to control the Val Tellina passes. England would be a further ally against Habsburg power.[38] By contrast Elisabeth expressed her disappointment in no uncertain terms, snubbing the wife of the French ambassador, saying she would 'neither receive nor listen to her'.[39] Henrietta Maria had always been Elisabeth's favourite sister. In letters she was her 'dearest sister', while Christine was merely her 'dear sister', but the Anglo-French match was aimed against Spain. Elisabeth's previously warm relationship with Henrietta Maria would never be the same. Bourbon–Habsburg rivalry would dominate European affairs for the rest of their lives and Henrietta Maria would prove to be her father's daughter in that struggle.

Part Two

TO LOVE A KING

'THE GAME AND PLAY OF FAVOURITES'

HENRIETTA MARIA'S APARTMENT IN THE LOUVRE WAS ON THE ground floor overlooking the palace gardens she loved. It was here on 8 May 1625 that she greeted her mother and sister-in law before her betrothal ceremony.[1] Anne of Austria was wearing pink and silver; Marie de' Medici was in black adorned with a thick collar of pearls and a huge diamond cross. They processed to Louis's Presence Chamber which was hung with red velvet trimmed with gold and so crammed with courtiers Henrietta Maria had difficulty making her way through the throng. She was in a formal 'gown of cloth of gold, cut upon cloth of silver, and richly embroidered all over with fleur-de-lys of gold, and chased and interlaid diamonds, rubies, pearls, and other rich jewels of inestimable value.'[2] Her sleeves trailed to the ground.

Henrietta Maria sat at Louis's right hand, on a throne set on a dais. Her face was framed with an open standing lace ruff of the kind that Marie had made fashionable. The terms of the marriage contract were read and then signed by Louis and Gaston, the seventeen-year-old Prince Charming of the court, by Marie, Anne, and the British ambassadors. These were Henry Holland and the forty-five-year-old James Hay, Earl of Carlisle. The latter – an ugly Scot known affectionately by Charles's sister, the Winter Queen, as 'Camel Face' – had been an early favourite of King James and had also been involved in the marriage negotiations.

With the ceremony over, Henrietta Maria emerged to find her dress had been badly creased, the gold and silver metal thread having been bent in the press of people. It had to be hung out and packed very carefully with the rest of her trousseau.[3] The wedding would take place three days later and as the countdown began there were sulks and tantrums amongst the invitees to the wedding at Notre Dame. Soissons, the prince who had hoped to wed Henrietta Maria, announced that he refused to attend. So did the Archbishop of Paris, who was furious that the elderly Cardinal de la Rochefoucauld (Richelieu's predecessor on the king's council), was to perform the marriage in 'his' cathedral. A number of the archbishop's clergy went on strike in sympathy, and new choristers had to be brought in from the royal chapels to perform at Notre Dame.

Those who weren't invited were desperate just to get a look and the crowds began gathering in the rain-swept cathedral square the night before the wedding. The next morning they piled up on stands from which they viewed an eight-foot high platform built for the procession. It was hung in violet silk embroidered with fleur-de-lys and ran all the way from the archbishop's palace and into Notre Dame. At 5 p.m. the patience of the crowd was at last rewarded with a hundred Swiss guards emerging from the palace with beating drums and whistling pipes. The king's guard and trumpeters followed, then 'the knights of the Holy Spirit, the princes, marshals, dukes and peers of France . . . their clothes strewn with diamonds.'[4] King Charles's ambassadors, Holland and Carlisle, came next, in silver and gold. These were the same fabrics that had been worn at the marriage of Henry VIII and Anne of Cleves, the last foreign consort to marry an English king.

Henrietta Maria now appeared in a glittering dress 'powdered with gold fleur-de-lys' and wearing a golden crown set with diamonds and 'a world of other precious stones'. She looked lovely, 'finely proportioned' with a 'perfect complexion', 'big eyes, black, soft, vivacious and shining.'[5] Even Henry VIII might have been impressed. On Henrietta Maria's left was Gaston. Remembered later as ' a man of war and a teller of jokes', he was close to his sister, who shared his sense of humour, and was anxious now to be given a place on the King's Council, as his heir.[6]

On her right Louis wore robes of state almost entirely covered in jewels, reflecting his status as the king 'that outshines all others'.[7] Three Princesses of the Blood held Henrietta Maria's pale blue velvet train, which was embroidered in gold thread so thick that a man walked underneath it to help carry its weight. Anne of Austria and Marie de' Medici followed, also dressed in silver and gold, then more Princesses of the Blood and the other senior ladies of the court. Like the king's moons and stars, each group 'in their several orbs, made all the place like the heavens sparkle'.[8]

As the spectators strained to see every detail a stand collapsed. Amongst those injured was the Flemish artist Peter Paul Rubens, who broke his foot.[9] The procession stopped at the west entrance to the cathedral where Henrietta Maria was to take her marriage vows. Charles would not attend a Catholic service and so his proxy, the Duke of Chevreuse, could not enter the cathedral. He was dressed in black velvet to represent Charles's mourning for King James, but his cloak was so thickly embroidered with gold and diamonds that when he moved it flashed like 'a living flame' around him. After the vows were made the procession continued to the choir. Fine white linen had been placed under the platform along with burning tapers reflecting so much light that an English witness thought the 'Church seemed like the palace of the Sun'.[10]

When the congregation had gathered, commemorative medallions of gold and silver were showered down from the choir. Each was stamped with an image of Charles and Henrietta Maria on one side, and the lily of France with the rose of England on the other. After everyone had settled, the nuptial Mass was sung. If grand ceremony was a way of paying homage to the king, then Church ceremony showed homage to God, while also attracting converts. In a world where music was a rare and valued entertainment, the Catholic Church showcased the work of the latest composers in breathtaking settings, to which the poor also had access. The voices soared into the vast vaulted space, the rich vestments of the celebrants glowed with gold thread, and the air was heavy with incense cast in clouds from the censors.

It was almost dark when the procession returned to the palace, cannons firing in celebration and bonfires lit throughout Paris. That night there was a banquet of 'unmeasured splendour', and afterwards Henrietta Maria was escorted to bed where Chevreuse got in beside her fully dressed.[11] They then touched legs as a symbol of consummation. The next day Louis found he had a sore throat. The plan had been for Louis to escort the three queens – his wife, mother and sister – to Amiens for a grand entry. They were then to proceed to Boulogne where Buckingham was to meet them. Over the following few days the rain continued, the Seine rose and Paris was flooded. Henrietta Maria also fell ill. Her onward journey was now delayed and there were concerns in England that this might be deliberate.

Suspicions were expressed that Louis was keeping hold of their new queen in order to pressure Charles into further concessions on the religious rights of British Catholics. If so, 'then we are fallen out of the frying pan [of the Spanish match] into the fire', one Londoner observed.[12] Questions were already being asked about the secret terms of the marriage treaty concerning Catholics, as well as the public promises made to protect Henrietta Maria's religious rights. Many were unhappy she should be given any such rights.

Charles's Lutheran mother, Anna of Denmark, is said to have converted to Catholicism in Scotland in the 1590s: but, if so, she had never dared practise her faith openly. After Anna's death in 1619 her French page had 'liberated' some of her secret possessions and brought them to Paris. They included a little crystal and enamel box with images of Catholic saints, and an English book of Catholic prayers, embroidered with gold, none of which had ever been revealed to the public gaze. By contrast Henrietta Maria had been guaranteed her own ecclesiastical retinue, headed by Richelieu's nephew, the twenty-nine-year-old Bishop of Mende. The devot leader Berulle was to accompany her as her confessor, along with twenty of his Oratorians, dressed in brown habits not seen in England since the dissolution of the monasteries. Henrietta Maria's baggage, meanwhile, held a wealth of religious pictures, silver and gilt plate as well as lavishly embroidered textiles.[13]

To allay Protestant fears, Charles was dragging his feet in arranging suitable places for his wife's private worship. A classical chapel on the periphery of St James's Palace had been commissioned during the negotiations for the Spanish match, but diplomats were reporting that 'scant solicitude' was being paid to finishing it. At Whitehall – the king's principal residence in London – there wasn't a chapel at all, a mere room having been put aside for her Mass.[14] Yet he couldn't afford to offend Louis. Charles needed France's might and French money to help fight the Habsburgs, and he was concerned the alliance he hoped for was already fracturing.

Louis had helped to pay for, and support, the army that Charles had sent in April to relieve Breda, but he had since announced he was only prepared to continue to fund it for a further six months. This was of little use to Britain. Charles had just learned that Breda had fallen to the Spanish and his army had been decimated by disease.[15] Charles wanted a formal offensive and defensive treaty, but the word was that Louis's focus was on the latest Huguenot revolt.

The rebel leader, the Duke of Soubise, had occupied the Île de Ré near the Huguenot port city of La Rochelle, and gained control of the Atlantic coast of France from Nantes to Bordeaux. Louis already had plenty on his plate in the Val Tellina passes in Italy where a proxy war remained in progress. His army – supposedly acting for his allies Savoy and Venice – had seized fortresses from papal and Habsburg forces. Richelieu was advising Louis that they could not afford to be distracted from the Huguenot revolt by fighting in yet another European battleground.

Rather than waiting for Henrietta Maria in Boulogne, Buckingham left for Paris to re-establish French support for a three-year plan he had formulated with Charles. This envisioned a co-ordinated European attack on Habsburg interests: France, Savoy and Venice would reclaim the Val Tellina passes in Northern Italy before attacking Habsburg Milan and Naples. Danish and German forces would fight in northern Europe, while English and Dutch fleets would create naval diversions and intercept Spanish treasure ships, bringing them gold from the New World.[16]

Buckingham had personal reasons to need the alliance to be a success. He was deeply unpopular in England both for his monopoly of power and, amongst Puritans, for his association with the Arminian movement within the Church of England. He had tried to win over the latter by boasting that he had outwitted Philip IV's favourite Olivares to spike the hated Spanish match, 'as if nations had been the game and play of favourites', one courtier noted with disgust.[17] It had not helped him much. His enemies would be quick to blame him for the failure of marriage negotiations to deliver on the Palatinate and for any relaxation of the persecution of Catholics.

Louis was still ill in bed on 24 May when the news arrived at the Louvre that Buckingham was to appear in Paris that night. The Duke of Chevreuse left immediately to meet him and escort him to his palace, where Buckingham would be invited to stay. Buckingham's first announcement was a pointed one: Charles, he said, was 'dying with impatience and love' to see his bride.[18]

Marie de' Medici hoped to pour oil on these troubled waters. A dinner, hosted by Richelieu, was to be given for Buckingham at her palace, the Luxembourg. Marie had begun building it the year after Henry IV's assassination and it crowned her as the most important patron of architecture of her day as well as standing as a monument to their marriage. The facade depicted twin-sculpted portraits of the couple, and the entrance carried their entwined ciphers, which was stamped throughout two identical apartments: the west dedicated to Marie and the east to Henry.[19]

Buckingham arrived dressed to impress. One outfit seen in Paris was of ecru-coloured satin embroidered with bands of graded pearls, and judged to be 'the finest outfit one could see in a lifetime'. He had accessorised it with a hat that had a 'plume of herons' feathers, at the base of which was a badge of five very large diamonds and three superb pearshaped pearls'. Around his neck he wore a collar of another six ropes of pearls, matched with pearl rosettes, a pearl garter, pearl buttons and buttonholes, while his mantle was embroidered in further bands of pearls. His diamond and pearl earring 'scarcely showed because his hair was so long and so much curled as to hide it'.[20] He appeared in such costume to be 'the best-looking and best-built man in the world'.[21]

The dinner that night was held in the gallery of Marie's apartment, which was newly hung with a cycle of twenty-four over-full-length paintings by Europe's leading artist – poor Mr Rubens with his broken foot. Twenty-two of the images depicted her life and triumphs. One showed Marie accepting the orb of state from Henry's hands in 1610. In another she was the Regent Militant, mounted on a war horse and carrying a marshal's baton. Richelieu, who wanted to streamline the monarchy and concentrate absolute power in Louis, had been so concerned to see the way they foregrounded her greatness, and promoted the tradition that members of the royal family had a right to a share in government, that he had tried several times to get Rubens sacked and replaced.[22] Marie de' Medici had resisted, dashing to see the pictures being unwrapped as they arrived, and pressing Rubens to have the cycle completed in time for the wedding.

Marie was now anxious to show off the cycle to Buckingham, as she had to Louis, who had seen them for the first time only a few days earlier. Rubens, still in bed and unable to walk, had been concerned about Louis's possible reaction: not least to the picture that showed Marie's 'heroic' escape from her imprisonment at his hands at the Château de Blois. Happily, Marie's chaplain served 'as interpreter of the subjects' for the king and 'most artfully diverted and dissimulated their meaning'.[23]

Buckingham admired the pictures principally as a display of great talent and promptly commissioned a portrait of himself. Rubens was to depict him escaping a personification of envy to ascend into the Temple of Virtue. The dinner was, though, soured by the Earl of Carlisle condemning Richelieu and the whole French nation for their lax support for the war. Buckingham, it was noted, did not make any effort to contradict him. He had already had a two-hour meeting with Richelieu which had left him in little doubt that Louis would not be shifted on the matter of the offensive alliance.

Buckingham took out his frustration on Henrietta Maria. Her godfather Pope Urban had sent his nephew Francesco Barberini to France as his legate to press Louis to come to an accommodation over the Val Tellina.[24] He had visited Louis the same day Buckingham had arrived in Paris. Barberini had asked for something Louis was not prepared to give: free passage through the Italian passes for Spanish troops needed for the Dutch and German wars. An agreement was, however, still possible. Barberini had also seen Henrietta Maria, and Buckingham berated her, having decided she had shown the legate too much honour.[25] Henrietta Maria responded tartly that 'it behoved her to treat with respect, the representative of the head of her religion'.[26]

The favourite's attack had been a disturbing, even frightening development. It suggested a possible future assault on her religious rights. Buckingham would need someone to act as the lightning rod for Charles's anger on the failure of the military alliance he sought. Henrietta Maria could be damned for being French in England, just as Olivares had damned Elisabeth for being French in Spain – and she could be damned as a Catholic too. For the time being, however, it was another marriage that Buckingham had in his sights.

On 23 May 1625 Henrietta Maria was carried out of Paris in a red litter embroidered with gold to 'shouts of applause'. 'Goodbye sweet banks of the Seine where I have enjoyed 1,000 amusements', announced a tract written in Henrietta Maria's voice, 'Goodbye gardens filled with delight . . . goodbye the marvellous buildings in which I have been so happy.'[27]

With her were 'a countless throng of people, accompanied by the guards, by the people of the city, by Buckingham, by the other English and by all her suite'. They included 4,000 of the greatest men and women of France, the ladies wearing masks of black silk lined with white satin to protect them from the sun, the carriages of the great nobles furnished in red velvet, gilded wheels flashing in the cloudy light.[28]

Henrietta Maria's family would soon join her, but following his illness Louis was no longer willing to accompany her to Amiens. He broke off early to say his farewell to Henrietta Maria at Compiègne, eighty kilometres from Paris. With Louis out of the way Buckingham's plan then sprang into action. In the nineteenth century Alexandre Dumas's novels would build on a historical tradition of a romance between Buckingham and the lonely Anne of Austria. In reality she was the intended victim of a honey trap. If French policy was to change in British interests – and more specifically his own – then Buckingham's hated rival Richelieu had to go. For this to happen Anne had to be won round to the enterprise and become the figurehead of an anti-Richelieu court faction.

Buckingham had a helpful ally in this regard. His hostess, Madame de Chevreuse, was now having an affair with Holland, and detested Louis who had blamed her for a miscarriage Anne had after the two women had been running in a corridor in 1622. The loss of the baby had ended the brief honeymoon in Louis's marriage: Anne had never forgiven him for his lack of sympathy, while Madame de Chevreuse was briefly banished from court. Richelieu had since had her removed from her post as superintendent of Anne's household. In revenge Madame de Chevreuse had been fanning Anne's distrust of Richelieu, 'as the creature of the king and the queen mother', who liked to keep Anne powerless.[29] She had also been undermining her marriage, giving Anne witty poems on the joys of carnal love, while encouraging her to enjoy the gossip about court gallants said to be in love with her.

As the wife of Charles's proxy Madame de Chevreuse had been instructed to help settle Henrietta Maria into her new role as Queen of England, serving as her closest body servant. She and her husband were therefore travelling to England with her. On the road Madame de Chevreuse made herself busy, chatting with Anne, 'forcing the queen's thoughts towards Buckingham, by perpetually talking about him, and removing what scruples she had [about a flirtation] by dwelling on the annoyance thus given to Cardinal Richelieu'.[30] Buckingham's friend Wat Montagu, who claimed he had made Charles fall in love with every hair on Henrietta Maria's head, was with the duke, as another cupid.

Venetian diplomats reported there was a lot of gossip on the journey to Amiens concerning Anne of Austria, Madame de Chevreuse, the Princess of Condé (wife of the anti-Habsburg senior Prince of the Blood), the British ambassadors and Buckingham, although it was 'all kept very secret'.[31] At Amiens it would explode into scandal.

Henrietta Maria was greeted at the gates of Amiens by the Marshal of France, the Duke of Chaulnes.[32] The gates were adorned with Charles's arms and she was dressed in a formal gown. She had one in green that was to be worn in London, so it may have been another in her trousseau of grey satin, embroidered with gold, silver and pearls. In this fairy-tale costume she was processed through seven triumphal arches to the cathedral where the Bishop of Amiens handed her a golden rose. In an accompanying text Pope Urban explained that in England he expected Henrietta Maria to be like 'a flower' amongst the thorns of heresy, reseeding the Catholic faith in England.[33] At Mass Henrietta Maria then stood godmother to Chaulnes's son, promising to care for the baby's spiritual welfare, just as the Pope had instructed her to care for that of Charles's subjects.

The next day the three queens, Anne, Marie and Henrietta Maria, visited the town's small Carmelite convent. It was here that one of the most revered women in France had died in 1618. Madame Barbe Acarie, who was a cousin of Berulle, had been married aged sixteen to a bully who had taken away her novels, leaving her with only religious books to read. In these, however, she had found direction. She became known for the help she gave the poor and had founded the main Carmelite convent in Paris. After her husband had died she had retired to this smaller convent in Amiens.

The three queens were reported to be very moved as they listened to the stories of Acarie's suffering during her last illness and were shown a crucifix that Acarie had gazed upon in a chapel next to her room. It was said that she bore the stigmata: the marks of Christ's crucifixion on her hands and feet.[34] The visit was intended to be an object lesson to Henrietta Maria: Acarie's life was a reminder that married women, and not just those in religious orders, could dedicate their lives to God through doing good works. Her good work was to be that golden rose. It was also supposed to be the immediate prelude to the last stage of her journey – but the weather was deteriorating and this time it was Marie de' Medici's turn to fall ill.

With Henrietta Maria's departure stalled again, the focus of the court turned from piety to parties. Buckingham had the opportunity to introduce Anne to the English style of dancing, in which couples 'touch hands and pass often near each other', their 'eyes, gestures' and 'a thousand other intangible things' speaking 'the words that the honour of such occasions forbids'.[35] Anne later admitted that she had enjoyed Buckingham's attentions, which, she claimed, 'flattered her glory more than it shocked her virtue'.[36] There was one evening, however, when it had come very near to shocking her virtue. Anne and Buckingham were walking in a garden when they disappeared from the view of her suite. She was heard to cry out for her equerry. Some said later that Buckingham had tried to kiss the queen, others that she had let him do so – until he began to reach below her waist. Anne insisted he had merely expressed himself too passionately in his words. Whatever had actually occurred, the story would annoy Louis and increase his estrangement from Anne, as Buckingham intended.

Charles, meanwhile, was sending frantic letters to his wife. He had left London for the English coast shortly before Henrietta Maria's arrival in Amiens and was so anxious to greet her that he had left his baggage and ridden for Canterbury – a journey of fifty-six miles – in one day.[37] Now he had learned she was delayed again. Henrietta Maria reassured him. Her mother's health was improving and she was on her way. In Amiens there was free wine for everyone as Henrietta Maria left the city. She promised that the next words Charles heard from her would be delivered from her own lips. At the outskirts of the city Henrietta Maria fell to her knees to say a formal goodbye to her mother. Marie gave Henrietta Maria her blessing and a letter with instructions, just as she had done for Elisabeth. Marie had written it in her own hand, 'so that it will be dearer to you'. Henrietta Maria would keep an extended version, written for her mother by Berulle, for the rest of her life.

'From now on, Queen of England, embrace only the interests of this [English] nation; forget in any way those of France,' Henrietta Maria was told. She had, nevertheless to try and cement the fraternal bond between Charles and Louis, whose current interests were far from aligned. Henrietta was further told to love her husband and obey him in all things, save those that were against her religion. On this she was reminded of the weighty responsibilities she had already sworn to uphold. She was to protect persecuted Catholics, who 'have been suffering for many years' and 'not forget the other poor English people. Although they are of another religion than you, you are their queen; you must help and edify them, and by these means gently to prepare them to part from error.'[38] Was this mission even possible? Could she be both a good queen of Protestant England and a good Catholic?

Henry IV had converted to the Catholic religion of the majority to please France, but a very different example was set before the fifteen-year-old. 'Show yourself a worthy daughter of the great St Louis, who went to die for the faith in strange lands,' her mother exhorted her.[39]

Marie then recalled the fate of the Catholic Mary, Queen of Scots, Charles's grandmother, a former queen consort of France, and executed in England dressed in martyr's red. Her parting words to her kneeling daughter were sworn aloud before the gathered crowd. If Henrietta turned apostate, and became a Protestant, the blessing she had just given her daughter would turn to 'a thousand curses'.[40]

While Henrietta Maria has been condemned in British history as a papal agent who turned Charles Catholic, the reality was that she was a fifteen-year-old girl and Charles a twenty-four-year-old monarch who was head of his own Protestant Church – and this was not a role he was likely to want to give up. The denial of Papal authority in religious as well as secular matters was part and parcel of his belief in divine right kingship. And while she was exhorted to inspire conversions by example, her opponents could wield the power of the law and the scaffold. Marie de' Medici realised the pressure to convert would be all one way – on her daughter, not on Charles.

Loud artillery salutes rang out as Henrietta Maria prepared to leave in her carriage, perhaps never to see her mother again. Her distress would be seen in her face days later.

Buckingham was, meanwhile saying his farewells to Anne. He was screened behind the curtain that covered her carriage window, weeping bitterly and kissing her gown. The Princess of Condé, who was sitting beside Anne, joked that while she could attest to Louis of Anne's virtue, if Anne did not look upon Buckingham with more pity she could also attest to Anne's cruelty. Anne viewed it as play-acting, a mere game of courtly love. Only when she was older did she admit these had been 'dangerous illusions'.[41] Both she and Henrietta Maria were pawns in a duel between their husband's leading ministers, Buckingham and Richelieu, but the dangers for Henrietta Maria were particularly acute.

Henrietta Maria's marriage represented an alliance with a Protestant power of a kind that had infuriated Henry IV's Catholic murderer.

Yet it did not please Protestants either. A British polemic had just been published in the Netherlands warning that God would have her murdered at the hands of fellow Catholics, just as had happened to her father, and as a punishment for her religion. Either way, it seems she was damned.

'WHAT SHE WILL THINK, AND SAY, OR DO'

HENRIETTA MARIA HAD NEVER SEEN THE SEA BEFORE, AND RAN to the shore to let the waves lap her feet. Although the weather on the road to Boulogne had been terrible, she had arrived 'in good health and very merry'.[1] The gales were dashing the little fleet of English ships that had been sent to fetch her and she was concerned that she would be seasick and not appear her best when she met her husband. She wrote asking Charles to wait a day or two after her arrival so she could recover from her journey. The next day there was a huge storm in which a sailor fell from his ship and drowned. Nevertheless, she insisted on taking a little boat out into the sea with Gaston to get her sea legs.[2]

In England Charles impatiently filled his time inspecting the navy and coastal fortresses, as well as organising matters for Henrietta Maria's arrival. He had changed his mourning black for mauve and ordered the courtiers who had followed him to Canterbury to wear colour again. The 'cavaliers and ladies' enjoyed their days 'in conversation and the nights in dancing'.[3] There was uncertainty about how to refer to the queen. It was difficult to pronounce the French 'Henriette Marie'. Prayers had been said in the king's chapel for 'Queen Henry'.[4] Since then it had changed everywhere to Marie or Mary. Eventually she would be given the name she is remembered by, the Italianate Henrietta Maria – a nod to her Medici heritage.[5]

Meanwhile everyone was curious to hear stories about Henrietta Maria from those who had travelled to Boulogne. Some had spoken of seeing sadness in her face, which they attributed to her leaving her mother, but they also noted she was 'full of wit' and 'a sweet lovely creature.'[6] There were reports too that Henrietta Maria had spoken to Buckingham's mother with the greatest courtesy.

It was a source of embarrassment to Buckingham that his mother had become a Catholic. Such conversions angered Charles as they had James, and it tarnished him with claims of 'popery'. This referred to a form of spiritual and political tyranny which was applied not only to Catholics but to any form of Protestantism short of pure Calvinism: many Puritans labelled Arminians as popish. His mother's conversion had some use, however. Under the terms of the marriage treaty Henrietta Maria's ladies-in-waiting had to be Catholic and so protect her from undue pressure to change her religion.

The queen's household would be an important alternative court and source of influence. Buckingham hoped his mother and then his Protestant friends and relations would be integrated into it before it could become a centre for plots against him. Richelieu already had allies like Bishop Mende installed, but for Buckingham a precedent had been set concerning Protestants: Lady Holland had been made a lady-in-waiting as a favour to her husband the earl, possibly granted by Marie de' Medici who had always liked him.

On Sunday 12 June – according to the English calendar – the wind dropped, and Henrietta Maria prepared to board the *Prince Royal*. She said a heartfelt goodbye to Gaston on the shore. He was the last family member she would see for many years. Her chief consolation was that 'Mamie' St George, who had cared for her since infanthood, was coming with her.

At 11 a.m. the *Prince Royal* set sail in 'a fair leading gale, fitting the entertainment of a queen.'[7] Henrietta Maria knew little of the kingdom she was heading for: neither the language nor much of its history, save that the English had a habit of cutting off the heads of queens.

Four queens had been beheaded in England over the previous century. Three of them had had strong French connections. Mary, Queen of Scots was half French, while Lady Jane Grey – the so called 'Nine Days Queen' – had been an ally of France. Then there was the queen consort, Anne Boleyn, who was French-educated and, in many ways, so very like Henrietta Maria: black eyes, witty and fierce, and holding religious beliefs feared and detested by the majority of her husband's subjects. Henrietta Maria was, however, much younger than Anne had been and had no English relatives to support her.

When they docked at Dover at eight that night Henrietta Maria was feeling extremely sick. She was escorted off ship, down a bridge that had been built especially for her and that was covered in red cloth. She was then carried in a litter up the hill to the little town of Dover.[8] There was an official welcome from the mayor, delivered in English, which the queen could not understand, after which she was taken in a coach to the castle. The cortège passed through the outer defended ward into the fortified inner bailey where she saw the largest keep in England – the last resort in a siege or attack on a castle – newly adorned with a porch bearing the royal arms. A magnificent supper had been prepared, but Henrietta Maria was still feeling unwell. She asked for another urgent message to be sent to Charles begging him not to come that night.

Although Henrietta Maria's servants later complained they had thought Dover Castle old-fashioned and poorly furnished, she slept well. Charles had taken great care to ensure the king's lodgings had been upgraded, lavishing over £2,600 on it. The next morning Henrietta Maria was feeling a little better and sat down to enjoy her breakfast. Her husband was already on his way, arriving at the castle at 10 a.m. in his ordinary riding clothes. He was told his wife was still eating and so he waited for her in the official Presence Chamber. Henrietta Maria 'made short work' of finishing her meal, and dashed down a 'pair of steps'.[9]

A royal marriage might be about alliances and dynasties, but it was also about two people bound for life. Henrietta Maria saw an elegant young man, with a slight, athletic figure, long curled hair, and a fashionably trimmed beard. Charles scarcely had seconds to absorb the blur of the 'nimble, quick, black-eyed, brown-haired' girl who 'threw herself into his arms with . . . boundless and inexpressible affection', before falling to her knees.[10] 'Sir,' she said in French, 'I have come to this country for Your Majesty to be used and commanded by you.' She reached to kiss his hand. He took hers instead, raised her up, wrapped her in his arms, and covered her in kisses.

Charles had been told that his wife was small and was surprised to find she came to his shoulder. Henrietta Maria noticed him glance at her feet to see if she was wearing stacked shoes. 'Sir, I stand on my own feet. I have no help by art. Thus high I am, and am neither higher nor lower.'[11] Charles asked for them to be left alone and for an hour they were uninterrupted. He was shy and reserved. Henrietta Maria was not, but told him she was worried that 'being young and coming to a strange country [she] might commit many errors'. She asked that if this happened he 'would not be angry with her' and to 'tell her . . . when she did anything amiss'.[12]

Buckingham and the Chevreuses joined them for lunch where Charles carved for his wife. Then they set out for Canterbury in a carriage and six: the latest fashion. The court and local gentry had gathered to greet the king and his queen at Barham Downs, about five miles from the city. They arrived to find the ladies ranked in rows, all dressed in fine clothes, although 'the country ladies outshine the court', a local witness reported.[13] It was Henrietta Maria, however, who was the star of the show.

'We have a most gallant new Queen of England who in true beauty is far beyond the long-wooed Infanta,' a courtier who had been in Spain reported. While the Habsburg princess 'was of a fading flaxen hair, big-lipped and somewhat heavy-eyed . . . this daughter of France, this youngest branch of Bourbon, is of a more lovely and lasting complexion, a dark brown, she has eyes that sparkle like stars, and for her physiognomy she may be said to be a mirror of perfection'.[14]

As they set off for Canterbury again, Charles began by ushering the most senior English ladies into his coach for the onward journey, and Buckingham insisted 'Mamie' St George make way for his sister Susan, Countess of Denbigh.[15] Mamie – who was the highest-ranking female officer in the queen's household – complained to the Duke of Chevreuse. He claimed that Henrietta Maria had agreed the matter with Charles and perhaps she had, with Madame de Chevreuse's encouragement, but it was an unhappy experience and there were other concerns.[16] The roads into Canterbury had been strewn with green rushes and roses to welcome the royal couple and people had clambered into every tree to shout and cheer their greetings. Charles did not, however, wave back.

The Scottish King James had taught his son that acknowledging crowds was unkingly. Yet the English had been used to a theatre of reciprocity under the Tudors, in which their kings and queens had played to the gallery with great success. A display of royal love would not have been amiss at a time of suffering. It was proving a hard summer. The rain was destroying the harvest and there was a severe outbreak of plague. Lymph nodes swelled to the size of eggs, oozing puss, and fever set in. Some victims went mad in their delirium, screaming and running wildly around the streets. Most died within days.

The royal couple spent their first night together at what had been a medieval abbey and was now a private house. The owner, Lord Wotton, had 'come out' as a Catholic in April and Charles had sacked him promptly from his role as a counsellor. Wotton had since retired to another of his properties. What the Protestants guests wanted to know, however, was whether Henrietta Maria could 'abide a Huguenot'? 'Why not,' she replied, 'was not my father one?'[17] This raised hopes that she might convert. It was a Catholic fast day and all eyes now strained to see what she would eat.

As one Catholic admitted, for Henrietta Maria the 'great enemy is great expectation'. She bore the weight of Catholic hopes as well as Protestant fears, 'the good angels are praying above, the ill ones are cursing below. And they of this world' were watching to see 'what she will think, and say, or do, or omit, upon which, her last account must be cast up'.[18] That night she ate meat. Protestants took this as an indication that she was willing to convert. English Catholics took comfort from reports that she had eaten only white meat.[19]

The queen's mind may not have been on her food at all. One observer thought she was 'suffering a touch of the green sickness'. This was not the seasickness that had troubled her when she arrived at Dover; it was an affliction of adolescent virgins, around the queen's age, who were believed to be so desperate to mate they almost lost their minds, not eating, weeping, becoming angry – behaving, in short, like distressed adolescents often do.[20] On some level the strain on her was showing: Henrietta Maria's marriage was about to be consummated in the proper manner, and not just by touching legs with a proxy groom.

After dinner the formal bedding ceremony took place in Henrietta's rooms. Madame de Chevreuse handed Henrietta Maria her night attire. Charles then entered her bedchamber. He came alone and asked his wife's servants to leave. There was 'much ado' to get out 'an old matron who attended on the queen, she alleging that she had engaged her promise to the queen mother not to leave her'.[21] Marie de' Medici wanted to have a witness confirm the marriage was validated. Charles locked all seven doors, only letting in two servants to formally undress him, before also shutting them out.

The next day the young couple remained in bed until 7 a.m. When they emerged, Charles seemed very happy. A groom of the king's bedchamber sent his wife a pair of Charles's ribbon shoelaces to celebrate their king and queen 'lying together'. 'Long may they do so and have as many children as we are like to have.'[22]

The court enjoyed further 'plentiful entertainment' at Cobham Hall in Kent that night. Here they were guests of the king's thirteen-year-old cousin, the Scottish James Stewart, Duke of Lennox – later also Duke of Richmond. He was destined to lose three brothers killed in the Civil War and his wife would travel with Henrietta Maria and her armies.

After dinner, Henrietta Maria put on a private performance of the sarabande for Charles. An erotic dance with castanets, popular in the Americas, it had been banned in Spain for 'arousing tender passions, captivating the heart with the eyes, and disturbing the tranquillity of the mind'. The French version was slower, but no less 'amorous', and its gestures were described as 'lascivious'.[23] Yet Henrietta Maria loved the sarabande. With her long arms, she was built perfectly for it, and she had a natural grace. Her 'whole body moves in music', a contemporary recalled, 'Nor indeed, can the set of looks or turn the head, or hold a flower of fan in her hand . . . but she performs it at such ease as if it was all flowing nature.' Her dancing 'binds the wildest heart . . . and breeds nothing but the bees honey without the sting'.[24]

Buckingham, observing Charles's reaction as he watched his wife dance from behind a screen, wrote to Louis crowing that he had no doubt Charles would soon be siring children – as Louis had not. The next morning the couple travelled by barge down the Thames towards London. At Gravesend the Royal Navy fired 'fifteen hundred great shot' in salute. It was 5 p.m. when they reached Charles's capital.[25]

Henrietta Maria now saw the strange and magnificent structure of London Bridge. Spanning over 900 feet it had been built in the twelfth century and had acquired its own little village, a crazy muddle of buildings that over 500 people called home. Many of these houses were over five floors in height and some burst forward, overhanging the river by as much as seven feet. There were shops too, and in the middle of the bridge stood Nonsuch House, so called because there was no other house like it. Prefabricated in the Netherlands it had onion domes, gilded weathervanes and a sundial that read 'Time and tide wait for no man'. This was true, as Henrietta Maria discovered, when they sped through the rapids between one of its nineteen mismatched arches, to emerge on the far side. There they found themselves amongst thousands of small boats full of curious spectators.

Fifty ships of the Royal Navy fired their ordnance as the king and queen stood at the barge's windows, both dressed in green. A heavy shower burst and in the sequinned light Henrietta Maria saw before her a vast cityscape of church spires, pitched roofs and tall chimneys. A quarter of a million people lived here and the lord mayor's instructions to avoid public assemblies for fear of spreading plague had been put aside. Londoners were crammed on the shore, on wherries, and in the windows of their tall plaster houses, all 'shouting amain' for the king and queen.[26] There had been 165 victims of plague and typhus only the previous week but London, like Canterbury, still remained in that strange period of disbelief that marks the early days of a major epidemic.

As the royal barge approached Whitehall Palace, London's bells began to ring out, not slowly, tolling for the dead, but loud and gay, proclaiming the arrival of England's new queen. Henrietta Maria got off the barge at the Watergate in her formal gown with its train and trailing sleeves, all embroidered in silver and gold and sewn with pearls. Whitehall's disparate collection of Tudor buildings had no equivalent to the Pavilion of the King at the Louvre, although alongside it there was a beautiful Italianate Banqueting House in bright bands of coloured stone. It had been designed by the London-born architect Inigo Jones and completed only three years earlier, its clean modern lines advertising order, harmony and authority, which was how Charles saw the future. The reality of his current situation was, however, challenging.

Elizabeth I had bequeathed a Crown mired in debt and King James had failed to engage Parliament in a desperately needed reform of taxation. On the journey from Dover many of Henrietta Maria's household had complained that Charles's 'penury appeared in all directions at table, in the coaches, waggons and horses.'[27] Where in 1620 her sister Christine had been given a Grand Entry to Turin in which she had been processed through a brand-new outer gate, then along a newly widened street to the royal palace, Henrietta Maria was greeted merely with new taffeta hangings for her apartment. Her rooms did, however, have some fine works of art, that included portraits of her parents, and she also had beautiful views of the Thames where swans bobbed on rippling pewter waters.

Charles would prove also as generous as he was able in his support of his wife's intention to renovate and refurbish her lodgings in the French taste. At the French court, for example, the bedchamber was a ceremonial space where important audiences would take place. Henrietta Maria's trousseau contained appropriate bedchamber furnishings in red velvet trimmed with silver and gold. It was to be set up at Whitehall on a red-covered dais, the bed crowned with four white ostrich feathers.[28] Meanwhile, the next morning Henrietta Maria went to the small room, or oratory, that had been set aside for her worship. Under the persecution Catholicism had been driven from public spaces into private homes where priests were hidden illegally: often by women. Fewer women than men had offices or wealth to lose and so women took greater risks. They also kept their faith alive by educating their children in their religion. As queen Henrietta Maria was a mother to the whole nation and it itched Protestant anxieties.

A witness reported sourly that Mass was 'mumbled over her Majesty at 11.00 at what time she came out of her bedchamber in her petticoat, with a veil upon her head'. The mumbling was the lowered voice of the priest during the consecration of the Eucharist. The veil was lace as it was there not merely to cover the queen's hair for modesty, rather it was a mark of reverence and an acknowledgement of what is sacred. The tabernacle was also veiled. To the witness, she was committing idolatry, the worship of a baker's wafer. The danger feared by many was that the habit might spread. Charles now banned his subjects from attending the queen's chapels: anyone who did so would risk arrest.[29]

Under the terms of the marriage treaty English Catholics would not be punished for attending Mass in their own homes, but with the religious and diplomatic climate so stormy, Catholics worried that even this modest gain would be denied them. It was being said already that the plague was God's punishment for permitting the queen her Mass and for the relaxing of the laws against Catholics. A five-man delegation, headed by the head of the English secular clergy (that is, of parish priests, not members of religious orders), braved heavy rain to arrive at the palace later that same day, looking for assurances of support from the queen.[30] The Bishop of Mende and the Duke of Chevreuse duly gave it to them, but Louis's refusal to give Charles military aid gave Charles little incentive to carry out his pledges concerning Catholics, and he soon had good political reasons not to.

On 21 June the articles of marriage were read at the Banqueting House. The room was hung with silk and cloth of gold and decorated with cupboards of jewelled crystal basins, ewers, cups and salts. The court and the French ambassadors had dressed in their finest clothes – the jewels worn by the Duke of Chevreuse were reputed to be worth £100,000. The couple were blessed by a Church of England bishop and they kissed to seal their union. There was a dinner and dancing. Yet it was soon clear that Henrietta Maria accepting a Protestant blessing would not make attacks on Catholics any less aggressive.

The first parliament of Charles's reign had opened on 18 June, with the king politely doffing his crown to his MPs. Parliament was a vital tax-raising body for the king: one capable of giving MPs considerable influence over royal decisions and so protecting the rights and property of their electorate. Charles had asked them to vote immediately for the subsidies he needed to fight the Habsburgs. Instead, a conference was set up with representatives from the Houses of Lords and Commons about how to restrict Henrietta Maria's Catholic influence and that of her household.

The MPs eventually demanded that Catholics be banned from visiting court without a royal warrant, that all anti-Catholic laws be executed to the maximum degree, and that the government take control of the education of Catholic children out of the hands of their parents. Buckingham gave the French private assurances that the king would mitigate any such laws, but in public he supported their imposition, triggering a series of furious arguments with Bishop Mende.

Berulle – the man who had assured the Pope that Henrietta Maria's marriage would kick-start the reconversion of the Stuart kingdoms – was in despair. He told Henrietta Maria that she was surrounded not just by plague victims, but also 'the dead and infected before God', heretics destined for hellfire.[31] He wrote to Mother Madeleine, the abbess of the main Carmelite convent in Paris, 'There is nothing in this country to recommend to you' and 'a great deal to fear'.[32] He planned to return home as soon as possible. Henrietta Maria did not have that choice.

'The great historiographers of Christendom have now taken their pens into their hands,' a contemporary noted, 'and already they are assembling notes for their great works, and they resolve to give, to this Majesty, a very principal part of those acts, which are to be represented to the life, upon the theatre of this world, whether they prove good or bad.'[33]

7

ROWS

IN HER LETTER OF INSTRUCTION MARIE DE' MEDICI HAD URGED her daughter to 'Be a model of honour . . . so that your bearing, your gaze, all your actions show cultivation.'[1] Henrietta Maria managed to live up to this ideal some days better than others. She kept her composure when the plague entered the palace on 2 July, killing a woman in the royal pantry and the baker's son. All the bread was given away, but the Venetian ambassador reported further cases among 'low officials'. How long until it spread closer?

Large numbers of visitors were permitted to watch Henrietta Maria dine at court, often in closed and stifling hot rooms. One day she appeared as a 'most delicate lady' with 'sparkling black eyes' whose 'deportment among her women [was] so sweet and humble' that a visitor found he could only sigh that she was not of the 'true religion'.[2] Another day a different visitor saw her drive everyone out from her dining room 'with one frown'. The queen might be small, he noted, but she had 'a more than ordinary resolution'.[3]

Henrietta Maria longed for fresh air. She walked whenever she could in the meadows by the Thames. One day she even took a rake and joined the haymakers at their work.[4] The attacks on Catholics in Parliament and the fractious relationship between Louis and Charles nevertheless began to show in the royal marriage. The king's duty to provide suitable places for her worship had been agreed before she had left France. Yet

72

when her priests inquired about the unfinished chapel at St James's Palace, Charles snapped that if the closet at Whitehall wasn't big enough for their purposes they should use the garden, and if not the garden, then the park.[5]

In public Henrietta Maria showed Charles due regard, but in private she was often in a 'humour of distaste'.[6] He, in turn, was irritated by the louche behaviour of her companions and the lack of respect it showed him. One of Charles's first actions as king had been to clean up the lax morals of his father's court and to reintroduce strict Elizabethan rules of precedence. The French enjoyed witty conversation above bowing and scraping, and it embarrassed Charles that they flouted his rules, insisting 'upon being French everywhere, retaining their freedom of speech and manners'.[7]

The problem was made worse by the poor vetting of Henrietta Maria's household. It had been increased from the sixty-five people who had served her since she was twelve, to 400, and included some of the 'most ordinary and ill-fashioned people in France'.[8] Bishop Mende felt that many of the women in the queen's household would be more suited to a brothel than to serving the queen. The only positive point of contact between Charles and Henrietta Maria were the Duke and Duchess of Chevreuse, who were liked by them both, but their sojourn in England was about to be cut short.

Mende had discovered that Madame de Chevreuse and Buckingham were 'shut up [together] five or six hours every day'. He feared that 'Holland has made over his prize' and told Richelieu that she was now having an affair with Buckingham.[9] Whether or not the duchess had taken on a new lover while nine months pregnant, Richelieu had good reason to be concerned that Buckingham was ensconced with such a troublemaker. Louis sent orders that the duke and duchess return as soon as Madame de Chevreuse had delivered her child. It proved to be a little girl and on 28 July 1625 Charles and Henrietta Maria attended the baby's christening at Richmond Palace. There they said their goodbyes to the Chevreuses.

The king and queen were also leaving London where deaths from the plague were now running at 3,500 a week.[10] Charles had prorogued Parliament which was set to reopen in Oxford on 1 August. Charles left for nearby Woodstock on the afternoon of the christening and Henrietta Maria the next day, travelling by barge. Wherever the court went, the plague followed. Two men died in Windsor in a house where the queen's priests lodged during a brief stopover. Others were already dying in Oxford where the reassembled Parliament proved no more anxious to grant Charles his subsidies than it had in London.

The loss of Breda, at the cost of several thousand English soldiers, the failure to extract any promises from the French over the Palatinate, and fears about the agreements made with Louis concerning Catholics were all of concern, and responsibility was laid at Buckingham's door.

The favourite's failures were put down to a combination of corruption and popery. More traditional members of the Church of England saw Arminians as little better than a Catholic fifth column and Buckingham was believed to be the leading influence on Charles's own 'Arminian' tastes. Get rid of Buckingham and, it was hoped, Charles might be brought back to the righteous path.

Yet Buckingham's enemies covered a wide political and religious range – and not all of them were opponents of Arminianism. Charles would have gained many friends if he had sacrificed Buckingham. Instead, the king tried to deflect MPs' criticisms of the duke with the reimposition of the penal laws against Catholics. No more would they be allowed to hear Mass in their own homes without fear of punishment. Henrietta Maria learned that her co-religionists were also forbidden from travelling further than five miles from their homes and again to be fined for refusing to attend Protestant services.[11] Many poorer Catholics ended up in prison for non-payment where they were unable to work and thus could not provide for their families.

In breaking his promises under the marriage treaty, Charles was, quite brutally, choosing his favourite over his wife. He was not the only king to do such a thing, but his relationship with Buckingham was a peculiarly intense bromance. His father had lavished love on Buckingham when Charles was in his early teens. It had hurt him that James would take Buckingham's side when they quarrelled. Everything had changed, however, after his mother's death in 1619, when Buckingham had recast himself as Charles's friend, rather than his rival. Buckingham had helped improve Charles's relationship with his father and eventually James had become the outsider in this familial threesome, with Charles and Buckingham conspiring together, not least on making war against the Habsburgs in spite of James's preference for peace. Charles, acting as Buckingham's protector, had now gone further in supplanting James. The lonely boy who had once looked up to the sophisticated older man had become a powerful king, a father to his friend in his role as a monarch.

Charles's actions against Catholics failed to spare Buckingham further criticism from MPs, and Parliament was dissolved without the king gaining his subsidies. Meanwhile Henrietta Maria wanted to do something to make her feelings felt. That September, when she was staying at Titchfield Abbey in Hampshire, she was told that a Church of England service was taking place in the Hall. She had no legal recourse to protect her fellow Catholics from being obliged to attend such services on pain of ruin but she could express her anger. She did so by bursting into the service with her friends, interrupting the sermon, and walking up and down with them, laughing and joking loudly.

Later the gang spotted the minister sitting quietly on a bench in the garden. They sneaked behind a hedge and fired a pistol, covering the terrified minister with hail shot.[12] Was this childish? Perhaps – but she had limited powers as an independent adult, nor did her elders set her a more mature example.

On another day at Titchfield the queen's new confessor, an ally of Richelieu called Père de Sancy, decided to compete with the king's

Protestant chaplain over who was to lead the prayers at the beginning and conclusion of the meal. The king's chaplain won the first round in alliance with the carvers who slapped down the food on the king's plate. Even Charles joined in, 'pulling the dishes to him'. At the end of the meal de Sancy tried again, praying so loudly he drowned the clergyman out. Charles then lost his temper, seized his wife by the hand and dragged her from the table.[13] That this was as much about Anglo-French rivalry as it was about religion is evident in Henrietta Maria rebelling on other matters.

Henrietta Maria was being encouraged by her servants to stand up to any interference in how they managed her affairs. When Charles sent instructions to Hampton Court that she was to order her household in the same manner as his mother had, she snapped at his messenger that she hoped he 'would give her leave to order her house as she list [wished]'. The next time Charles saw her he reminded her that she should never 'have affronted me in such a thing publicly'. She duly gave him 'so ill an answer' that he couldn't bring himself to repeat it, even to Buckingham.[14] Charles found it difficult to read people and was bewildered by the change in the eager girl he had met at Dover, so he sent his friend to talk to her. Buckingham duly delivered a vicious dressing-down, reputedly even going so far as to remind her that queens in England had been known to lose their heads. Henrietta Maria was unmoved.

One night, when they were in bed together, Henrietta Maria handed Charles a piece of paper listing the officers she wished to manage her jointure. Charles told her she couldn't have any French managing income from English land that he had settled on her. She replied that she and her mother had already made the appointments, Charles told her they had no right to do so. She then turned on him, he recalled, and, 'bade me plainly to take the lands to myself; for if she had no power to put in whom she would in those places, she would have neither lands nor houses of me'.[15] Charles told her 'to remember to whom she spoke'. This triggered a further tirade, with the enraged teenager telling him 'how miserable she was' and how this was all his fault. Charles tried to interrupt, but 'she would not so much as hear me. Then she went on saying, 'she was not of that base quality to be used so ill'.[16]

Diplomats from states like Venice and Savoy, who opposed the Habsburgs in Italy, and wanted to see an effective Anglo-French alliance, were appalled at the deterioration in the royal marriage. The Venetian ambassador in Paris went to see Marie de' Medici and pleaded with her to smooth relations between the couple.[17] She seems to have done so for Charles was soon (rather pompously) informing Buckingham that his wife had begun 'to mend her manners'.[18] Richelieu too seemed anxious to improve relations and was making fresh promises of joining a wider alliance against the Habsburgs, that would include the Danes and the Dutch, as well the Venetians and Savoyards.

Henrietta Maria began to show generosity to favoured Protestant women, even kissing them in greeting. By Christmas she seemed happier.[19] She was spotted at London's main shopping centre, the Royal Exchange, where she 'went nimbly from shop to shop, and bought some knacks, till, being discovered, she made away with all haste'.[20] Yet there were few such carefree days. Rather than wait for the French alliance to be in place Buckingham, as Lord Admiral, had launched a naval assault on Cadiz. It had ended in failure with the ears of British sailors decorating Spanish hats. Hoping to blunt Puritan criticism Buckingham was now saying that it was more important to British interests to support the Huguenot rebels in France than to fight the Habsburgs.

Henrietta Maria tried instead to improve Anglo-French relations. She wrote to her mother asking her to press Louis to moderation towards the Huguenot rebels and expressed anguish about the quarrels between her husband and brother. She also planned a masque with a theme designed to further foster Anglo-French goodwill. Charles had made her a generous New Year's gift of his mother's palace, Denmark House, which overlooked the Thames on the south side of the Strand. It was the first of seven houses he would give his wife during their marriage. Now known under its earlier name of Somerset House, this was to be her principal residence and she was having Inigo Jones build a theatre in it. At first, Henrietta Maria hoped to show the play at the time of Charles's coronation, which was to be held on 2 February 1626. But then her role in the coronation ceremony became the source of another row.

Charles's persecution of Catholics was beginning to bite hard. The Venetian ambassador reported in January 1626 priests were being imprisoned almost daily and ordinary Catholics were being taxed two-thirds of their income. One recusant – that is, a Catholic fined for refusing to go to Protestant services – wrote from the Fleet prison that twenty-three of his fellow inmates had died recently of plague. Imprisonment for being unable to meet the fines was, for some, a death sentence. Letters to Henrietta Maria from Berulle in France reminded the queen she had a duty to these suffering Catholics. [21] Her confessor, Père de Sancy, told her that she should demonstrate this by standing with the recusants and boy-cotting court ceremonies that had any Protestant religious content.

Henrietta Maria duly refused to take part in Charles's coronation. This has been quoted as an example of her 'bigotry', but seven months earlier, in June 1625, she had been willing to have her marriage blessed by a Protestant bishop. It was a response to the renewed persecution and to the deterioration in Anglo-French relations prompted by Buck-ingham's threats to interfere in France's internal affairs. Being crowned would have given her greater status, as it had her mother, but her brother Louis was also against it, reminding her that 'a heavenly crown is better'.[22] Berulle assured her that it wouldn't risk her marriage because Charles would one day return to the Catholic fold of his grandmother, Mary, Queen of Scots.

Berulle's view had no basis in anything other than wishful thinking, but Buckingham ensured that Charles didn't press his wife on the mat-ter of the coronation. Neither Puritans nor moderate Calvinists wished to see a Catholic queen crowned, and he hoped his action would help ameliorate their attacks on him. It did, with the Venetian ambassador reporting, 'the duke has caused more satisfaction over this than by all his other devices to save himself'.[23]

On coronation day Henrietta Maria stood at the window of a private house near the palace gate and watched as Charles was processed to Westminster Abbey. He had dressed in white satin beneath a mantle of purple velvet. It was said during the Civil War that Charles had been warned by the Earl of Pembroke that the only kings of England to have been crowned in white were Richard II and Henry VI, both of whom were overthrown and murdered.[24] In fact King James had dressed in white. It is in the significance of the date – the Feast of Candlemas – that the origins of the myth of the white king are found.

It was traditional to choose a holy day for a coronation. This was problematic as holy days were Catholic. James had chosen the feast of St James, who, as an apostle, was more acceptable to Protestants than lesser saints. Charles chose Candlemas. In Catholic tradition this is the feast of the purification of the Virgin Mary, when all the candles to be used the following year are consecrated. Charles, however, had chosen Candlemas as a means to drawing attention to his religious role as head of the Protestant Church of England. Charles, like his father, saw the coronation as anointing him as a combination of layman and cleric. Candlemas highlighted that he was being purified for his spiritual role in the reign ahead.[25]

There are no surviving accounts from 1626 describing the white suit as a novelty, but there was a report of a prayer that drew attention to Charles's having the care of his subjects' souls, as well as their bodies.[26] The prayer was said to date back to the reign of Henry VI, whose rule had ushered in the Wars of the Roses before his eventual overthrow. Already – over eighteen years before the story of the Earl of Pembroke's warning about the white suit was first recorded – Charles was being linked to a failed king and to civil war. Why was this?

If military success raised a king to greatness, then military failure was often their undoing. Henry VI had an unpopular French wife, but it was losing the Hundred Years' War, not his marriage, that had triggered the Wars of the Roses. Charles's reign was less than a year old and already it had seen military failure at Breda and Cadiz. This was hugely damaging, but the mention of Charles having care of his subjects' souls is also significant.

The rich ceremonial of the coronation with its use of relics and holy oils was little different to that of earlier Protestant monarchs, but it may have acted as a reminder of Charles's love of ritual. Where Puritans hoped for further reform of the Church of England on Calvinist lines, Charles's Arminianism threatened an entirely different sort of reform. This was one that Charles saw as restoring to the Church of England the traditions of the ancient Christian Church, before corruption by Rome, but which Calvinists, with their fierce tradition of iconoclasm, did not recognise as true Protestantism.

There was also another piece of gossip doing the rounds. It was said that during the coronation procession the queen's ladies were seen in the window of the house at the palace gate dancing behind her. The suggestion is not merely of high spirits, but a display of disrespect, even of a witches' revel: as if Henrietta Maria, god-daughter of the Antichrist, rejoiced in the knowledge the king would lead his people to doom, just as Henry VI had done.

On 4 February 1626 a new Parliament opened and there was another argument between the royal couple. It was a ridiculous dispute – Charles insisted Henrietta Maria cross a muddy garden to get to rooms from where she could watch the procession with Buckingham's mother. She refused to risk getting her feet wet until persuaded otherwise by the French ambassador. The fact she had listened to the ambassador, but not to him, annoyed Charles so much that he sent Buckingham to order her to return to her own apartment. It was two days before the tantrums and sulks were resolved – notably by Henrietta Maria asking to see Charles in private. They slept together that night, but the tensions with France continued to damage their relationship.

A truce was signed between Louis and the Huguenots on 5 February, with the English having persuaded their fellow Protestants to agree terms. There also seemed to be progress on the military alliance against the Habsburgs. Christine's husband Victor Amadeus of Savoy had been offered the command of French troops against Spain in Italy. However, the Savoyard ambassador in Paris, the abbot and art collector Alessandro Scaglia, had warned Buckingham not to trust Richelieu to hold good on any of his promises. He suggested the duke still needed to have the cardinal removed from power. The French court was 'a heaven full of comets', Scaglia noted. Should Richelieu's star fall then an ally could seize control of French foreign policy.

While Buckingham considered how Richelieu might be destroyed, the cardinal's nephew, Mende, was making alliances with a group of anti-Arminians in Parliament who planned to have Buckingham impeached for corruption. Their decision had been made after a conference was held at Buckingham's house on the writings of an extreme Arminian cleric called Richard Montagu. Holland's elder brother, the great anti-Spanish privateer Robert Rich, 2nd Earl of Warwick, had hoped to see Montagu's writings condemned and Buckingham help change the direction of Charles's religious policy. By 17 February it was clear this was not going to happen.

Warwick shared with his brother 'a pleasant and companiable wit', but having inherited the family estates he was free from the necessity of the court career that Holland needed to support his flamboyant lifestyle.[27] He could afford to take the risk of angering Charles.

A client of Warwick's in the Commons, a Puritan MP called John Pym, who had a reputation of working with the relentlessness of an ox at the plough, was picked to ensure the charges against Buckingham would be as hard-hitting as possible.

On Shrove Tuesday, as Pym's work began, Henrietta Maria held the masque she hoped would encourage good relations with France. She and twelve of her ladies had been rehearsing it for weeks.[28]

Charles's mother Anna had performed in masques, but she had not had any speaking roles. Henrietta Maria did, and was rumoured to have learned over 600 lines, 'no normal thing here' it was observed.[29] Perhaps it was because this was so radical that the audience, sitting in her new theatre at the upper end of the hall in Somerset House, was restricted to senior members of the nobility and a few foreign dignitaries.

The masque was a pastoral – a romance set amongst shepherds in an imaginary rural idyll. Inigo Jones, who had spent twenty years mastering the technology of scene changes, had been instructed to do an illusionist setting that encompassed the different locales into one complex scene. It would look old-fashioned to those used to his work, 'a French antique' some later called it, but the result was stunning nonetheless. It included a village street with thatched cottages, grand houses, a ruin and an eight-columned temple.

The script, adapted from a French original, focused on a heroine called Artenice, played by Henrietta Maria. For dynastic reasons Artenice is promised to a man she does not love. Her heart is with Alcidor, who comes from the other side of the river and is therefore forbidden to her. Alcidor represented Charles, born in another kingdom, across the narrow waters of the Channel. In the course of the pastoral the lovers discover they share the same roots. This referred to Charles's half-French, Catholic grandmother, Mary, Queen of Scots. Their shared heritage means the lovers can marry.

The audience had to wait until the opening of the third scene before Henrietta Maria delivered her first speech. In the voice of Artenice, Henrietta lamented the gap between human laws and natural laws, expressing her longing to be like the birds who can sing freely of their love. Divine law is seen in nature, which is God's Creation, and so nature trumps human convention. This gave Artenice the right to act in accordance with her conscience rather than the diktats of men. The pastoral concluded with the lovers united, having discovered they had much in common after all. The queen and her ladies then stepped down from the stage to dance with the audience. Behind them shutters closed to reveal a painted image of Somerset House from the Thames. They had moved from an imaginary world to the reality of London and the court, French and English touching hands to the music.[30]

Henrietta Maria hoped the masque would act as a reminder of the images of a harmonious union promoted at their wedding, as well as the kindness on religion that had been promised.[31] It was 'beautiful', a Tuscan diplomat reported, 'the decoration and the changing of the scene, as well as the gestures and elocution of the ladies, among whom the queen outdid all the rest'.[32] Yet the pastoral drew no positive comment from the English. 'I hear not much honour of the queen's masque,' one gossip reported, 'for, if they were not all, some were in men's apparel.'[33]

Masculine style had been fashionable at James's court, where it imitated the androgynous clothing of the infamous pipe-smoking cutpurse Mary Frith.[34] It was, however, also seen as transgressive. It suggested an attempt by women to usurp male authority. Nor did Henrietta Maria's assertion of her French-Catholic identity endear her to her audience who were about to discover that Louis had betrayed all his promises to his would-be allies against Spain.

On 5 March 1626, after any hint of secret peace talks with Philip IV had been denied, Louis signed a treaty with Spain. It agreed that France's allies in northern Italy, the Protestant Grey League, would keep their overlordship of the Val Tellina passes, with the pro-Spanish Catholic Val Telliners given local political and religious rights. Richelieu was concerned that the costs of war to France had become prohibitive. They had caused annual state expenses to rise to over 40 million livres in the previous year – 25 million more than was taken in.[35] Nor did he believe that France's internal security was yet established. England, Savoy and Venice were bitterly disappointed. 'Broken faith, false promises, secret intrigues, plain trickeries, "Yea" in the mouth, and "Nay" in the heart have between them ended in a treaty,' a Venetian commented.[36]

Diplomatic observers noted that Henrietta Maria's French household did nothing to help dissociate her from Louis's act of treachery, keeping her 'thoroughly French, both in her sentiments and habits'. 'The marriage has not changed her one whit.'[37] She spoke French, ate French food, enjoyed French amusements. Nor was there any attempt to be discreet about her religion with Henrietta Maria still aiming to set a pious example. Her household prepared for Holy Week in the run-up to Easter on 2 April by turning Somerset House into a virtual convent. There was a gallery divided and fitted up with cells, a refectory for dining and an oratory for religious services.

This was to be a retreat time of peace and meditation for Henrietta Maria, who waited on her servants, as a reminder of Christ's service to mankind. For many Protestants, however, the queen's acts of humility looked more like humiliation at the hands of her priests: an attempted assertion of the power of the Church over the Crown. Protestant distrust of a celibate clergy fed into other prejudices. It was said the queen's priests used her confessions as pornography and would salaciously 'interrogate her how often in a night the king had kissed her'.[38] Charles admitted he was jealous of the time she spent with them, complaining they were 'stealing her away'.

The king also had other anxieties. A pamphlet had appeared accusing Buckingham of having murdered James with a poisoned plaster and syrup that he had supplied for the king when he was dying. This was a piece of Habsburg – not French – black propaganda, but it was being used by Buckingham's English enemies who were being wooed by Bishop Mende. A parliamentary select committee cross-examined James's doctors and discovered Buckingham had twice violated rules that only the royal physicians could prescribe and administer drugs. In May the House of Commons laid formal charges before the Lords against the duke. Framed largely by Pym the charges alleged not only political corruption but also 'injury' to King James, leading to his death.

This was treason, and if proven, was a capital offence. Mende was, in effect, plotting with Buckingham's would-be killers.

In France Buckingham's allies were repaying the compliment in a plan to murder Richelieu. It was, however, the queen consorts, Henrietta Maria and Anne, who would have the worse summer ahead.

WINNING THE KING

BUCKINGHAM'S FLIRTATION WITH ANNE OF AUSTRIA WHILE escorting Henrietta Maria from Paris had succeeded in annoying Louis. The question it had not answered was how easily Anne might be detached entirely from loyalty to her husband. There were now new reasons to believe it was worth pressing.

In March 1626, Louis and Marie de' Medici had announced Gaston's betrothal to the richest heiress in France: Mademoiselle Bourbon de Montpensier, daughter of Henri de Bourbon, Duke of Monpensier. Louis wanted to avoid a dynastic marriage with the daughter of any ruler that would have allied Gaston with a foreign kingdom. This would have given the 'rising sun' of France far too much power and potentially limited Louis's choices in foreign policy. The marriage would also ensure that her wealth would be kept within Louis's immediate family and not enrich one of the other princely houses. It did, however, threaten the position of the still childless Anne. Charles's former ambassador in Paris, 'Camel Face' Carlisle, who was back in France, spoke to Madame de Chevreuse about how to exploit this.

The duchess, who 'often suggested expedients so brilliant they seemed like flashes of lightning', described Louis as 'an idiot who is incapable of governing'.[1] They could declare this incapacity and remove him from rule – an idea which had featured in the rebellion of the 2nd Earl of Essex against Elizabeth I in 1601. Louis's marriage would be dissolved and Gaston would then marry Anne. This, it was hoped, would help neutralise any Spanish opposition to Louis's overthrow. Anne's sibling, Philip IV, would simply be exchanging one brother-in-law for another.

Buckingham had wanted Anne as a figurehead around whom to build an anti-Richelieu court faction. He now saw she could be used not only to overthrow the cardinal, but Louis as well.

Gaston, who was being denied the say in government affairs he believed to be his right, proved to be a willing conspirator and other recruits were not hard to find. The twenty-two-year-old Soissons, who had been thwarted in his hopes of marrying Henrietta Maria, now wished to marry Mademoiselle Bourbon de Montpensier. Then there was that serial rebel the Prince of Condé, whose wife had been in the carriage with Anne and Buckingham at Amiens. Condé's long-standing allies, Louis's illegitimate half-brothers César and Alexandre Vendôme, were also recruited, as was one of Louis childhood playmates: the popular and handsome Marquis of Chalais, who had fallen madly in love with Madame de Chevreuse. 'Since my life depends on you, I fear not to hazard it for you,' Chalais promised her.[2]

What would become known as the Chalais conspiracy began to unravel on 4 May 1626, with the arrest of the superintendent of Gaston's household. He had been particularly vociferous in calling for Gaston to have a share of power and Richelieu was anxious to discover if he had a plan to do anything about it. A number of the plotters decided they needed to act before the superintendent gave anything away in prison. They discussed inviting Richelieu to a dinner party at which an argument would erupt. Swords would then be drawn and he was to be killed 'by chance' in the melee. These plans were leaked by a panicked conspirator. Richelieu did not yet know the full details of the conspiracy, but a series of further arrests and interrogations soon began. Meanwhile Louis gave the cardinal a bodyguard of musketeers for life.

*   *   *

In England King Charles was desperate to prevent the impeachment case against Buckingham, launched in the House of Commons, from reaching the Lords. He had not yet persuaded MPs to grant him the subsidies he needed for his war, but he couldn't afford to wait longer. On 15 June 1626 Charles dissolved his second parliament. He was angry that his MPs had attempted to dictate to him on his choice of leading counsellor and a few days later Charles entered Henrietta Maria's apartment at Whitehall to find her women also breaching his rules on court etiquette, dancing and amusing themselves with her.

Charles grabbed Henrietta Maria's hand, pulling her to his apartment, which lay next to her own, and locked her in his rooms. He then ordered her friends into the park. There he told them he was sending them home. From her locked room above, Henrietta Maria saw her women weeping. Unable to discover what was happening she 'grew very impatient and broke the glass windows with her fist'.[3] Yet within a few days calm had returned and, with 'her rage appeased', the king and queen were seen 'very jocund together'.[4] Others too noted that 'in spite of all these troubles they behave towards each other with great affection'.[5] What on earth was going on?

The truth was that the problems in the royal marriage were caused largely by external forces: 'The king is most good-tempered and without vices,' a Venetian diplomat wrote, 'unless his poverty is one, and his affection for the duke [another].' As for Henrietta, she was naturally ebullient, 'a very perfect character [with] a lively and firm disposition'.[6] Both Charles and Henrietta Maria wanted their marriage to work and were attracted to each other. Even sleeping apart for two nights caused comment. But the people they loved fanned any problems between them, and in this regard a misunderstanding helped to trigger what would prove to be a major turning point in Henrietta Maria's life and marriage.

Urban VIII had declared a Jubilee year in which Catholics were encouraged to travel to Rome to hear Mass, in return gaining a papal indulgence offering a partial remission of sins. Since British Catholics were too impoverished to travel to Rome, and also fearful of drawing attention to themselves, Henrietta Maria had successfully petitioned her godfather to extend the Jubilee to British Catholics who attended Mass in England. On 26 June 1626, Henrietta Maria retreated to Somerset House to celebrate the Jubilee. There, it appears to have been suggested to her that she set an example to Catholics by walking publicly to her unfinished chapel at St James's Palace to hear Mass.

Afterwards the queen went to Hyde Park to enjoy the open air.[7] This was close to Tyburn where numerous Catholic priests had been executed. To Catholics the priests had died as martyrs; to Protestants they had been traitors. Stories soon spread that the queen had been processed barefoot to where the scaffolds usually stood, 'her luciferian confessor riding alongside her in his coach', lording it over her.[8] It was said she had then prayed for the Jesuit, Henry Garnet, executed following the Gunpowder Plot in 1605.[9] The French angrily denied any procession to Tyburn. Buckingham, however, seized the opportunity to press Charles for his instructions on how to respond.[10] Charles promptly ordered the immediate expulsion of his wife's French household.

Henrietta Maria was left with only two priests, her cook, musicians and dressmakers.

In the place of Mamie St George and other old friends came Buckingham's allies and relations. Henrietta Maria was particularly distressed by the inclusion of the twenty-six-year-old Lucy, Countess of Carlisle, wife of 'Camel Face' and a first cousin of Henry Holland. Described as 'the glory of her sex and the ornament of the age', Lucy was reputed to be Buckingham's mistress and Bishop Mende believed Buckingham intended to plant her in Charles's bed.[11] If so, she posed a serious threat. Lucy was 'full of enchantment', but also ferociously ambitious. It was said she had 'more lions and more leopards' in her character than the king kept in the Tower zoo.[12]

Henrietta Maria's mental and physical health collapsed, with her French doctor reporting having to treat her for stomach pains and melancholy.[13] Buckingham's sister, Susan, Countess of Denbigh, tried to gain the queen's favour and restore her well-being by reinstating two of her most long-standing servants and their families. They included her nurse, who had been with her since 1615 when her mother had gone into exile. These servants were, however, now in Buckingham's pocket. The Venetian ambassador noted that Henrietta Maria was watched closely, something she felt keenly.[14] 'I try to hide (as much as I can) to write to you,' she told Mende, 'being like a prisoner who cannot talk to anyone, neither to describe my misfortunes, nor to call out the name of God, to have pity upon a poor oppressed princess.'[15]

Henrietta Maria wanted her friends and family to use all their powers to force Charles to accept her household back. She begged Louis as his 'most affectionate sister' to take pity on 'the most miserable creature in the world'. She warned her mother she was 'on the point of death'. She flattered Richelieu that no one was better able to help her than he was.[16] As Charles reminded Marie de' Medici, however, her sisters Elisabeth and Christine had long since lost their French servants and 'there can be no exceptions taken at me, to follow the examples of Spain and Savoy in this particular'.[17]

Onlookers soon noted approvingly how Henrietta Maria's English ladies waited on her with the decorum the French had lacked, while Charles spoiled her with generous gifts of 'golden vessels'.[18] People assumed that Henrietta would soon accept the Englishwomen as her new servants. But even as a little girl Henrietta Maria had found it hard to let things go, 'all of a sudden'.[19] In September, the queen was reported to be 'unhappy as usual' and still 'under the influence of youthful passion'.[20] She refused to allow Buckingham his victory, snubbing his friends and favouring his enemies. As a result, 'The duke and his sister are in a great fit of jealousy,' she wrote to friends in France. She had learned that Louis was sending an ambassador, the Marshal de Bassompierre. She had a plan, she confided, 'I will tell Monsieur de Bassompierre in more detail . . . Show this letter to the queen and then burn it.'

Yet Henrietta Maria ended her missive on a more plaintive note. She had never truly left France while she was surrounded by a French retinue. Now they had gone and she wanted to go home, even if only for a short while. 'See to it I am able to see my mother. I'll owe you all that one can.'[21]

Richelieu's influence in England had received a lethal blow. With the expulsion of Henrietta Maria's household his spies and agents had returned home. The arrests and interrogations of the early summer had, however, revealed the full extent of the plot in France against Louis and himself. The cardinal called it 'the most frightful conspiracy of which history has ever made mention.'[22]

Louis forgave his heir for the 'repose of the state' but on 5 August 1626 Gaston was obliged to marry Mademoiselle de Montpensier, which he did in an old suit. Their illegitimate half-brothers were imprisoned. Alexandre would die in jail in 1629, while César would only be released a broken man in 1630. The Prince of Condé begged and received forgiveness. Soissons fled France, as did Madame de Chevreuse, whom Richelieu believed 'did more harm than anyone else.'[23] In Lorraine the ruling duke soon became the duchess's latest admirer.

Chalais paid the ultimate price. He was executed on 9 August 1626, and it was a grim end, witnessed by Gaston. His friends had spirited away the official hangman, hoping that delay would allow time for Louis to forgive him. Instead a condemned prisoner had been offered a pardon to take the job. A cobbler from Toulouse, he had no idea how to wield an executioner's sword and set about his task with an adze – a tool normally used for smoothing and carving wood. It took thirty blows to cut off Chalais's head. Less than a month later the former superintendent of Gaston's household died in prison under suspicious circumstances – a loss that affected him deeply.

It wasn't until two days later, on 5 September 1626, that Louis could bring himself to ask his wife what she had known of the plot. Anne was summoned to a royal council meeting attended by Marie de' Medici and Richelieu. Instead of an armchair she was given a folding stool like a prisoner at the bar.[24] Louis stated baldy: 'You wished my death and to marry my brother.'[25] Anne replied that she had no need to sully her reputation for so paltry a prize and if anyone believed it, then 'knowing We are a queen, my tears will turn to sparks of fire.'[26] Louis did not believe her and diplomats reported she was in disgrace.

The arrest of the Chalais conspirators had also damaged Buckingham's influence in France. Yet the rivalry between the English duke and the French cardinal was far from burned out. Buckingham sent his right-hand man, the still-beardless Wat Montagu, to France, ostensibly to deliver Charles's congratulations to Gaston on his marriage. His secret role was to continue developing Buckingham's contacts with Richelieu's enemies. Montagu's first action was to meet up with an English agent who had been delivering money to Madame de Chevreuse in Lorraine.[27] This did not escape notice and Louis declined to accept Wat at court.

Charles did, however, receive the French ambassador, the Marshal de Bassompierre, whom Henrietta Maria was expecting and who arrived in London in October. A trade war between the two kingdoms had begun and the full-scale war that this threatened was not in Charles's best interest. His uncle Christian IV of Denmark had suffered a crushing defeat at Habsburg hands on 27 August – one that Christian blamed on a lack of English support. Even 'Camel Face' Carlisle was hoping that the political temperature with France might be lowered so that Charles could now focus on the war with Spain. Louis, for his part, also sought peace. He did not want England stirring up his troublesome Huguenot minority.

Bassompierre was under instructions to tell Henrietta Maria to patch up her quarrels with Charles. In this the ambassador succeeded – it was what she wanted. She warned him that Buckingham might try and encourage quarrels later. For the time being, however, Buckingham needed her goodwill. He wanted Henrietta Maria to persuade Louis to allow him to return to France. This would be ascribed in court memoirs to his love affair with Anne and wish to see her again. According to one English account Anne had even sent him a diamond garter as a mark of her affection, along with 'an exceedingly rich jewel' – a story that Dumas would expand on in his novel *The Three Musketeers*.

In fact, Buckingham hoped Louis would accept him as a mediator over disagreements on the implementation of the peace treaty of February 1626 with the Huguenots in the port of La Rochelle. If it succeeded Louis would benefit while Buckingham would gain credit with his Calvinist enemies in England and they would call off their attack dogs.

Shortly before Bassompierre's arrival Buckingham presented Henrietta Maria with a special gift, that was delivered in a pie at a banquet held in her honour. As the pastry was cut a perfectly formed boy, only eighteen inches tall, emerged. His name was Jeffrey Hudson, and he was seven years old.

The pie was a reference to the fashionable story of Tom Thumb, and Jeffrey, who was a butcher's son from Rutland, was now to become one the most prized members of the queen's household. Royal families across Europe valued the unusual in their servants. Henrietta Maria had a giant called William Evans, who was seven foot six and served as a guard at Somerset House. Her mother and sisters had many dwarves. Marie de' Medici's favourite was called Mathurin. Jeffrey, who would be known as the 'human thumb', was not only smaller than all the court dwarves of Europe, he was also exceptionally pretty: 'the most perfect imperfection of nature that ever was born', one diplomat admitted.[28]

In November 1626 Henrietta Maria showed Jeffrey off to Bassompierre in a masque she held with Buckingham. During the interlude her giant, Evans, appeared sitting down on stage. He then pulled a loaf of bread out of one enormous coat pocket. From the other, instead of cheese, he plucked Jeffrey.[29] The little boy would become 'much beloved by his mistress', and while many dwarves at others courts were little better than the possessions of their masters and mistresses, Jeffrey was to be raised as a courtier and a gentleman.[30] Meanwhile she agreed to help persuade Louis to invite Buckingham to France, if in return she was allowed to accompany him and see her mother. Her efforts failed. Louis refused to entertain the man who had insulted him and plotted with his enemies. Buckingham warned in turn that 'since he was forbidden to enter in a peaceable manner into France, he would make his Passage with an Army'.[31]

If Buckingham wanted war, it would be a dangerous moment for Henrietta Maria. Even long-standing Hispanophobes like Carlisle saw that it was a mistake for a medium-sized power like Britain to take on the two great powers of Europe at the same time. Buckingham would need to undermine any pro-French influence at court and the most significant of these was Henrietta Maria.

When Philip IV's favourite, Olivares, had wanted Spain to go to war with France, he had attacked the reputation of Spain's French-born queen, Elisabeth. Richelieu was worried that Buckingham might instead have Henrietta Maria poisoned – just as he had reputedly done with King James.[32] But England already had an example in how to dispose of the French influence of a king's consort. Anne Boleyn had been accused of adultery by Henry VIII's leading minister Thomas Cromwell, and then had her head chopped off.

On 14 January 1627 Henrietta Maria held a theatrical at the heart of the king's court at Whitehall. With their quarrels made up, Charles was now said to love Henrietta Maria 'extremely'[33]. The move to Whitehall was a mark of her improved position. Her performance that night, with fourteen of her ladies, was judged 'very beautiful' and the after-party and dancing went on until two in the morning.[34] Only a few hours later the court musician, Jacques Gaultier, who was her lute tutor, was arrested. Gaultier was sent to the Tower on the express orders of the king who went with Buckingham to interview him personally. The charge was the rape of a nine-year-old girl, but this was cover for allegations concerning the queen.

Overweight, with thick black brows and an explosion of frizzy hair, Gaultier had fled Paris a decade earlier, after being charged with the murder of a nobleman. He remained extremely violent, capable of biting a fellow London musician in the face, leaving a gaping wound 'an inch or more on the left side at the corner side of the mouth and nether lip down to the lower part of the jaw'.[35] It was Buckingham who had saved Gaultier from extradition for the nobleman's murder. Gaultier was the first person in England to use a double-headed twelve-course lute, and for Buckingham his exceptional talent was more important than his lack of moral worth. He had even brought Gaultier to Madrid when Charles was wooing the infanta.

The story of the child rape may have been Buckingham's idea. He had once extricated another man from a similar charge: his private astrologer Dr John Lambe, who also carried convictions for witchcraft. Buckingham was now hoping to use Gaultier to damage the queen and Carlisle, who had been urging a peace policy with France. Charles had been told that Gaultier was boasting that he could seduce the queen by the sweetness of his music. The fall of Anne Boleyn began with allegations that she was having an affair with the court musician Mark Smeaton. Gaultier was also supposedly threatening to murder Buckingham – the man who saved his life and career. This conveniently distanced Buckingham from the scandalous story concerning the queen.

Under questioning, Gaultier insisted that the comments attributed to him about the queen and Buckingham were untrue (he had no intention of following Smeaton to the block) – and Charles refused to believe his wife was in any way likely to be in lust with such a man. While Henry VIII was no longer in love with Anne when Smeaton was arrested, Charles was head over heels with his wife. Buckingham's mud wouldn't stick on the queen, but Carlisle was not to be so lucky. Gaultier 'confessed' to an affair with a daughter that Carlisle had by his first wife.[36] Charles, who had worked hard to clean up the morals of his father's court, was appalled at Carlisle's failure to control his family.

Gaultier was soon back at work in royal service, while Carlisle now found he was shut out of the king's confidence. Blocked from access to the king, he turned instead to Henrietta Maria. She responded positively and even softened towards his wife, Lucy, to whom she had previously expressed a 'great aversion'.[37] She would always prove pragmatic in embracing old enemies when they developed common interests. She realised Lucy – although judged by some to be the 'killing beauty of the world' – now posed no threat to her marriage. This was confirmed in April 1627 when Charles gave Henrietta Maria a beautiful diamond as a mark of his devotion.[38] She also enjoyed Lucy's company.

Lucy's gossipy supper parties were much more fun than being fawned over by Buckingham's relations. Henrietta Maria was 'in her conversation extremely sweet and sharp', that is 'sharp in understanding' and was someone 'who knows how to hold up a discourse'. When others were witty she didn't 'let it die in her hand but applauds it' and all this made her 'rare company'.[39] Lucy, ten years older, complimented the queen, 'approving the bon mots spoken in her presence, moderating the excess of compliments, passing over a dull jest without a sweet smile, giving the wise answer to an extravagant question'.[40]

Without her trusted French servants, Henrietta Maria was taking control of her own agenda. Henrietta Maria recognised that Lucy's love affair with Buckingham made her a useful point of contact with the duke. This was increasingly necessary as a war with her brother, Louis, approached. Buckingham had persuaded Charles that Richelieu's build-up of French naval forces posed a threat to British sea power and that it was his duty to stand by the Huguenots of La Rochelle in their disputes with Louis. In the absence of Parliament, forced loans of doubtful legality were now being used to pay for a planned invasion. Charles was ignoring property rights to pursue a war Henrietta Maria had tried to avert as best she could. The loans triggered mass defiance; almost equally unpopular was the billeting of thousands of soldiers near the coast as the invasion fleet was prepared.

The plan was to capture the Île de Ré, with the objective of controlling the approaches to La Rochelle and encouraging a revolt in the city. In Europe they would call it 'the war of the favourites'.[41] Even Buckingham's mother suspected that Buckingham's personal rivalry with Richelieu had played a role in the coming conflict. She told him not to make 'God part of these woeful affairs', in cloaking it in the guise of a religious crusade.[42] As he pushed ahead, she turned to Buckingham's personal fortune teller Dr Lambe for advice. Lambe duly looked into his crystal ball to discover what the war would bring for the duke. Troublingly he saw an assassin armed 'with a long dagger'. The description he gave of the man fitted that of an officer called Gray who was on the ship Buckingham was due to sail in for France. Gray was taken ashore before 17 June, when over a hundred great ships crossed the Channel for France, carrying 5,934 Irish, Scots and English troops under Buckingham's command.

Henrietta Maria hid her disappointment that war had not been avoided. She told Lucy 'she must prefer her husband's honour before all the world' and was reported to be very 'merry'.[43] Charles told Buckingham he and Henrietta Maria were indeed 'never better together', assuring his favourite she was 'showing herself so loving to me, by her discretion upon all occasions, that it makes us all wonder and esteem her'.[44] She, in turn, acknowledged Buckingham's letters to her as showing 'great servility', and wrote back politely.

When it came to kings, absence rarely made the heart grow fonder, and Buckingham's wife fretted to her husband that he needed to 'remember your promise in making haste home, for I will assure you, both for the public and our private good here in court there is great need of you'. One sure barometer of the strength or weakness of his position was the attitude of Lucy Carlisle, who 'uses your friends something worse than when you were here'.[45] This, Buckingham hoped, was temporary and all favour would be restored in victory, he reflected, 'whereby . . . the worst of our ill-willers . . . might know all'.[46]

Unfortunately, victory was elusive. A chaotic landing on the Île de Ré on 12 July 1627 saw 409 men killed or drowned. The following three months were spent in a fruitless siege of the island's garrison fortress. Richelieu took personal command of the French response as Buckingham's men grew weakened by hunger and died of disease. On 27 October 1627 Buckingham launched a desperate attack on the fortress without artillery cover, and with ladders that proved too short to scale the walls; 3,895 men were killed during the assault and the subsequent retreat to the ships.[47]

The defeat was judged 'the greatest and shamefullest overthrow the English have received since we lost Normandy'. This had happened during the reign of Henry VI. Once again Charles was being linked to the failed king who had triggered the Wars of the Roses. 'Poitiers, Cressy, Agincourt, all lie buried in one Île of Ré,' one writer moaned.[48] It was the people of La Rochelle who were to suffer now. They had rebelled at Buckingham's encouragement, and Louis was going to starve them into submission unless Charles could stop it.

BECOMING A LEADER

HENRIETTA MARIA'S SISTER, CHRISTINE, GENEROUSLY REWARDED the messenger who arrived in Turin with the news of her brother Louis's victory at Île de Ré. Britain's defeat was celebrated with cannon shot and fireworks. Yet the following month, November 1627, when Henrietta Maria turned eighteen, it emerged that all had not been as it seemed. Richelieu's agents captured Buckingham's right-hand man, Wat Montagu, in Lorraine, where he had been visiting Madame de Chevreuse. The papers he was carrying revealed Savoy was acting secretly with Lorraine and Britain to encourage the Huguenot rebels and against Richelieu. Most of Wat's letters were in cipher so he was taken under heavy escort to the Bastille in Paris for further interrogation.

With England and France at war, Henrietta Maria was forbidden formal contact with her mother. She was in touch, nonetheless, determined to use her influence in France to help Charles and his kingdoms. Henrietta Maria pleaded successfully for Wat's release, which came four months later, and he was spared torture – reputedly after Marie de' Medici's intervention. That Christmas a number of British prisoners of war were also returned to England as a present from Louis to his sister.[1] Her earlier requests for her brother to treat the Huguenots kindly were, however, ignored. The starving inhabitants of La Rochelle ate all the horses, mules, cats 'and other creatures', then 'scattered themselves along the Fens where the salt pans were, to make war with eels and other little fishes'; they had gone to the coast for cockles and eaten herbs, 'boiling them in three parts water to take away the bitterness'. Soon they would be reduced to eating tallow – the rendered animal fat used for making candles and soap.[2]

A new invasion to save La Rochelle was an urgent priority for Charles, but he did not dare repeat the unpopular forced loans. That meant he had to call another parliament. It opened on 17 March 1628. Charles warned his MPs bluntly that if they didn't vote him the subsidies to fight France, he would again use extra-parliamentary methods of tax-raising. They feared that he might then never call a parliament again. Hoping for compromise they voted for a bill that would grant the king £300,000. In exchange, on 7 June 1628, Charles signed a Petition of Right that agreed the liberties of his subjects on such matters as the billeting of soldiers and forced loans. This goodwill ended when MPs drew up a protest document, called a Remonstrance, against Buckingham calling him 'the cause of all our miseries'.

If Charles had been prepared to punish Buckingham for La Rochelle and the forced loans it would have undermined those who also opposed his Arminian policies, but he still refused to sack his friend. The risk now was that if the king would not bend, something would break. MPs' accusations against Buckingham were being widely disseminated in print and popular ballads. People believed Buckingham must have cast a spell over Charles, just as Concini was supposed to have done over Marie de' Medici, with the help of Leonora. Less than a week later on 13 June 1628 Buckingham's astrologer Dr Lambe noticed a group of aggressive boys following him as he left a popular lower-class London theatre called the Fortune. They pointed him out to others, calling him 'the duke's devil'. A larger crowd began to gather.

Having also spotted a group of men, who later turned out to be demobbed soldiers, Lambe asked them to act as his bodyguard. Like many of the survivors of Île de Ré, they had been left unpaid. They accepted his money.

While the soldiers kept the crowd at bay Lambe ate his lunch at the

Horseshoe tavern off Moor Lane. When he left, however, the mob was still outside. They pelted him with stones and attacked his bodyguard. He took shelter in another tavern – the Windmill – and then left by a back entrance, dashing to hide in a neighbouring house. He was seen. With the mob threatening to tear the house down the frightened householder called the constables. Four of them escorted Lambe out – but he was grabbed from the constables and beaten to the ground. A crystal ball fell out of his pocket as they went on hitting and kicking. Lambe was left dying in the care of men who showed him little respect, charging Londoners tuppence a piece to see the corpse. This was four times more than they would later be asked to pay to view the body of Charles I. The men who had Lambe's body made £20 – at least 4,800 viewings must have taken place.[3]

A few days later, a demobbed soldier called John Felton went to see a clerk he had commissioned to draw up petitions for his back-pay. He also wanted to ask for a promotion – not that he was likely to get one. He had been left badly wounded in the hand and was suffering from the trauma of the retreat. His sister often heard him screaming in his sleep.

Felton found the clerk in his shop transcribing copies of Parliament's Remonstrance and, after leaving, he took one away with him. Back in his lodgings he read the accusations made against Buckingham and it struck him that his suffering was part of a much larger picture. 'Popish' Arminian innovations in religion, the dangers to liberty, all these were tied up with the military failures at Île de Ré. Felton told his sister he was going to ask Buckingham personally for the money he was owed.

On 17 August 1628, Buckingham left London for Portsmouth and Felton followed. Parliament had been prorogued for the summer on 26 June and a new fleet was being made ready for the relief of La Rochelle. The sailors and soldiers in Portsmouth were not, however, very welcoming to their Lord Admiral. No sooner had Buckingham arrived than a group of 300 surrounded his coach demanding their arrears.

One managed to drag him out. He was very fortunate to be rescued. Lambe's murderers had said that if they had caught Buckingham instead of his 'devil', they would have 'minced his flesh' and each of them would have 'eaten a bit of him'.[4]

The man who had grabbed Buckingham was arrested, and on 22 August he was hanged. That night Buckingham dined with Wat Montagu, who told him the navy was being overcharged for supplies in the town. The next morning Wat had better news. Buckingham was in bed with his pregnant wife at the Greyhound Inn when Wat arrived to tell him that an advance English force had relieved La Rochelle.[5] Buckingham literally danced with joy. He ordered a coach to take them to the king. In the crowd downstairs John Felton was waiting. Like the man Dr Lambe had seen in his crystal ball the previous summer, he was carrying a knife.

With Charles in Portsmouth, Henrietta Maria had set off on her own progress to Wellingborough in Northamptonshire. She intended to enjoy the waters of a new spa she had visited the previous year. She had now been married three years and she hoped it would help her conceive a child, the vital task of a queen consort. Other elements of the mission her mother had laid out for her were also on her mind.

Two Catholics in Lancashire – a priest and a yeoman – were facing execution. The yeoman was on a charge of murder after a pursuivant fell while chasing him across a field, broke a leg and died. The man had sworn on his deathbed it was an accident, but the local JP was determined to make an example of the yeoman. Henrietta Maria was pleading for both the priest and the young man.[6]

The queen's second concern was to advocate a peace with France. Henrietta Maria's former almoner, the young Bishop of Mende, had died of wounds in the fighting for La Rochelle.[7] Holland had also lost his younger brother at Île de Ré. How many more losses might there be while 'the two favourites dye red the swords of the two young kings', as one Savoyard put it?[8] She told her mother she had barely 'held back from the fire' to do 'everything that was in my power' to carry out what her mother 'ordered'.[9] Namely, she was confronting a faction at court who wanted Charles to make a peace with Spain in order to focus on the war with France.

To advertise her position Henrietta Maria was planning an outside theatrical that would include thrilling battle scenes. Her mother's Italian dance masters had also taught fencing, a skill used in choreographed duels and battle scenes known as *combattimento*. Henrietta Maria's cousin (Marie de' Medici's niece), Eleanora Gonzaga, wife of the Holy Roman Emperor Ferdinand II, had put on an all-female version in 1626. Eighteen court ladies had performed as fighting Amazons armed with cuirasses, daggers and spears, as well as taking part in choreographed jousts.[10] Henrietta Maria had commissioned a set of blue calico tents, decorated with gold fleur-de-lys, pyramids and stars, as well as a turreted mock castle, also in painted cloth. Her battle costumes included 'thirteen caps made of tinsel and taffeta in the fashion of helmets', along with wooden swords and sheaths. It would have been the talk of the court, but the drama of real-life events overtook her plans.

A letter marked 23 August arrived for the queen with shocking news. The author described seeing Buckingham leaving the Greyhound with Wat Montagu 'betwixt nine and ten of the clock in the morning'. As he was going through a doorway a man in the press of the crowds stepped forward and stabbed him in the chest. Buckingham cried out 'Villain' and pulled out the long blade. He then fell against a table. Those standing nearby thinking he had suddenly taken ill held him up, 'till they saw the blood come gushing from his mouth'. The screams of Buckingham's pregnant wife when she saw his body were such that Henrietta Maria's correspondent hoped 'never to hear the like again'.[11]

Henrietta Maria had resented having Buckingham's other relations amongst her attendants, but 'Camel Face' Carlisle told his wife Lucy that the 'comfort she gives these many distressed ladies' who were with her 'must affect all the world'.[12] Henrietta Maria added the news of the assassination to her latest letter to her mother, with other details as they came in. Buckingham had been 'stabbed with a knife'. His last words were, 'I am dead'. The murderer – John Felton – had been caught but remained unrepentant, saying he had 'done very well'.[13] Marie de' Medici passed her daughter's letter to Richelieu, asking that Louis look upon his distressed sister with 'compassion'. With Buckingham dead Marie hoped there might be new opportunities for a peace.

In September Henrietta Maria travelled to London to be with Charles, who had returned to his capital, and still shed 'many tears' for his friend.[14] Aware that her every gesture would be watched and interpreted, she expressed grief for Buckingham to 'parallel herself in lamentation' to the king, albeit 'rather out of discretion than out of a true sensation of his death.[15]

Charles had Buckingham buried in the Henry VII Chapel in Westminster Abbey, where his father and his first son had been laid to rest, as if he too was a member of the family. The burial had to take place at night to avoid any attacks on the funeral cortège and when Felton was executed in November his action was still being celebrated. In the view of many he had indeed 'done very well'. Yet Buckingham had his mourners besides the king.

Buckingham's sister, Susan, erected a monument in Portsmouth Cathedral, 'in tears and everlasting grief'. His bowels were buried there, as she hoped hers would be. Meanwhile, she kept the ten-penny knife that had killed her brother as a relic. It remains with her descendants today.

In the shadow of Buckingham's murder, two other deaths a few days after his had attracted little notice and are long-forgotten. The two Catholics Henrietta Maria had tried to save had both gone to the scaffold. In the case of the yeoman the judge had visited the foreman of the jury in his home to insist on a conviction. He had been particularly irritated by Henrietta Maria's attempted intervention, in which she had even gained some support from Buckingham and the king.

The news that Buckingham had been given on the day of his death had proved false: there was no victory for Charles in France. Instead, in

October 1628 La Rochelle fell to Louis. Henrietta Maria was convinced that nothing lay ahead for Charles in this war but further humiliation. On the other hand France might now be prepared to make the alliance aimed at Spain that Charles had hoped for when they married. The Bourbons and the Habsburgs were clashing, once again, in Italy.

The death of the last male heir of the House of Gonzaga, rulers of Mantua and Montferrat, had left a disputed inheritance. While Charles was busy negotiating to buy the fabulous Gonzaga art collection, France and Spain hovered over greater prizes. The territories were vital to Spanish interests as they protected the so-called Spanish Road: their supply line to the war in Europe. They were equally important to Louis XIII because they lay next to France's unruly southern provinces. Louis had discovered that the peace he had made with Spain in 1626 over the Val Tellina passes had cost him more than he had wished. The Val Tellinas had allowed Spanish troops passage through the region, a concession he had refused the papal legate Barberini in 1625.

A proxy war had begun – the so-called War of the Mantuan Succession – with France backing the Duke of Nevers and Spain backing his distant cousin, the Duke of Guastalla. In October 1628 when Charles's new ambassador was leaving for Madrid, Henrietta Maria was asked if she had any messages for her sister Elisabeth. She 'answered him she would have nothing to do with Spain, nor with any persons there.'[16] In doing so she was claiming leadership of a court faction that backed an aggressive foreign policy against Spain. It was a role last held by Charles's elder brother, Henry, and before then by Elizabeth I's favourite, the great Protestant hero of the war with Spain, Robert Devereux, 2nd Earl of Essex.

Henrietta Maria's followers were an eclectic group. They were dominated, however, by moderate Calvinists who were also protectors of Puritans, now under assault from the king's Arminian policies. Several were diplomats who had been associated with her marriage negotiations in 1624–5. Wat Montagu, whom she had freed from the Bastille, and was loved by the queen for his 'wit and conversation', was one such.[17] The most notable was her steward, Henry Holland, whose mother had been Essex's favourite sister, and whose brother, the Earl of Warwick, was a leader of the parliamentary opposition.

In pursuing a foreign policy that would see a Protestant state – England – allied with France against the Habsburgs, Henrietta Maria was following in her father's footsteps. If she was to secure her position, however, as a figure of real influence she needed to have a son and, if necessary, she had to fake it until she could make it. Soon the word went out that she might be pregnant, for she had cravings 'and had sent all about the town for mussels to satisfy her longing'.[18]

Although courtiers were quick to grab the offices that became vacant with Buckingham's death, there was one unofficial position no one wanted. This was the role of 'evil counsellor', the figure commonly blamed for a monarch's unpopular decisions. In 1628 the buck had stopped with Buckingham. Yet now that Buckingham was dead unpopular decisions continued to be made. Charles was pushing ahead with his Arminian reforms of the Church of England, and when Parliament reassembled in January 1629 religion was the focus of the first debates. It transpired that MPs differed widely in what they wanted for the Church of England. Puritans wanted more radical Calvinist reform; other MPs approved of the Arminian beautification of their churches. There were divisions too on taxes.

The self-proclaimed 'patriot' party already distrusted the king as anti-parliamentary and wished to deprive Charles even of those subsidies traditionally granted for life. The 'royalists' feared this would tip power too far away from the monarch and into the hands of powerful political cliques. With matters at an impasse Charles asked the Speaker to adjourn Parliament for eight days, hoping to negotiate a back-room deal. On 2 March, when the Speaker rose from his chair to make the announcement, he was seized and held down by patriot MPs, who were convinced he was about to dissolve Parliament, perhaps forever. The session ended in chaos and on 10 March Charles did exactly what the patriot MPs had feared. He dissolved Parliament and he did not plan to call another if it could possibly be avoided. Someone had to be blamed and the figure alighted on was Henrietta Maria who, as a foreigner, a Catholic and a woman bore all the characteristics of a stock villain. There was a rumour that Charles had been 'well inclined' to his MPs until, in bed on 9 March, Henrietta Maria had poisoned his mind against them.[19]

Anxieties about the queen soon increased. While Henrietta Maria had not been pregnant when she had reported cravings, she had become so soon afterwards and on 22 March this was confirmed with bells pealed across England 'for joy the queen is with child'.[20] Having a son would give her a supposedly even greater hold over her husband.

The truth is that Parliament had always been, for Charles, merely a tool to be used to help him rule or not, as he saw fit. In this he was influenced by his father's theories on divine right, not by his wife. The queen's feelings about the dissolved Parliament were concerned principally with the immediate impact it had on foreign affairs. Without a Parliament, and until Charles found some new means of raising large sums of money, he could not afford to continue to be at war. On 10 May 1629 peace with France was proclaimed at the gates of Whitehall.[21] Charles referred to it bitterly as a mere cessation of arms, but Henrietta Maria celebrated with a hymn of thanks sung in her chapel at Somerset House. It looked set to be a good summer and she was reported to be 'full of strength and courage' as she laid plans for the birth of her child.

England did not, as yet, have any equivalent to the Paris Guild of Midwives, and Henrietta Maria looked to her mother to find her one in France. Louise Bourgeois, who had delivered Henrietta Maria in 1609, had gone on to deliver Gaston's daughter, Anne-Marie-Louise, in 1627, but sadly Gaston's wife died of a post-partum infection. The male physicians at court had blamed the midwife and although her writings on childbirth had received many accolades, her career at court was finished. Marie de' Medici suggested instead the services of a Madame

Peronne who came from a family of midwives, one of whom had been a long-standing rival to Louise Bourgeois.[22]

On 13 May 1629, months before her due date, and while Peronne was still in France, Henrietta Maria went into labour.[23] The baby was breech and the doctor said he could save either the mother or the child. Charles told him to save his wife.[24] It was a boy, 'but', it was reported, 'the flower had been cut down the same instant it saw the light'.[25] Their little son was buried at Westminster Abbey that night in the tomb of his grandfather King James. Charles was distraught. Only nine months after Buckingham's funeral here was another burial in the dark: the death of a male heir was a source not just of pain, but of shame.

A message was sent to France to stop the arrival of Madame Peronne. The midwife travelled instead to Savoy, where Henrietta Maria's sister Christine was also due to have a baby.

Writing to Richelieu, Henrietta Maria admitted that her miscarriage was a bitter 'affliction', but she played this down with her sister.[26]

Christine and Victor had lost a six-year-old son only the previous year, and when they had a little girl on 27 July Henrietta Maria wrote to congratulate them. 'As to my loss, I wish to forget it in order to participate with you in the pleasure which my sister's happy delivery has brought you,' she told her brother-in-law, and asked Christine to kiss her baby niece, 'for love of me'.[27]

Henrietta Maria's eldest sister, Elisabeth of Spain, was also pregnant. She had thus far delivered five short-lived daughters and insults had been heaped on her for her failure to deliver an heir for Philip IV. This all changed when she gave birth to a healthy son, Balthazar Carlos, on 17 October. Suddenly she began to be praised for her beauty, which was judged to be a reflection of her political virtues. Henrietta Maria, meanwhile, was acutely aware that her miscarriage also had political ramifications. Diplomats were reporting how some of Charles's subjects were looking to his sister as his replacement.

Henrietta Maria made an effort to appear carefree, to give an impression of confidence that a living heir would soon follow. This only earned her the disapproval of the new French ambassador, Charles de l'Aubespine, Marquis of Châteauneuf. An abbot aged almost fifty, Châteauneuf saw only a frivolous teenage girl, whose husband would tease her about her long lie-ins and extravagant shopping. The morals of the witty and clever men she liked as company also sometimes left much to be desired.

George Goring, the son of the queen's Master of the Horse, Lord Goring, was recently married and rapidly working his way through his rich bride's £10,000 dowry.[28] Then there was the tall, charming but self-centred young Gentleman of her Privy Chamber Henry Jermyn, whom Charles would later lock in the Tower for impregnating one of her maids of honour. It was a woman amongst her favourites, however, who really concerned the abbot: her friend Lucy Carlisle.

Part Three

A GOOD CATHOLIC AND A GOOD QUEEN

FOREIGN AFFAIRS

THE DEPTH OF HENRIETTA MARIA'S AFFECTION FOR LUCY CARLISLE had been evident in the immediate aftermath of Buckingham's assassination. Lucy had caught smallpox and Henrietta Maria had to be prevented from risking her own life to go and see her. Lucy was given special permission to return early to court that October 1628, wearing a mask while her skin healed. When it came off it seemed it had left no 'danger of an imprinted face', but then she was an expert with make-up.[1] She had even given the queen lessons in how to 'paint'. Some wondered what other 'debaucheries' she might lead Henrietta Maria into.[2] This was not, however, what most concerned Châteauneuf. He had learned that Lucy's husband 'Camel Face' Carlisle had 'turned hugely Spanish'.

Although he was a long-standing Hispanophobe, Carlisle had come to believe that peace with Spain was currently in Charles's best interests. Philip IV was desperate not to have to fight France over the Gonzaga inheritance in Italy while fighting Britain as well. Carlisle hoped that Philip might be prepared to give up the Palatinate in return for peace with Britain. Philip had already sent the fifty-one-year-old artist Peter Paul Rubens as his personal envoy. Carlisle, for the Spanish faction, and Holland for the French, faced off at court in a fashion war, each trying to outdo the other in the extravagance of their clothing, while Lucy 'made game' of Châteauneuf. The abbot was none too amused, and ensured that Henrietta Maria was told that Lucy also 'bore herself with little respect' towards her, 'going so far as to make sport of her actions' behind her back.[3]

Lucy often turned her humour on her friends. As one victim noted, her wit had 'a sharpness, and strength, and taste, to disrelish, if not to kill, the proudest hopes which you can have, of her value of you'. Charles advised Lucy to leave the court until his wife's temper had cooled. Lucy did so for a month, returning in January 1630 to find Holland so close to the king and queen that he would sit casually in their carriage with his hat on. Henrietta Maria, meanwhile, was so popular with the anti-Spanish faction that Holland, Warwick and the Puritan John Pym considered naming their latest project in the Caribbean after her (though in the end they chose 'Providence' island over 'Henrietta').

Rubens was, nevertheless, making headway with Charles. The king had commissioned him to paint ceiling canvases for Banqueting House that would glorify the Stuarts, but he was a man 'capable of much more than producing pictures'.[4] Indeed he succeeded in arranging an exchange of official ambassadors between Philip and Charles. His only concern as he left court in February 1630 was that Henrietta Maria might undo his good work. She was pregnant again and refused to even grace Rubens with a leaving ceremony, deeming him 'not of that quality to require . . . [a] solemn reception with the attendance of her great ladies about her'.[5]

Just as Rubens left England so did Henrietta Maria's beloved dwarf Jeffrey Hudson, who was sent to France to fetch the midwife, Madame Peronne. The ten-year-old Jeffrey caused a sensation in Paris. Marie de' Medici and other ladies at the French court gave him £2,000 in jewels as an expression of their delight. On the return trip, however, Jeffrey and Peronne were captured by privateers based in the independent Flemish state of Dunkirk. Dunkirkers were notorious for stealing English ships, but there was more upset at court than 'if they had lost an entire fleet'.[6] Henrietta Maria asked the ruler of the Spanish Netherlands, the Infanta Clara Eugenia, for help. No peace treaty had yet been signed, but this childless sixty-three-year-old daughter of the Armada king, Philip II, nevertheless had Jeffrey and Peronne freed. [7]

At midday at St James's Palace on 29 May 1630, Peronne was with the Huguenot physician, Théodore Mayerne, attending on Henrietta Maria as she went into labour. She delivered a son in a red velvet birthing chair like the one in which her mother had delivered Louis XIII.[8] Henrietta Maria had fulfilled her principal duty as Charles's wife. Afterwards, the king sat on the green satin cover of his wife's bed and wrote to Marie to give her the good news and Henrietta Maria added a shaky signature. The future Charles II was 'so dark I am ashamed of him' she joked later to Mamie St George: brown skin was associated with those who worked in the fields. He was also very large, a throwback to the king's grandparents Mary, Queen of Scots, and Henry, Lord Darnley, both of whom had been exceptionally tall.

Charles insisted on a Protestant christening. Henrietta Maria acquiesced despite her promises to the Pope. She knew this was not a battle she could win: Charles's Protestant faith was as firm as her own attachment to Catholicism and he was the king. There was another fight she would also lose. Charles needed peace with Spain as well as France if he was to avoid calling another parliament. He signed a treaty with Spain, without any agreement on the Palatinate, less than six months later on 15 November 1630.

The end of the debate over the peace was good news for Lucy Carlisle. It meant the queen was prepared to accept her back into her favour. Lucy encouraged this by becoming closer to the queen's favourite, Holland; indeed they were soon rumoured to be lovers. Henrietta Maria, meanwhile, intended to continue to pursue her own foreign policy agenda – and she had a new enemy in her sights.

Wat Montagu had been dispatched to Paris with the official announcement of Prince Charles's birth and had returned to England in August 1630 with a large quantity of diamonds as a christening present from Marie. She had also sent some secret messages for Henrietta Maria concerning Richelieu. Marie was angry with her former servitor. She believed Richelieu had encouraged Louis in his quarrels with her son-in-law Philip IV in Italy and complained that the 'yellow-faced, arrogant invalid' seemed to possess her son's mind.[9]

Regular bouts of illness were something Richelieu and Louis had in common, and Louis had been seriously ill that summer. By September 1630 Louis believed he was dying. Marie and Anne of Austria took advantage of their constant access to Louis's bedside to persuade him to make peace with Spain. On 14 October a treaty was signed and as Louis recovered from his illness Marie decided the time had come to persuade him to sack the cardinal. First, on 10 November 1630 Marie relieved Richelieu of all his appointments in her household. Richelieu sent messages to Gaston begging him for help, but Gaston's and Anne of Austria's dislike of Richelieu was also as strong as ever and both were working with Marie. Gaston was bitter about the death in prison of his half-brother Alexandre Vendôme the previous year, and they all believed that without Richelieu, Louis would be easier to manage.

The next day Richelieu went to Marie's Luxembourg Palace to hand over his keys of office. Marie had invited Louis to say his goodbyes to her before heading to his hunting lodge at Versailles. She wanted him to witness the scene. Marie greeted Richelieu dressed in black, as the widow of Henry the Great. Richelieu fell to his knees and begged Marie for forgiveness. She berated him instead for his lack of gratitude to her and then turned to Louis to demand he sack him. Louis asked her to be patient. He then left to go hunting, ordering Richelieu to follow him to Versailles, 'with a visage revealing indignation'.[10]

Marie, Gaston and Anne believed they had triumphed, but as Louis had demonstrated in the past, while he could not stand up to his mother to her face, he could do so behind her back. Louis had learned to value Richelieu's service and he believed the terms of the October peace were far too generous to Spain. He would refuse to ratify it and much tougher terms would be agreed the following year. Meanwhile, instead of sacking the cardinal, many of his enemies were removed from senior court positions and replaced with Richelieu's candidates. The most senior position, Keeper of the Seals, was given to Abbot Châteauneuf, who had returned from England in February and was considered one of Richelieu's most effective allies.

Henrietta Maria learned of what came to be known as the Day of Dupes not much more than a week after it happened. Her mother was refusing to attend council meetings if Richelieu was present, but once again, Louis chose the cardinal's side. On 23 February 1631 Marie was placed back in internal exile, reviving painful memories for Henrietta Maria of the period she lost her mother as a little girl.

Marie sent Louis a stream of letters signed, 'the mother of the king and subordinate of the man who rules his mind' telling him his actions 'would find neither the approval of God or man'.[11] He remained unmoved. On 1 April 1631 Gaston wrote to Louis blaming Richelieu for causing family divisions and for the suffering of the poor, who bore the tax burden of Richelieu's aggressive policy towards the Habsburgs. He was, he declared, ready to 'spill his blood' for the people. A copy of the letter was sent to the Parliament of Paris. Gaston then fled to Lorraine, where he promptly fell in love and married his cousin, the duke's daughter, without Louis's permission. Two months later Marie left for the Spanish Netherlands seeking 'a haven', she said, 'where I could escape the storm'.[12] From there she launched a new propaganda war. Pamphlets were churned out in which Marie argued her care for Louis was inspired by a mother's love, while Richelieu's expressed mere ambition; and that she represented the Christian character of the French monarchy, as mother of the king, while he was subverting its moral politics in favour of an authoritarian, statist tyranny.

Marie's court began attracting a growing number of exiles, adventurers and troublemakers. She intended to travel on to England and Charles scrambled desperately for excuses to prevent Marie's arrival. The expense was something he could ill afford: nor was she a popular figure in England where her Counter-Reformation zeal was well known. He wrote to her citing the example of his father King James (a wise and compassionate king) who had been obliged, for reasons of state, to refuse his beloved daughter the Winter Queen a refuge. He offered, instead, to intercede on Marie's behalf with Louis 'as befits a good son in law'.[13]

Henrietta Maria understood, however, that there could be no reconciliation for her mother with Louis while Richelieu remained in power. She was already in touch with Richelieu's old sparring partner, Madame de Chevreuse having brokered her return from exile in Lorraine the previous year. Remarkably, Madame de Chevreuse had convinced Richelieu she was no longer a threat. The conspiring duchess had not been caught out in the Day of Dupes and was now bringing Richelieu what he thought were useful bits of information. He even found he very much enjoyed her visits. The same was true of his powerful ally Châteauneuf, who was falling completely under her spell.

Henrietta Maria was, meanwhile, proving as subtle a conspirator as her former lady-in-waiting and mentor. 'She embarks not herself rashly, to gain her ends, but seeks to takes her time, and (as if her journey were by water) she can handsomely look one way, when yet she rows another', a contemporary observed of the queen. Henrietta Maria had patience. 'And she knows how to apprehend an occasion, and how to let it also fall . . . to have either the bridle or the spur.'[14] She was now biding her time.

Espionage is a dirty business, and when it emerges into daylight often causes diplomatic embarrassment. This was the case in England in June 1631. Louis's new ambassador, the Marquis of Fontenay-Mareuil, was having the London house of the French exile François de Roches closely watched. Known as the Chevalier de Jars, he had been a junior figure in the 1626 'Chalais' conspiracy to murder Richelieu.[15] A 'man of great vivacity', he was a confidant of Henrietta Maria's and played tennis with Charles regularly.[16] Richelieu wanted to know who the chevalier was corresponding with in France, but his letters were proving hard to intercept. Fontenay had, however, conceived a plan.

The ambassador dispatched his steward and another gentleman servant to the chevalier's door. Having watched the house, they knew he was out. They told his maid that they needed to see one of the chevalier's other servants who, they claimed, owed them money. When she confirmed that the servant was also out, they said they would wait for him and asked her to fetch them a beer. She returned to find them walking out of the chevalier's chamber. One of them had a bundle under his cloak. The ambassador's henchmen left with what was, in fact, a casket of papers potentially linking Henrietta Maria not only to a conspiracy she was leading against Richelieu in France, but to another at home, directed against Charles's Lord Treasurer, Richard Weston.[17] After a blazing diplomatic row the casket was left on the door of the chevalier's lodgings. The papers were not.

Happily the casket letters did not reveal the names of all the plotters, nor the extent of what the conspirators were planning in France. The majority concerned Weston. The Lord Treasurer was a Hispanophile and crypto-Catholic detested by Holland and the queen's 'Puritan' followers (courtiers who came from moderate Calvinist families and who protected Puritan clergy), while she also resented his interference in her financial affairs. As one friend of Weston's observed, Henrietta Maria liked to wear 'such jewels as may add to the glory of her greatness'. She also spent on 'noble designs of building, and adorning her princely houses'. She was half Medici, after all. Somerset House had new private and state apartments, with one exquisite room designed by Inigo Jones painted in her mother's livery of blue, white and gold. She had planted new gardens, importing trees and plants from France, and built fountains. As a result she was in debt 'and would perhaps have been in more than that if she had not a rare servant to take upon him the care of the treasure; who makes her business his more than her own'.[18]

Richelieu now wrote to the Lord Treasurer to suggest a pact, 'for the individual preservation of each other in their charges and places'.[19] Weston agreed to give Richelieu information about his enemies in England. Henrietta Maria was, however, building up her own network in France.

In July 1631 she succeeded in brokering a pardon for the chevalier with Louis in return for his giving information on the Chalais conspiracy of 1626. With the help of Abbot Châteauneuf, the chevalier soon gained so much influence in Paris that he was being touted as Louis's next ambassador in London where Henrietta Maria was making it impossible for Fontenay to do his job.

The queen usually gave French ambassadors privileged access to her household. This meant they could casually bump into Charles when he was visiting his wife, rather than having to rely on appointments: a huge advantage over the Spanish. Now, while she was polite to Fontenay in public, out of respect for Louis, she 'never assented him a gracious look'.[20] The French believed she was encouraged in this by Wat Montagu, to whom Richelieu gave the rather flattering code name, 'the wolf'. The cardinal's greatest enemy, Marie de' Medici, was, meanwhile, still hopeful that she would soon be back on her son's council.

We have an image of Marie painted in Antwerp in October 1631 by Rubens's finest pupil, the young Anthony Van Dyck. She would soon send him to England where Van Dyck would be appointed 'principal painter in ordinary to Their Majesties' the following year. Unlike many of Van Dyck's sitters, Marie de' Medici was not afraid of showing her age and he depicted her as the formidable middle-aged woman she was. Marie's face is narrower than in her youth, and her chins are several. A crown is placed beside her, and beneath her a rich Persian carpet is set on bare earth. The picture suggests her exile is only temporary, and the crown at her side, as queen dowager of France, is just waiting to be retrieved.[21]

Marie hoped to spend a 'brave Christmas' with Gaston in London before her return to France and sent Henrietta Maria's illegitimate half-brother, the Chalais conspirator César de Bourbon, Duke of Vendôme (elder brother to the late Alexandre), to London to arrange it. Henrietta Maria was heavily pregnant and on 4 November she gave birth to a daughter in a room overlooking the gardens at St James's.[22] Less than ten hours later Henrietta Maria invited Vendôme to her bedchamber.

Vendôme – who had been present at Henrietta Maria's birth – had been released from prison the previous year, but Henrietta Maria had not seen him since she left France. Her room was scented with 'spirit of roses' and had been sumptuously decorated. The main feature was a state bed of tawny velvet, adorned with 'French network trim of silver' and surrounded, in the French court style, by a gilded and carved balustrade.

The queen greeted her half-brother in special birthing clothes, which included a train-length surcoat furred with ermine. Marie was certain Vendôme would get her invitation to come to London and she had already begun to pack when Charles sent his bedchamber servant William Murray to see Marie in Antwerp and ward her off.[23] Thwarted in her hopes of joining her youngest and favourite daughter, it was only a small consolation that the baby was named after her. The little girl would always sign herself as Marie, although she is remembered as Mary Stuart.[24]

Henrietta Maria planned a new pastoral for Christmas 1632 that would advertise her support for Marie de' Medici's attacks on Richelieu. It was written by Wat Montagu and rehearsals began in September with the cast given daily lessons from the leading actor of the Globe theatre. News soon reached her of a setback for her mother. Gaston had led a failed invasion of France, with 5,000 cavalry and troops on 1 September with the purported aim of 'freeing' Louis from Richelieu's control. Once again there was the execution of a leading supporter and once again Louis forgave Gaston his treason. The two brothers remained locked in their roles as king and heir, like planets trapped in their orbits, leaving Richelieu still vulnerable.

In December 1632, when Henrietta Maria's pastoral was performed, the Venetians and French remarked that the queen was regal and beautiful, 'above all the rest' of the cast. They were particularly impressed by the 'grace' with which she delivered speeches in English for the first time.[25] And there was also good news for Henrietta Maria from France.

Richelieu had fallen gravely ill. It seemed certain he would die and Anne of Austria began to throw parties. By January 1633, however, Richelieu was back at work and Weston had information for him. Henrietta Maria had been overheard saying Richelieu's trusted ally, Châteauneuf, 'was her particular servant, and that he would guide the state better than the cardinal, when the latter should be dead'.[26]

Richelieu took another look at an intercepted letter between Châteauneuf and Madame de Chevreuse. It had been written during his illness, and the abbot did not seem entirely sad at his close colleague's possibly imminent demise. Châteauneuf was arrested the next month. Numerous letters from England were discovered amongst his papers. They included thirty-two from Henrietta Maria. The roles of Madame de Chevreuse and the Chevalier de Jars were also exposed. Châteauneuf was imprisoned. Madame de Chevreuse was exiled to Touraine and the Chevalier de Jars was condemned to death.

The chevalier cannot have forgotten the fate of his friend Chalais in 1626 and the many, many blows it had taken to chip off the young man's head. As he was about to lay his head on the block it was, however, announced that the death sentence was commuted. Henrietta Maria had written secretly to Louis to plead for his life. In England Charles chose not to arrest any of the queen's circle of co-conspirators in the plot against Weston. It seemed to him the least said was soonest mended and he did not wish to embarrass his wife.[27] Henrietta Maria's loyalty had been emphasised in December when he had fallen ill with small-pox, and she had insisted on sleeping in his room until he had recovered.[28] Still, there were aftershocks.

Weston's son, Jerome, had intercepted Henrietta Maria's letter to Louis pleading for the Chevalier de Jars. She had posted it in a package under Holland's name, hoping to avoid detection. Holland took Jerome's search of his post as a personal slight, and challenged him to a duel. These deadly sword fights were absolutely forbidden, representing, as they did, a contempt for law and order which a king was expected to uphold. Both men were placed under house arrest. Charles was so angry, and Henrietta Maria so distressed, that there were fears for her latest pregnancy (she would give birth to the future James II in October 1633). With her life seemingly at risk Charles relented and matters were patched up with letters of apology and confession.

Henrietta Maria was overwhelmed with gratitude for Holland's support. When Weston tried to cut off Holland's contact with the queen, she wrote to the Earl, promising 'I will not act independently from you . . . I would rather die than be so cowardly as to act without telling you, for I have too high a regard for you and am too much indebted to you for what you have ensured on my account.'[29] The scapegoat for Henrietta Maria's plotting was to be Wat Montagu, who had helped compose the letter to Louis as well as the December pastoral. He was expelled from Britain, 'as being too busy in many matters'.[30]

Charles was irritated with Wat, not only for his meddling in the plot, but also because of the aftermath of the pastoral. A Puritan gentleman called William Prynne had printed a long polemic that accused women who acted on stage – especially those who spoke and dressed in men's clothing – of being 'notorious whores' and attempting to usurp male rule. Prynne had his ears cropped for insulting the queen. Nevertheless, his accusations had struck home with Charles.

Henceforth Henrietta Maria would appear in court masques looking lovely but always mute.[31] Yet her promotion of an ideal of platonic love continued to place women centre stage and her message on the value of the female perspective spread far beyond the court. Henrietta Maria was a patron of many theatres in London. She liked to sit as a private citizen in the audience and would blend in with the crowd as unsuccessfully as a 'bird that thrusting but her head into a bush, is said then to think all her body hidden'.[32] It became more fashionable for women to go the theatre and there were soon complaints of 'many wanton ladies of all sorts resorting by troops unto our plays'.[33]

Writers, knowing a successful play could become a means to court preferment, chose 'lady' titles to grow their audience, while a few bold actresses projected femininity as a mobile and vivid force in current affairs. Women's involvement in politics and their assertiveness even became dramatic tropes. There were jokes that 'in some country / Ladies are Privy Counsellors' and 'all the women / Wear swords and breeches'.[34] If Henrietta Maria was silent in court masques, she was not silenced. Far from it.

THE ROAD TO ROME

SOME SAID THAT HENRIETTA MARIA HAD TREATED WAT MONTAGU badly, letting him take the blame for much of her plotting against Richelieu. Well, that was realpolitik and the 'pleasures of life' he boasted of enjoying with Henrietta Maria were not behind him. Expelled from England he presented himself in September 1633 at the French court, hoping to see Anne of Austria. This chutzpah did not impress Louis XIII, who refused to receive him so he travelled on to Turin, arriving on 6 October 1633 in the company of another of Henrietta Maria's merry favourites, the playboy Robert Dormer, Earl of Carnarvon.

Aged twenty-three, with long, blond, wavy locks, Carnarvon came from a Catholic family, but after his father died he had been raised as the ward of the Protestant Earl of Pembroke. Such arrangements were intended to snuff out a Catholic child's birth religion. In the case of Carnarvon the wardship had not succeeded in making him anything more than nominally Protestant and his recently arranged marriage to Pembroke's daughter was a trial to them both. He was 'extremely wild' and after enjoying 'an excellent supper and with a good bed ready', liked to swear, 'by God's blood he will have three whores'.[1] The young men visited the Jesuits, attended a comedy given at court, climbed the hill to a Capuchin monastery, and afterwards saw a charlatan, or quack, in the plaza.[2] Later they watched Henrietta Maria's brother-in-law, Victor Amadeus – who had become Duke of Savoy in 1630 – dine in state.

Wat found that Christine, the thirteen-year-old 'baby bride' of 1619, had at the age of twenty-seven matured into 'a worthy daughter of Henri IV [having] inherited such of her father's virtues, as compose the proper ornament of her sex, and with regard to what are termed the foibles of great souls, her highness had in no wise degenerated'.[3] These 'foibles' referred to Christine's lovers. Christine and Henrietta Maria were alike in many respects, but not in this. As Wat later observed, Henrietta Maria was a woman who 'does nothing by halves, save in one regard', by which he meant she offered her favourites no sexual favours. While Wat's closeness to Henrietta Maria had raised eyebrows it was 'without scandal'.[4]

Henrietta Maria loved Charles, who was a young man with a high sex drive. Christine was married to a much older man. There was, however, another reason for the difference in their romantic lives. Henrietta Maria had informed the French ambassador earlier that year that she still wished very much to fulfil her mission, 'to work for the benefit and consolation of the Catholics of this country [Britain]'.[5] She could not do so without maintaining a high moral standing. Christine, by contrast, shared the religion of the majority in Savoy.

Christine's lovers had, thus far, included a French courtier called Pommeuse, who had been sent into exile after the birth of a daughter in 1629. Another French lover, called Saint-Michel, had followed. She was currently linked to a Piedmontese, the musician, poet and artist Count Philippe San Martino d'Agliè.

'Practically every evening he is seen by all to visit Madame in a small remote room, where he remains with her three hours at a time,' one witness recorded.[6] Christine maintained, nonetheless, a 'great power' over her husband, who expressed no doubts about the legitimacy of the healthy son she had given him the previous year.[7] Indeed, having an heir had inspired him to relaunch an old claim to the crown of Corsica.

With the help of Count Philippe (who had a genius for the choreography of the *ballet de cour*) Christine had ensured that the House of

Savoy's royal claims had an appropriately impressive and sophisticated setting. In common with Henrietta Maria in England, her sister Christine had brought a strong French influence to Turin. Some judged she had 'rendered her little court the most agreeable in the world'.[8] Yet the great powers refused to recognise the claim to royal status. Particularly galling for Christine was Richelieu ignoring her title of 'Madame Royale' in favour of the mere 'Madame de Savoye'.[9] A mutual dislike of Richelieu, as well as affection for Wat, bound Christine and Henrietta Maria closer.

Christine sent gifts of gloves for Henrietta Maria's children, and she, in turn, sent Christine richly embroidered garments for herself and horses for Victor Amadeus. Christine was pregnant with what would prove to be another son when Wat moved on to Venice on 18 November 1633.[10] From there Wat went to Rome, arriving in January 1634. Henrietta Maria's relationship with her godfather, the Pope, ensured that, despite Wat's Protestantism, he had the best possible introductions. Wat's leading patron was the Pope's nephew, Cardinal Francesco Barberini, who had been made the Church's Protector of England and Scotland. Wat also very much liked the Pope's domestic prelate, the thirty-one-year-old Jules Mazarin. The future cardinal had 'a charming face, graceful manners', was 'lively, likable, polite, with a penetrating mind', and 'clever at dissimulation, in a word fit for everything'.[11] Better yet, he 'spent money freely' on his English visitor.[12]

Mazarin and Barberini wined and dined Wat and they talked theology, the Italians hoping to convert him. They also tried to discover whether it might be possible to persuade Charles to accept a Papal envoy to his court. They had heard great things of Henrietta Maria's Catholic mission. It was said her 'sweet and virtuous carriage' was bringing 'the Catholic religion, great respect and honour' in England.[13] No Catholics had been executed for their faith since the summer of 1628, when Henrietta Maria had failed to save the Lancashire priest and the recusant yeoman farmer. More miraculous still, Henrietta Maria had been granted permission to build a beautiful chapel for her worship and it promised to be a very grand affair.

In a country where attending Mass was banned for Charles's British subjects, Henrietta Maria made sure she heard Mass almost every day. Indeed, it was noted, 'in so many years, since she was first a queen, where she has had so many indispositions, so many childbirths: and so many long journeys on progress, she has never perhaps failed three days in causing the highest art of her religion to be said by her own chaplains'. If there was no house suitable, then 'even cottages and poor cocklofts were made to serve the turn'.[14] The beautiful chapel she had commissioned would, however, be a more suitable setting for the magnificent baroque services she wished to showcase in England.

Henrietta Maria had the aid of ten or eleven Capuchin friars who had arrived after full diplomatic relations between England and France had been restored in 1630. Although few in number they were impressive men. Richelieu's famous éminence grise, François Leclerc du Tremblay, was a Capuchin. They had a significant royal history in England as part of the favoured order of Observant Friars patronised by the early Tudor kings. Their particular band of piety also appealed to the queen. It was inspired by the writing of the thirteenth-century Franciscan Bonaventure and his belief that, since the existence of God cannot be proven, faith begins in instinct. Only then can it be developed by the intellect. 'The heart has its reasons that reason knows nothing of,' was how Blaise Pascal phrased it.

The Capuchin had learned English and British history to enhance the appeal of the colloquial style of their sermons, but the setting as well as the words were important. In 1625 Charles had told her priests that, if they didn't like the oratories and the unfinished chapel at St James's Palace provided for her worship, then they could hold their services in the garden. Things were very different now. Charles had, at last, fulfilled the terms of the marriage treaty in giving the queen £2,000 for a new chapel. She had chosen Somerset House as the location. It had been the home of Edward VI's uncle, the Protector Somerset, who had introduced the first Protestant prayer book in 1549, triggering a huge rebellion. 'This was the place from which the religion was changed in this unhappy kingdom,' one of her friars observed.[15] They would now use it to return England to the Catholic Church, one conversion at a time.

Henrietta Maria had commissioned Inigo Jones, who was planning a magnificent building, separate from the main palace, a hundred feet long and thirty feet wide, with arches and columns. This was, in effect, to be a semi-public church with a friary attached. She had laid the foundation stone on 14 September 1632. The crowd had been so big, 'it seemed as if all the inhabitants of London had concerted to attend', one friar recalled. A tented church was created for the ceremony with tapestries for walls and a floor of flowers. The queen, heavily pregnant with James, heard Mass kneeling on a red velvet cushion, while music 'ravished the heart'. Then she had laid the stone, taking a trowel with a velvet fringed handle and plunged it into 'a glittering basin of silver gilt' before showering the mortar over the stone.[16] That night parties had continued along the Thames, so that it seemed that the firelight and the water were one.

With the work on the chapel still in progress, the queen's monks were currently based in buildings on the old tennis court, where they were the object of great curiosity. Londoners 'came to see them, as one goes to see Indians, Malays, savages and people from the extremities of the earth'.[17] The friars showed Londoners around their cells, where they slept on bare boards, and recalled with their visitors how 'England was formerly full of monasteries and of holy friars'.[18] Charles, however, did not view the queen's chapel as a great threat to the Church of England. Like his Archbishop of Canterbury, William Laud, Charles believed their brand of Protestantism was England's aboriginal faith, the true heir to the early Christian Church and the apostles.

Charles was certain that once English 'Reform' Protestantism had been properly ordered, his beautified Protestant ceremonies could surpass Catholic services in their appeal – and his subjects were obliged to attend these services. Charles was collecting recusancy fines against Catholics who did not attended Church of England services at ten times the rate of what he had achieved in the 1620s. Victims regularly petitioned the queen for help but her power had its limitations. Poor Catholics often remained imprisoned for years for non-payment.[19] Pope Urban hoped that a personal envoy might help Henrietta Maria move her mission forward – and there was another objective.

The Catholic clergy in Britain were quarrelling bitterly over the degree with which they should compromise with the state, with those associated with France usually being the more flexible. The issue of the Oath of Allegiance, which denied the Pope's power to depose princes, was one live issue. The Pope wanted a bishop to oversee and discipline the clergy on just how high they should 'jump . . . in obedience' to the king.[20] In February 1634, a month after Wat's arrival at the Vatican, the Pope briefed a priest called Gregorio Panzani, warning him that he was considering sending him as his personal representative to achieve this. Wat had suggested a way to win Charles round to accepting an emissary.

A view of Greenwich painted by Adriaen van Stalbemt and Jan van Belcamp depicts a summer day in 1634. In the foreground is Charles with Henrietta Maria holding the hand of the young Prince of Wales. A number of courtiers are standing around. One is climbing the hill – perhaps Inigo Jones. Behind them are wooden platforms on which builders work on a garden pavilion for the queen to his design, but under her direction.

What would become known as the Queen's House was a balustraded rectangle with the lower storey in rusticated stone – that is, the stones would be cut back leaving the central portion raised. The next storey was to have tall windows, plainly framed, and there would be a pillared portico on the park side that would function as a viewing platform for activities in the park. It was far less plain than it is today. The upper portions of the garden front appear to have been painted with colourful grotesques, while the queen's bedchamber and withdrawing chamber had balconies, as well as a terrace above, to enjoy the views of the garden, the river, Greenwich Palace and, on a clear day, the City of London.[21] The plans for the interior of the house were equally striking. They included a hall in the shape of a forty-foot cube and a balustraded gallery halfway up that the queen was to paint in white and gold. There would also be a stunning circular open-well staircase, the earliest of its kind in England. Modelled on those at the Villa Rotonda and the Carità, it was a wrought-iron balustrade depicting the lilies of France – although it is today misnamed 'the tulip staircase'.

Naturally Henrietta Maria's new house would require works of art. Van Dyck had been employed full-time by the king since 1632. He was currently painting Henrietta Maria's three children as a gift from the queen for her sister Christine: the prince, black-eyed, with his hand rested on a large and fluffy-coated hound; Mary, pouting with golden curls; and James wearing a little lace cap. Henrietta Maria explained to Christine the portrait was taking longer than expected, because Mary would not sit still for it. The queen also hated sitting for portraits, and as often as not Van Dyck had to work from a template of her facing him in three-quarter profile. The king kept one in his bedchamber at Whitehall of her in a white dress trimmed with cut satin that looks as fine as lace and as fresh and frothy as cow parsley.

Despite her reluctance to sit for long, Henrietta Maria had a close personal relationship with Van Dyck. She had worried that he would be lonely far from home and had asked for his brother Theodore (a Catholic priest) to be sent to join him as one of her chaplains. That way he could enjoy 'contentment from conversation with his brother and security while living under her protection'.[22]

The artist who was to be most closely associated with the Queen's House in Greenwich was, however, Orazio Gentileschi, who, like Van Dyck, had previously worked for Marie de' Medici and was commissioned to do a number of ceiling paintings for the great hall. Wat had visited Orazio's daughter Artemisia in Naples a few months earlier in March 1634, and had also been impressed by her work.[23] She would later join her father in working for the queen. Meanwhile, Wat was hoping to worm his way back into Charles's favour by helping to expand his art collection and was busy purchasing several moulds of classical statues in Rome, to be later cast in bronze for Charles. He had also encouraged Cardinal Barberini to send a monumental picture of Bacchus the god of wine by Guido Reni as a gift to Henrietta Maria. It was this – and the suggestion of what might follow for Charles – that had helped to smooth the arrival in England of Gregorio Panzani on 15 December 1634.

Panzani unpacked his goods at a private house in London. His agency had not been given any official status – he was invited only as an individual who happened to be from the Vatican. Nevertheless, it was as the Pope's representative that he was given an audience with Henrietta Maria.

Panzani found a young woman of just twenty-five, who liked perfumes, beautiful dresses and 'lively young men' with whom she loved 'to gossip and hear lively stories and witticisms'.[24] Charles had an awkwardness that made those around him also behave awkwardly. Henrietta Maria was the beating heart of the court's *joie de vivre* – but not everyone approved of this gaiety. The Earl of Newcastle, who had spent a fortune entertaining the king and queen at Welbeck Abbey that summer, later complained that 'mean men' jeered at nobles who could not 'dance a sarabande with castanets off their fingers'. He even believed this loss of due deference led to the Civil War.[25] Yet Henrietta Maria did fulfil her royal obligations to be patient with the dull but important.

As another observer noted, while Henrietta Maria 'delights in good company, so she is troubled to keep that which is not' and 'she never wrangles nor chides . . . much less does she disgrace or affront' but, after tolerating whatever boredom was inflicted on her, would 'after a while retire herself.'[26] There were, admittedly, a few occasions when she reacted differently. Henrietta Maria found something innately hilarious in pomposity. There was an occasion when an ambassador delivered a speech to her in Latin, a language she didn't speak. It went on for over an hour and a half and her secretary got so bored he gave up translating. She, meanwhile, tried so hard to suppress giggles that when the ambassador finished she could only manage 'a very concise and almost voiceless answer'. It caused 'great merriment at court and among her ladies for the rest of the day.'[27]

Happily Panzani spoke French. He told Henrietta Maria of the Pope's gratitude for the work she was doing for suffering Catholics and gave her a number of gifts. They included a bottle of oil made from cedar wood, never seen before in England. It was well known that Henrietta Maria loved presents, 'And acknowledges, even by rewards, all those poor little presents which are made to her (though it exceeds not that sometimes a fruit or a flower)', but then, as this onlooker noted, 'who loves it not when the present is choice?'[28] While Henrietta Maria's love of luxury goods has been used to accuse her of frivolity, the fact is that leading men also loved expensive perfumes and accessories. Think of the late Duke of Buckingham, who took golden perfume pans to war, or the fashion wars between the earls of Holland and Carlisle. Then, as now, it was also big business. Henrietta Maria's role as a seventeenth-century 'influencer' supported a whole network of traders in London, including many women who depended on her custom and the following she inspired.

More significant than the cedar oil was a gift of an 'exquisite' crystal reliquary containing the bone of an early Christian female saint whose tomb had been rediscovered only two months earlier.[29] The gratitude Henrietta Maria showed for this has also been used against her, described as a mark of her superstition and stupidity. There was, however, great rivalry between the most sophisticated European courts over such historic and holy artefacts. Christine and her husband had the famous Turin shroud, in which, it was said, Christ's body had been wrapped.

The shroud was central to all the great religious ceremonies at their court, and acted as a lure for foreign princes who came to Turin hoping to be permitted private access to it.

Henrietta Maria told Panzani that just before his arrival in London a small piece of the true cross had been found at the Tower, where it had been hidden for generations. Charles's servants had planned to display it with other curiosities, but he had agreed that she could have it for the new chapel she was building at Somerset House.[30] In Europe relics were about national prestige as well as faith, but as a Catholic queen in a Protestant country, Henrietta Maria also had more reason than most to make a public point of her Catholic piety. This explains why, when the Pope sent the queen pictures, she would announce that she wished he had sent more devotional objects. The reality was that Henrietta Maria was every inch the daughter of the great patron of Rubens, of Van Dyck, of Gentileschi: Marie de' Medici. Behind the scenes Henrietta Maria was seeking to acquire works by Leonardo and Andrea del Sarto, as well as ordering a bust of the king from the great sculptor Bernini. In due course the bust would stand in the hall at the Queen's House, a lone male figure in a room decorated, ceiling and walls, with images of women by Gentileschi.

Wat arrived in England in January 1635 with the Guido Reni painting of Bacchus for the queen in his baggage. He was 'well received' by Charles as well as Henrietta Maria. He even attended on their old enemy, Lord Treasurer Weston, who was now Earl of Portland – although he was not to enjoy his earldom for long.[31] Weston was gravely ill and died the following month. His death removed Henrietta Maria's leading rival for the ear of the king and Wat hoped she would now help his star rise again at Charles's court.

Henrietta Maria later said that she had always regarded her Scottish confessor Father Robert Phillip of Sanquhar a 'prudent and discreet man', not least because he 'always told her . . . to live well towards the Protestants, who deserved well from her'.[32] She was particularly close to the Earl of Holland, 'and deeply respects his advice', Panzani noted.[33]

Henrietta Maria was married to Charles I aged fifteen, in 1625, 'a lovely, Sweet young creature' with 'an extraordinary directness and quickness'. The marriage represented a French alliance with a Protestant power of the kind her father, Henry IV ('the Great'), had pursued, and which had cost him his life.

Marie de' Medici hurried Peter Paul Rubens to finish a cycle of twenty-four monumental paintings depicting her many triumphs, in time for Henrietta Maria's wedding. Here she is depicted as the Regent Militant, carrying a marshall's baton. She had encouraged her daughters to believe that women were capable of exercising power for good.

Marie de Rohan, Duchess of Chevreuse, lover of Henry Rich, Earl of Holland and intimate of George Villiers, Duke of Buckingham, was later Henrietta Maria's co-conspirator in her plots against Louis XIII's leading minister, Cardinal Richelieu. She was painted by Diego Velázquez in Spain in 1637–8, aged thirty-six. This is believed to be that portrait.

The beautiful George Villiers, Marquess (later Duke) of Buckingham, painted naked, with his wife, Katherine Manners. Richelieu believed that Buckingham's enmity towards Henrietta Maria could extend as far as murder.

Inigo Jones's set design for Henrietta Maria's first masque in England. Foreign diplomats thought the 1626 pastoral beautiful, but the elite British audience did not like it because the women, 'if they were not all, some were in men's apparel'.

Despite early quarrels, by early 1627 Charles was said to love Henrietta Maria 'extremely', and in April he gave her a diamond ring.

An image of an ideal marriage: the hilt of Charles's sword is pointing at the queen's womb. Henrietta Maria is wearing orange bows, the colour of the Protestant anti-Habsburg cause in Europe that she supported.

Cardinal Armand Jean du Plessis, Duke of Richelieu, former servitor of Marie de' Medici and later her deadly enemy. He complained bitterly that in politics he was a victim of 'the impertinence of the [female] sex', Marie, Henrietta Maria and the Duchess of Chevreuse in particular.

Henrietta Maria sent this portrait of her three eldest children, Charles, Mary and James, to her sister Christine, Duchess of Savoy, in Turin. She complained Mary wouldn't sit still, so it took longer than intended.

Marie de' Medici was the greatest patron of architecture of her day and Henrietta Maria was every inch her daughter. She loved to spend on 'noble designs of building and adorning her princely houses'. Somerset House was her principal residence, and here she introduced to England parquet floors, sash windows and garden designs inspired by Le Nôtre.

The drama and beauty of the baroque Mass held great popular appeal and encouraged conversions to Catholicism, making Henrietta Maria's chapel at Somerset House the most controversial building in Protestant England. Large numbers of candles, like those seen at this Forty Hours Devotion at the Brompton Oratory in London, were a particular feature of services held there.

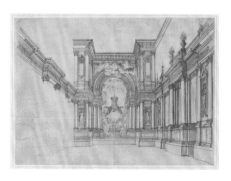

Perspective tableaux, such as that built at the Somerset House chapel, were very fashionable in Rome where artists like Bernini, and leading clerics like Cardinal Barberini, competed to create the most lavish and striking examples. Of the one at Somerset House it was said that Inigo Jones, 'never did a more curious piece in all the masques at Whitehall'.

Henrietta Maria's eldest sister Elisabeth was the first queen of Spain to be portrayed on horseback. Her husband Philip IV later made her regent while he was away from his capital fighting rebels, a role Henrietta Maria was never given by Charles I.

Louis XIII and Gaston Duke of Orléans leading the French armies. Kings were expected to win their wars. Henrietta Maria's brother Louis did so. Charles I did not, and his failures in this regard were an important factor on the path to the civil wars.

Henrietta Maria pregnant: she would deliver four sons and five daughters, but only three of her children would survive her.

William Prynne called women who spoke on stage – as Henrietta Maria did – 'notorious whores'. Charles obliged her to give those appearances up. Nevertheless, she continued to encourage female-centric plays that advocated a voice for women in public discourse.

Henrietta Maria took the advice of the Poet Laureate William Davenant in trying to persuade Charles to woo parliament and the people after he lost the Bishops' Wars. Contrary to myth she was a willing conciliator and flexible in negotiations, without being weak.

He was surprised by her affection for her 'Puritan' followers, but he was reassured that they were better placed to 'speak boldly for Catholics' than closet Catholics, who 'do not want to be discovered' for fear of the impact on their lives and livelihoods.[34]

How much Henrietta Maria's Protestant friends actually did help Catholics is another matter – two years earlier a French envoy had singled out Holland and Wat as making their efforts to advance the Catholic religion more difficult.[35]

Panzani's arrival had also coincided with a period of increased Protestant anxiety. It had emerged that Lord Treasurer Weston had died a Catholic and this fuelled concerns about how many other closet Catholics there might be at court. The fact the king seemed to enjoy Panzani's company also troubled many. The Italian was a man of charm and tact who knew how to get on the right side of Charles. He assured the king that the Pope wished to encourage the loyalty of British Catholics to the Crown, offered to further build Charles's art collection, and they discussed the possibilities for the reunion of Christendom, a subject as close to Charles's heart as it had been to his father, King James.

Charles declared himself a Catholic – that is a member of the Universal Church – just not Roman Catholic, and he said that, 'so long as a man believed in Christ, he could save his soul whatever religion he was born, baptised and bred.'[36] In October 1635, Barberini told Mazarin that Panzani was even speculating on Charles's possible conversion. Barberini admitted he would 'rob Rome of her most valuable ornaments, if, in exchange, we might be so happy as to have the King of England's name amongst those princes who submit themselves to the apostolic See.'[37] He did, not, however, think it a likely occurrence. Charles was 'naturally tenacious and not easily moved from the principles in which he has been educated'. Nor did Barberini think there was any genuine possibility of the Church of England reuniting with the Church of Rome. The English are 'a mysterious people', he warned Panzani, and 'the sea which you passed to meet them is an emblem of their temper.'[38]

In both the matter of Charles's conversion and the reunion of the Church of England and Rome, Barberini was correct. Charles's Archbishop of Canterbury, William Laud, refused even to see Panzani.

A short, slight figure with a love of tabby cats, Laud was a very focused individual, often brusque to the point of rudeness. 'I have no leisure for compliments,' he once said.[39] With his short hair and plain dark clothes he resembled a Puritan and, like them, he believed in the rigorous self-examination of conscience. He kept a diary in which he recorded all his sins and illicit fantasies – once recalling a dream in which he had taken the Duke of Buckingham to bed with him. In his daylight hours he took on vested interests both inside and outside the Church to root out corruption. He wanted to restore the Church of England to the authority of the medieval church, but cleansed of its 'Romish' errors. When Henrietta Maria began pressing Charles, on Panzani's behalf, to give permission for a Catholic bishop to function in England, Laud told the queen, 'plainly, when she spoke to him about it, that he would oppose it as much as he could'.[40]

Someone else was, however, being supportive of Panzani's efforts on another matter: persuading Charles to establish an accredited papal agent – Wat Montagu.[41]

Henrietta Maria later explained to a friend 'it was necessary' for royals to 'behave as confessors who must know all and say nothing so that those who approach them may tell them of their necessities, and often display for them their passions, their hearts, their malice and the injustice that comes from the harm they do one another, and it is necessary, charitably, so as not to embarrass anybody, never to speak again of all these things'.[42] A contemporary confirmed that 'Above all things she knows how to be secret' and 'was able to do so, beyond the usual custom of queens, and beyond the almost portable imbecilities of women, especially of women in the tender part of their years'.[43]

Now Wat had told Henrietta Maria his secret. He was considering converting to Catholicism, but did not want to rush matters. Doubtless he had much reflecting to do on spiritual matters. There were, however, worldly considerations to take into account. He was hoping that Charles would make him the queen's vice chamberlain. Charles had never knowingly give a senior court position to a Catholic.

Henrietta Maria spent the following months talking to Wat and urging him to show courage. By October 1635 it was evident Charles was not going to make Wat her vice chamberlain. And Wat decided to break cover. The queen summoned Panzani to Hampton Court and told him 'in the greatest secrecy' that Montagu wished to become a Catholic. It was clear to Panzani that she had played a role in this and he reported that he had never heard her talk with such emotion.

Henrietta Maria was proud of the guidance she had given Wat and happy about his decision, but when it became public it was a huge scandal. Charles saw any conversion to Catholicism as a blow to his authority. He was so angry that Wat fled to Paris. From there Wat wrote to his father, the Earl of Manchester, explaining that he found only the Catholic Church offered an 'unbroken thread of doctrine from age to age'. He sent a copy of the letter to Henrietta Maria's Scottish confessor, Father Phillip – evidently so that it might be made public. His view was a direct contradiction of Charles's belief that the Church of England was the true heir to the early church.

If Charles was angry, Wat's father was distraught. He accused his son of thwarted ambition. 'The court of France, nor yet all the princes' courts of Christendom (most of which you have visited) could never till now taint your faith,' he wrote; 'But now Italy hath turned you because England has discontented you.' Wat's reaction was to become more defiant. In Paris he was seen everywhere wearing a diamond cross that Mazarin had given him, as well as 'a chain of beads . . . at his neck'. He wrote to his friends in England 'that he is ready to die a martyr for his religion'.[44]

At Christmas Montagu was in Turin where he was entertained by Christine as if he held the rank of an ambassador. Nevertheless, she told Henrietta Maria he seemed strangely deflated. The queen explained that he had a thoughtful, melancholic side to his personality, an attribute they shared. Panzani had noted that when Henrietta Maria reflected on the future 'she likes silence' and would meditate and pray, putting her trust 'entirely in the king'.[45] Wat knew that when it came to court conversions there was always a price to pay. The question was only how great it might be. Yet Wat's spirits were restored by the time he reached Rome in January 1636. He stayed with Cardinal Barberini who acted as his godfather when he was formally received into the Church. He would now never hold any formal position at the English court, but his conversion at Henrietta Maria's hands, and the sacrifices that went with it, would bind them close until her death nearly thirty-four years later.

THE GOLDEN ROSE

ON 8 DECEMBER 1635 A CONGREGATION GATHERED IN HENRIETTA
Maria's new chapel at Somerset House for its first public Mass. It was
the Feast of the Immaculate Conception celebrating the Virgin becoming the Mother of God. The ceiling above them depicted the end of her
earthly story, the Ascension of the Virgin on her death to reign as
Queen of Heaven.[1] It was, however, the extraordinary scene before
them that held their gaze: a columned archway and forty-feet-high
curtains opened to reveal an altar with a vision of paradise.

Clouds, angels and cherubs had been set in a series of ovals with
'hidden lights which kept increasing, so that the distance appeared very
great, and the number of figures double what they were'.

The Mass was sung in eight parts by an invisible choir, the voices
seemingly emanating from the angels in their clouds, 'as if the whole
paradise was full of music' and so 'melodious that one would have a
heart of stone not to be moved'.[2] The air was scented with incense, and
the windows of the chapel covered to highlight the lighting effect of
the tableaux, while the priests moved in fine embroidered vestments,
saying the words of transformation at the consecration. The congregation became participants in a living scene and tears were seen pouring
down Henrietta Maria's face, adding to the intense emotion of bread
and wine becoming Christ's body and blood.

It had been extraordinary, allowing the congregation to feel suspended somewhere between the physical reality of the chapel and the infinite space of the spiritual world suggested by the heavenly images.[3] The last sense to be called on was taste as diplomats and foreign workers 'thronged to receive Holy Communion', along with a few English Catholics, risking arrest. And it was not yet over. That evening, after dinner, the queen returned for Vespers. The sermon was taken from a text in the Psalms, 'This is the Lord's doing and it is marvelous in our eyes'. And what was marvellous, the priest announced, was that the Mass, 'abolished and forbidden for so many years in all England, Ireland and Scotland', was performed again. There were cheers and, as the congregation followed the queen out, they found a huge crush of curious visitors pushing their way in to see the chapel and the Exposition of the Blessed Sacrament.

For forty hours worshippers came to pray before the transformed host. It was exposed in a golden sunburst and brilliantly illuminated by over 400 lights at the epicentre of the tableau. For three days it was impossible to shut the chapel doors as people continued to flood in. Charles, who had donated a magnificent Rubens of the crucifixion for the altarpiece, went to see what all the fuss had been about.[4] He was stunned by what his wife had achieved and 'said aloud that he had never seen anything more beautiful or more ingeniously designed' than the tableau.[5] Another visitor admitted 'Inigo Jones never presented a more curious piece in all the masques at Whitehall'.[6]

The queen kept the decorations up until Christmas and, on 28 December, she delivered her fifth child, a little girl called Elizabeth. Henrietta Maria was proving as fecund as her mother had been. The Venetian ambassador reported that people were actually happier that it was a princess because the kingdom was 'relieved of the danger to which states sometimes succumb from there being too many Princes of the Blood'.[7] In fact, in contrast to France, her children would prove very loyal to each other in the years ahead.

*   *   *

In the Scottish tradition the princes and princesses were each placed with a governor or governess to raise them. This had led to some confusion the previous summer of 1634, when an ambassador came to deliver his farewell to the queen and mistook her dwarf, Jeffrey, for her eldest son. His frantic apologies when he had realised his error had only made her laugh the more.[8]

Despite living apart from her children for much of the time, they were a close family. Charles and Henrietta Maria would often take their children 'out maying in the park'. They shared a sense of fun: she once raced against her ladies along the Thames and won while Charles kept his eldest son in St James's Gardens so late that the boy caught a cold. 'Never', it seemed to the queen's Master of the Horse, Lord Goring, 'was there a private family more full at peace and tranquillity in this glorious kingdom.'[9] This was the height of the period described by the poet Thomas Carew as 'halcyon days' 'when [Henrietta Maria] the queen of Beauty did inspire / The air with perfumes, and our hearts with fire'.

In Greek myth the halcyon were birds who hatched their young in the calm before the winter storms: a time of peace that was in great contrast to the horrors in war-torn Europe. Van Dyck's images captured a court that liked to imagine itself set in a rural idyll of gardens and countryside, hunting and romance, and that prized elegance, gallantry and wit.

Henrietta Maria kept in touch with Wat Montagu in gossipy and affectionate letters. She said she missed him and wished for his return 'with great passion'. He replied that he took nourishment only from her letters and her living image was printed on his soul.[10] He told her about the progress on the bust portrait of Charles by Bernini the queen had requested and had seen Van Dyck's sketches for it. He was also working to promote her choice of candidate for an accredited papal agent. Charles had agreed to formal diplomatic relations with the Vatican, having been persuaded the Pope might offer support for the restoration of the Palatinate. Panzani described the kind of man who would best fit in at Charles's court as one who led an exemplary life, but was not strait-laced, and got on well with women. This was most important as, he noted, a great deal of court business was done through Henrietta Maria and her ladies.[11]

Henrietta had in mind a suave Scot from near Aberdeen called George Conn, who was 'graceful in his person, of a fit age, affable in conversation, well acquainted with the methods of courts'.[12] He had been in exile for much of his adult life, but he had the advantage over Panzani that he spoke English. He was also the author of a famous hagiography of Charles's grandmother, Mary, Queen of Scots. With Wat's help Henrietta Maria got her way and George Conn arrived in England on 17 July 1636. The court had fled London from another summer of plague and Conn and Panzani caught up with Henrietta Maria at Apethorpe Palace in Northamptonshire on Sunday 24 July.[13]

Henrietta Maria gave Conn an audience after she had attended Mass and he gave her more gifts from Pope Urban. They included a cross with diamond bees (inspired by the bees that adorned the Barberini arms) and an unframed picture of St Catherine. She promptly tied the cross around her neck and promised she would pin the picture of St Catherine to curtains on her bed. Charles then arrived along with the Earl of Carnarvon (Wat Montagu's former travelling companion) and the Earl of Holland. The king gave Conn a friendly hand and Conn soon found himself deluged with invitations. There was dinner hosted by Holland and hunting with Lucy Carlisle's brother, the Earl of Northumberland. He was even befriended by Lucy herself. She was briefly suspected of popery for it, though as Conn observed, 'she has no religion beyond her own beauty'.[14]

Conn also met Charles's nephews, the eighteen-year-old Charles Louis and his sixteen-year-old brother, Prince Rupert of the Rhine. Their father Frederick had died on campaign four years earlier, in 1632, leaving Charles Louis uncrowned King of Bohemia and the Elector Palatine.[15] There had been high hopes for his cause in 1633 when the Swedes had forced the Imperialists to surrender his capital, Heidelberg, but the

Habsburg reconquest of the Palatinate had been even more devastating than the first: the starving inhabitants were reduced to cannibalism. The one bright hope was that the French had felt sufficiently threatened by the Habsburg successes to return to war with Spain in 1635 after a hiatus of four years. For the first time they had formally declared themselves in the Thirty Years' War – and Louis did so on the 'Protestant' side. The Palatine brothers were in England hoping that Charles too might enter the war.

Thousands of Charles's subjects were already fighting in Europe as volunteers and mercenaries, and the princes were popular at court. Van Dyck painted them in armour, their long hair curling over expensive lace collars, Charles Louis holding a baton in his hand: a symbol of command. He had inherited his father's morose temperament and rather less of his mother Elizabeth's Stuart energy. His handsome black-haired brother Rupert – or Robert as King Charles sometimes called him – was very different. Brilliant and hot-tempered he had been a warrior since he was thirteen, fighting for the Prince of Orange.

Conn observed that the court was divided into three principal politico-religious factions, each with their own foreign policy agenda. The first were the Calvinist zealots who wanted further Calvinist reform of the Church of England and war with Spain in alliance only with Protestant powers – and a parliament to pay for it. These were small in number as most of them preferred to stay away from court where they risked being snubbed by the king, The second wished to remain at peace with Spain so that Charles could continue without a parliament. This helped protect the position of those likely to be attacked by MPs: 'Arminian' Protestants such as Laud and a circle of crypto-Catholics that hovered close to the Crown.[16] But this was not the faction Henrietta Maria supported.

The queen was allied to the moderate Calvinists who were prepared to achieve their ends over the Palatine in alliance with France. This group covered the spectrum from those largely hostile to the court, represented by men such as Holland's elder brother, Robert Rich, Earl of Warwick, and those like Holland, who was very close to Henrietta Maria. She was also on good terms with the Palatine princes. She had even had Van Dyck paint her, in a portrait with Jeffrey Hudson, wearing orange bows – the colour associated with the Protestant cause.[17]

Charles was keeping his own opinion on the future direction of foreign policy close to his chest. The only thing that was certain was that he did not want to call another parliament. To avoid the necessity of doing so Charles had been hyper-exploiting prerogative taxes – those raised by royal right alone. Holland, who was now Groom of the Stool, his closest body servant, was in charge of executing the Forest laws. The most effective tax, however, was Ship Money. This had always been imposed on coastal areas to raise money for the navy in times of war. Charles began raising it in peacetime to build up his navy for leverage in the European conflict and to protect British coastal villages from North African slavers. In August 1635 it had been extended inland and some areas had resisted paying it.

Charles ordered that as the court passed through towns and villages on his progress the local sheriffs should be visited and instructed to ensure the previous year's tax was paid before the 1636 writs went out. Charles and Henrietta Maria receive a muted welcome when they entered Oxford on 29 August, where they were guests of Archbishop Laud. The royal procession through the city met with only a few cheers. There were suggestions that the unpopularity of the tax played a role. Another reason given was that Laud's insistence on order and decorum left no room for spontaneity. One witness believed the people did not dare 'cry *vivat* [God Save the King] in that disorderly manner which would have become good subjects'.[18]

Order and decorum were a cornerstone of Charles's religious reforms, and while Henrietta Maria retired to her lodgings, Charles went to Christ Church to set an example, kneeling to pray at the south door of the cathedral before he entered. What Charles saw inside would have greatly pleased him. The university chapels had all been 'much beautified' and 'extraordinary cost bestowed upon them'. There were stained-glass images in the windows, while Communion tables were covered in rich tapestries and hangings.[19] The effect was disconcerting for many Catholics and Protestants.

On the one hand Catholics fretted that so called 'Church Papists' (who avoided fines by attending Anglican services) would be seduced by this new-look Protestantism. 'Do not their churches begin to look with another face? Their walls to speak a new language? Their preachers to use a sweeter tone?' Catholics observed anxiously. Even Conn expressed fears that Charles 'resolved to deal with his master the Pope, as wrestlers do with one another, taking him up to fling him down'.[20] On the other hand, Puritans like William Prynne – the man who had suggested the queen was a whore – argued that Laud's 'beauty of holiness' would confirm Catholics in their errors, 'for they see us running, if not flying so fast of late, that they say they need not come towards us, since we are posting so fast to them'.[21]

Laud had spent a fortune on a banquet that night followed by a production of William Strode's *The Floating Island*. The story and themes delivered messages designed to appeal to Charles. There were arguments in favour of a powerful navy along with the taxes needed to support it. There were also satirical attacks on Puritans – notably William Prynne. Yet it was as misogynist in tone as anything written by Prynne. Henrietta Maria and her ladies made their dislike of the production very plain. Happily the plays on the following two nights were better received. Both praised the virtues of women and the second, William Cartwright's *The Royal Slave*, highlighted the value of female advice at court. Henrietta Maria later ordered it to be played again by the king's men.[22]

Panzani had been correct in observing the importance of the good opinion of women in the court of Charles I – and especially of the queen. 'She hath a very quick apprehension . . . and her Judgement is also naturally good; and now much matured', one Catholic observer noted. This was because of 'the great experience, which she is growing apace to have, both of Persons, & Things'. She had been queen for eleven years.[23]

Conn frequently met the king in Henrietta Maria's apartments. Like Panzani he found Charles enjoyed discussions about religion. One day the queen issued a defence of the significance of the Virgin Mary, against her husband's view that prayer to the Virgin was a distraction from the proper worship of God. Quoting the medieval Franciscan theologian and philosopher Bonaventure, she argued God could not deny the Virgin Mary's requests, because she could command her son, Christ, as his mother. This was the basis of Marie de' Medici's belief that because a woman wielded power in heaven, so women could also do so on earth.

Charles reacted to his wife's arguments 'with much pleasantness'.[24] Conn judged correctly that there was, however, no possibility of his conversion. Nor was there any likelihood of a reunion between the churches. Instead Conn encouraged the queen to influence the religion of her children – she had already taken Prince Charles to Mass – and to expand her protective net around British Catholics. He hoped that together they might even create a Catholic party at court, resembling the devot party of her mother in France. Their first success was to persuade Charles to permit Wat Montagu to return home in April 1637.

Charles refused to see Wat for weeks, but Henrietta Maria, who had only just recovered from the birth of another daughter, Anne, on 17 March did so with 'infinite goodwill'.[25] This encouraged the rest of the court to accept him. Meanwhile, they found in each other their 'habitual joyful familiarity'. Henrietta Maria would even go to his house to dine with him in secret.[26] In the past there had been no hint of scandal between them, but in Europe there were now rumours that they were having an affair. 'He is not in the king's best graces, but the queen does all she can to make him another Count Philippe,' one of Mazarin's correspondents wrote, referring to Christine's Piedmontese lover. 'Sometimes he has to do without the queen's embraces for two months at a time, but only because the occasion is lacking.'[27]

An affair with Holland was also hinted at – Henrietta Maria gave him a full-length Van Dyck of herself dressed in blue at about this time: the most expensive she ever paid for.[28] This was, however, malicious chatter. While she was forgiving about her friends' rackety private lives she had 'an extraordinary innocence', Conn noted. Her Scottish confessor also admitted her sins were more of omission than commission.[29] Henrietta Maria had found fulfilment as a wife and mother, and purpose in the protection of Catholics and as an inspiration to conversion. Wat was a reminder of what she could achieve – and her chapel in Somerset House was fulfilling its missionary role with remarkable success.

The rules against Charles's subjects attending Mass in the queen's chapel in Somerset House had broken down after a particularly unpleasant incident when pursuivants dragged a heavily pregnant woman out of the chapel, causing a miscarriage. She was the wife of one of Henrietta Maria's servants and the queen had complained so vociferously to Charles about the loss of the baby that the congregations at her chapel had been left largely alone thereafter.

Mass was now being said several times a day by her Capuchins. Their music showcased the latest Italian compositions by contemporaries of Monteverdi (whom Wat had seen perform in Venice). The sermons were equally stimulating, being designed not only to confirm Catholics in their faith, but also to convert Protestants. Those who argued back (seventeenth-century congregations were less supine than today's) were invited for private talks in which their views might be changed.

On Sundays and holidays the crowds became so thick at the chapel that it was often difficult to get in, and people had to wait two or three hours to find a priest to hear their confession. Converts included 'An English Countess', 'Dr Vane, Almoner, otherwise chaplain, to His Majesty', 'two other young ministers', the 'daughter of a Puritan father and a Catholic mother', an 'English Gentleman of the Protestant religion, who . . . was a member of the King's Council in Ireland', and 'Catholics were so exceedingly multiplied' in parts of London that it was said that in 'Bloomsbury there are as many or more than Protestants'.[30] Conn opened another chapel at his London house where he hosted a society Catholic wedding and he too soon gathered converts.

What more could the Pope hope for, Henrietta Maria asked Conn? 'For the conversion of England,' he replied. 'Then we must act and not talk,' she said with a laugh – and she was as good as her word.[31] Henrietta Maria set up two voluntary associations of laypeople: the confraternities of the Rosary and of St Francis. These associations bound ordinary people and court Catholics as brothers and sisters across class boundaries to promote special acts of charity and piety. They met every Saturday in her chapel, where 'the litanies of the Blessed Virgin and other reverential services were sung'. Yet more converts were gathered through their processions and by intimate contemplative groups that met in a number of public places and also welcomed Protestants.

The next step for Conn and the queen was to find some means of persuading Charles to give Catholics freedom of worship across the country. Henrietta Maria dreamed of an English equivalent to her father's Edict of Nantes, which allowed Protestants and Catholics to co-exist with freedom of religion for both under his rule. Such toleration already existed in a new colony in the Americas named after her as Maryland.[32] The main difficulty, as they saw it, was that the Pope would not agree to Catholics accepting the Oath of Obedience, which denied his right to depose princes. The answer, Conn believed, was for them to highlight Catholic loyalty in contrast to Puritan sedition. On 14 June 1637 an important case was to be held in the Star Chamber against a number of such dissidents.

They included the name of a figure very familiar to the queen: William Prynne.

Conn made sure he attended proceedings to learn what he could. On the morning of the case he sat in a box with the Catholic Countess of Arundel to watch what unfolded.

Aged thirty-seven, Prynne had been a Lincoln's Inn lawyer but he had only one case he really wished to prosecute, and that was against Charles's reforms of the Church of England. He sat at a desk all day, his eyes shielded from the light by 'a long quilt cap'. Every three hours or so a servant would bring him a roll and a pot of ale to sustain him, while he studied and wrote dire warnings against popery. He was a man who saw Jesuits around every corner and under every bed. They could 'metamorphose themselves into any shape', and his imagination was 'stuffed with plots'.[33] He appeared now in the Star Chamber with his 'long meagre face' and 'strange, saturnine complexion' alongside two other Puritans.[34]

Prynne's co-accused were both acquaintances of his: a physician called John Bastwick, aged about forty, and a bushy-eyebrowed cleric called Henry Burton who was almost sixty. Bastwick had described the bishops as 'the tail of the beast' and the Church of England 'as full of ceremonies as a dog is full of fleas'. Burton had delivered sermons against Communion tables being railed off and resembling altars, against crucifixes, and bowing to the east. As for Prynne: his latest work (which he had carefully avoided putting his name to) raged against King Charles's *Book of Sports*, which permitted 'lawful recreations' on a Sunday, including dancing.

Together the men faced twenty-five judges, accused of writing and publishing seditious, schismatical and libellous books against the Church of England hierarchy. All three had refused to either plead or to submit to interrogatories under oath. 'They are mad factious fellows,' one witness commented, 'and covet a kind of puritanical martyrdom, or at least a fame of punishment for religion.'[35]

Since there could be no trial as such, the law took them to have confessed their guilt. On 30 June they were fined the enormous sum of £5,000 each and sentenced to life 'in three remote places of the kingdom, namely the castles of Carnarvon, Cornwall and Lancaster'. They were also to have their ears cropped, in Prynne's case for a second time. The letters SL ('seditious libeller') would be branded into his cheek.

The punishment was both horrible and insufficient. In England any theft over five shillings earned the death penalty. They could have been hanged: Henry VIII would have had them executed in a heartbeat. Instead, they were turned into living martyrs. Conn attended the mutilations and was shocked to witness that the three men were permitted to speak out before they took place. Burton declared the day as being like his wedding day, Bastwick urged onlookers to 'fight on against Gog and Magog [the evil forces ranged against the godly]', while Prynne told the gathering crowd that it was 'for the general good and your good that we have engaged our own liberties'.[36] Some in the crowd were angry at this defiance, but Conn saw the more thoughtful 'were very reserved', and many wept. Handkerchiefs were dipped in their blood to be kept as relics and their journeys to their various prisons became a procession in which they were 'mightily courted by the people'.[37]

Charles told Conn angrily that the Puritans were putting 'everything into confusion'.[38] The introduction of a new Church of England-style prayer book in Scotland had triggered a major riot on 23 July 1637 in St Giles, the main Edinburgh kirk. Presbyterians complained that the Calvinist belief in the absence of the Physical Presence of Christ in the Eucharist had not been expressed in sufficiently robust terms in the new text. Charles believed, however, that the riots were less about religion than an attack on his rule. It seemed to Conn to be the perfect time to highlight Catholic loyalty – and that month there was also a reminder to Charles of the benefits of friendship with Rome.

Bernini's stunning bust, commissioned by Henrietta Maria for her husband, had just arrived at the Queen's House. It depicted Charles in all his princely glory. Wat claimed it did 'more for the doctrine of icons than [the Jesuit theologian] Cardinal Bellamino ever achieved'. A curious incident was, however, later recalled. As the bust was being placed on its pedestal, a hawk carrying a partridge cast a drop of blood from the sky. It fell and trickled a bloody line across the marble neck.[39]

'LAST OF THE 'HALCYON 'DAYS

IN THE LATE SUMMER OF 1637 HENRIETTA MARIA'S FAVOURITE masque writer, William Davenant, set off with two friends on a progress to Bath. Davenant, the thirty-year-old self-made son of an innkeeper, was focused, ambitious, and his sins were as plain as the nose on his face – or rather the nose he did not have on his face: he had lost it having 'got a terrible clap of a black, handsome wench that lay in Axe yard Westminster'.[1] The more notorious of Davenant's companions was the twenty-eight-year-old soldier-poet, Sir John Suckling.

A small, slight man with a sandy beard that curled naturally, Suckling had a 'ready and sparkling wit' inherited from his mother, along with a fortune from his father, who had been a comptroller of James I's household. Described later as 'the greatest gallant of his time', he was also an angry young man. He had experienced the horrors of Île de Ré when he was only eighteen. Later, while fighting in the Protestant cause in Europe, he had picked up a gambling habit that made him England's most famous 'gamester, both for bowling and cards'.[2]

Suckling had invented the game of cribbage and just as Davenant had lost his nose to one vice, so Suckling was losing his fortune to another. It was said shopkeepers couldn't trust him with a bill of sixpence, as 'one day he might, by winning, be worth two hundred pounds, and the next day he might be worth half so much, or perhaps be minus'.[3] He disliked the 'damnably proud' lords at court and specialised in satires about the powerful.[4] This included Lucy Carlisle who had become a notorious powerbroker since her husband's death the previous year and 'grown greater in her own conceit than ever she was'.[5] Henrietta Maria had introduced a new style of salon culture to England that Lucy was imitating and that he mocked. Every week the queen would open her presence chamber – usually at Somerset House – and a select group of ladies and gentlemen would gather round under her canopy of state to gossip and chat. Lucy invited others to her house on the Strand, which acted in part as a gateway to the queen's salon and also enabled her management and manipulation of political factions. Where poets saw the queen as affectionate, giving as well as receiving love, Lucy was judged seductive but disdainful.[6] Suckling wrote a poem imagining himself taking off her clothes as she walked in Holland Park and made lewd puns on the kind of access a man might desire from her.

The third young man on that summer progress, Jack Young, was a member of Suckling's favourite drinking and literary club, the Order of the Fancy, 'whose practice was to speak excessively and talk nonsense'. Many were veterans of Île de Ré and they would often recuperate from their excesses by taking the waters at Bath. 'The wine drinkers to the water takers, greetings', a letter from Suckling to his fellow members of the Fancy began, 'Colonel Young' was to reinforce their journey with 'some slight forces of Canary [malmsey] and some few of sherry' to be followed by 'regiments of claret' while a lieutenant would bring up the rear 'with Rhenissh and white [wine]'.[7] It was no wonder Suckling had a red nose, but at least he had a nose, and that summer his finances were better than they had been for some time.

Suckling's writing had been gaining royal attention. Charles, who was then hunting in the New Forest, was having Suckling's latest ballad sung to him. It imagined a contest taking place in front of Henrietta Maria between Suckling, Davenant, Thomas Carew and Ben Jonson, to be judged by Apollo, the god of poetry. Thomas Carew was the poet of the 'halcyon days', Ben Jonson had been Poet Laureate until his recent death on 17 August. Young had been passing his grave as it was being covered in Westminster Abbey before he left London. He gave eighteen pence to the stonemason to engrave the blue marble, 'O Rare Ben Jonson'. Davenant liked the phrase so much he would later ask for the same compliment for his own tomb.[8]

Suckling had packed thoroughly for their journey and 'came like a young prince for all manner of equipage and convenience', as well as 'a cartload of books' to research his latest work. ''Twas as pleasant a journey as ever men had; in the height of a long peace and luxury, and in the Venison season', Davenant later recalled. On the second night of their progress the friends stopped at Marlborough and walked the downs behind the town while their supper was being prepared. They came across 'maids . . . drying off clothes on the bushes'. Young 'espied a very pretty young girl, and got her consent for an assignation at midnight'. Unluckily for him Davenant and Suckling were on the other side of the hedge, and having overheard him were 'resolved to frustrate his design'.

The friends usually played cards after supper, but Young, 'pretending weariness', said he had to go to bed and was 'not to be persuaded by any means to the contrary'. When Young had gone, Davenant and Suckling confided in the landlady that Young's yawns were symptoms of a coming fit, from which he suffered about twice a year, often at midnight. They asked her to lock him in his rooms and get a good strong man to watch out for him. At midnight Young got up and, finding himself locked in his room, thundered and shouted at his door while Suckling and Davenant were 'ready to die with laughter'. Eventually Young broke out only to be pinned down by the hired man, 'a huge, lusty fellow' who 'fell upon him, and held him and cried, "Good sir . . . you shall not go out to destroy yourself."' Young 'struggled and strived, insomuch as at last he was quite spent and dispirited and was fain to go to bed to rest himself'.

Young was told what his friends had done only after they had left for the next stage of the journey. They spent that night at a fine house that was destined to be burned down during the civil wars, and then with Davenant's elder brother, where they 'stayed a week – mirth, wit and good cheer flowing.'[9] In the sober hours of day Suckling wrote a short 'Account of Religion by Reason' at the kitchen table. He argued that much established religious teaching was shared even with heathens and that a solution to quarrels between religions could be found through reason. It delighted him that an oral version had already 'frighted' a lady into 'a cold sweat' and 'had like to make me an atheist at court'.[10]

Suckling's tolerant words went unheard. These were the last of the halcyon days before the storms. Winter was coming.

As the Scots had discovered, Charles wanted all his subjects to worship just as he did. In Ireland Laud's friend, Thomas Wentworth, who served as Charles's Deputy Lord Lieutenant, had introduced a policy they described as 'thorough'. Spiritual as well as political obedience to the king was imposed on Catholics and Protestants alike. Scotland was not, however, a colony as Ireland was. Their Kirk, which had a much purer Calvinist tradition that the Church of England, was popular and powerful. The fact the riots in Edinburgh had come as such a shock to Charles was a mark of how little he knew the country of his birth. He had only returned once as an adult, for his coronation in 1633.

Henrietta Maria had never been to Scotland and had been given a very distorted view by the nature of Charles's court. As little as 1 per cent of the Scottish population was Catholic, yet at court Scottish Catholics were highly visible. The Kirk had made life so difficult even for Catholic aristocrats that a large proportion of them had made their way to England. The Scottish lords Douglas, Nithsdale and Abercorn had all played leading roles in the diplomatic initiative to Rome that had brought Conn, their fellow Scot, to court. When Charles claimed that only a handful of troublemakers lay behind his Scottish problems, Henrietta Maria had no reason to disbelieve him, especially since her old sparring partner, Richelieu, was suspected of playing a role.

France had a long history of using Scotland as their 'bridle' on England and Richelieu had excellent motives to twitch on those reins now. The Winter Queen's hopes of an Anglo-French alliance against the

Habsburgs had ended that summer. Charles had feared tipping the balance of power too far in France's favour if the Spanish Netherlands were further weakened.[11] Richelieu was concerned that Charles might even make an alliance with Spain. Marie de' Medici had sent agents to England in July 1637 to promote this policy, and in September her ally Madame de Chevreuse escaped her exile in Tours and headed for Spain.

The duchess rode astride, dressed in black, in the guise of a young nobleman escaping the consequences of a duel. Blood seen on her saddle when she dismounted was ascribed to a sword thrust in her thigh. She slept on straw and rode across the Pyrenees. Her first night in Spain was spent in a monastic hospice where she awaited permission to travel on to Madrid. It soon came, Elisabeth and Philip sending her a coach and clothes 'befitting her sex and station'.[12] On 25 November 1637 King Philip met Madame de Chevreuse en route at Guadalajara and they 'discussed the business that had brought her to Spain'. This was, primarily, the Franco-Spanish peace Marie de' Medici had always wanted, but Madame de Chevreuse also suggested an English marriage alliance between Henrietta Maria's daughter, the six-year-old Mary, and the eight-year-old Prince Balthazar Carlos.[13]

It was not an alliance that Henrietta Maria had shown any enthusiasm for in the past. Philip's council had observed that the French-born sister queens of England and Spain had 'no relationship', even after the Anglo-Spanish peace was made in 1631. Madame de Chevreuse hoped that this might be turned round and was carrying a miniature of Henrietta Maria as a gift for Elisabeth. While Henrietta Maria had always been an enemy of Spain it was possible the troubles in Scotland, and the rumours of French involvement, would change all that.

In Paris Richelieu moaned that he was a victim 'of the impertinence of the [female] sex' – and worried about Henrietta Maria. 'Besides it being in the nature of women to follow their humours, rather than reason, the particular constitution of this princess makes her incapable of following any other opinions but those she draws from her own [unreasonable] mind.'[14]

'Scottish affairs continue to growl, but I hope they will not bite,' Montagu observed to a friend as he left England in the new year of 1638. Although opponents of the prayer book had set up what amounted to a provisional government, he believed that in the end Charles would 'translate the Church of Scotland into English' – that is, bring it in line with the practices of the Church of England. Wat admitted he would rather 'it would all be in [Catholic] Latin' and in this regard he was in trouble again.[15]

Holland's half-brother, the Earl of Newport, had complained angrily to Charles that Wat had convinced his wife to convert to Catholicism. Laud had insisted Charles expel Wat from court, but Henrietta Maria had lessened the blow by pleading with Charles to send him to Paris, where, she argued, his knowledge of French affairs might make him useful.

This time Louis agreed to accept Wat at court where he soon saw Anne of Austria. She was pregnant with the future Louis XIV, a fact that court wags in France ascribed to the royal couple having been shut up in the Louvre during a snowstorm, with only one bed made up. Wat also had meetings with Richelieu. The cardinal was irritated when Wat asked for the release of his enemy the Chevalier de Jars from prison, but felt it was politic to agree. He wanted Charles's permission to raise 5,000 mercenaries in Scotland for the war with Spain and Henrietta Maria offered her support. She was not yet persuaded to a Spanish alliance and thought it better to have Scotland's fighting men in Europe than making trouble for Charles at home.[16]

Wat was back at Charles's court by the spring and on 14 April 1638 he was at Portsmouth to greet Madame de Chevreuse, who arrived from Spain in an English galleon. Parties were thrown in the town to celebrate. Afterwards Wat escorted her by coach to London, along with a train of 'most of the young lords and gallants then at court'.[17] There was plenty of time on the journey to exchange their news. Madame de Chevreuse could tell him about the magnificent formal entry to Madrid she had been given on 16 December 1637, and how she was greeted with great warmth by Philip and Elisabeth – or Isabel as she was known in Spain. The queen now 'had a Spanish intelligence' and dressed with a hairstyle as stiff as topiary, yet something of the French princess remained with her 'cheerful and lively spirit not completely suffocated by the court etiquette'.[18]

Elisabeth was guiding Balthazar Carlos's education not only in his academic studies, but also in the dance, music and court theatre that she and her sisters loved and which he often attended with his mother alone. Treatises dedicated to Balthazar Carlos also flattered Elisabeth, praising royal 'mothers, daughters or sisters' for their political role – especially as negotiators in diplomatic marriages. This was something Madame de Chevreuse had to consider while enjoying a dizzying round of banquets, and dances, plays and tournaments. The whole Spanish court found her 'a very attractive presence', pretty 'with a fair complexion and golden hair' as well as a 'free air'.[19] She discovered, however, that she had a French rival for Elisabeth's ear. This was Marie de Bourbon, the sister of Henrietta Maria's former beau, Soissons.

Marie de Bourbon had married Christine's brother-in-law, Thomas Francis of Savoy, Prince of Carignano, a key figure in the developments unfolding in Turin. Christine's husband Victor Amadeus had died after an episode of abdominal colic on 7 October 1637. This had left Christine's five-year-old son vulnerable to the ambitions of his uncles, Thomas Francis and Cardinal Maurice, who were demanding a share of the regency. Since Christine was pro-French, Philip IV was anxious that Thomas Francis be encouraged to look to Spain. To this end Philip expected Elisabeth to keep Marie de Bourbon happy, which was no easy task. She was extremely volatile and there was an embarrassing incident when she stormed out of the queen's box at a tournament, because she felt Madame de Chevreuse had a more honourable place, sitting in a box with Prince Balthazar.

Elisabeth must have been relieved when the complicating presence of Madame de Chevreuse ended with an invitation from Charles for her to travel to England. Her parting words to Olivares had been to reassure him that Henrietta Maria hated Richelieu – and she now hoped to use this to encourage the marriage match.[20] We don't know whether she shared this with Wat before their carriage journey ended at Brentford, just outside London, but it was clear she was to be treated with all honour, a fact that was bound to annoy Richelieu. With Wat's role as her principal escort over, her former lover, Holland, took his place, accompanying her to Hyde Park with twenty-five noblemen following them in their coaches.

Henrietta Maria sent a coach to collect the duchess for the last leg of her journey. It travelled at walking pace for the crowds to enjoy the spectacle, six pages running alongside the coach and with two further coaches of the queen's ladies joining the procession. Henrietta Maria and Charles then greeted Madame de Chevreuse at Whitehall and she was offered the privilege of being seated in the royal presence. This was something the wife of the French ambassador was refused, a fact that did not go unnoticed in Paris where the wife of the British ambassador was told that henceforth she would be expected to stand also. The king gave her lodgings at the end of the Privy Gardens at Whitehall next to King Street, and she was soon enjoying herself with the many French exiles in London, as well as charming the English.

She 'makes our court so gay', Montagu wrote to a friend of the duchess.[21] After Whitehall she stayed for a time at Somerset House and then she moved into Wat Montagu's London home. She must have found the number of new converts at court striking. Protestants commented anxiously that it seemed 'our great ladies fall away every day', with the Masses in the queen's chapels said to 'contribute much to it'.[22] Laud had tried to insist that something was done to reduce the number of visitors to Somerset House, but without success, and Catholics, it was observed, 'now have both fair words and good looks, who not long ago were continually frowned on'.[23]

Henrietta Maria even seemed to hope that toleration of religion for Catholics was in sight. Her optimism was advertised in a new masque, first shown in February, and which she had kept in rehearsals for Madame de Chevreuse.[24] Written (at least in part) by the new Poet Laureate, William Davenant, *Luminalia* opened in darkness. Henrietta Maria then appeared as the Goddess of Brightness, bringing day into the night where, the masque hinted, Catholics had been forced to stay hidden. This optimism seemed justified when in May 1638 Charles allowed Henrietta Maria to have a Catholic appointed to the key position of her secretary. This was an astonishing departure from previous royal policy.

Madame de Chevreuse hoped Charles's new attitude might go far enough to overcome the confessional difficulties of a Spanish match. Mary – who now had the French-style title of Princess Royal – was later remembered as carrying a rosary given by her mother while Madame de Chevreuse took her to Mass. With the duchess's encouragement letters from Henrietta Maria were exchanged with Elisabeth, as were family portraits. Yet the marriage proposals found little traction. Charles was convinced that Spanish talk of a match was simply a means of keeping England passive in the European war, just as it had been in 1623. Nor was an alliance with Charles of much use to Spain while he remained focused on Scotland.

Charles had declared that Scots who refused to accept the prayer book were traitors. In reply the rebels had issued a public contract known as the 'National Covenant' whose signatories swore to protect the Kirk against popery and deny loyalty to any king who was not a Presbyterian: that is, a member of a Church governed by Calvinist councils rather than bishops. The Covenant was sweeping Scotland and the rebels had many supporters south of the border. Charles believed ceremony was bringing order to Reform Protestantism, but Puritans saw his 'order' as popish idolatry. Other Protestants, who were less concerned about the ceremonial style of the 'beauty of holiness', were instead angered by the support Laud's bishops gave to Charles's rule without Parliament.

Yet Sir John Suckling mocked fears of an uprising in Scotland, followed by an invasion of England, commenting that the worriers 'have made the little troop of discontents a gallant army'. Charles's confidence also received a boost in June 1638 when judges found in favour of the king in a trial against a gentleman called John Hampden for non-payment of Ship Money. The imposition of the tax in peacetime and inland was ruled legal. Many of the king's opponents were left despairing that there would ever be another parliament.

A new plan now began to form in the mind of Madame de Chevreuse. Henrietta Maria's 'great affection' for her mother had been noted by the Venetian ambassador who commented that the 'violent passion' of worrying about Marie 'prejudices her health'.[25] Marie de' Medici had been trying hard to persuade Louis to allow her to return home. She had even claimed that she had been kept in the Spanish Netherlands against her will. This had annoyed the Spanish, while failing to soften Louis. Madame de Chevreuse considered that having won the Ship Money case Charles might be prepared to risk inviting the controversial Marie to his court for the pleasure of thumbing his nose at Richelieu and pleasing his wife.

Seizing this opportunity, Madame de Chevreuse now launched 'so flat and sudden a surprisal as, without our ports should have been shut against [Marie de' Medici], it was not to be avoided'.[26] So commented Charles's horrified Secretary of State, Sir Francis Windebank. After seven years of trying to foist herself on Charles, Marie de' Medici was on her way.

THE BISHOPS' WAR

MARIE'S SHIP APPEARED UNEXPECTEDLY AT HARWICH IN ESSEX ON 28 October 1638, having blown off course for Dover. Astonished locals watched as six of her coaches were disembarked along with seventy horses and assorted monks and dwarves, foreign nobles and soldiers of fortune. The 'mother of three queens' as she was known (being the mother of two and the mother-in-law of another) recovered from her stormy arrival in the town that night, her likely refuge giving the queen her first experience of an English pub: the Three Cups, which had a good room with a plaster ceiling of English Tudor roses and French fleurs-de-lys. The next day her cavalcade set off for London.

'Imagine now the impatience of Her Majesty on the expectation of the honour and contentment of seeing the queen her mother,' one of Marie's train boasted confidently.[1] In fact, far from being impatient to see Marie, Henrietta Maria was extremely anxious: 'Farewell my Liberty,' she is said to have wailed. Henrietta Maria was concerned not only about 'the constraint' but also the expense.[2] Charles was short of money, having given huge sums to the Prince Palatine, Charles Louis, for his latest military ventures in Europe and was also shelling out the cost of their failure. He was paying ransoms for 600 Scots and numerous English mercenaries captured in Flanders at the Battle of Kallo four months earlier, on 20 June, and would soon be paying for more. News was just reaching England that Prince Rupert was amongst the prisoners captured at the Battle of Vlotho in Germany on 17 October.

Henrietta Maria convinced herself that after only a few days her brother Louis would pay for Marie's keep. After all, Marie was the mother of the King of France, and only the mother-in-law to the King of England. Meanwhile Henrietta Maria prepared Marie's rooms at St James's Palace with care. The Presence Chamber was hung with tapestries sewn with flowers and the state bed with velvet in Marie de' Medici's signature black, trimmed with gold and lined with coloured silk in aurora – a light orange. A lavish state entry to London was organised, and on 8 November Charles met Marie for the beginning of the procession on the outskirts of his capital. There was a howling gale, 'the watermen call it the queen mother's weather' it was reported, while Laud described a veritable tempest on the Thames.[3]

Trumpeters and gentlemen pensioners rode in pairs before the royal coach. Marie's richly embroidered litter followed with the captains of the pensioners and the guard in their rich coats, then came the coaches of the British nobility and other courtiers.[4] At the City gates the lord mayor and aldermen greeted Marie standing on carpeted platforms and dressed in scarlet gowns. The roads from Temple Bar to St James's Palace were lined with the Yeoman of the Guard, then the London and county militia bands, their banners and streamers flying in the high wind. Londoners pressed behind, hoping to catch a glimpse of Marie, as fascinated and appalled to find this icon of the Counter-Reformation in their midst as dogs confronted by a voluptuous and well-protected cat.

At the palace Henrietta Maria, heavily pregnant, and accompanied by her children Charles, Mary, James, Elizabeth and Anne – who was only nineteen months old – greeted her mother on her knees. The future parliamentarian amazon, Lady Brilliana Harley, remarked that Marie de' Medici 'was so transported with joy' to see her daughter after an absence of thirteen years 'that she was in a trance'.[5] It is possible, however, that Lady Brilliana had misread Marie's expression. Henrietta Maria confided in Christine by letter that their mother was not at her best after her storm-tossed journey. Marie had greeted Charles's council while seated and showed the most 'rigid hauteur', offering them only a few words. She then gave the great ladies and lords of the court the same treatment.[6] Happily, she softened after Charles gave her a large pension, becoming pleasant to the ladies and expressing 'extraordinary satisfaction' at what her daughter had achieved for the Catholics in Britain.

Marie had brought her own gift: a miraculous statue of the Virgin. A metre tall and decorated with silver, gold and diamonds, she stood on the prow of a boat as the Star of the Sea that had brought her to these heretic shores. The icon was made from the wood of a holy oak tree that grew at Scherpenheuvel (in modern-day Belgium) on the front line between Catholic and Protestant lands. The Virgin had appeared by the tree and was said to have performed miracles especially 'to confuse the heretics and exterminate heresy'. Accounts of other miracles associated with objects made of the wood had been 'found to be true by sundry [English] Protestant gentlemen'. These were taken as evidence of the superiority of the Catholic Church and kept in the libraries of many English Catholic families and religious houses, both at home and abroad.

The statue was presented to Henrietta Maria's Confraternity of the Rosary to use in their processions.[7] Meanwhile, with Marie content, Henrietta Maria suggested to Christine that if she had anything she wanted to ask of her, now was a good time.[8] Christine needed whatever support she could get. Earlier the previous month, on 4 October 1638, Christine's elder son had died aged six, leaving her 'the most afflicted princess on earth this day'.[9] The crown now rested on the fragile head of her only remaining son, the four-year-old Charles Emmanuel II. Christine's brothers-in-law were plotting invasion in alliance with Spain, while Richelieu wanted to take control for France, and was expressing contempt for Christine's 'weakness of judgment, her feebleness of mind' and her confidence in the 'young, impudent Piedmontese' Count Philippe.[10]

As Christine sought a middle way between France and Spain, rumours were still growing in Europe that Richelieu was involved in the rapidly deteriorating situation in Scotland. Catholic refugees were fleeing south from 'the madness and hatred' that was growing 'fiercer every day' there.[11] Yet in England the suspicion was that British Catholics were behind the crises. Where the papal agent George Conn had seen an opportunity in existing Protestant divisions to seek freedom of worship for Catholics by demonstrating loyalty to the king, Protestants saw a conspiracy to create splits, to divide and rule. Many believed that Conn had encouraged the imposition of the new prayer book on Scotland hoping to bring about a civil war that would see Church of England bishops allied to Catholics, with Charles the victim of evil counsellors of whom Henrietta Maria was the chief.[12]

Less than a month after Marie de' Medici's arrival in London the Puritan rector of St John the Evangelist gave a sermon on Genesis 3:17 in which God cursed Adam, 'Because thou has harkened unto the voice of thy wife, and hast eaten of the [forbidden] tree.' Few doubted whose wife's advice he was worried about.[13]

By that Christmas 1638 it was clear that a war with the Scottish rebels could not be avoided. The General Assembly of the Kirk had backed the Covenanters, condemned the new Scottish prayer book and declared episcopacy unlawful. For Charles, the stakes could hardly have been higher. He saw an episcopal Church as a pillar of the monarchy and instituted by Christ himself. Thousands of Scottish mercenaries had begun returning from Europe to serve in the Covenanter army. They included senior commanders, even generals. France's allies against Spain, the Dutch and the Swedes, were also giving the Scottish rebels material support, allowing them to buy and ship munitions.[14]

Royalists like Sir Arthur Aston who came with 'as many soldiers of note as he could bring' were also returning from Europe, but their numbers were fewer.[15] In England Charles sent out letters to 'all noblemen . . . signalling his resolution to go northwards, and requiring them to attend him with their retinues'.[16] Holland promised twenty horse. More junior figures did even more. Sir John Suckling, who had been made a Gentleman of the Privy Chamber, raised a hundred horse for the king and clad them 'in white doublets and scarlet breeches, and scarlet coats . . . hats and feathers'.[17] George Conn persisted in believing that British Catholics would benefit from also showing their loyalty.

With Conn's encouragement a letter was circulated amongst the English Catholic clergy asking them to urge their flock, 'to make some expression of our readiness to serve His Majesty'. They were assured that Henrietta Maria 'knows how much good this expression of our duty at this time would work upon the king his most clement disposition towards his Catholic subjects'. They were also warned that if they did not help and the rebels won, Catholics would 'feel the ill effects of it more than others'.[18] The Catholic refugees from Conn's native Scotland were already evidence of that.

On 29 January Henrietta Maria's seventh child was born. The birthing room at Whitehall had a freshly plastered and gilded ceiling, a new chimneypiece, and was hung with religious pictures taken from several royal palaces. At least three depicted the Virgin and Child, including a Raphael and a Van Dyck. Wat Montagu contributed a picture of the Holy Family with St John.[19] Sadly the little girl born that night lived for only an hour, 'to the deep grief of her mother'. Henrietta Maria and Charles commissioned elegies and verse to memorialise the girl whom 'God had called back to heaven': she was the first baby they had lost since their firstborn son in 1629, and this must have brought back sad and difficult memories.

Anne, Elizabeth and Mary had been given family names, but this daughter was named Catherine. Perhaps Henrietta Maria had been studying the face of the fifth-century princess and martyr St Catherine of Alexandria in the miniature the Pope had given her and which she had pinned to the curtains of her bed. The saint seemed to haunt her. Henrietta Maria had Van Dyck paint her in the guise of St Catherine and even sat for him so he could paint her from a new angle and not use the usual template.[20] Catherine – whose saint's day, 25 November, was Henrietta Maria's birthday – was known for her many conversions. There were other reasons, however, to feel especially close to St Catherine now: she used to appear to Joan of Arc, France's great female martyr-warrior, and would offer her counsel.

Henrietta Maria was working hard to support Charles's military efforts and she surely felt she needed counsel. In February 1639 she dispatched an English priest called George Gage, supposedly to offer thanks to Our Lady of Scherpenheuvel for her survival from childbirth. In reality he was to ask his brother, Henry Gage, a colonel in the Spanish service, to treat for mercenaries. Charles needed arms too and the money to buy them. War was expensive and getting more so. At the beginning of the century France's military expenses had amounted to less than 5 million livres. In the 1620s Louis had spent 16 million livres annually. In 1640 it would be 38 million.[21] Meanwhile Louis's mother remained a financial burden on Charles. Henry Jermyn was dispatched to France to persuade Louis to accept Marie back. He saw Richelieu several times, but the cardinal was only prepared to help Marie go to Florence, 'whither she is most determined not to go'.[22]

On 21 March the devastating news came that a Covenanter army under Alexander Leslie, a former mercenary general in the Swedish service, had taken Edinburgh.[23] On 4 April, with the king headed north to confront the rebels, Henrietta Maria called a meeting of leading Catholics at Conn's house. The intention was to organise an efficient method of fundraising amongst Catholics. It transpired that there was little enthusiasm for this task. English Catholicism had survived because its adherents kept a low profile. They had no wish to be associated with a war against Scottish Protestants. Conn pointed out that if they didn't give money willingly the king would simply take it from them by putting up their recusancy fines. Eventually a list was drawn up of fifty Catholic gentlemen who would raise money in the counties. Three letters were then sent out in support of the project: one from the clergy, another from leading lay Catholics, a third from the queen, also asking for prayers and a fast as Holy Week approached.[24]

It was not only Catholics that the queen turned to for help. Henrietta Maria hoped that the ladies of the realm would offer up their jewels for Charles. She made Lucy Carlisle and the late Duke of Buckingham's sister Susan Denbigh her collectors.[25] Meanwhile the noseless poet Laureate, William Davenant, had supplied the queen with carrier pigeons to allow her to keep in touch with Charles and his army.[26] On 4 June 1639, when the king reached Berwick on the northern border Holland was sent to reconnoitre the Scottish position. He came across what appeared to be a vast army. Sir John Suckling, who was with him, described seeing huge clouds of dust. It was a trick. The rebel general, Alexander Leslie, had strung out 10,000 men in a thin line, with cattle being driven behind then to give the illusion of far greater numbers.

By the evening of 5 June there were rumours the Scottish army was 45,000 strong. Charles sent a page to start negotiations. A treaty was signed before the month was out, but the money being raised from Catholics was still rolling in. The queen personally received the famous English nun Mary Ward during this period.[27] By mid-July Henrietta Maria's collectors had raised £10,000 in what had become known as 'the queen's subsidy'.[28] This almost matched the amount Charles had been given by his Protestant subjects who were far greater in number and, embarrassingly a large proportion of that had come from the Church of England's bishops. Laud was said to have personally donated £3,000. It was their funding of the royal army, as well as the Covenanters' attack on episcopacy, that gave this bloodless confrontation its sobriquet of the Bishops' War. It would not be the last so named.

The treaty amounted to a mere cessation of arms. Episcopacy remained illegal in Scotland and this threatened Charles's religious authority across his three kingdoms. Battle had simply been put off for another day. Conn would not live to see it. Ailing with what would prove to be a terminal illness, he returned to Rome in August leaving his fellow Scottish Catholics facing annihilation. In England too

Catholics found that Conn's call to back the Crown had left them dangerously exposed.

Charles was not the only ruler in Europe to be facing rebels. On 27 July 1639 Turin had fallen to Prince Thomas in alliance with Spain. Christine might well have been killed had it not been for the bravery of Count Philippe. With sword drawn, her lover had led the horsemen of the noble guard and forced a passage through Spanish troops for her carriage. Richelieu blamed Christine, listing the faults of the duchess, moral first and then political. Christine was 'blind', an 'enemy to herself', she had 'a light and inconstant mind', a 'fearful and avaricious nature', she was 'obstinate', but also 'irresolute between her madness and her malice, between the weakness of her advisors and the malice of others who are supporters of the princes'. She was, in short, 'a miserable princess'.

When she fled to France Richelieu was determined to make her Louis's client: a nominal ruler of Piedmont but obliged to follow French policy. Her son would be raised in Paris along with the dauphin.[29]

Christine courageously made the cardinal understand that while she needed French support, they could not renounce Piedmont and give up their strategic intervention in Italy. She duly gave Louis the minimum guarantees to continue his action in Italy, pushing back her brother while forcing him to support her in pursuit of one shared policy: the weakening of Spain.[30]

The French duly plotted Christine's return – 'so secretly', Richelieu observed, that in Turin, 'even their own shadows know nothing about it'.[31] On 20 September 1640 they retook Turin and in November Christine made her formal entry with Count Philippe leading the guards, his horse in trappings of embroidered buffalo skin.

'I never doubted your courage, but on this occasion it was extraordinary,' Henrietta Maria told her sister. Richelieu demanded, however, a personal price for Christine's restoration.

On 31 December 1640 Count Philippe was arrested after a supper party in Turin. He cried out to Christine, but she told him she could do nothing to save him; 'we must yield to the force that will separate you from me.'[32] Count Philippe was now a prisoner in the French castle of Vincennes and Richelieu talked disdainfully of Christine to her own ambassador as the captive's 'wife'. In fact, in due course, she would take a new lover.

In Spain, meanwhile, Henrietta Maria's eldest sister, Elisabeth, was supporting her husband Philip IV, who faced an uprising in Portugal. The taxes needed to fund Spain's wars and rivalry with France had generated disorder across Philip IV's kingdoms. Marie de' Medici and Madame de Chevreuse nevertheless hoped Philip would find the money to conclude an alliance with England. Marie had been trying to contact Elisabeth in Spain since the summer, sending gifts, hoping her envoy could get an interview. If the Princess Royal was married to Balthazar Carlos then in due course Charles's heir could be married to Gaston's daughter, helping to bind the peace between the Bourbon and Habsburg families that Marie had always desired.

Philip IV had, however, been irritated by Marie's claims to Louis that she had been kept in the Spanish Netherlands against her will, and Elisabeth was told to reply to her mother only in the most general terms. Madame de Chevreuse did better, persuading Olivares to send a top-flight ambassador armed with proposals for an alliance that would 'restore the King of England's fortunes in Scotland'.[33] The key figure and gatekeeper to royal policy was currently Charles's former hardman in Ireland, the forty-six-year-old Thomas Wentworth, soon to be made Earl of Strafford.

The king recognised that he needed his next campaign against the Scots to be better managed and financed than the last. He considered Strafford – who had helped rule Ireland with a rod of iron and who was judged 'a man of great parts and extraordinary endowments of nature' – well qualified for the task.[34] Henrietta Maria had often quarrelled with him in her efforts to defend Catholics in Ireland so she was not the best person to introduce Madame de Chevreuse. Nor could Madame de Chevreuse turn to her former lover Holland. Seven years earlier Strafford had suggested Charles should have Holland executed for his near duel with Jerome Weston. Holland detested him.

By contrast Holland's cousin Lucy Carlisle enjoyed a close relationship with Strafford. Ireland's Lord Deputy had found Lucy a powerful ally at court, 'extremely well skilled how to speak with advantage and spirit for those friends she professeth'.[35] He, in turn, had protected her interests in Ireland. No one was considered to hold more influence with him – they had even exchanged full-length portraits. Chevreuse now engaged Lucy's friendship by ensuring she became 'more in favour [with the queen] than she has been for a long time'.[36]

Lucy duly introduced the duchess to Strafford, whom Henrietta Maria described as 'ugly, but agreeable enough in person' and with 'the finest hands in the world'.[37] Chevreuse told Strafford she believed that Philip could lend Charles £100,000 for his war. Strafford made it clear he was interested in learning more.

Henrietta Maria had seen her brother face rebellions in France. They had been crushed and she was optimistic about her future in England. Charles had given her a new palace – Wimbledon. It was small and there were to be no official state rooms or divisions between inner and outer lodgings; with only a tiny number of rooms for servants and friends. This was to be an intimate hideaway for the king and queen: an expression of their love for each other. Inigo Jones was involved in the building work, while André Mollet and Lawrence Cousin were to plan a French-influenced garden that could be accessed straight from the house.

The king too seemed to be without anxiety, and Lucy Carlisle's brother, the Earl of Northumberland, was astonished at how dedicated the king and queen were to arrangements for their latest masque. Rehearsals began in early December 1639 for William Davenant's *Salmacida Spolia*, and Northumberland observed, 'Their Majesties are not less busy now than formerly you have seen them at like exercise'; indeed the king seemed 'to think of little else'.[38]

The title of the new masque referred to a Greek myth in which the invaders of Salmacis were pacified after drinking from a magical fountain. So, in the masque, the sight of Charles, as Philogenes, lover of his people, supported by Henrietta Maria, as Chief Heroine, would be enough to pacify his unsettled kingdoms. Jeffrey Hudson and the usual ladies were due to take part, although Northumberland wondered if the Countess of Carnarvon would do so. She had become so pious that she refused, in the Puritan manner, to dance or sing on a Sunday. It was a mark of the growing divide at court between those who had some sympathy for the Scottish rebels and those who did not. The former had come to include many of the queen's former Puritan followers: moderate Calvinists that included Henry Holland.

The masque opened on 21 January 1640, the day after Strafford was raised to his earldom. It took place in a vast temporary room built of oak on the river side of the Banqueting House. The Rubens ceiling paintings celebrating the Stuart dynasty had been installed in the Banqueting House only that summer and Charles was anxious they not be damaged by candle smoke.

The sets and costumes designed by Inigo Jones were, as usual, spectacular. Charles climbed the craggy rocks of discord in a plumed helmet and silver breeches before making himself comfortable on a golden throne. Henrietta Maria's appearance was then heralded by a chorus of 'the King's Beloved People'. They addressed Marie de' Medici, as a queen on whose bosom Henry IV had 'laid his weary head', her beauty and wisdom keeping his martial courage alive and allowing it 'to thrive'. Henrietta Maria then appeared from the heavens, emerging from 'a huge cloud of various colours'.

It had been over fifteen years since Henrietta Maria had played the role of a sunflower for her mother at the French court. She was now thirty, and mimicking her mother as the supportive partner of a king. Marie de' Medici sat in the audience alongside the new papal agent, the twenty-eight-year-old Italian count and cleric, Carlo Rossetti. But, as Henrietta Maria recognised, the situation for Catholics remained dangerous. In contrast to Conn, Rossetti was managing his chapel discreetly and urging all Catholics to keep their heads down. Henrietta Maria had dressed as Chief Heroine in 'carnation [red-pink] embroidered with silver', a helmet on her head and a sword at her side, a symbol of her heroic love for Charles. The masque concluded with her enthroned by the king, surrounded with rays of light and armed women, harmony restored.

Scots in London ignored the masque's themes of the supportive wife and referred sourly to Whitehall as her 'Amazonian' castle and already it was being said she wore 'the breeches'.[39] In reality it was Strafford Charles was listening to, on how to deal with the Covenanters.

Part Four

TRANSFORMATION

15

TO REBEL WITHOUT FEAR

THE THREE SPANIARDS WHO MET WITH STRAFFORD ON 29 APRIL 1640 found him an impressive, even 'great' man: if rather more direct than they were used to. Strafford estimated Charles needed £300,000 to fight the Scots. He wanted to know how much Philip IV was prepared to lend Charles and how serious was the suggestion of a marriage alliance. 'He has a peculiar way of coming right out with his proposals,' one of the Spaniards observed, 'and gives you no time to prepare your reply.' The envoys told him everything was up for discussion.[1]

The Dublin Parliament had voted Charles £90,000 of subsidies in March and Strafford had advised Charles to call the English Parliament hoping MPs would vote the rest. The first parliament for eleven years, it had opened just over two weeks earlier on 13 April. Madame de Chevreuse had attended the ceremony, but had left England shortly afterwards. She was heavily in debt and her husband was threatening to fetch her to France.[2]

Henrietta Maria had greeted the Spanish warmly, her hair uncovered. Chevreuse had done her work well in softening Henrietta Maria's former antipathy to Spain.[3] The queen also supported her husband in laying aside her former quarrels with Strafford, observing that 'she esteems him as the most capable and faithful of the king's servants.'[4] She had been anxious, nevertheless, about the new parliament. With her mother she had begged Charles to protect her co-religionists from attacks. She would prove prescient in her fears, and the focus of MPs thus far had been on grievances, not the subsidies Strafford hoped for.

Moderates and radicals were united in anger against the king, and with reason. The military costs of war had lain within Parliament's jurisdiction since the Hundred Years' War. It had also had a role in shaping the national Church since Henry VIII. Yet Charles had once again gone to war without calling Parliament. Last time it had been against France. Now it was a war about religion against fellow Protestants. In Scotland the rebels were, meanwhile, on the move. Five days after Strafford's meeting with the Spanish agents, news reached London of a skirmish with royal troops at Edinburgh Castle. War had begun. Yet with the news announced, MPs continued to refuse the king his subsidies even in exchange for his promises to give up his right to collect Ship Money.

Preserving their religion and protecting the institution of Parliament was of more concern to MPs than the latest Bishops' War. Fears of a deep state plot by Catholics and Arminians persisted. It was evident to Charles that leading Puritans like the MP John Pym, and Holland's more radical elder brother, the Earl of Warwick, had no wish for Charles to beat the Scots at all.

Strafford, believing he had Spanish gold in the bag, advised Charles to dissolve Parliament. He could raise an army in Ireland and was 'as confident as anything Scotland shall not hold out five months'.[5]

Lucy Carlisle's brother, Northumberland, urged the king to instead stick to the 'known ways', of working with Parliament, as did Henry Holland, but rather than heed her old friend, Henrietta Maria continued to back Strafford, 'loudly'.[6] If Charles beat the rebels, it would free him to face down his opponents at home. If he did not, then all Henrietta Maria's work for Catholics over the previous eleven years would be undone. Even Holland's wife – the longest-serving English member of her Privy Chamber – was openly discussing with her friends their hopes that Parliament would destroy any 'Romanism' in Britain.[7]

On 5 May 1640 Charles dissolved what became known as the Short Parliament. Yet, against tradition, the deliberative body of the Church of England, known as Convocation, continued to sit and issued orders to the clergy to make regular pronouncements on the divine right of kings. This provoked a backlash. Broadsheets were pinned up calling for the murder of Laud, Strafford and the papal agent Rossetti. When threats were made to burn his house Rossetti took refuge with Marie de' Medici at St James's Palace. Charles ordered out troops to guard them.

On 11 May an organised mob of youths stormed Laud's Lambeth Palace. The archbishop fled across the river to Whitehall, but even here, in the king's principal residence in London, there was sympathy for the rioters. A windowpane in an antechamber to Charles's rooms was scratched with a diamond, 'God Save the King. God confound the Queen with all her offspring. God grant the Palatine to reign in this realm.'[8] Henrietta Maria was again heavily pregnant.

It was at this violent juncture that news arrived of a major rebellion against Philip IV in Catalonia. Elisabeth was to be regent in Madrid while Philip led his armies. Both the Queen of Spain and her court ladies were selling their jewellery to help pay for the war effort. There was not going to be money spare for Charles. Laud advised the king that he now had to undercut the Puritan propaganda of popery within the Church of England by renewing the persecution of Catholics. Laud led the way, ordering the public burning of Catholic books and the arrest of priests.

Henrietta Maria argued against Laud promising Charles that Catholics would produce more money for him. They had just delivered a tranche of £4,000. At least forty-seven priests had been arrested by the time she gave birth to her fourth son, Henry, at Oatlands Palace on 8 July. It was traditional to make gestures of mercy during times of celebration. Charles sought a halfway house between his wife's wishes and Laud's advice, ordering the release of Catholics from prison, but solely for the period during which she recovered from her delivery. Henrietta Maria hoped to persuade him the priests should stay free once he had won his war.

* * *

The king set off for York on 20 August 1640, bringing reinforcements for the royal commander at Newcastle. There was no question of Henrietta Maria being made regent during his absence fighting the rebels, as Elisabeth was for Philip IV in Spain. Charles had not given her such a role when he had gone to Scotland for his coronation in 1633 and he was not giving it to her now. His seventeen-year-old godson and namesake Charles Porter was already in York awaiting the king's arrival. His father, Endymion Porter, a groom of the king's bedchamber and who was accompanying the king, had found him a post as a cornet of the horse serving under the boy's uncle, Lord Newport. The anxious and excited teenager had written asking for his father to send him a black sword hilt like that of his older brother, George, 'and let it be deep enough that I might thrust both my fingers into it, for I like a good sword extremely'. He added as a postscript, 'Pray, sir, remember my most humble duty to my mother.' Mrs Porter had been serving the queen at Oatlands as she recovered from the birth of little Henry.

The king's party had not yet arrived in York when the royalists engaged the Scots six miles to the west of Newcastle at Newburn on 29 August. Charles Porter took part in a gallant cavalry charge that briefly checked the Scottish advance, but the Covenanters were far more numerous and better positioned. He was killed 'a youth as much pitied as famed for his brave carriage and valientness', a witness recorded.[9] By that evening the English were in full retreat. The Scottish commander, Alexander Leslie, did not pursue them. He was in league with leaders of the English opposition, Pym and Warwick amongst them: a massacre would have complicated matters for his allies. As it was, the English army had 300 dead.

In London blame for the war and the slain was cast on Henrietta Maria and her mother. It was said that Marie de' Medici had given the king advice 'against the religion and liberty of the realm'.[10] A well-known zealot called Anne Hussey also accused Marie of being behind a plot to murder Protestants in Ireland, working in league with her Irish confessor, who was reportedly planning to cut the king's throat. Charles's

Secretary of State, Sir Francis Windebank, imprisoned the priest for a week, hoping the hysteria would pass. It didn't and the priest's release provoked howls of outrage.

Meanwhile, Henrietta Maria was again being cast in the role of the seductress Eve. 'We know as well what the honest king does in his bed-chamber, as that papist wench that lies by his side,' a Scottish propaganda sheet observed. She was 'the only animator of the best sort of men against us'.[11] Others complained how she tempted ordinary folk into wickedness: 'Doth not all the world know that she is a papist and by means of her example . . . are not many thousands, both in court and city and other places, brought into her snare?'[12] Her efforts to promote a positive image of her faith had brought a storm of hatred on her head.

Marie was already under guard. Now, with Charles still in York, the Privy Council ordered out troops to defend the queen and her children at Whitehall. Gunpowder was sent to defend Portsmouth in case she had to flee to Europe at short notice. Henrietta Maria did not express fear, however, so much as anger. She was disgusted with the terms of the armistice that Charles had signed with the Scots. The king guaranteed to pay them a large allowance to support their armies in England. Essentially the English would be paying for their own occupation.

The treaty was, the queen declared, 'full of indignity and likely to lead to fresh inducements to other subjects to rebel without fear, secure from this example'.[13] Yet she would prove more flexible than her husband in her response to events as they unfolded.

Henrietta Maria 'apprehended . . . rightly', that Charles needed to make a populist gesture and split their opponents. A petition was now circulating, signed by twelve leading opposition peers. They demanded not only structural changes to dismantle Charles's ability to rule without Parliament, but also that 'evil' counsellors be given up to Parliament for punishment. She wished Charles to engage the support of the most significant of these peers: Robert Devereux, 3rd Earl of Essex. As the son of

Elizabeth I's last favourite, Essex was heir to a legend of anti-Spanish heroism. He had fought for the Protestant cause in Europe and his parliamentary career had seen him emerge as a champion of the rights of the people and of the nobility. She 'instantly wrote' to Charles advising he take Essex into his service.

Charles refused to have a man who had been a long-standing opponent of royal policy foisted on him as a counsellor.[14] The queen nevertheless agreed to see Essex, along with his brother-in-law, William Seymour, Earl of Hertford. In the past, when Henrietta Maria had looked to the future, she had been content to trust in the king. She was no longer content to do so. Hitherto her involvement in politics had been in the field of foreign affairs, and in her role as Britain's leading Catholic. Charles's losing the war against the Scots had transformed her into a much more active player.

Essex and Hertford had little reason to feel comfortable in her presence. The forty-nine-year-old Essex had a difficult history with women. He was badly scarred by smallpox and was cuckolded by two wives. Nor did he have much reason to care for queens. He had been ten when Elizabeth I had cut his father's head off for attempting a palace revolt. His brother-in-law, the fifty-two-year-old Hertford, had also suffered at royal hands. Both his grandmother, the Tudor princess Lady Katherine Grey, and his first wife, Arbella Stuart, had died while imprisoned for marrying without royal permission.

The rebel earls had spent most of their lives outside the court and were rough and ready men, but they found Henrietta Maria down to earth. Her beloved brother Gaston had long opposed Richelieu's pursuit of royal absolutism and was popular with the French people. She assured them she would do her best to now try and convince the king that a parliament was necessary. Charles needed parliamentary subsidies to pay the Scots to leave England and since this meant he had to call a parliament, it would be better, she believed, if he were not to try and fight the inevitable.

The subsequent elections took on the character of a referendum on the proper constitutional place of a Parliament in England. Was

England a 'mixed monarchy', where authority lay with the king in Parliament, rather than one defined by divine right, as King James had argued? And if it was a 'mixed monarchy', where should the balance of power lie?

The cultural influence of Henrietta Maria and her long assertion of the right of women to express political and religious opinions may have inspired the two single female freeholders in Suffolk who tested their right, as property owners, to cast their votes.[15] Their votes were not counted, however, the high sheriff being concerned not to give the inferior sex 'dominion over the superior', regardless of a woman's status.

On 31 October Henrietta Maria met Charles just outside London at Theobalds, on his return from York. She had brought with her a number of horsemen – or cavaliers, as such royalist swordsmen were coming to be known, from the Spanish '*caballeros*'. They set off together and were escorted through London 'in pomp and with a kind of ovation . . . restored to the affections of his people with the most splendid cavalcade'.[16] For most people in England, their support for the institution of Parliament did not translate into antipathy for the king. They were glad of his return and hopeful of peace with the Scots and his reconciliation with their Parliament.

At 1 a.m. on 3 November 1640, the day Parliament was due to open, Count Rossetti was woken by a thundering and shouting at his door. Two justices of the peace had arrived with an escort of a hundred swordsmen and warrants to search his house for arms. The turnaround in the fortunes of the Catholic community since the Bishops' Wars had been sudden and the fall precipitous. The Venetian ambassador was predicting 'the total desolation of the Catholic faith in England'.[17] Many had begun 'hurriedly selling their goods with the intention of living quietly in some other country'.[18] Rossetti's life had been threatened and so he had good reason to be fearful now.

The priest George Gage, who lived next door, was called over to interpret for Rossetti. With Gage's help the papal agent reminded the JPs that he had diplomatic protection. For half an hour there was a stand-off in the rain. Finally, it was agreed to send messengers to the Secretary of State, Windebank, asking him to validate the warrant. Rossetti invited the JPs into the dry while they waited. The mood changed as they chatted and he showed them his art collection. When the messenger returned it was to announce that the warrant had been declared invalid. The JPs left sheepishly. Rossetti had no idea when or if they would be back.

A few hours later Charles left Whitehall by barge to open his new parliament. Lucy Carlisle was amongst the courtiers who watched the ceremony in the Lords. She saw her cousins Essex, Holland and Warwick. There was Pym too, Warwick's man, in his black suit and white linen collar: the voice of the radicals in the Commons. Barberini had written to Rossetti from Rome predicting that the new parliament would not be dissolved for a long time, if ever. The opposition intended to create a new regime, dominated by themselves, and they would not risk that with elections. Charles gave a brief opening speech in which he spoke of the urgent need to free the north from the Scottish invaders. The electorate shared this priority. Those who had been in secret alliance with the Scots did not.

In Parliament Pym now regaled the House of Commons with Mrs Hussey's stories about Marie de' Medici's plot and said that Catholic clergy 'were in pay to be ready to cut all Protestant throats'.[19] The aim of the opposition was to scare moderate MPs so badly they would vote for radical legislation that would reduce Charles to the status of a puppet king. Pym was practised at lighting the touch paper of popular fears, and what could have been easier than blaming England's troubles on a hated minority? A parliamentary committee was set up to discuss how to restrain ordinary Catholics. In London's narrow and huddled streets, their homes were overrun in the search for arms and 'plundered, their goods carried off'.[20] Pym wanted them to wear

distinctive clothes that would mark them out and oblige them to register with Parliament. The Venetian ambassador reported fears that this
was a prelude to a mass expulsion that would leave them 'like the Jews'
as wandering exiles.

On 11 November 1640 Strafford recommended to Charles that opposition figures known to have been in contact with the Scots be charged
with treason. It was too late. By the end of the day it was Strafford who
was under arrest, accused in Parliament of having fomented war with
Scotland so he could use an Irish army to 'bring in the papist party'.
This was the man who had spearheaded the persecution of Catholics
in Ireland with a policy labelled 'thorough'.

That Laud faced the same possible fate was signalled on 28 November, when his bitter opponents William Prynne, and his fellow Puritan
martyrs John Bastwick and Henry Burton, were released by order of Parliament. Around 2,000 horsemen accompanied them as they entered
London, along with a hundred coaches and cheering spectators: not
'without scandal to right-minded people', the Venetian ambassador
noted.

Henrietta Maria was by now under mob attack. She had seen a crowd
advance on 'my own [Somerset] house' where they stoned the congregation as they left her chapel. When she was told Parliament intended
to deprive her of her English Catholic servants she responded that if
that was the case she would not have Protestants either. She then wrote
to Louis for help. Despite their quarrels Louis promised his sister he
would defend her religious rights. 'Tell your husband I do not want to
meddle in Parliament's affairs', but, if necessary, 'I know well what I
shall have to do.'[21] Charles, however, had been unable to prevent Strafford's arrest and other leading servants had little faith he could protect
them either.

Windebank heard that he was to be questioned about Strafford's
supposed treason and fled his house in Drury Lane for France during
the early hours of 3 December, carrying letters from Henrietta Maria.

On 18 December Laud was arrested and charged with high treason. Amongst the accusations were that he planned for the Church of England to reunite with the Church of Rome and had encouraged the war with Scotland. Henrietta Maria and Laud had been bitter enemies, but she 'feels very strongly at seeing her husband not only deprived of his most faithful ministers, but so effectively despised by his own subjects', the Venetian ambassador reported.[22]

There was also a private blow to absorb. There was an outbreak of smallpox, and the three-year-old Princess Anne, who had often had coughs and other respiratory diseases, proved unable to fight off the infection. She was buried at Westminster Abbey before Christmas 'to the intense grief of Their Majesties'.[23]

Henrietta Maria's mother was also ill. Rubens, who had depicted Marie de' Medici's greatest triumphs, had died seven months earlier, on 30 May 1640, and it seemed that Marie's world of glory had departed with him. She had been under constant attack and Charles had been obliged to cancel her pension.

Marie had dismissed her household and was now living 'the frugal life of a private lady . . . reduced to the last extremity'. To the Venetian ambassador her fate offered 'a singular example to the world that even the royal state of the greatest princes is subject to the same vicissitudes as affect the fortunes of private houses'.[24] But it was not over for Charles Stuart just yet. The Venetian worried that Henrietta Maria would urge him 'to throw himself into desperate courses'.[25] He misread her: she was still urging Charles to act tactically.

For many years Henrietta Maria had worked closely with moderate Calvinists at court. She was keen to work again with old friends like Holland. They could help build bridges with the opposition, who had now grown so powerful they were known as the Junto. For this to succeed she needed sweeteners: money and offers of important court positions.

The queen wrote to Pope Urban asking for £125,000. She described how Catholics had been banished from London and were again being prosecuted under the penal laws 'which go right to death'. Charles was already suffering 'for his bounty towards those of our religion', but cash might 'forestall a great part of their violence'.[26] She also redoubled her efforts to persuade Charles to take opposition figures onto his council. It proved an uphill task.

Charles had ignored Henrietta Maria's pleas to employ Essex in August and in early December Lucy Carlisle was reporting that Charles still 'made merry' at the idea of placing leading Junto figures on his council.[27] Then something shifted. On 14 January 1641 Lucy heard that 'we shall have a great change of officers' and that Pym was to be Chancellor of the Exchequer.[28] Charles's problems, however, encompassed more than a few discontented nobles and embittered Puritans. The queen's next task was in line with advice that the soldier-poet John Suckling had written to one of her favourites: his cousin, Henry Jermyn.

Suckling urged that 'the great interest of the king is a union with his people'. He needed to regain their love and 'do something more . . . something of his own . . . giving them things they expected not'. Suckling hinted at the need to sacrifice Strafford. Blaming servants for their mistakes was something kings had always done, but only the queen would be able to convince Charles to do so. 'How becoming a work for the sweetness and softness of her sex,' Suckling had observed, 'and how proper for a queen, reconciling King and People.'[29]

There was nothing Jermyn enjoyed better than gambling with men like Suckling. Even later in life 'all his delight and expense was in play'.[30] It seems he passed Suckling's advice over to the queen. William Davenant and Suckling then presented her with a poem. It compared a 'King's (perhaps) extreme obdurateness' to the hardness of a diamond, which only another diamond could reshape. It also hinted at the need for a scapegoat, 'Though what you gain with tears, cost others blood.'[31]

That Christmas, Davenant saw the effect of their arguments: the queen on her knees begging Charles not to do anything to annoy Parliament. Lucy Carlisle also noticed that Strafford was again 'not in any degree acceptable' to her.[32] Henrietta Maria and Jermyn now shut themselves up with Charles for hours at a time, trying to get him to act with the ruthlessness and imagination the situation required. But if Strafford was convicted of treason Charles wanted to be sure he could use his royal powers to pardon him. He suggested a test case, a man whose fate struck at the core of the queen's sense of her purpose.

A Catholic priest called John Goodman was due to be executed on 23 January for practising his office. It was to be the first such execution since 1628 and also followed efforts by Henrietta Maria to seek a reprieve. On the night of the 22nd Charles wrote out an order in his own hand, suspending the sentence against Father Goodman on the grounds that he did not wish to execute a man on a matter of religious conscience alone. If Goodman lived, 'the king holds on to his authority', Rossetti reported to Barberini. If he died, 'Parliament would be free to proceed against anyone with impunity.'[33]

16

THE ARMY PLOTS

MPS ARRIVED AT BANQUETING HOUSE ON THE AFTERNOON OF 23 January 1641 and entered the Italianate double-cube room. It was an awe-inspiring sight: 110-feet-long walls covered in priceless tapestries of gold and silver, the ceiling decorated with Rubens masterpieces and their king seated at the end on a raised throne under his canopy of state. Charles had chosen to address both Houses of Parliament not at Westminster, but here, in this royal space, to remind them that authority lay with him and government was based wherever he was. Nevertheless, his speech offered a significant accommodation.

Charles told MPs he wished to give up his rights to tax his subjects without parliamentary scrutiny. Yet there were no cheers for what might, in other circumstances, have been judged golden words. MPs had been infuriated to learn that morning of his reprieve of the priest John Goodman's life. To their minds, Charles's action had combined high-handedness with a casual disregard to the popish threat – and that was something they were determined to respond to.

If one priest's life had been saved, other Catholics were to suffer for it.

In the next few days diplomats found themselves caught up in the mass arrests of recusants. On 2 February Henrietta Maria stepped in to try and calm the situation. The role of mediatrix was a traditional one for a queen, and she met with Pym and other leading members of the

Junto to urge compromise. She was working to persuade Charles to sign a bill that meant he would have to call Parliament every three years. Thus far the calling of Parliament had been entirely a matter for the king. She also discussed a possible way forward over Strafford. This allowed some progress.

The following day Strafford's trial was deferred to give him more time to prepare his answers to the charges.[1] Lucy Carlisle noticed that Strafford was now also 'very confident of his overcoming all these accusations' and 'you cannot believe he can be happier'.[2]

Charles in turn agreed to remit Goodman's fate to Parliament, albeit on the understanding he would be imprisoned rather than hanged. He further announced a series of measures against Catholics: priests and Jesuits were to be expelled from England, the papal emissary Rossetti would no longer be welcome at court, and he promised measures to discourage English Catholics from attending Mass at the queen's chapels, or at embassy chapels. Henrietta Maria followed this up with a personal message to Parliament on 4 February expressing her goodwill and also promising to discourage English people from attending her chapel.

The queen's message was received in silence. She was the face of the popish threat. The Junto now continued on the attack. Wat had been questioned by MPs in January on his role in fundraising amongst Catholics for the Bishops' Wars, and on the powers delegated to the papal agents. He was considered to have been evasive and on 13 February he was described in Parliament as 'dangerous' and accused of being in league with foreign rulers.[3] Charles's powers were also unravelling fast.

The Triennial Act was passed; parliamentary committees were appointed to abolish any court that did not adhere to Common Law. These included the Star Chamber (used in trials for sedition) and the ecclesiastic Court of High Commission (used against dissident clergy). When on 19 February Charles agreed to the appointment of seven new councillors from the opposition – including both Essex and Hertford – things began to look more positive. Junto leaders hinted that they might agree to spare Strafford's life when the time came, as they had that of the priest Goodman who was destined to die in prison.[4]

Unfortunately, five days later, on 24 February the Covenanter Scots – whose army still occupied the north of England – put a sporran in the works. They demanded death for Strafford, and the abolition of episcopacy across the three kingdoms. The first was a blow to Charles's sense of honour, the second struck at the fault lines within English Protestantism.

Twenty thousand Londoners had delivered a petition to Parliament in December demanding that episcopacy be abolished 'root and branch'. But these were radicals.[5] The majority of the political nation wanted a return to the traditional moderate Calvinism of the Church of England. They did not wish to get rid of bishops, or the royal supremacy, which hitherto were integral to England's constitutional arrangements. On 27 February there was a ferocious debate in Parliament that saw the Junto split between the hardliners behind the 'root and branch' petition and moderates. Nothing was concluded and the Scottish demands were left standing.

With the Spanish alliance defunct, Charles needed to look elsewhere for military help against the Scots and their allies. Marie de' Medici had suggested a match between Mary, the Princess Royal, and the fourteen-year-old William of Orange, heir to the ruling house of Holland. William was Calvinist, which would please British Protestants of all stripes, and he was rich. Indeed, Marie de' Medici believed the Prince of Orange could help provide Charles with an army of 20,000 men.[6] Marie, it should be remembered, had married her own daughter to a Protestant king.

Henrietta Maria held on to hopes of French support also. They were, after all, allies of the Dutch against the Habsburgs and as she was a French princess her difficulties might be seen as a matter of family honour. She wrote to Louis's foreign minister warning that she faced her 'ruin on earth' and asking for 'the help of the king my brother', hoping to travel to Paris to see Louis in person.[7] But Richelieu was determined to keep her away. The French ambassador in London scoffed that she had no real fears for herself, and if she fled to Paris, it would be to save Montagu and Jermyn. Richelieu also wrote to remind her that those who fled into exile – as her mother had – 'were the losers on these occasions'.[8]

There was, however, an army that was already at the king's disposal – his own. The soldiers who had been betrayed by the Junto to the Scots had not yet been disbanded. They remained in the north where, on 6 March, they learned that £10,000 due as back pay was being diverted by Parliament to the invaders.

On 21 March a letter arrived in London from a group of discontented officers. Addressed to Lucy Carlisle's eldest brother, Northumberland, who was the Lord General of the army, it complained bitterly how they had to live off the people of the north, 'which both they and we are weary of'.[9]

For reasons that remain mysterious the twenty-four-year-old officer who brought the letter – one James Chudleigh – showed it to the masque-writer and Poet Laureate William Davenant. Having read the letter Davenant told Chudleigh that it was 'of greater consequence than he imagined'.[10] He then took Chudleigh to Jermyn and Suckling. They in turn asked to show a copy of the letter to the queen. Strafford's trial, which she planned to attend, was opening the next day. Charles had made it very clear that he would not permit Strafford to be executed. If Strafford was, nevertheless, beheaded it would be evident that Charles could not protect his supporters. Waverers would not invest in a loser, while Charles's enemies would be greatly emboldened.

Parliament's decision to pay the Scots before England's own troops had demonstrated how MPs were vulnerable to military pressure. If it worked for the Scottish rebels it could work for the king too. The army in the north might be brought south and used to save Strafford's head and Charles's crown.

* * *

At 9 a.m. on 22 March 1641, Henrietta Maria was in Westminster Hall for Strafford's trial. She sat in a box alongside her daughter, the Princess Royal. Mary was a pretty, brown-haired girl and the queen was anxious to show her off as the future bride of William of Orange. Their box was positioned on the left of the dais, on which sat an empty throne. The chair represented the 'state', which, MPs declared, was vested in Parliament while it was in session. The king sat in his own box on the right of the dais. Prince Charles was seated on the steps, below his father.

The ten-year-old's striking dark colouring, physical grace and wilful temperament were characteristics he shared with his mother, and the last ensured they were already clashing. Henrietta Maria had written to 'chide' the prince for refusing his medicine when he was ill and she warned 'I must come to you and make you take it for it is for your health.'[11] Henrietta Maria would always be determined he would do what she believed to be good for him.

Beneath the prince, sitting on benches in two parallel lines, were the judges and the peers. The Commons were seated in a rising grandstand. All watched as Strafford was escorted into the hall.

A tall man with a stoop, Strafford wore black and looked dishevelled: a statement of grief. There was no axe, usually carried before the prisoner in a treason trial. Charles had specifically ordered that it be omitted, so publicly staking his reputation on his servant's life. The prisoner was taken to an open box facing the throne. Twenty-eight articles of impeachment were read to him. The following day John Pym opened the prosecution. He was a convincing orator, but less effective when his certainties faced contradiction: humourless and slow on his feet where Strafford was witty and scornful.

Wat Montagu was seen sitting in the queen's box, laughing at Strafford's jokes and talking loudly over Pym. It was not the only provocation of which he was guilty. Wat had more than doubled a list of priests attached to the queen, who were to be excluded from the order expelling Catholic clergy from England. On 27 March the House of Lords demanded his banishment along with that of other court Catholics.

Holland, on the queen's behalf, pleaded the cause of two of her servants, but Wat was not an official member of her household and had
to go.

Henrietta Maria sent a letter to France asking that good care be taken
of Wat, 'since he suffers for as good a cause as for his religion, and also
for being too affectionate to me'.[12] She had hoped to promote him as a
possible future cardinal – something that had prompted even Barberini
to wonder 'whether the queen truly bears him a special affection, as has
been rumoured'.[13] With Wat in exile, Jermyn was left as her new leading
favourite.

Lucy Carlisle had noticed that Jermyn had grown in the queen's favour
'to a strange degree' during the period when they had been trying to persuade Charles to sacrifice Strafford.[14] Now they were working together
on a very different plan – one in which the king's army could be brought
to London under the command of another of the young men in the
queen's circle. This was the talented, if dissolute, George Goring, who was
colonel of one of the northern regiments. Once in London, Goring was
to seize the Tower and overawe the city.

There was, however, an alternative and less dramatic plan which
Charles had been discussing with another young man who was close to
the queen: Lucy Carlisle's younger brother, Henry Percy. This was to present a petition from the army demanding that episcopacy be retained,
that the king's revenues match those he had during the Personal Rule, and
that the royal army in Ireland not be disbanded before that of the Scots.
Charles asked Percy to meet with Goring and Jermyn, which he did on 29
March. Goring then leaked what he had learned through Holland's half-
brother, Newport, to whom he was related by marriage.[15]

The revelations concerning the army plot horrified the Junto. On 6
April they ordered that the army and the Yorkshire-trained bands
(that is, the local militia) could not be moved without the express
command of the king and endorsed by Parliament. But why had Goring leaked the information? It is possible that Goring acted as he did
because he feared the plan was compromised. The young officer, James

Chudleigh, who had brought the letter from the discontented army officers, came from a Puritan family. After a brief flirtation with royalism (that may or may not have been genuine) he would fight for Parliament during the Civil War. It is also possible – indeed probable – that Goring had acted on the king's instruction.

Goring had now gained the trust of the Junto and he remained a powerful figure in the port town that was viewed as the queen's leading escape route to Europe. Henrietta Maria had paid secretly for Portsmouth to be fortified and had packed up her best plate, just in case she needed to leave England in a hurry. The indications are, furthermore, that Charles only wanted to frighten the Junto with the threat of force. Charles tended to pull his punches: 'He was very fearless in his person, but not enterprising.'[16] The king's resolve would have been further weakened by the fact it did not seem necessary to use the army to save Strafford. The case against him was going badly and on 10 April 1641 the trial collapsed. Yet Strafford remained at risk.

There were means of getting round the difficulties of a trial and these were now deployed. A Bill of Attainder was introduced in the House of Commons. If passed by both Houses, Strafford's guilt could simply be declared by Act of Parliament.

On 20 April 1641 the fourteen-year-old Prince William of Orange arrived in London for his marriage to Mary. He was escorted directly to Henrietta Maria's Privy Chamber at Whitehall, accompanied by the Prince of Wales and the seven-year-old Lord Admiral of the Fleet, James, Duke of York. The younger brother was as fair as the elder was dark but shared the same Stuart energy, 'an active soul [who] delighted with quick and nimble recreations'.[17] Henrietta Maria greeted William affectionately before he was taken to see Marie de' Medici and his child bride.[18]

Mary had caught a cold sitting in the box with her mother watching the last day of Strafford's trial and had been in bed with a fever and a swollen face. This may be why William was not allowed to kiss her. The

Venetians heard, however, that, young as she was, she had made it plain she did not wish to be married. They also reported that he had not been allowed to kiss her grandmother. The story reflected the assumption that Charles and Henrietta Maria were disappointed to be marrying Mary to a future stadtholder, a chief magistrate of the United Provinces of the Netherlands, rather than the heir to a throne.

William had, however, reportedly brought gifts worth upwards of £23,000, as well as a substantial sum in gold. The Junto feared Charles would use this to buy the loyalty of the army and fund the arrears in their pay.

The Junto responded with a show of strength. The following day, 21 April 1641, a crowd of 10,000 descended on Westminster, 'at command' of the Junto's hardliners.[19] Its leaders carried a petition calling for Strafford's death. MPs duly passed the Attainder Bill and sent it up to the Lords. At this juncture Henrietta Maria made another effort to seek a compromise.

Using her friend Holland as her intermediary the queen reached out to members of the Junto, meeting with the very 'worst' of them in secret, down backstairs, where they would stand with their faces lit only by the torches they carried.[20] Charles had promised Strafford 'upon the word of a king, that you shall not suffer in life, honour, or fortune'.[21] This was not a promise he could afford to break. Yet the Junto also had reasons to step back from the brink. Many MPs considered the use of Attainder to be an attack on Common Law and little better than judicial murder.

On 29 April Henrietta Maria returned to Westminster Hall to hear the final day of arguments as the Lords debated the Attainder. The key moment arose when Charles's Solicitor General, Oliver St John, stood up to speak. Henrietta Maria knew his name well. He was one of the members of the Junto she had urged to be brought into the king's service the previous winter. To her shock St John announced that Strafford was like a 'marauding beast'. In attacking the law Strafford had made it imperative that Parliament defend itself and it was not cruel 'or foul play to knock foxes or wolves on the head'. Henrietta Maria stood up and left.[22] If the king was to save Strafford's life they needed again to review all options.

The Tower, which overshadowed Elizabeth Nutt's home, was never short of interesting gossip. Its current prisoner, Strafford, was, however, the most infamous of her adult life – and she was curious to see him. As the wife of a merchant she had plenty of important friends who worked in the Tower and money for small bribes, so it was easy enough to get access for herself and three companions – even to the very door of Strafford's locked room. There she bent down and looked through the keyhole.

Strafford was talking to another man. Mrs Nutt heard Strafford discuss a ship his brother George had waiting for his escape. Strafford wanted to know where it was docked. Something was said about the Lieutenant of the Tower, Sir William Balfour, but Mrs Nutt could not quite make out what.[23] It would later emerge that Strafford had offered the Lieutenant of the Tower £20,000, and a good marriage for his son, in return for opening the gates to Sir John Suckling and a hundred men. The plan was that with London distracted by Mary's and William's wedding celebrations, Suckling and his men would overwhelm the Yeomen of the Guard at the Tower and spring Strafford.

On the wedding day, 2 May, Suckling arrived at a rendezvous point at the White Horse tavern near St Paul's to wait for his men. Henrietta Maria and her mother were, meanwhile, entering the king's chapel at Whitehall. The two queens took their seats in a raised closet. They were there as witnesses to the marriage rather than participants in what was to be a Protestant ceremony – one that exemplified Charles's attachment to the concept of the 'beauty of holiness'.

Painted and carved images covered the chapel walls. A tapestry depicting a scene of the crucifixion hung behind a railed-off Communion table, which was itself covered with expensive fabrics. There was to be music too. One hymn had been written especially for the wedding, and the celebrant, Matthew Wren, Bishop of Ely, was well known for Protestant services that resembled the baroque Catholic Mass.

Charles gave away his daughter, who wore a pearl necklace William's mother had given her worth an astonishing £3,000, and a dress of white and silver: the same colours Henrietta Maria had worn for her wedding in Paris sixteen years earlier. William, who wore red and gold, put a ring on her finger and by 2 p.m. the wedding service was over. The couple were then taken 'to Their Majesties' most cheerful reception in the queen's withdrawing chamber'.[24] Charles had insisted on a private wedding breakfast, 'where none should sit as guests but the king, the queen, the queen mother [Marie de' Medici], the prince [of Wales], [James] the duke of York, and the married couple'. The five-year-old princess Elizabeth also joined them. A few nobles were permitted to watch, but there was also an absence that was 'wondered at'.[25]

The king's nephew Charles Louis had come to England, hoping to marry his tiny cousin himself. It was a strange time to be looking for a dowry from his cash-strapped uncle. Radicals had often suggested they would prefer him to be King of England to any of the Stuart children, so it seems quite possible the ungrateful youth hoped a marriage would raise his chances of replacing them.

After the breakfast Henrietta Maria took the children and their assistants for a walk and play in Hyde Park and there was time to rest. The next ritual, the symbolic consummation, was not to take place until 10 p.m. that night. If Henrietta Maria knew about the plot to free Strafford she must have wondered how Suckling was doing. There had been a curious incident that morning that suggested trouble. Holland had, at the last minute, replaced his brother Warwick as William's escort in the carriage procession. The Junto leader had announced he was too busy with matters of state to attend. Had Warwick learned something from Mrs Nutt of the plan to spring Strafford?

After the children had played and rested the king joined the queen and the bride, her brothers and the groom for supper. Henrietta Maria then took Mary to be undressed while Charles and a group of nobles joined William.

What followed was to be merely representative of the sexual act. Charles and Henrietta Maria had insisted on a clause that after the wedding their daughter would remain in England until she was twelve and that consummation not take place until she was fourteen at least.

When everyone was in place the ambassadors were escorted from the withdrawing chamber to the bedchamber. Multi-tapered candles of the whitest wax lit the scene before them, 'burning against the walls' where they 'diffused a bright and glorious light'.[26] Mary had been placed in a state bed of blue velvet trimmed and embroidered in silver and gold, and surmounted with great white feathers. Henrietta Maria sat in an alcove along with her dwarf Jeffrey Hudson, and was surrounded by the great ladies of the court.

When Charles and William arrived they had to struggle through the press of courtiers and ambassadors to make their way to the bed. Having reached it William kissed his brothers-in-law goodnight and got in 'very gently'. He kissed Mary three times. The onlookers then witnessed 'as much of the consummation of that marriage as so young years and the form used in that kind could afford' the Venetian ambassador reported. Three-quarters of an hour later William got up. He realised he had lost a slipper. It was found near Mary. Finally, after William knelt before Mary's parents for a blessing, the king escorted him to his room to sleep for the night.

It was now that the king and queen learned what had happened to Suckling. No more than sixty men of the hundred he had hoped for had turned up at his rendezvous so Suckling had decided to put off taking the Tower until the following night. Unfortunately, his sixty swordsmen had been noticed. If Warwick had known something was being planned his spies would have been on the lookout for a large group of armed men.

As word spread a huge crowd of Junto followers had descended on the Tower to defend it. Come the morning the angry crowd shifted to

Westminster. There, MPs arrived to learn of the attempt to free the king's 'marauding beast'.

Over the following few days arrest warrants were put out for a group of the queen's favourites: Henry Jermyn, John Suckling, William Davenant, and Henry Percy. Percy and Davenant were captured but Suckling and his cousin Jermyn escaped via Portsmouth. George Goring claimed he had been asleep when they arrived early in the morning of 7 May and that the warrant for their arrest did not arrive until after they had left.[27] Happily for Goring the Junto believed him. The men left in a royal pinnace, the *Roebuck*, along with Wat's former travelling companion, the Earl of Carnarvon, who was also suspected of involvement in the plot.

The refugees split when they reached Dieppe. Jermyn headed for Rouen where Wat Montagu was waiting for him. Wat had a powerful new ally at the French court – his friend from Rome, Mazarin, was now in Richelieu's service. Suckling, meanwhile, made for Paris in the company of the Earl of Carnarvon. Back in England the Junto fury expressed itself in further violence against ordinary Catholics. Mobs attacked foreign embassy chapels to 'overthrow their idolatry'.[28] The queen's tenants – Protestant and Catholic – were also assaulted, while lampoons were posted claiming Henrietta Maria was the lover of the fugitive Henry Jermyn.[29] This made her not only an adulteress, but the mistress of a man accused of treason: a double traitor.

Meanwhile, thousands continued to gather around Parliament. Pressure from the London radicals saw a bill passed that ensured Parliament could not now be dissolved without its own consent. It had become, Henrietta Maria observed caustically, a 'perpetual parliament', its MPs having granted themselves jobs for life, just as Barberini had predicted to the papal agent Rossetti the previous November. Henrietta Maria now had a last-ditch meeting with Rossetti to ask once again for money from the Pope for Charles. In return she promised Charles would allow Catholics to practise their religion freely. This was a bluff, and the Pope knew it.

Charles had broken such promises in 1625, when he had continued to impose recusancy fines against the terms of the marriage treaty. The Pope suggested Charles convert to Catholicism instead, reminding Henrietta Maria that her father's conversion had stabilised France. Her response was that the issue was 'exceedingly difficult'.[30] She knew very well that Charles would rather die than become a Catholic. Nor would a Catholic conversion help stabilise England. The queen's Scottish confessor Father Phillip was thoroughly alarmed about what might now follow.

Marie de' Medici's life was already being openly threatened. She had 'sent twice or thrice, to express her Apprehension, and her Fear' to the House of Lords and ask for a guard. None had been given.[31] Next it would be Henrietta Maria.

'The Puritans, if they durst, would pull the good queen in pieces', Father Phillip wrote to Wat in France. Surely King Louis could not allow 'a Daughter of France, his sister, her children, to be thus affronted'? Father Phillip advised the queen not to wait for an invitation and to leave England immediately.

On 5 May 1641 – only three days after Mary's wedding – the French ambassador saw the queen's coach packed up and ready to depart for Portsmouth. Fully aware that Richelieu did not want her in France he told her French almoner, Jacques du Perron, Bishop of Angoulême, that she must stay put. The Junto were informed and the next day Holland was deputed by the House of Lords to ask the king that Henrietta Maria's journey to Portsmouth be deferred. Henrietta Maria pretended she didn't know what Holland was talking about, and 'answered with spirit that she was the daughter of a father who had never learned how to fly, and she had no idea of doing any such thing either'.[32]

On 8 May the 'perpetual parliament' passed the Attainder Bill and it was sent for Charles to sign. A number of Church of England bishops spent the entire day trying to convince Charles to thereby condemn Strafford to death. They failed and so further pressure was applied. That night as crowds of up to 12,000 gathered at the gates of Whitehall

Palace, the Prince Palatine, Charles Louis, saw his uncle break down at the council table. Writing to his mother, the Winter Queen, he described Charles protesting 'that if his person only was in danger he would gladly venture it to save Lord Strafford's life, but seeing his wife, children, and all his kingdom were concerned in it, he was forced to give way . . . which he did not express without tears'.[33]

The Junto's success was an opportune moment for Holland to again ask his fellow peers for a guard for Marie de' Medici. He was concerned there were plans to attack her residence, he told them, and 'If anything should happen to the queen, it would be a great Dishonour to the Nation, she being come hither for Protection from the king and queen: she is to be considered as a Lady that is a Mother to the greatest princes in Christendom. Besides, she hath lived here with such Modesty and Moderation, as everybody near her doth wonder at it: there hath not been a Person complained of, or punished, belonging to her Family: She hath often desired His Majesty might so govern, as to have the Affections of his People, and particularly, by Parliament.' [34]

Marie de' Medici was granted a guard of a mere five men. Another plea – this one delivered by the Prince of Wales – was still less successful. The king sent his son and heir to beg for Strafford's life. The Lords replied that mercy would put the royal family at risk. On 12 May Strafford's execution went ahead on Tower Hill. The watching crowd was exultant. 'My Lord's condition is happier than mine,' was Charles's comment.[35]

As for Henrietta Maria: Charles Louis observed to his mother, 'my Lord of Stafford's death' had left her very angry. [36]

Lucy Carlisle had been cross-examined about what she knew of the attempt to spring Strafford, which was nothing – or at least nothing she ever gave away. Her sister, the Countess of Leicester, updated her on the royalist refugees arriving in Paris where her husband was ambassador. Charles's former Secretary of State Windebank, who was bisexual, was seen regularly partying 'with a coach full of boys', while Suckling was a regular visitor at the countess's house. She found him still 'good company, but much abated in his mirth.'[37] He had little money and soon had less. Parliament had stopped his pension from the king.

It is a mystery what happened to the 'greatest gallant of his time', but 23 July 1641 is the last date we know Suckling was alive. By the next summer news tracts concerning the refugees from England no longer mentioned him. It was later said that he was living above an apothecary shop when he took poison, 'which killed him miserably with vomiting.'[38]

Davenant, the noseless friend who had accompanied Suckling to Bath in 1637 on 'as pleasant a journey as ever men had', would never forget their happy summer progress. But imprisoned and under interrogation the jokes they had played on Captain Young, Suckling writing his book on quarrels between religions being addressed through reason, must all have seemed a distant dream.

THE STRUGGLE FOR LONDON

HENRIETTA MARIA HAD TO WATCH HER AILING MOTHER, MARIE de' Medici, being driven out of England on 22 August, 'for the quieting of . . . His Majesty's well-affected subjects', as Parliament had put it. Marie was now in Cologne, where she would meet up with the papal agent Rossetti a month later. Meanwhile, Henrietta Maria apologised to Christine that she had not 'written more often'; 'I swear to you I have gone almost mad with the sudden change in my fortunes, having gone from the highest degree of happiness to fall into the greatest misery and despair; not just for myself but for others.'[1]

Henrietta Maria described how their friends were pursued to the death, 'Catholics persecuted, priests hanged'. The first had died the previous month, on 26 July 1641. A bad-tempered old scholar of eighty-one, he was drawn and quartered for having failed to comply with the expulsion order. It was said that the fact he was a convert had put him at the front of the queue of those condemned to die. His head and limbs were now pinned around the City. 'I feel worse about the suffering of Catholics and others who serve the king than I do about myself,' she wrote.[2] She was desperate to do something about it. She had suggested to Charles that he travel to Scotland to sign a new treaty that had been agreed and would see the invaders return home. He had duly travelled to Edinburgh, but she had been refused permission to accompany him.

Unable to see Scotland for herself and learn something of the country, Henrietta Maria had hoped instead to take her daughter Mary to Holland. She hinted to Christine that she would have preferred a greater marriage for Mary, but she hoped for the best: 'although [William] will never be a king, I have no doubt she can be just as happy'. After all, she reflected, 'I know well that it is not kingdoms that bring happiness'.[3] Charles now needed to firm up the Dutch marriage alliance, which, Henrietta Maria confided in Christine, could 'be greatly advantageous' to them.

William had left England on 15 May, just three days after Strafford's execution. Instead of his bride he had taken Van Dyck's marriage portrait of her holding his hand, observing wistfully 'I think she is far more beautiful than her picture'.[4] He had since written begging for Mary to join him. Henrietta Maria and Charles had reiterated that they did not want the marriage consummated until she was fourteen, but had agreed for Mary to leave England. Henrietta Maria had asked Parliament for a passport to travel with Mary, ostensibly so she could also visit Spa to take the waters, her health having deteriorated 'in body and in mind'.

The queen's claims were backed by her doctor who informed MPs he gave her opium to help her sleep and feared she was so weak 'she would not recover' from her ailments. MPs were, however, suspicious. They had a report 'of great quantities of treasure, in jewels, plate and ready money, packed up to be covered away with the queen . . . and that divers papists, and others, under the pretence of Her Majesty's goods, are like to convey great sums of money, and other treasure, beyond the seas . . . to the fomenting of some mischievous attempts'.[5] The passport was refused with the parliamentary commissioners assuring Henrietta Maria that everything possible would be done for her health – in England.

Henrietta Maria had thanked MPs for their concern. 'I hope I shall see the effect of it,' she observed drily.[6] To the Venetian ambassador she was more defiant, telling him 'she was prepared to obey the king but not 400 of his subjects, as this did not befit her spirit or her birth'.[7] She 'felt like a prisoner', she told Christine. She acknowledged her sister had endured 'enough afflictions' of her own, but she had 'done something' about it. The rebellion in Catalonia had weakened Spain and put Christine's regency in a stronger position, especially after Henrietta Maria's former beau, Soissons, had accidently shot himself in the head in July; Christine's sister-in-law had become his heir and Prince Thomas became a supporter of her Francophile policy, in order to secure his wife's inheritance.

Henrietta Maria had no comment to make about Soissons, her sole focus being Charles, and her advice that he go to Scotland had, at least, yielded some positive news. He had been received in Scotland 'with great joy, and such as they say was never seen before', the queen told Christine. She hoped the same turnaround might be achieved in England.

Henrietta Maria had witnessed how on Charles's return to London from York a year earlier, in 1640, he had been greeted by crowds 'with a kind of ovation'.[8] There were signs that the popularity of the Junto was now waning. Extreme Puritan congregations known as 'secretaries' were emerging from the shadows to the horror of orthodox Protestants, while many feared their real king was being usurped by a 'King Pym' and an oligarchy of ambitious nobles. If Charles processed through London again, playing to the crowds as Elizabeth I had done, he might regain the hearts of the people. Suckling's advice still resonated: 'the great interest of a king is a union with his people'.

'God be with you,' Henrietta Maria concluded her letter to Christine; 'We also have need of Him.'[9] She now had a new plan to lay. Meanwhile, on 10 September, a second priest was executed.

Henrietta Maria had warned that Charles's failure to punish the Scottish rebels would offer 'fresh inducements to other subjects to rebel without fear'.[10] When the peace terms Charles signed in Scotland became public, the native Catholics of Ireland rose up to demand the same freedom of religion and political rights as the Presbyterian Scots. In their words they intended 'to imitate Scotland, which got a privilege by that course'.[11]

Reports reached London on 1 November 1641 that the rebels 'surprised some castles, slew the Protestants who offered resistance, burnt their dwellings and subsequently took possession of several strong positions in the country.'[12]

The English presses began churning out images of the horrors that were taking place in Ireland, redoubling 'the odium against the English Catholics as well as their danger', the Venetian ambassador reported; 'a proclamation has been published commanding all of them, under severe penalties, to bring their names to Parliament. The intention is supposed to be to force them to leave the kingdom or at least to involve the loss of their property.'[13] The ambassador was forced to intervene to save the life of an English cleric in his own service, who had diplomatic immunity from the crime of being a priest. Seven others were on trial for their life, including one, John Hammond, who was in service to Henrietta Maria. The Venetian further reported that 'parliamentarians have conceived some suspicion that the queen may have given some encouragement to these movements in Ireland, in secret ways.'[14]

The Irish rebellion was to be the breaking point in the queen's relationship with Holland. Formerly so close that people had wondered if they were lovers, they had grown increasingly estranged since Charles had lost the first Bishops' War in 1639. Holland had not enjoyed seeing the likes of Jermyn and Montagu overtake him in Henrietta Maria's affections, but his sympathies had lain with the Scottish rebels, not with the king. He now saw the rebellion in Ireland as a war to the death between the Calvinist settlers and the native Catholics, and he did not trust Charles to deal with the Catholics as ruthlessly as he believed was necessary.

Holland was also concerned that when the English army, which had been disbanded following the peace treaty signed in Edinburgh, was recalled to use in Ireland, Charles would deploy it against his opponents at home. There had been an 'incident' in Edinburgh in October that had exposed a plot to arrest, or even assassinate, leading Covenanters, along with the king's former negotiator, the moderate Marquess of Hamilton, who had developed a close relationship with the Covenanter leader, Archibald Campbell, Earl of Argyll. Charles denied any involvement, but was not believed, and if he was prepared to see Hamilton murdered, was even Holland safe from arrest if the king was restored to his full powers?

The Junto began to have meetings in Holland's house in Kensington. Wat Montagu's elder brother Edward, Viscount Mandeville, a man 'of a gentle and generous nature, civilly bred', was one attendee.[15] Like the rest of Wat's family he was a moderate Calvinist and was Warwick's son-in-law. Holland's cousin Essex also went, as did a more surprising figure – Lucy Carlisle. Since Strafford's execution she had reinvented herself as a Puritan 'she saint', taking notes in sermons, and making King Pym her latest gallant. Had she moved to where power now lay, or was she a spy for the queen? We know Lucy had recently shown Charles's new Secretary of State, Sir Edward Nicholas, secret papers she had got from Mandeville.

It may well have been Lucy who warned Henrietta Maria that another family member – Holland's half-brother, Newport – had suggested that if the king tried to hatch a plot against them (as he had against Hamilton and Covenanter leaders in Scotland), then 'the person of Her Majesty and her children should be seized upon'.[16] Henrietta Maria acted promptly to get her eldest sons out of the country.

Parliament had replaced the Prince of Wales's governor, the Earl of Newcastle, with Essex's brother-in-law, Hertford, whom the king had raised recently to the title of marquess. She knew Hertford had grown anxious about the radical shift of the Junto since she had first met him in August 1640 and she now asked him to send her sons Charles and James from Richmond Palace to her at Oatlands. Hertford complied, but the Junto found out and sent Holland to retrieve the prince and the duke. Holland was instructed to advise the queen that the boys needed to return to Richmond so they might 'continue their studies'. He arrived with armed men.

According to the future Charles II – speaking in 1651 – Holland smashed up 'an altar, crucifix and silver candlesticks of his'.[17] Father Phillip was accused of trying to convert the royal children, but whether these items were Arminian or Catholic we can't be sure. In any event Father Phillip was taken away for interrogation concerning his 'involvement' in the Irish rebellion, and after he refused to swear on a Protestant Bible, he was put in the Tower. Having lost her children and her confessor, Henrietta Maria prepared the fightback.

Together with Charles's Secretary of State, Sir Edward Nicholas, the queen was planning something that would help renew Charles's bonds with his people and turn the tables on the Junto's populist rhetoric. She informed the royalist Mayor of London, Richard Gurney, that the king wished to process through the City on his return to London.[18] Nicholas had advised Charles how to conduct himself, showing 'yourself gracious to your people, by speaking a short word now and then to them as you pass amongst them, to cheer and encourage them in their dutiful affections to your royal person'.[19] They did not, however, have long to pull something spectacular together: Charles was already on his way.

In mid-November 1641 Van Dyck arrived at Wat Montagu's house in Pontoise, seventeen miles north-west of Paris. He had travelled from Antwerp with his heavily pregnant wife, Mary Ruthven. The artist had returned to the continent in 1640 hoping to pick up commissions from former patrons of Peter Paul Rubens. Richelieu had urged him to come on to Paris, but it was evident to Wat that Van Dyck was ill, 'to the point of being unable to work'. Even his mind seemed disturbed. His wife was now desperate to get back to England to have her baby. Wat begged Van Dyck to stay and rest so he might recover, but his wife's tears 'were stronger than human reason'.[20]

The London to which Van Dyck returned was suffering from another severe outbreak of plague. Most MPs were avoiding the capital. On 22 November Pym took advantage of their absence to introduce into

Parliament a Grand Remonstrance against Charles's rule. Its long list of complaints and accusations painted a picture of popish conspiracy that necessitated a radical response: legislation that would remove all meaningful power from the king. One plague victim responded by sending Pym 'an abominable rag full of filthy bloody puss', calling him a 'Traitor and other opprobrious names' and expressing the hope that the puss 'should kill him by infection'.[21] Many felt the king had already given up enough powers to dangerous and power-greedy radicals.

The Remonstrance passed at two in the morning of 23 November with a narrow majority of eleven. The king's supporters were, however, about to be given an opportunity to express their loyalties. On 24 November 1641 the lord mayor asked his aldermen to order 'a good substantial, treble watch' in their wards while two of the trained bands were put on call.[22] A royal entry to London on a scale not yet seen during Charles's reign was planned to go ahead the following day, and no violence would be allowed to spoil the celebrations or damage the message of royal strength.

The following morning, on the outskirts of London, Charles left Theobalds with the queen, and the princes Charles and James, in a glittering cavalcade of peers and cavaliers. The mayor, his aldermen and 500 mounted liverymen greeted him as he arrived at Moorfields, outside the City walls, 'habited in plush, satin, velvet and chains of gold', the liverymen all bearing swords and each horseman with a liveried footman attending on him.[23] The mayor presented Charles with the keys of the City. Charles in turn delivered a speech in which he vowed to protect the Protestant religion as established by Queen Elizabeth and King James.

Charles and the princes then mounted horses and rode into the City at Moorgate, with Essex's brother-in-law, the Marquess of Hertford, bearing the processional sword before him. Bringing up the rear, in a display of military might, were 1,000 armed cavaliers from the disbanded royal army in the north. As 'drums beat . . . muskets rattled . . . and flags were displayed', it seemed as 'if Mars himself, the God of battle, had been their conductor'.[24] The streets were hung with tapestry and trumpet blasts greeted the king. As the procession continued the conduits ran with wine, the crowds cheered and Charles 'courteously saluted the people by often putting off his hat . . . a favour which til then neither he or his father had ever bestowed on the vulgar'.[25]

That evening at the Guildhall, the aldermen feasted the king and his nobles. Henrietta Maria sat with Charles beneath a royal canopy, his nephew, Charles Louis, on his left and their two elder sons on their right to advertise their superiority in line of succession. Down the centre of the room, at two long tables, the favoured peers and their wives enjoyed 500 dishes served in ten courses. Holland was there, in acknowledgement of his role as mediator between the king and the Junto. His brother, Warwick, was not. Nor was Lucy Carlisle's eldest brother, the Earl of Northumberland, whose relationship with the king had deteriorated after he had failed to support the second Bishops' War.

After the feast the king and queen were escorted to Whitehall where bonfires were blazing and the crowds cried 'The Lord preserve King Charles'.[26] It was a heartwarming sight for royalists, but this was a divided kingdom. The procession was not only a means of recruiting supporters, the display of strength was also a threat to the king's enemies. In this regard a pamphlet commissioned to celebrate the occasion issued a warning against traitors to the king: 'those that were inclined / To practise mischief . . . shall have / A regal judgment and a legal grave'.[27]

Charles and Henrietta Maria were anxious to help the ailing Van Dyck if they could. The king offered a huge reward to any doctor who would save the artist's life, but this proved impossible. Van Dyck died aged forty-two on 9 December, at his house in Blackfriars. His eight-day-old baby daughter was baptised the same day. She was named Justinia, perhaps after the emperor who had recovered from the first great plague epidemic in Constantinople – an expression of hope now lost.

Charles ordered that Van Dyck be buried on 11 December in the choir of the Protestant Cathedral of St Paul's, despite the artist's Catholic faith. He also composed the Latin epitaph for his tomb. It translates as 'Anthony Van Dyck / Who, while he lived, gave to many, immortal life'. John Suckling and Henry Holland, Lucy Carlisle and Marie de' Medici, Robert Warwick, Charles Louis and Rupert of the Rhine – in Van Dyck's portraits their faces are vivid still.

The following day Charles issued a proclamation. The Junto intended to pass an impressment bill through Parliament. This would allow them to neutralise the danger that the disbanded royalist army would be recalled to fight the rebels in Ireland and then deployed against them. Instead they could recruit an army of draftees who would fight under the Junto's hand-picked officers. Lined up to stop the bill were the king's supporters in the House of Lords, where the numbers of nobles who backed him was increased by the presence of the bishops. Henrietta Maria had been urging peers to return to London for weeks and they now gave the royalists an overall majority. The Junto still dominated the Commons, but only because moderate MPs kept away from London. The proclamation would force them back. It summoned 'all members of both Houses of Parliament' to return to Westminster by 12 January.

There were now 'continual petitions from all counties for and against bishops', who held the balance of power.[28] On 15 December the Junto published the Grand Remonstrance so their accusations could be disseminated across the country. It had immediate impact.

On 21 December royalists lost their majority in elections to the Common Council of the governing body of the City of London. This gave the Junto access to the 8,000-strong City militia. Charles's thoughtless response was to replace the pro-Junto Lieutenant of the Tower with a pardoned murderer called Thomas Lunsford. Further riots followed and although Charles quickly replaced Lunsford with a less controversial figure, the rioting continued. On 27 December the bishops in Westminster listened to the roar of the crowd outside, not daring to leave the Lords Chamber. They were still there when night fell, the Marquess of Hertford warning 'these people vow they will watch you at your going out, and will search every coach for you with torches so you cannot escape'. Yet they could not stay there forever.

Some of the bishops 'by secret and far-fetched passages escaped home'; others were hidden in the coaches of peers known to support the Junto, but who had no wish to see the clergy lynched. On the road: 'ten thousand apprentices were between York House and Charing Cross with halberds, staves and some swords', one peer reported, 'and though it were a dark night their innumerable links [ropes dipped in resin] made it light as day. They cried "No bishops! No papist lords!", looked in our coaches whether any bishops were therein, so we went on in great danger.'[29] The next day Charles issued an order to the mayor to use the militia 'to suppress all such tumults . . . by shooting with bullets or otherwise to slay and kill such of them as shall persist in their tumultuary and seditious ways and disorders'.[30]

On 29 December the mobs arrived at the palace gates carrying clubs and swords and crying once again 'No bishops! No papist lords!' Cavaliers leapt over the rails and beat them back with the flat of their swords. 'In all these skirmishes they have avoided thrusting, because they would not kill them,' a witness reported – yet how long would that last? 'Both factions talk very big, and it is a wonder there is no more blood yet spilt, seeing how earnest both sides are. There is no doubt, but if the king do not comply with the Commons in all things they desire, a sudden civil war must ensue, which every day we see approaches nearer,' one observer reported.[31] Another noted 'that we talk now of nothing but drawing of swords'.[32]

The Archbishop of York, John Williams, who had been an early supporter of the Junto and had advised the king to sign Strafford's death warrant, had now turned against them. He urgently petitioned the king for a suspension of parliamentary business. With the violence preventing bishops from attending, he argued, the Lords was not properly constituted. The Junto-packed Commons responded by having ten of the twelve petitioner bishops arrested and imprisoned. The royalist majority in the Lords was lost. If Charles did not take drastic action the Junto could push through the impressment bill that would allow them to take charge of future army recruitment.

On I January Charles attempted a truce, offering Pym the post of Chancellor of the Exchequer that it had been rumoured he would get a year earlier. Whatever might have happened then, Pym now turned him down. Time was running out for Charles – and also for Henrietta Maria. According to the Venetian ambassador, the Junto had 'decided to accuse her in Parliament of conspiring against the public liberty and of secret intelligence in the rebellion in Ireland'.[33] She believed she could be locked in the Tower, even executed: 'They said publicly that a queen was just a subject and could be punished like anyone else,' she told Christine.[34]

On 3 January the king launched the same process Parliament was using against the imprisoned bishops – impeachment – against five members of the Commons, including Pym. One member of the Lords was also picked out on a charge of treason: Wat Montagu's elder brother, Viscount Mandeville, the future Earl of Manchester, whose secret papers Lucy Carlisle had handed to Charles's Secretary of State, Sir Edward Nicholas. Henrietta Maria expressed her relief to Lucy. The king was poised to reclaim his realm, 'for Pym and his confederates are arrested before now'. But when the king's serjeant-at-arms arrived at the Commons to arrest the five members, he was turned away. The Junto then returned to their attack on the queen.

For months Pym and his allies had been drawing a psychological portrait of the royal couple. Holland was a useful informant as was Lucy Carlisle, communicating 'all she knew and more of the dispositions of the king and queen'. Far from being a spy for Henrietta Maria she had been a double agent. When it came to friends for Lucy, 'They whom she is pleased to choose are such as are of the most eminent condition, both for power and employments.'[35] It was King Pym and the Junto who were now most eminent for 'power and employments'. The execution of Strafford had made that very clear to Lucy. For weeks Lucy had been carefully manipulating Henrietta Maria, encouraging the queen to believe the worst of what the Junto intended for her, hoping it would provoke Charles into one of his periodic losses of control. 'There is great danger in that face,' Suckling had once written of her.

When news reached Whitehall that Parliament was to deprive the queen of most of her household clergy, Henrietta Maria was led to believe this was the prelude to her own arrest. That was 'a fate worse than death', she told Christine, as it would make Charles vulnerable to blackmail. At 10 p.m. on 3 January Charles ordered that the cannon at the Tower be armed and made ready to overawe the capital and defend his family. What happened the next day, was not, however, to be the result of any careful planning the night before, but a reckless gamble the king made at a moment of high passion.

The shops in London were shut on the morning of 4 January 1642. With the guns at the Tower trained on London, people were braced for violence, 'every man his halberd and weapons in readiness'.[36] Yet the capital remained quiet until, at 3 p.m., Charles entered the guardroom at Whitehall Palace and 'called in a loud voice, "My most loyal subjects and soldiers!" '[37] Five hundred armed cavaliers followed him out through the Great Court and down the stairs of the palace. At the gates the king found the road thick with mud. He hailed a passing coach to take him the half-mile to Westminster and Parliament. A French spy raced ahead to warn the five MPs due for arrest that Charles was on his way.

Charles's targets fled the Commons Chamber just as the king and his cavaliers entered Westminster Hall. 'He proceeded to the Commons Chamber,' the Venetian ambassador reported, and there, forbidding any [of his cavaliers] to enter at peril of their lives, he went in alone, and looking keenly round he noticed that the accused were not there according to his expectation. He then said that a very serious incident had forced him to betaken himself to that place, and this was that having accused five of their members of high treason he desired them to be handed over to him at once, and he looked for obedience in this. But no answer was given and he went out with the same following [of cavaliers], leaving Parliament greatly inflamed. Arrived back at the palace again the king commanded the heralds to try every means to take these men, but without result.[38]

Yet again Charles had made it appear he was set on a course of violence. This time his action had crystallised fears that he was the enemy of Parliament and of the people who elected it. But what had prompted his sudden and disastrous decision? Henrietta Maria has always been blamed. It was later said she had told Charles he had to go Parliament in person, 'Pull those rogues out by the ears' and arrest them, or 'never see my face more!' Others described it more broadly as 'the women's council', with Charles goaded that if he 'were King of England he would not suffer himself to be baffled about by these persons'.[39] The Venetian ambassador, who had excellent intelligence, reported something rather different.

On 3 January Charles had reissued his commands concerning the five members and ordered that they be obeyed. Instead, on the morning of 4 January, the Commons had 'denounced the accusation against these members as an infamous libel and an unlawful blow'. The king's orders, even on a matter of treason, carried no weight. It was this that had triggered Charles's reaction. 'When the king was informed of these insubordinate and disrespectful actions, he came out of his chamber immediately.'[40] From there he had proceeded to the guardroom, collected his men, and left the palace.

Charles had always believed that it was enough to 'show myself, like myself' to bring his subjects into line. He was King Philogenes of William Davenant's masque, the lover of the people whose mere appearance could settle a kingdom. The Commons had disobeyed and threatened to arrest his officers. He had been certain they could not disobey an order from his own mouth. It was only as he stood in the Commons Chamber, impotent in his demands, that he realised he was mistaken.

SAVING THE KING

ON 8 JANUARY 1642 LONDON'S COMMON COUNCIL APPOINTED A CLOSE friend of the Earl of Essex as the captain of the City militia.[1] Fearing Henrietta Maria's arrest, Charles wrote that same day to the royalist captain of the ship *Bonaventure* asking that he 'carry [the queen] presently with the first opportunity of wind to St Helens point near Portsmouth'.[2] Next, he had to get her out of London. He informed the Junto that the royal family were leaving for Hampton Court. They could not force him to stay without announcing his arrest.

Holland and Essex were dispatched to persuade Charles to remain in London, while Lucy Carlisle spoke to Henrietta Maria.[3] Charles turned the request round, asking Holland and Essex to demonstrate their loyalty to their king by accompanying them in their roles as royal servants. They refused. Holland feared an 'incident' would occur in which they would be murdered. On Monday 10 January the royal family left Whitehall by barge, 'discontentedly, attended not with many lords or old courtiers, but with the officers of the late army in good numbers'.[4] The fires at Hampton Court were not laid. Beds were not set up. Charles, Henrietta Maria and their eldest children had to share a room.

'My heart pities a king so fleeting and so friendless yet without one noted vice,' a knight told his wife. The king was 'so poor he cannot afford to feed those that follow him. I was told that one night the prince wanted wine and another candles.'[5] Here Charles was confronted with the fact that he had lost London – his 'Imperial Chamber' as he called it.[6] It was a devastating blow. Yet the danger to the queen appeared to have been only narrowly averted. The next day a letter was read in the Commons claiming that Henrietta Maria, along with other Catholics, were concocting a plot against Parliament and people.

The royal family kept on the move. First they travelled to Windsor where, once again, they were 'forced to lie with their children' in one room.[7] A Commons delegation there found 'a disconsolate court, saw not one nobleman and scarce three gentlemen'. Endymion Porter, whose son had died fighting the Scots, was one; 'my duty and my loyalty have taught me to follow my king and master, and by the grace of God nothing shall divert me from it', he wrote to his wife.[8] From there the royal family went to Greenwich. Henrietta Maria was now so ill she was losing teeth.

On 17 January Charles sent further secret orders to the captain of the *Bonaventure* asking 'as soon as you arrive there [in Portsmouth] . . . send us advertisement thereof by an express and trusty messenger'.[9] The execution of Catholic priests continued in London. Two were hanged, drawn and quartered on 21 January. On 3 February it was reported that 'almost all the king's servants are declared enemies of state and not to be permitted to attend the king; nay, they have shaved him so close that poor Tom Davies [the king's barber] must not trim him'.[10]

The news emerged, however, that Parliament was no longer opposed to Henrietta Maria's leaving for Holland with Mary. The Venetian ambassador noted that a faction within the Junto now believed the king would be a weaker opponent without her advice and support, while her leaving the country was a less controversial means of separating the royal couple than placing her under arrest. Charles and Henrietta Maria seized the opportunity.

On 13 February the king and queen were in Canterbury. Preparations for the fleet to take her to Holland were being done as quickly as possible, in case the Junto changed their minds. One captain complained that 'I never heard the like for the voyage of persons of so great a dignity.'[11] To smooth matters further Henrietta Maria 'prevailed with the king' to agree to an 'exclusion' bill, which prevented the bishops from sitting in the House of Lords.[12] Henrietta Maria reassured him it could later be repudiated as done only out of 'fear of danger to my person.'[13]

Back in London, as news of the queen's imminent departure spread, the thousands of tradeswomen whose livelihoods depended on her as a leader of fashion petitioned Parliament against her going. They complained she had been frightened with 'tumultuous assemblies' and the 'unpunished printing of many scandalous and licentious pamphlets' against her.[14] They were ignored. Three days later Charles and Henrietta Maria were at Dover. The castle had a small plaque to mark the place where they had first met: 'all places of this castle only this / where Charles and Marie, shared a royal kiss.'[15] They stayed for a week, separated from most of their children. James, Duke of York was with the Marquess of Hertford, while the younger children were at St James's Palace, also in Parliament's care.

There had been repeated efforts to remove the Prince of Wales from his parents, but he remained with them. Henrietta Maria urged Charles not to hand the boy over when she had left and she urged him to stick to a plan they had agreed. Irresolution would lead to a loss of confidence, she explained and, with it, foreign aid. Charles promised that he would not come to any new accommodation with Parliament without her knowledge and agreement.[16]

Their final parting came on 23 February 1642. The king clung to his wife, as if he 'did not know how to tear himself away', the Venetian ambassador reported, neither of them able to 'restrain their tears.'[17]

As her ship, the *Lion*, sailed away, Henrietta Maria stood on deck watching Charles ride along the shore, where 'taking off his hat he waved it around several times, bidding her a very affectionate but very sad and painful adieu.'[18] The darkening skies heralded a storm that engulfed her flotilla of twelve ships. A baggage ship sank with only a few men saved while the material losses were huge, amounting to 60,000 pounds sterling. The late Duke of Buckingham's sister, Susan Denbigh, mourned, 'I have lost all my goods which is and has been to both me and all who belong to me, a sorrow beyond expression.'[19] The queen's chapel ornaments and the relic of the true cross also went to the bottom of the sea. 'The queen laments this not only on religious grounds, but because of the venerable antiquity of that relic, which has been preserved over a thousand years in the Tower of London' the Venetian ambassador reported. 'St Helena deposited it there with her own hands, when the faith of Christ flourished in those parts.'[20]

Charles's sister, Elizabeth – the Winter Queen – greeted her sister-in-law after her ships had docked in Holland. A red-faced hunting lady, in widow's black she was every inch a Stuart in her physical energy, her sense of humour and intelligence, but also in her lapses of judgement. Her son Charles Louis had led her to expect a harridan. She must have been shocked by the 'very weak and dejected' creature she now met.[21]

In the shared coach Elizabeth's eleven-year-old daughter, Sophie, was cold-eyed in her appraisal of her traumatised and ailing aunt. 'Van Dyck's portraits had given me such an idea of the beauty of all English ladies, that I was surprised to find the queen (so beautiful in her pictures) a small woman with long slim arms, uneven shoulders and teeth protruding from her mouth like guns from a fort.'[22]

Henrietta Maria now had to face a formal entry to The Hague, which had been arranged with as much entertainment 'as the short warning did permit'. The queen duly sat through an execrable ballet that had been vetted and censored by a board of Calvinist ministers.

Over the next few days Henrietta Maria's natural charm worked its magic on Elizabeth and her daughter. 'She uses me and my children extremely well both for civility and kindness,' Elizabeth admitted – and Sophie agreed: 'She did me the honour to say she thought me rather like her daughter. So pleased was I that from that time forward

I considered her quite handsome.' Indeed, 'After careful inspection I found she had beautiful eyes, a well-shaped nose, and an admirable complexion.'[23]

A letter waiting for Henrietta Maria from Christine had also brought 'great consolation' in her distress. 'I have barely slept,' she confided in her sister. 'It is no small thing being forced to leave my husband the king and my children.'[24] She allowed herself to hope that Charles might be able to persuade Hertford to hand James over to him, and even that Parliament would agree to allow the younger children to join her in Holland.[25] It was hard, meanwhile, to forget the treachery of old friends like Holland and Lucy Carlisle – whose name she took as her own code name. She felt, she told Christine, that 'everyone had betrayed us' and that she and Charles only had themselves to rely on.

Henrietta Maria now had to get used to her new surroundings at the Oude Hof in the Noordeinde Palace supplied by the Prince of Orange. His family had earned their ruling status from their role as leaders of the Dutch rebellion against the Habsburgs in 1579.[26] Louis XIII had recognised the current prince's role as a great general by elevating him from being referred to at the French court as 'Excellent' to 'Highness' – the term for minor royal sovereigns. William's marriage to England's Princess Royal had further raised their prestige and the Noordeinde Palace was being redone in Mary's honour. The Orange court was at its zenith: cosmopolitan and exciting. But, Henrietta Maria grieved, this was not 'our country', England.[27] Nor did it feel comfortable to be in the heart of a republic. Many of the Dutch were unsympathetic to Charles's cause.

Henrietta Maria had brought jewels and other valuable goods to sell or pawn to raise funds with which she intended to buy arms and men. Her ships would then transport them to royalist forces at home.[28] Henrietta Maria knew she would also have to use her diplomatic skills to prevent Parliament gaining access to the same European weaponry that she sought. Loyal friends were, however, on their way to help. Wat Montagu and Henry Jermyn were coming from France and others from England, her masque writer William Davenant amongst them.

Davenant might very easily have been executed by Parliament for his role in the army plot – Jermyn had been found guilty of treason *in absentia* – but he had played the innocent with all the skill he had learned in the theatre. The fact he had gone on the run when the Commons had called him for interrogation 'did proceed from a reverend awe your displeasure bred in me', he had told MPs: it was his 'befitting bashfulness' rather than a 'sense of guilt'. He reminded MPs of a poem he had written for 'the Queen Majesty in praise of her inclination to become . . . the people's advocate' in early 1641, and assured MPs that while he 'may be guilty of some misbecoming words' against Parliament, 'loose arguments, disputed at table, perhaps with too much fancy and heat', nothing more serious was involved.[29]

There had, by all accounts, been a tremendous row between MPs over what to do with Davenant. Happily, there was something about 'The poet' that people didn't take seriously. A piece of doggerel about his capture described how 'They flew on him as lions passant / And tore at his nose, as much as was on't!' It's tempting to say that Davenant's liaison with a prostitute had cost him his nose, but had saved his life. He had been freed in 1641 to return to his home in the neighbourhood of St Martin-in-the-Fields where he had remained, until the queen called him.

From July Davenant and Jermyn would be used as the queen's messengers and agents, criss-crossing the Channel at considerable risk to their lives, while Wat would be used for correspondence with France. Meanwhile, Henrietta Maria invited buyers to see some of the best jewellery she had with her. There were collars of pearls and of rubies, and a famous Burgundian jewel, a pin of rubies and diamonds known as the 'Three Brethren'.[30] Their value was intimidating – rumoured to be as much as 1,265,300 guilders or about £35 million today. The knowledge that the money would be put to a political and military purpose further complicated matters. Nor could her activities be kept secret. 'God knows the queen is very narrowly watched here . . . and I durst pawn my life that Parliament has some agents here merely to attend that business', one onlooker observed.[31]

The Junto asked their Dutch friends to put obstacles in the queen's way and so they did. She found she was able to sell only smaller items in The Hague. These included some pearl buttons belonging to Charles which she had reset into a chain. 'You cannot imagine how pretty your pearls were,' she told him. Even so they went for half what they were worth. It was a buyers' market, she acknowledged, 'You may judge, now, when we want for money, how they keep their foot upon our throat.'[32] Nevertheless she managed to send jewels to Amsterdam (which had a substantial Catholic minority), to Antwerp (in the Spanish Nether-lands), and to Denmark (which was ruled by Charles's cousin, Christian IV). She also persuaded the Prince of Orange to act as guar-antor for anything she sold.

Parliament soon learned the queen had flogged a pearl collar in Amsterdam for £16,000.[33] Purses had begun to open, and money was flooding in: 140,000 guilders from Amsterdam, 40,000 from Rotter-dam, 160,000 from The Hague.[34] She began to buy gunpowder, arms and cannon. She sent Charles Barbary horses and other useful gifts she had from the Prince of Orange and even returned the money she had brought with her; 'I am left without a sou but it matters not. I will reimburse myself as soon as I can. I had rather be in want than you,' she told Charles.[35]

The king had reached York on 19 March 1642, in accordance with their rearranged plan. The queen was happy to learn that Hertford had escorted James to his father with upwards of 900 horse. After a lifetime in opposition to the Crown, Hertford had swung to the royalist cause, as she had hoped he would. Henrietta Maria now wanted Charles to secure a northern port where her ships could land the munitions she had bought. She suggested Hull, Berwick or Newcastle as suitable, but she reminded Charles, 'we must have Hull'. Arms vital for the conflict ahead had been kept there since the Bishops' War of 1640. Now was the moment to seize the magazine. Charles had been well received in York, but 'the affection of the people changes like the wind, therefore you should make good use of it while it lasts . . . you write to me that everyone dissuades from taking Hull by force, unless Parliament make the first move – have they not done so?'

They had indeed: Parliament had ordered that the munitions be transferred to London, without the necessary royal warrant. The king needed to move fast. It was Charles's right to enter Hull, so refusing it would be a declaration of war, Henrietta Maria reminded him. 'Having Hull is not the beginning of anything violent. It is only taking action against the rascal who would refuse it to you.' She worried about his tendency not to follow through with plans after they were laid; 'you have already learned to your cost that lack of perseverance has ruined you.'[36] Thinking ahead she added, 'If you have to get Hull by force you will need some powerful aid for besieging places. The Prince of Orange will send some if you wish it. As fast as I write something always comes into my head; but Adieu, I have such a bad toothache that I scarcely know what I am doing.'[37]

Hearing nothing further from Charles, Henrietta Maria remained concerned about his tendency to procrastinate, reminding him 'the longer you wait the worse it will be'. She feared he would also give way on the matter of England's military forces, the county militia, which were traditionally raised in the king's name, and which Parliament now wished to control. 'Perhaps it is already done,' she continued angrily, 'and . . . I should never have quitted England because you will have rendered my journey ridiculous, having broken all the resolutions that you and I had taken, save going to York, and there to do nothing.'[38]

As it turned out Parliament had passed a Militia Ordinance in March, giving themselves command without royal assent. Charles had then carried out his own plans for Hull. On 22 April 1642, he sent the eight-year-old James there along with a small escort that included his sour-faced nephew, Charles Louis. The little duke had ridden right into the town before he was noticed.[39] The governor, Sir John Hotham, felt obliged to receive them officially. This allowed James to inform Hotham publicly that the king was approaching and expected to be granted entry. Hotham considered keeping James hostage, but thought better of it. When Charles arrived at Hull the next day he was, however, refused entry: Parliament had effectively declared war.

When Henrietta Maria heard the news she imagined herself in James's place: 'I would have flung the rascal [Hotham] over the walls, or he should have done the same thing to me!' Now Charles had to take Hull, she urged. She would pray for 'the man of sin who has married the Popish Brat of France, as the preacher said in London!'[40] 'Go on boldly . . . the time is come since I see there is no hope of an accommodation. May heaven load you with as many benedictions as you have had afflictions and may those who are the cause of your misfortunes, and those of your kingdom, perish under the load of their damnable intentions!'[41]

Charles now began openly recruiting men to fight against the Junto and they responded in kind. Many – perhaps most – people in England hoped the coming war would pass them by, but towns and villages, even families, were dividing into cavaliers and roundheads – a description associated with Puritans who wore their hair short. The royalist Hertford saw his brother-in-law, Essex, named as Parliament's Lord General. Warwick, Parliament's acting Lord Admiral, saw his elder son rally to the king. In The Hague too there were divided families. The queen's lady-in-waiting Susan Denbigh wrote to her eldest son Lord Feilding without avail, begging him not to betray the king.[42] Even Charles's family was split. His nephew Charles Louis would soon return to Holland as a friend to Parliament. By contrast Prince Rupert, released from Habsburg captivity, was anxious to leave for England to fight for his uncle, as was his strapping younger brother, Prince Maurice.

Henrietta Maria judged Rupert 'capable of doing anything', although 'He should have someone to advise him, for believe me, he is yet very young and self-willed. I have had experience of him,' she wrote.[43] It appears the battle-hardened twenty-two-year-old and his diminutive aunt had already had a stand-off on how best to support his uncle. It would not be their last. Meanwhile, in June, it was Henrietta Maria who struck the first blow for Charles, dispatching her ship, the *Providence*, back to England with gunpowder, small arms and seven or eight pieces of heavy artillery. Warwick ordered three ships to intercept her at the Humber, but the *Providence* evaded capture for long enough for the arms to be unloaded.[44]

Henrietta Maria planned to return to England herself as soon as possible. 'I cannot refrain from telling you the joy I feel about getting away,' she wrote to Charles, 'in truth I am afraid it will turn my brain for I do nothing in the world but think about it.'[45] For the time being, however, the royal palaces of England remained like stage sets, awaiting the actors to bring them alive. Lucy Carlisle, who had kept her rooms at Whitehall, wandered echoing rooms where tapestries 'had for their pride been taken down' and 'clapped close prisoners in the wardrobe'; here was 'A Palace without a Presence' a poet wrote, 'a Court without a Court'.[46] Lucy hoped it would not be for long and the king would lose the war quickly. Charles had arrived in York with only thirty or forty men. Even now his recruits were far fewer in number than theirs – and they had the vital munitions in Hull. Lucy and Holland imagined Charles returned to his throne chastened, the Church of England fully reformed, while they would earn the gratitude of the king and queen who would need their good offices with England's parliamentary masters.

By 1 July 1642 Marie de' Medici was too tired and ill to get out of bed. Her face had a red rash and she had gangrene in her leg. The doctor suggested amputation. She refused. She was living in a former brewery that had once belonged to her favourite artist, Peter Paul Rubens. Despite these modest circumstances, when Rossetti joined her in Cologne the previous September she had hoped she still had much to achieve. Rossetti had arrived as the Pope's Nuncio Extraordinary for a peace conference he had been trying to bring together since France and

Spain went to war in 1635. It was a golden opportunity for Marie de' Medici to help end what she saw as Richelieu's bellicose foreign policy.

The peace agenda had become seemingly more urgent after January when the Elector of Cologne had broken the neutrality of his domains. He had called in an Imperial army against Hessian troops who had their winter quarters on his lands. The Imperialists had been defeated, leaving Cologne 'deserted and wasted' and even the richest spending 'their life in sadness and grief'. But amidst this misery Marie's poor health had gone into a steep decline. Henrietta Maria had asked for a passport to see her, but it was refused. Marie had lost half her body weight that year, her abdomen and legs filled with fluid, and while she drank thirstily, she produced very little urine.

Marie had taken comfort in the visits she received from the abbess of a nearby Carmelite convent. They spoke, they prayed, and the abbess admired the statue of Our Lady of Scherpenheuvel, which Marie had brought back from England. According to later accounts the nun had had a vision of the statue, dressed in white, the symbol of peace, hovering above the tiller of a small boat sailing from the Low Countries towards England.[47] The miraculous statue, which had been used in the processions of Henrietta Maria's Confraternity of the Rosary, was said to have 'brought great spiritual benefits and the conversion of souls'.[48] The Virgin had not brought peace to England, however, having arrived on the eve of the Bishops' Wars. Perhaps she would bless Cologne instead. On 2 July 1642, Marie told Rossetti she wanted the statue to go the Carmelite nuns in Cologne and wrote her will.[49]

Marie divided her pearls amongst her servants and her other important jewels amongst her daughters, the Pope and the Elector of Cologne. She left her wedding ring to Anne of Austria and other possessions to her sons. Marie was asked if she would leave Richelieu a bracelet, but she said she thought that was more than he deserved. Instead Marie returned to Richelieu a parrot he had given her. We don't know what words she had taught it.[50]

Marie had recognised Richelieu's talents early. He had learned from her the power of mass communication, the need to control the visual and print media. She had used the arts in painting, sculpture, architecture, theatre and print to justify her rule as a queen regent and protect a vulnerable boy-king, emphasising the properties of divinely anointed kingship. But he had turned his back on the familial model of her society of princes in favour of an absolutist-nationalist vision. It would see France become the dominant power in Europe, but at a heavy cost.

On 3 July Marie's fever grew worse. Her servants heard her say 'Louis, Louis' and then, with a prayer on her lips, Marie de' Medici died. Her body was embalmed, so it might later be taken for burial at the Basilica of Saint-Denis in Paris. Her entrails were interred in the Chapel of the Magi in St Peter's Cathedral in Cologne: a suitable resting place for the mother of three kings. In Holland, Henrietta Maria went into mourning black. Many children live to see parents who were once powerful personalities sadly diminished in old age: few mothers have been quite as large in life, and become so reduced, as Marie de' Medici.

TO 'KILL A QUEEN

THE KING RAISED HIS STANDARD AT NOTTINGHAM ON 22 AUGUST 1642. Battle was coming and Henrietta Maria sought news-sheets with accurate information from home. One day, as she disappeared into a bookshop, she realised she was being followed. She hoped she could soon leave The Hague.

Henrietta Maria later entertained friends with stories of how Dutch citizens would plonk down beside her with their hats on or face her and simply stare. In reality such behaviour was no laughing matter. It was intimidating. Many of them were in Parliament's pay. The eleven-year-old Mary complained she even had 'spies in her apartments', and spoke to her mother-in-law, 'clearly expressing her contempt, hatred and dissatisfaction' with this state of affairs.[1]

The Junto also had friends in the Dutch States Provincial, their equivalent of Parliament. Henrietta Maria ensured that their envoy was denied a public reception, but, she complained to Charles, 'still they have sent to the rogue in private'. The envoy asked the Dutch to stop her sending any further 'money, men or arms' to the king. The Dutch complied, declaring 'they do not wish to irritate [the English] Parliament by permitting the export of munitions to His Majesty'.[2] Henrietta Maria then adapted, sending 200 men and arms to England in small boats to escape detection.

Envoys had also been sent from the English Parliament to France.

Louis was told that Henrietta Maria, Wat Montagu and others 'of the evil English party', had been involved in the latest conspiracy against Richelieu. This had been promoted by Gaston and ended in the execution of another former favourite of Louis, the twenty-two-year-old Marquis of Cinq Mars on 12 September.[3] Henrietta Maria, had, however, written four days earlier, to the Count of Chavigny, the French Secretary of State for Foreign Affairs, reminding him that the envoy 'comes from rebels against God and against their king'.[4] She said they were full of lies, telling the Dutch that she and Richelieu were working together to impose Catholicism on England.

Happily for Henrietta Maria, Louis was anxious for reconciliation following their mother's death, and Richelieu was seriously ill. Chavigny responded positively to her letter and she was soon thanking him for stopping a shipment of 'arms prepared for the rebels'.[5] She was also told she would be 'extremely welcome' in France.[6] The question that now confronted Henrietta Maria was whether to go to there or England. What did Charles wish, she wanted to know?

'All my friends from [France] persuade me extremely to go, assuring me that there I should be very useful for your service,' she told Charles, and 'France, with the power it possesses, may help us much.'[7] On the other hand going to England was dangerous: 'You may be sure that the rebels will do all they can to prevent me from joining you, and to take me, believing that they will thus make a better bargain with you . . . These are reasons you must now think over . . . although, you may imagine my inclination leads me to England.'[8]

Charles wanted her home: but first there was a battle to face. One he had long been expected to lose.

On 21 October 1642 the king's army came across a squire who, 'not knowing of the war', was out hunting. Charles engaged him as a last-minute recruit.[9] The next day, they faced Parliament's forces under the Earl of Essex at an escarpment called Edgehill, near Kineton, Warwickshire. The queen's young sons Prince Charles, aged twelve and

James, Duke of York, aged nine, were with their father and 'within half a musket shot' of the enemy. Many of the king's soldiers were barefoot and armed only with agricultural implements. Parliament's forces not only had the munitions from Hull, they also had arms taken from captured ships sent by the queen. A substantial portion of the queen's arms had, nevertheless, reached their intended destination. Henrietta Maria had given the royalists a fighting chance.

At 3 p.m. Essex ordered the opening salvos of artillery. The children heard the screams and smelt the blood. They watched their cousin Prince Rupert lead a cavalry charge and then the slow advance of the royalist infantry. James remembered all his life their 'steady pace [and] daring resolution'.[10] On the parliamentarian side Wat's brother, the future Earl of Manchester, beat his men with cudgels to make them stand and fight. As bullets flew over the children's heads, Charles ordered them escorted from the field. A parliamentarian soldier rode at their party, sword drawn. He was shot and dispatched with a poleaxe. Such were their schoolboy lessons now.

The boys waited out the battle with the wounded and the dying, whose numbers grew hour after hour. The royalist supplies of ammunition held and it was only the falling night that ended the killing. Three thousand were left dead or mutilated on the field. The hunting squire was knighted that night. He had survived and so had the royalist cause: Edgehill had not proved to be the knockout blow that Parliament had expected.

In London there was panic that Prince Rupert would now march on the capital and fire the City. Henrietta Maria's youngest royal children, Elizabeth and Henry, were taken from their sickbeds to be used as human shields, 'carried from St James's' into the City for the place's security, 'though the women with tears besought the contrary'.[11] Charles headed instead for Oxford. It would become his wartime capital. Meanwhile, rumours of disaster and a lost battle reached The Hague.

Susan Denbigh complained 'the perpetual fear I am in of hearing worse news of my poor Majesty makes me abound with sorrow'.[12]

Henrietta Maria was told that Charles was dead and their eldest son a prisoner: 'As to Prince Rupert, there are men here who have seen and touched his corpse and that of Prince Maurice,' she told her husband when, at last, she had learned the truth.[13]

Susan Denbigh discovered her husband, who had been with the king's guard at Edgehill, and their son, Lord Feilding, who had fought with Parliament, had also survived. Another lady-in-waiting, the Duchess of Richmond, daughter of the late Duke of Buckingham, was told her brother-in-law, the twenty-four-year-old Lord d'Aubigny, had not. He was to be buried in Oxford. Charles had also made a decision. He would now either be returned to his throne 'a glorious king', or he would be 'a patient martyr'. He was haunted by his having signed Strafford's death warrant: 'No consideration whatsoever shall ever make me do the like again.'[14] He would be true to his word.

Henrietta Maria's focus now was on gathering a fleet to take her home. As she told Richelieu she had 'great hope of returning soon – to England'. It seemed that 'at the very time you have taken my part in my troubles, our affairs have changed'.[15] She would not see her old enemy again.

Richelieu died on 4 December 1642, aged fifty-seven, having survived Marie de' Medici by only five months. 'I never forgot what I owed the queen mother – whatever slanders have been said to the contrary,' he recalled in his last days.[16] Perhaps not, but it would be his version of events that would survive, damning not only Marie's reputation but also that of Christine. It had annoyed the cardinal that rather than permit Savoy to be annexed by France as Richelieu had wished, she was successfully building Savoy as an intermediate power, had reconciled with her brothers-in-law and retained control of her son's government.

Wat Montagu's close friend Mazarin now took Richelieu's place as Louis's leading counsellor. Henrietta Maria sent Wat back to Paris to see what help he could get from him. For her, France could wait. 'I need the air of England,' she observed, 'this country [Holland] is too trying to the patience of persons who, like me, scarcely have any.'[17]

* * *

A Venetian diplomat reported that the national assembly of the United Provinces, the States General, had made 'a display of their lack of respect for Her Majesty, saying that ten ships were too many for her and that she ought to rest content with two' as her escort to England.[18] The queen made sure she got her way and on 19 January 1643, her flagship, the *Princess Royal*, bobbed alongside a further eight men-of-war, and five smaller vessels at the port of Scheveningen.

The day was calm and bright, but the good weather did not last. When the queen's fleet was a day from shore a storm broke and her ships were 'tossed and riven to and from on the Dogger Sands'. Henrietta Maria didn't sleep for days as 'the sudden gusts and blasts' of the wind 'ducked and drowned the sails in the seas'.[19]

The queen had George Goring's father Lord Goring with her, as well as her dwarf Jeffrey Hudson, and her ladies-in-waiting Susan Denbigh and the Duchess of Richmond. As the storm worsened two ships sank with eighteen hands and twenty-eight horses lost. The ladies were so frightened they 'confessed their sins aloud, and the horror of death made them forget the shame of broadcasting their sins, so that they might receive absolution . . . believing that day must be the last of their lives'.[20] Henrietta Maria also prayed to the Black Virgin of Liesse, to whom the founder of the French Carmelites, Madame Acarie, had been dedicated.[21]

With no nearby English port in royalist hands and despairing at 'this sad and unsafe condition', Henrietta Maria ordered that the flotilla return to Holland. The admiral thought this could be still more dangerous and, indeed, in the harbour at Scheveningen, they saw four ships lost in the tempest, including 'the bulk and ribs of an English one which had perished . . . before our eyes'. A shot was fired to warn the town of the queen's return and the news was carried to The Hague. When the fleet docked Henrietta Maria was greeted by carriages carrying her daughter Mary and all the princes and princesses, who 'did drive and ride into the sea for joy and haste to see that happy sight of Her Majesty's safety'.[22]

Henrietta Maria's and her ladies' vomit-encrusted clothes had to be burned, and it was reported that the queen, 'having suffered all this so long with a princely patience and courage', was left 'in poor health.'[23] 'I confess I never expected to see you again,' Henrietta Maria told Charles, 'a storm of nine days is a very frightful thing'. Yet she had not been afraid of death itself, she wrote to Charles. 'The only regret I felt about dying was this accident might encourage your enemies and discourage your friends.'[24] She managed even to see comedy in what had happened, teasing her friends about the sins they had declared when they thought they were about to drown.

Henrietta Maria would later commission the best goldsmith in Paris to produce a silver ship, with all its parts working, as a gift to the shrine to the Black Virgin in Liesse. She would also pay for a low Mass to be said in the chapel every Saturday, and on the anniversary of her survival, for the rest of time.[25]

As soon as the storm had dropped Henrietta Maria hoped to set out again, but she found her ships were trapped. Warwick had sent his navy to watch her fleet. It was evident they were preparing to either capture or sink her ammunition ship, which was anchored along the Mass river. The munitions it carried included two Dutch demi-cannon nicknamed 'the Queen's pocket pistols'.[26] The royalists were already on the back foot. The parliamentarian commander Sir Thomas Fairfax had taken Leeds on 23 January while Henrietta Maria was at sea. The royalist Earl of Newcastle had fallen back to York, abandoning plans to take the Midlands. Without fresh supplies they could lose the north altogether, while the king's main field army at Oxford was also short of men and munitions. Henrietta Maria was determined her ammunition would reach its destination, 'knowing how much the king's service, and his good subjects and soldiers in the north were concerned in it'. The Junto were equally determined to thwart the queen.

Parliament's allies in the local States Provincial ordered the Dutch admiral, Martin Tromp, to seize the ammunition ship and take any arms he found. Tromp, anxious not to anger the Prince of Orange, deferred the orders to the superior States General – which represented all the States of the United Provinces and not just Holland. Henrietta Maria then went on the attack, insisting she needed arms for her personal protection and threatening a grave breach between Charles and the United Provinces, 'the consequences whereof will be very dangerous'.[27] With tensions high, Parliament's supporters in The Hague began uttering 'many gross speeches of her' and attacked the Anglo-Dutch marriage alliance. Henrietta Maria responded by piling pressure on the Prince of Orange, who argued vigorously in her favour with the States General.

The result was a triumph for Henrietta Maria's diplomatic efforts. Tromp was ordered to enforce the protection of the queen's flotilla from any hostile force, including the ammunition ship, which his fleet was to accompany from the river Mass. When the vital ship duly reached open water Warwick's sailors 'made three shots at it', but Tromp returned fire, at which point the parliamentarian guns fell silent. They had no desire to provoke a war with the Dutch.

Henrietta Maria was greatly relieved when the ammunition arrived at Scheveningen. She had spent three days there, and to some travelling with her it appeared to be no more than 'a poor fishing village'. Henry Jermyn, who was recently returned from France and was with the queen, was one of those who liked his creature comforts.[28] Happily when Henrietta Maria's fleet set sail for Newcastle on 16 February it was in 'a soft and gentle gale'.[29] She had been pestered by people warning that a 'strange conjunction of the planets (not seen in 2,000 years) was due', but 'Her ardent desire to hasten to her husband's side, removes all fear from her heart, and animates her to encounter every danger', one diplomat observed.[30] This was just as well. Parliament had ordered Essex to preserve 'the king's person' in battle. There were no such orders concerning the queen.

Henrietta Maria was now Warwick's target and sixteen ships, under his vice admiral Sir William Batten, were sent to capture, 'burn, sink and destroy', her fleet.[31] It had got as far as Scarborough when the wind changed. Henrietta Maria's ships could not go further so they dropped anchor in Bridlington Bay on 20 February 1643. A message was sent to the Earl of Newcastle, who was about twenty miles away, warning him of her arrival. Local royalists brought provisions and expressed relief that she had not reached Newcastle, 'considering the dangers, both of the haven, and ships, which lay in wait for her there, fitted with men of desperate minds'.[32] She was, however, not yet safe. Parliamentarian spies had reported her change of course.[33]

On Wednesday 22 February an advance guard of the Earl of Newcastle's cavalry arrived at Bridlington Bay and the queen disembarked to spend the night in a humble thatched house on the quay.[34] The next day the Earl of Newcastle arrived and had dinner with the queen. A former patron of Ben Jonson and Sir John Suckling, the fifty-year-old nobleman 'liked the pomp' of his position, 'and preserv'd the dignity of it to the full'.[35] Nevertheless, he needed a professional to serve under him. Henrietta Maria had provided him with Lord Eythin, a Scot who had fought for the Swedes, and who also came to see her. They parted that night after a good dinner, with Henrietta Maria promising to review the troops the next day. Batten was already on his way.

It was dark and foggy at 4 a.m. when the parliamentarian ships entered the harbour. Henrietta Maria, who was still asleep, described to Charles what happened next.

'One of these ships had done me the favour to flank my house, which fronted the pier, and before I could get out of bed, the balls were whistling upon me in such style that you may easily believe I loved not such music.' People shouted for her to get out, 'the balls beating on all the houses'. She dressed, gathered her little dog Mitte, and ran with the women, 'for the soldiers remained very resolutely to guard the ammunition'.[36] The men worked frantically to unload thirty-two cannon, up to 10,000 small arms and seventy-eight barrels of powder while the firing continued, 'the balls singing around us in fine style'. They ran to the shelter of a ditch, with Henrietta Maria acting 'the captain . . . although a little low in stature', she joked. Before they managed to reach shelter a sergeant 'was killed twenty-paces from me'. The queen and the other women plunged into the ditch, and lay there under fire for two further hours, 'the balls always passing over our heads and sometimes covering us in dust'.[37]

There was no exaggeration in Henrietta Maria's description of events. A witness estimated the ships had fired 'above a hundred shots at the houses in the quay, for two hours shooting cross bar shots, and many bullets of twelve-pound weight'. He confirmed that 'One of those ships was directly planted against the house where the queen lay' and described how 'lords and ladies', their own houses shot through, had run with the queen, 'the bullets flying about them in the streets and fields as they went'. He further reported the death of the sergeant, 'not far from the queen's lodging'.[38] The cannon only stopped when Admiral Tromp warned Batten that he would 'fire on them as enemies' if they continued.

As the tide turned, Parliament's ships were forced out to sea and Henrietta Maria returned to her house, saying Parliament would not have the satisfaction of reporting she had retreated from the village. She had three eggs for breakfast and then reviewed the 'army of foot' and 2,500 horse, 'riding through and through', as she had promised she would. There she saw Lord Goring's son, George, who was now serving as Lieutenant General of the Horse. He had managed to keep the pretence of being loyal to Parliament right up until August 1642, being 'so rivetted in their good opinion and confidence, that they would give no countenance to any information they received . . . of anything to his prejudice'.[39]

George Goring's past life as a spoilt courtier was over and the life of a soldier of more modest means had begun. He owed his wealth and position to the king and it was a debt that would be paid in full. 'I had it all from His Majesty,' he later observed, 'and he had it all again.'[40] Others from the queen's old circle of playboys and playwrights felt the same way. Carnarvon was back from France and was a royalist commander, while the Poet Laureate William Davenant was serving as

Newcastle's Master of the Ordnance. War was quite a show to keep on the road, but contrary to the prejudices of some, he proved rather good at it.

Waiting in Bridlington for wagons to carry the ammunition and baggage to York, Susan Denbigh was 'very sick and weary'.[41] Yet there was work to be done. Henrietta Maria was already busy meeting and greeting. Royalists – and not least the king – expressed outrage at the attack on his wife, but the attempt to kill her was a mark of how formidable their enemies judged her to be. Henrietta Maria's arrival had left parliamentarians with 'some apprehension, not so much because of the succour she has brought [in the form of arms], but . . . the fear that her ardent French temper inspire the king's phlegmatic one to vigorous resolution'.[42]

An anxious figure came to see the queen: Sir John Hotham, the man who had lit the touchpaper to the Civil War by denying the king entry to Hull. One of the three leading parliamentarian commanders in the region, he wanted to make a deal. Like many others he had believed that Charles would be defeated quickly. Thanks in large part to her supplies of arms to the king in 1642, those hopes had proved misplaced. Now they faced the prospect of seeing the entire kingdom made bankrupt by the war. Hotham, like other members of the parliamentarian gentry, was also concerned about the attacks on the traditional Church of England and on the rise in social disorder.[43]

Hotham knew that Holland was leading a delegation to Oxford, representing a moderate pro-peace party in Parliament, who hoped to open negotiations with the king. The war was proving disastrous for Holland personally as part of his income was controlled by the king and part by Parliament. Nor did he wish to see England fall to the rule of soldiers. If Charles could be brought to agree the gains Parliament had made thus far, Holland hoped a solution could be reached. He was in touch with the queen, whom he respected, and Henrietta Maria had responded positively to his approaches. Despite her personal feelings towards Hotham – whom she had wanted to fling over the walls of Hull – she also listened carefully to what he now had to say.

Hotham was not willing to become a turncoat, but he did wish to make a secret treaty with the queen. If the royalists kept away from his estates and headquarters, he would not hinder her passage to York. He hoped this might later ensure that his execution was not made a condition of any peace treaty. The queen was happy to agree to Hotham's terms, intending to recruit him more fully later.

Meanwhile, no sooner had one parliamentary commander left Bridlington than an emissary from another arrived. On 27 February Lord Fairfax had dispatched his nephew, Sir William Fairfax, with a letter from him for the queen. A tall man with brown hair and dark eyes, William Fairfax was ushered into the queen's presence after dinner by Henry Jermyn and William Davenant. Amongst the men he saw standing with Henrietta Maria was the Earl of Newport. This was Henry Holland's half-brother, the man who was said to have suggested in 1641 that the royal children be held hostage to the king's good behaviour. Where, however, had this intelligence come from? The most likely culprit is Lucy Carlisle, who had hardly proved a reliable source of information to the queen. He had now been cast under fresh suspicion. Newport had been fighting for the king as Newcastle's lieutenant general until a quarrel blew up over Newcastle's willingness to employ Catholic officers. Newcastle argued that it was an insignificant issue. Newport passionately disagreed. It was widely believed that Newport had turned coat and it had been reported he was planning a kidnap attempt against the queen.

Loyalties were often slippery things, as Henrietta Maria knew all too well. She believed, however, that parliamentarian agents were using Newport's well-known antipathy to Catholicism to spread fresh disinformation about him. He had come to assure her of his loyalty. The queen, later damned as a bigot, had not only accepted his word, she had him standing beside her to send a message. She was not to be fooled a second time.

Henrietta Maria was certain the letter from Lord Fairfax also contained a trap and so she refused to read it. Eventually William Davenant persuaded her to do so. It proved to be as Henrietta Maria suspected. Ostensibly, Fairfax's letter offered the queen safe escort to York and expressed the wish that her 'powerful influence' be used with her husband in favour of a peace treaty. It all sounded so innocent, but these bland phrases could not be taken at face value. She did not believe she was being offered safe passage. She was being asked to give herself up to be used as a hostage. Fairfax did not want her to mediate a peace. Warwick, Pym and the war party in the Junto wanted to blame her for the war, which they wished to continue until they had gained an absolute victory. They had already ensured the terms of the peace the king was offered were tougher than he was likely to accept. They had also launched a series of initiatives guaranteed to irritate royalist moderates: the sequestration of royalist property being one such.[44]

Henrietta Maria told Fairfax's emissary that she had nothing to say to him. It was evident, however, that she was very angry.[45]

Lord Fairfax's letter was published shortly afterwards in a pro-parliamentarian newsletter to demonstrate Parliament's commitment to peace in the face of the warmongering of a fanatical papist queen.[46] Newcastle's army was referred to simply as 'the queen's popish army'.

Henrietta Maria's chief concern now was not whether or not it was inevitable that the war continue, but whether it would spread to encompass all three kingdoms. There was a view that this was inevitable. William Fairfax may have spotted another controversial figure standing alongside the queen: one very different from the Calvinist Newport. This was the tall, red-haired Catholic, Randal MacDonnell, Earl of Antrim.[47]

A powerful figure in Ulster and western Scotland, Antrim wanted Charles to accept a ceasefire agreement between the Irish Catholic rebels – known as the 'Confederates' – and royalist Irish Protestants. He would then lead his own forces in an invasion of the Western Highlands of Scotland. There they would meet up with Scottish royalists led by James Graham, Earl of Montrose. He also now came to see Henrietta Maria at Bridlington having been told she was the person whose support he most needed. Her 'court by many is judged very confident and fixed, whereas other courts [namely the king's] are too moveable'.[48]

A former Covenanter, Montrose had spent some time at court in the 1630s, where he had come to loathe the overbearing arrogance of the English nobility. He had also felt humiliated at the king's hands. His brother-in-law had run away with one sister while being married to another and Charles was highly sensitive to scandal, as Lucy Carlisle's late husband had discovered in the matter of the lute player and his daughter. In any event, Montrose had turned against his erstwhile Covenanter allies. He was envious of the power of the Earl of Argyll and appalled by the threat that Argyll's supporters posed to the monarchy, as well as by their imperialist demand that Presbyterianism be imposed on the whole of Britain.

Montrose was certain Scottish neutrality would not last indefinitely and that the King needed to strike first. He told her that 'The king has loyal subjects in Scotland – they have wealth and influence and hearts stout and true, they want but the king's countenance and permission [for a rising] . . . The only danger is delay, if the army of the covenant be allowed to make head, loyalty will be overwhelmed. The rebellious cockatrice must be bruised in the egg, physic is too late when disease has overrun the body.'[49] Antrim added that once the royalists in Scotland and his Irish army had defeated the Argyll Covenanters they would march south and join Charles's army.

A ruthless strike against those who had caused so much trouble to the king appealed to the queen, but she wasn't reckless. The Marquess of Hamilton – whom she liked – had worked hard to persuade Charles that the best way to keep his fellow Scots out of the war was not to alarm moderate opinion north of the border. Commissioners from Edinburgh had recently arrived at Oxford to discuss a way forward, and while Montrose was judged to have a 'generous spirit', Hamilton was thought to have the 'better headpiece'.[50] In any case she needed Charles's agreement to Montrose's plans – so she asked him to see her again for more detailed discussions in York.

On 4 March 1643 the queen left Bridlington for the capital of the north, laughing and joking with her soldiers on the route.

Part Five

THE GENERALISSIMA

HER POPISH ARMY

AT DAWN ON 20 MARCH 1643 SIR HUGH CHOLMLEY SNEAKED out of Scarborough disguised 'with a black patch over one eye'.[1] Cholmley was the third member of the triumvirate of parliamentarian commanders in the north (the others being Sir John Hotham and Lord Fairfax). He was also military governor of this Yorkshire port. He had used it successfully as a base from which to capture ships carrying arms for Henrietta Maria from the Low Countries and Scandinavia. He had hoped his success in taking it for Parliament would aid a negotiated settlement. He no longer had faith that Parliament wanted one. With 'the queen's promise' of safe passage he was now heading to see her at York.

A well-built, attractive city of 12,000 souls, York had been the home of Charles's court in 1642. Clusters of half-timbered houses and shops with projecting upper storeys stood in narrow medieval streets separated by gardens, orchards, and open spaces. Henrietta was soon to move into a gentleman's house in the city, but for the time being her headquarters were just outside it. Here she sat on the Earl of Newcastle's Councils of War. Henrietta Maria was not entirely impressed by his abilities. He was told that one of her ladies-in-waiting had said 'you were a sweet general, lay in bed until 11 o'clock and combed until 12, then came to the queen and so the work was done'.[2] He was a little too used to fine living: 'fantastic and inconstant' was how Henrietta Maria described him.[3] Nevertheless, as Henrietta Maria told Charles, she and Newcastle remained 'very good friends'.[4]

It was almost dark when Henry Jermyn brought Sir Hugh 'to kiss my hand', as she told Charles. Sir Hugh had made it plain he wanted to defect, but he wanted assurances, first that she would not discourage Charles from sticking to the promises he had already made to Parliament, and second that she would promote a peace.[5] Henrietta Maria did so and Sir Hugh agreed to hand over his garrison in three weeks. This would have given him the time to retrieve his wife and children from London, return his commission to General Essex and inform the garrison of his decision. He wanted to give them the choice to either leave or turn royalist with him. There was one difficulty: Sir John Hotham got wind of Sir Hugh's plans.

Sir Hugh narrowly avoided being assassinated by two Dutchmen on his return to Scarborough. This forced him to tell his men immediately of his plans. Only twenty, including the Dutch lieutenants, left to rejoin parliamentarian forces and on 30 March, an unusually hot day, Henrietta Maria wrote to tell Charles that Scarborough was theirs. It was an important success. The port was difficult to blockade, being more open to the North Sea than Newcastle. It was conveniently close to York and brought some immediate gains: a royalist ship that had been captured by Parliament with its arms was retrieved, and two parliamentarian pinnaces taken, 'which brought . . . ten pieces of cannon, four barrels of powder, four of bullet'.[6]

Henrietta Maria would soon have other good news to deliver. The dashing George Goring was, that very same day, leading his cavalry to victory against Thomas Fairfax at Seacroft Moor, north-east of Leeds. He would present her with 200 of the 800 prisoners he took.[7] Meanwhile, the queen had qualifications to make concerning her promises to Sir Hugh: 'I want a peace more than any', but 'I would the disbanding of this perpetual parliament first'. She appreciated that people would be fearful that a royalist parliament would then revoke statutes already passed, but, she believed, assurances could be made. On the other hand, if Charles did not dissolve it, he was in no better position than he was before the war. 'Why then have you taken arms?'[8] Nor was she 'willing again to fall into the hands of those people, being well assured, that if power remain with them, that it will not be well for me in England'.[9]

Indeed, in London, the queen's chapel at Somerset House was being destroyed that very afternoon.

30 March 1643 was Maundy Thursday, which marks Christ's Last Supper before the crucifixion. Yet there was no public Mass at Somerset House and the crowds of the past were gone. As the MPs Sir John Clotworthy and Henry Marten strode across the great court at Somerset House, the silence of the empty space was broken only by the discordant music of the soldiers clattering behind them. The war party had ordered the men to oversee the arrest of the Capuchin friars and the obliteration of all 'superstitious' images. Holland had argued that this would break an international agreement with France – the marriage treaty – to no avail. The chapel was a monument to Henrietta Maria's Catholic influence.

Marten and Clotworthy made a strange couple: Henry Marten was 'a great lover of pretty girls' and 'as far from a Puritan as light from darkness'. He had taken grave offence after Charles had once called him 'a whore master' and was motivated for the task ahead by little more than pique.[10] Clotworthy, by contrast, was a 'firebrand' Presbyterian who had murdered a hundred Irish prisoners in Ulster the previous year. He was possessed with a pious zeal.[11] There was now an explosion of sound as the soldiers smashed the doors to the friary. The friars inside were terrified, 'their house filled with soldiers and a multitude of other persons . . . pouring forth all sorts of abuse against papists, laughing at the Capuchins, taking away their slender store of provision and their furniture'.[12]

There was a pause in the violence with the soldiers given time to sell everything they could before returning to Somerset House that afternoon. The assault on the chapel then began. Clotworthy led the way, climbing on the altar to look at the Rubens crucifixion in its gilt frame.

'Calling for a halberd he struck Christ's face in contempt with such offensive words it would be shocking to repeat them' a French witness recorded. 'His second blow was at the Virgin's face, with more hateful blasphemies, and then thrusting the hook of his halberd under the feet of the crucified Christ, he ripped the painting to pieces'. The remains of the masterpiece were thrown in the Thames.[13]

The soldiers returned the following day, Good Friday, to take down Matthew Goodrich's and Thomas de Critz's enormous oval ceiling painting of the Assumption of the Virgin. They destroyed that too. A further order was now made against all idolatrous images at Whitehall, Hampton Court and Greenwich.[14] The medieval great cross at Cheapside was torn down by workmen who were guarded from angry Londoners by troops of horse, while orders went out against other crosses in churches across London. Even the royal tombs at Westminster Abbey weren't spared attack. The altarpiece in the Henry VII chapel – designed by Michelangelo's rival, Pietro Torrigiano, the sculptor who brought the Renaissance to England – was totally destroyed. It had featured under the altar a figure of Christ lying dead. It was, the Venetian ambassador mourned, 'one of the finest ornaments of this city, admired by all foreigners for its antiquity and the perfection of the beautiful marble carving'.[15]

If carved angels and figures of Christ were objects of fear and hate, still more so was the flesh-and-blood queen. It was being said there were 'six or seven thousand' Catholics in her 'popish' army and that Protestant soldiers in the East and West Ridings of Yorkshire had deserted, 'because the queen would have a new popish standard carried in front'.[16] It wasn't true, but the fact that Newcastle was willing to accept Catholics in his army at all helped to give it credence.

Susan Denbigh's husband died of his wounds after the royalist victory on 3 April 1643, when Prince Rupert sacked Birmingham. The queen comforted her lady-in-waiting, while also considering a political downside to the latest royalist success. Argyll's Scottish Covenanters believed Presbyterianism in Scotland would never be safe if Charles won the war in

England. In York Montrose reiterated his warning to Henrietta Maria that it was only a matter of time before the Covenanters invaded England on Parliament's side. She promptly dispatched a Scottish sergeant major to Scarborough with orders to send munitions to Scotland, some of which were intended for Montrose's ally, Antrim.

If Charles's armies were to be outnumbered by an Anglo-Scots alliance, the king needed urgently to recall the royalist army currently fighting the Catholic rebels in Ireland. To achieve that he needed first to make peace with the rebel 'government' – the Confederates. A royalist uprising in Scotland could, meanwhile, help delay the expected invasion – except the ammunition due to be sent to the Earl of Antrim was stopped.[17] Sir Hugh later claimed he managed to persuade the queen that helping Montrose would only encourage the Covenanters 'to take part with the Parliament' in the war.[18] In fact Charles had sent Hamilton to York to argue the case for restraint.[19] Charles, ever the procrastinator, was anxious that 'the first breach [with the Scots] should not come from his party; but they should draw things out as long as possible before they hazarded on a rupture'.[20]

Hamilton duly informed the queen 'That stout and warlike nation [Scotland] is not to be reduced by force of arms, but with gentleness and courtesies'. He then personally guaranteed Scottish neutrality.[21] This 'made the queen give little countenance to Montrose'.[22]

When Charles raised Hamilton to a dukedom on 12 April 1643, he told him it was given at her encouragement. Yet Charles made Hamilton's task that much more difficult after the duke returned to Scotland to argue for neutrality. When the Scottish commissioners arrived in Oxford, instead of tactfully demurring over their desire to see Presbyterianism established across the three kingdoms, he reminded them angrily that England's religious affairs were none of their business. By the time the Scots had left Oxford on 19 April Parliament had also recalled their peace delegation. Charles needed urgently to shore up the position of the moderate Covenanters. Letters were duly sent north assuring his Scottish subjects that their Covenant was safe in his hands.

He warned, prophetically, that it was Parliament's support from independent Protestants sects, many of which they regarded as heretical, that posed the true threat to Scotland. Henrietta Maria, meanwhile, was backing an aggressive military strategy in Yorkshire, anxious to win the war before any alliance was in place.

Rotherham fell to the royalists on 4 May, when they captured arms and £5,000 in cash. On 6 May they took Sheffield. Henrietta Maria was, however, given a brutal reminder of how finely balanced the opposing forces in England were on 20 May 1643. Parliamentarian forces under Thomas Fairfax captured George Goring and retook the garrison of Wakefield, which had fallen to the royalists only a few weeks earlier.[23] With Charles formally rejecting Parliament's peace terms the same day it became all the more urgent to find some means of matching the numbers. Henrietta Maria offered Charles's uncle, Christian of Denmark, the formerly Danish-held islands of Orkney and Shetland ('it only being a thing that concerns Scotland') in return for help in winning the war.[24] She also had fresh hopes of French help following the death of her brother Louis on 14 May.

Louis's health had never been good and he seems to have died of intestinal tuberculosis.[25] Anne of Austria was now regent for the four-year-old Louis XIV and Wat was close to her. 'I am, perhaps, the only disinterested person from whom you can take advice,' Wat had told her.[26] Anne had agreed, and had done as he suggested, keeping his friend Mazarin – who had been made a cardinal in 1641 – in office. Writing to Hamilton, Henrietta Maria relegated her grief for her brother to an afterthought, crowing that 'from France (except the death of the king my brother) I have very good news'. Already she was thanking Mazarin profusely 'for the proofs I daily receive of your affection.'[27]

Yet Charles was still going to need the royalist army brought back from Ireland. Henrietta Maria duly dispatched Antrim from York 'to persuade the Irish [Confederate rebels] to make reasonable propositions' for a ceasefire.[28] Charles pressed Henrietta Maria to now join him in Oxford, but she wanted to stay north: 'The rebels are grown strong and we are weakened since our loss [at Wakefield] . . . leave me to do what I shall judge fit for the good of your affairs in this country,' she asked.[29]

The Parliamentarian war party wanted Henrietta Maria's head more than ever. As the Venetian ambassador noted, they believed, 'without [the queen's] encouragement and aid the king would never have put himself into a position to resist'.[30]

On 23 May, three days after the final collapse of the peace talks with Charles, a debate was launched in the Commons on whether or not to proceed with the impeachment of the queen for treason. Pym argued that 'all the danger and mischief that has befallen this state has proceeded from her'. Another MP, Sir Peter Wentworth, concurred. It was 'high time to lay the axe to the root, as she was, of all their calamities'. Henry Marten, the MP who with Clotworthy had destroyed her chapel, added for good measure that they 'should not fear the dignity of her person, for he knew no person so high (he excepted none) but was subject to the law' and that he 'would not have her impeached by the name of queen, but of Henrietta Maria, wife to the king'.[31]

Moderate MPs rallied to the queen's defence. One warned that to put the king's wife on trial was 'a rejection of all means of peace and a sentence to fight it out to the last man', and 'so far from subduing papists, they were now under [i.e. subject to] the law, and if the sword were to decide the question the sword would be the law'. Another agreed that putting the queen on trial would be the law of brute force and that 'it would put all to trial by the sword' and that whatever they gained, 'must and would be maintained by it'.[32] Pym, nevertheless, convinced a majority that an impeachment 'may be for her good and theirs'.[33] So 'it was debated and fully agreed, that she was liable to the censure of the law, as any subject in the kingdom' and that her 'actual performance with her popish army' was 'high treason'.[34]

The template for beheading a consort had been set with the trial of Anne Boleyn, the first of Henry VIII's queen consorts to be executed.

Yet many of those who had voted with Pym preferred to obfuscate on whether or not they wished to see Henrietta Maria executed. Some convinced themselves that a guilty verdict at trial would result in nothing more than having the requirement to pray for her cut out of the Book of Common Prayer! This delusion reflected a nervousness concerning what the nature of the treason charge against her actually reflected. Anne Boleyn, like Katherine Howard, Jane Grey – and even Mary, Queen of Scots – had been found guilty of treason against the monarch. Henrietta Maria had committed treason against 'Parliament and kingdom (not naming the king but as included in these two words)', as one observer noted.[35] This was an attack on monarchical government and if Henrietta Maria was guilty of this new form of treason so, surely, was the king.

Twelve days later two parliamentarians, Henry Marten and the MP Sir Henry Mildmay, arrived at Westminster Abbey to take an inventory of the coronation regalia. Marten announced that 'there would be no further use of these toys and trifles' and dressed up an old Puritan called George Withers in the crown and relics. The man 'marched about the room with the stately garb' and exposed the once sacred objects to 'contempt and laughter'. Both MPs were future regicides.[36]

When Scottish forces in Ireland captured the Earl of Antrim in late May the queen assured Charles 'he has nothing of mine in writing'. Her name was exposed, nonetheless, when one of Antrim's servants revealed his plans to invade Scotland, 'for the ruin of religion, and overthrow of His Majesty's loyal subjects in all three dominions'.[37] Parliamentarian newsletters had a field day with the story and in Scotland too it caused a sensation. If Hamilton had ever stood any chance of keeping Scotland out of the English Civil War it was now blown. As one Scot observed, it 'wakened in all a great fear of our safety, and distrust of all the fair words that were or could be given us'.[38] Yet a rising in Scotland was still possible, 'For my own part, I shall contribute to the utmost of my power,' the queen told Montrose; 'When the arms that are coming from Denmark, and which I daily expect, have arrived, you shall have of them whatever you require.'[39]

Meanwhile Henrietta Maria had been ordered to come to Oxford with her army. She was 'enraged', she told Charles, that she had to leave York before they had taken Leeds, anxious that 'if I go away [the rascals] will not be beaten'.[40] Nevertheless, she realised she now had to go to him. On 3 June Henrietta Maria wrote to the Earl of Newcastle to suggest they meet twenty-eight miles from York at Pontefract for a Council of War. They did so the next day. The subject under discussion was whether the army should 'march up with the queen and so join with the king [as he wished] or . . . only give order for some regiments to wait upon Her Majesty'. Despite Charles's orders it was decided the bulk of the army should stay in the north, 'to lay siege to my Lord Fairfax in Leeds or fight him in the field'.[41]

Newcastle stayed in Pontefract, to prepare an assault on Bradford, while Henrietta Maria headed for Newark in Nottinghamshire. Situated on the Great North Road, the town connected the king's headquarters at Oxford with York and Newcastle in the north. She arrived on 16 June and took up residence in a modest two-storey house with projecting eaves that still stands.[42] The town's old medieval walls had been supplemented with earthenwork defences that had shrunk the size of the town, while its population had been increased by the garrison. The result was overcrowding, and an epidemic of typhus had broken out.

Two days later, a letter arrived from Charles insisting that the Earl of Newcastle bring his entire army to Oxford. Marie de' Medici had instructed Henrietta Maria in 1625 to obey her husband in all matters save religion, but Henrietta Maria had got used to keeping things from Charles when she took her mother's part in her conspiracies against Richelieu. She still got irritated when he opened letters to her from Wat Montagu and told him so.[43] Henrietta Maria now wrote to Newcastle to warn him that she was instructed by Charles 'to command you absolutely to march to [the king], but', she reassured him, 'I do not send it you, since I have taken a resolution with you that you remain'.[44]

Nor did she pay close attention to Charles's order that she hurry to Oxford.

Instead on 21 June the queen's forces attacked Nottingham. They were repulsed and although the parliamentary press greatly exaggerated their modest losses, a nephew of the Prince of Orange, the nineteen-year-old Heinrich zu Dohna, was killed in the assault.[45] He was buried in Newark on 27 June.[46] Henrietta was keen to attack Derby next, but Charles forbade any further delay to her journey. It was later said that when the women of Newark petitioned her to stay until she had taken Lincoln, she replied that she was obliged instead to set them an example in obedience to their husbands. She agreed to leave Newark on 30 or 31 June. As she set out for Whatton and then Ashby de la Zouch in Leicestershire, she discovered her decision to leave most of the army with Newcastle had paid off. Newcastle enjoyed a major victory over Lord Fairfax on 30 June at Adwalton Moor outside Bradford. The parliamentarians suffered over 500 dead and 15,000 prisoners were taken.

More disappointing was the news that Sir John Hotham, the parliamentary commander she had hoped to recruit, had been arrested. He had come under suspicion, as had his son, who had quarrelled with a Puritan MP and army officer called Oliver Cromwell, a cavalry commander serving under Wat's parliamentarian brother, Edward, formerly Viscount Mandeville and now Earl of Manchester. Cromwell 'had a special care to get religious men in his troop' who 'were more apprehensive of the importance and consequence of the war, and making not money but that which they took for the public felicity'.[47] Young Hotham had regarded them as mere fanatics calling them, 'Brownists, Anabaptists, [and] factious, inferior persons'.[48] A handkerchief embroidered with Henrietta Maria's image was found amongst their possessions.[49]

In London Pym was now pressing the House of Lords 'to pass the impeachment against the queen, and a proclamation for her appearance to answer the same by a certain day'.[50] Still, she remained optimistic.

'I leave two thousand foot, and where-withall to arm five hundred more, and twenty companies of horse,' Henrietta Maria wrote to Charles, 'all this to be under Charles Cavendish who the gentlemen of the country have desired me not to carry with me – against his will for he desired extremely to go.' Indeed, their relationship was the latest of her rumoured affairs, largely forgotten after Cavendish was killed in battle on 28 July, run through with a sword by a Captain Berry.[51] 'We have done our business,' Cromwell is reported to have said on learning of his death.[52]

'Harry Jermyn commands the forces that go with me as colonel of my guards,' she added. They included 'three thousand foot, thirty companies of horse and dragoons, six pieces of cannon and two mortars'. She listed other commanders, concluding with herself, who was in charge of 150 wagons of baggage, 'as she-majesty generalissima . . . in case of battle'.[53] As reports spread of her advance, 'with an army of outlandish papists to destroy the religion of the land', fear was struck into parliamentarian hearts.[54] Instructions were issued in churches for people to 'oppose that accursed popish army of the queen's', and to destroy medieval church monuments and market crosses: symbols of the old faith.[55] Here was a 'Hogen-Mogen [High and Mighty] Princess' ready with her Dutch weapons 'to swallow up us and our religion'.[56] The roundheads would soon discover they indeed had good reason to be afraid.

OXFORD

BURTON UPON TRENT HAD BEEN FAMOUS BEFORE THE Reformation for its alabaster carving, selling goods across Europe. Now it was just a poor cloth town, but it possessed a strategic river crossing that was judged 'the chief passage from South to the North'. It lay only eight miles from Ashby de la Zouch: a tempting target for Henrietta Maria. It was strongly parliamentarian and garrisoned with 200 foot, sixty dragoons, as well as cannon, but the town lacked walls or, except on its east side, natural defences. Twice, on 4 July 1643, the military governor Colonel Richard Houghton was asked to surrender the town. When 'he had that rebellious impudence to stand it out the third time', the royalist Colonel Thomas Tyldesley led the charge across the twenty-nine-arch Trent bridge.[1]

For eight hours the roundhead garrison and the citizens of Burton battled to keep the queen's forces out of the town, 'the women making bullets while the men fought it out bravely'.[2] Elsewhere in the Civil War, other women took the same role for one side or the other. Eventually the royalists broke through, entering Burton on three sides and there was a 'bloody' and 'desperate' fight. In St Modwen's Church in the marketplace thirty roundheads were holed up, protecting their gunpowder store. They killed several cavaliers before setting light to the gunpowder and fleeing. It exploded, blowing out the church windows and destroying the roof as well as killing several more cavaliers.[3]

The victorious royalists took their revenge, brutally plundering the town, not leaving anything 'worth a groat'.[4]

There were later reports that there was also mass rape with women throwing themselves into the river, and over twenty bodies retrieved.[5] A parliamentarian newsletter nearer the time mentions only one murder of a civilian who was 'cut to pieces' after he was mistaken for a cannoneer who had killed a large number of cavaliers 'with his great shot'.[6] A royalist newsletter also noted that the queen 'forbad any violence to be offered to the town'.[7]

The fact the women had helped make bullets that had killed royalist soldiers may well, however, have given some men all the pretext they needed to justify rape – and it is clear there was anger against the role women had played. The 400 parliamentarian soldiers and officers taken prisoner included Houghton's wife, a 'seditious lady who (to the disgrace of her sex) showed herself as active against the queen's majesty as her husband and his fellow rebels had been against the king'.[8] She was taken to Ashby with her husband and the captain of the garrison. There they were to be bartered for royalist captives.

The ordinary men were marched in ropes to Tamworth where they were imprisoned with no food for several days, and little water. There wasn't, perhaps, much food to give them. Even Henrietta Maria complained of hunger. She hadn't eaten meat for days and was soon on the road again. The queen spent the night of 7 July at Croxall in a house belonging to the Countess of Dorset, governess to her youngest children. It was about seventeen months since Henrietta Maria had last seen Harry and Elizabeth. Her daughter was now seven while Harry turned three the next day. She spent his birthday on the road to the Staffordshire town of Walsall. She had little time to think of a missed celebration, she had scarcely slept three hours a night since she had left Newark. Yet, she told Charles, 'all this is a pleasure for me because it is done for you and to let you see by all my actions that I have no delight but to serve you'. She intended to rest for a day with her army so her men could sell their loot; they had taken so much plunder at Burton 'they cannot walk with the bundles which they will not quit'.[9]

Meanwhile the queen had good news from France to share with Charles. Wat Montagu had informed her that 'thence you shall have what you desire'. Not only arms but perhaps ships also, and that Madame de Chevreuse 'governs all there and has declared herself your agent'.[10] Charles ordered Prince Rupert and his forces to now join the queen, concerned 'for the more secure conveying of our dearest consort'.[11] If she came to him via Stratford, he feared 'the Earl of Essex may force her to fight'. It was, as Charles had thought, a dangerous route. On the night of 10 July Henrietta Maria was at King's Norton, heading for Stratford-upon-Avon when the governor of Warwick, Colonel John Bridges, attacked part of her baggage train. There were reports too of the 'grinning dwarf', Lord Grey of Groby, and Oliver Cromwell drawing their forces towards Dunsmore Heath 'to intercept the queen in her passage'.[12] Rupert and his army had, however, joined the queen, 'His dragoons double-armed' according to a parliamentary report, riding their horses 'with a musket in front and behind an Irish whore furnished with a strong water bottle'.[13]

When the queen escaped interception, a royalist newsletter crowed that Rupert's appearance had sent the roundheads scuttling away and 'the brave captains [Grey and Cromwell] made so much haste as any, to hide their faces from the dreadful prince'.[14]

Meanwhile, the bells of Stratford rang for the queen and the prince as they entered the town: Henrietta Maria in a coach with porters and footmen sent by the mayor. A feast awaited the hungry queen: chicken, quail, red meat, beer, bread and cheese with the biggest expense lavished on cakes.

According to a story dating back to at least 1733, Henrietta Maria stayed at the house of Shakespeare's granddaughter Elizabeth and her husband Thomas Nash. It is probable that she did so. The only house that was grander belonged to a Puritan. On the other hand, Elizabeth was close in age to the queen while her mother, Shakespeare's daughter

Susanna, who lived with her, was 'witty above her sex'. Henrietta Maria knew Shakespeare's work well (she had once sponsored a performance of *Richard III* for the king) and could hardly have resisted the opportunity of the amusing company of the child and grandchild of a writer who was already a legend.[15]

The next day Prince Rupert took a coachful of Henrietta Maria's ladies to a local manor house, to pick fruit in the gardens. The queen, meanwhile, prepared for her reunion with her husband and elder sons, which was to take place at Kineton, by the battlefield of Edgehill. When she was in Holland she had been assured many times that Charles and the Prince of Wales were captured or killed. Now she would be able to embrace them again. On Thursday 13 July Henrietta Maria set off on this last leg of her journey while Charles, 'attended by many of his Lords, the gentlemen of his troop, and many others of his officers and faithful servants' rode from Banbury to meet her, 'Prince Charles and the Duke of York, riding also forth to receive the blessings of so dear and so renowned a mother'.[16]

There had been 'much preparation for the queen's entertainment' at Kineton and 'great multitudes' of country people from the surrounding district came to witness the reunion, with its 'due solemnities and mutual caresses'.[17] Henrietta appeared with her army and all the munitions she had brought, sending up clouds of dust, the mighty queen 'by the help of Holland, Generalissima'.[18] A royalist account described the queen greeting Charles with 'cheerfulness', her smiles 'breaking like daylight from her face'. The crowd was ecstatic, the 'loud and joyful acclamations' of the husband and wife's reunion making 'it little less triumphant than their wedding day'.[19]

'You're come at last!' a poet announced, 'In vain whole hosts desir'd t'oppose your course / And wished but for your Spirit to meet your Force / 'Tis here a woman leads; but one would swear / The armies did consist of women there'. In other words she had unmanned the enemy. For Charles she achieved the opposite. Here was 'Henry's child', daughter of a French warrior king, but also the wife of an

English king at war. What 'Brought the most artillery' the poet asked, 'her train for war' or 'The warm embraces of a fair, chaste wife'?[20] The latter was linked to a royalist victory that took place that day. Charles and Henrietta Maria were in Moreton when news arrived of a major royal success at Roundway Down in Wiltshire: 'two happy stars conjoined . . . Ye kissed and thousand rebels straight were slain'. A medal would be struck in commemoration, depicting king and queen, with a dragon – representing rebellion – dead at their feet.

The next day, 14 July 1643, they left Moreton and entered the king's Civil War capital at Oxford, sitting together on view in a carriage, Prince Rupert and the Duke of Richmond riding beside them in a great procession of soldiers, nobles and heralds. The streets had been strewn with flowers and were lined with soldiers, 'their muskets charged', while behind them, 'every house by or near which she was to pass thronged with spectators to behold her'. A speech was delivered at Carfax and the queen was presented with a purse of gold. At Christ Church, where the king was based, 'she was waited on by the vice chancellor and the heads of houses' who presented her with a book of poetry dedicated to her and pairs of fine gloves. She was then taken to Merton College, 'which was provided for her lodging', and where private passage had been created running through the gardens to the King's rooms in Christ Church, 'the common people following all the way with loud acclamations'.[21]

On 15 July, '150 carriages of cannon arms and ammunition which the queen's majesty bought with her' was brought into town.[22] On 26 July, Prince Rupert made good use of both the arms and her men to take the port of Bristol. Charles was now winning the war.

It was from a position of strength that, on 30 July, the king issued a declaration advertising his commitment to a peace process. He reaffirmed his promise to uphold the true Protestant Reformed Religion, as well as the liberties of Parliament and the known laws of the land. He attached all blame for the war to a 'committee of a few men' – namely the leaders of the parliamentary war party – and promised mercy to all those who returned to their loyalty to the king. The end, it seemed, was at last in sight.

Did Henrietta Maria find her elder sons, now aged thirteen and nine, much changed after the battles they had witnessed? Their cousin Lord d'Aubigny, killed at Edgehill, had had a state funeral in Oxford in January. The driver of the black velvet-covered hearse showered money as he drove through the streets, the pikemen in the procession trailing their pikes on the ground, the musketeers giving three volleys of shot as the body entered Christ Church Cathedral. There had been many other funerals since and men left mutilated. Thirty cartloads of injured soldiers had arrived in Oxford on 12 July alone.[23] Sir Nicholas Slanning had returned from Bristol on 26 July shot in the thigh, but the wound 'swelled, grew black, stank, whereof he died'.[24] Charles Cavendish was killed two days later.

James was always playing at soldiers and showed more interest in guns than books. It seemed less of a game to Prince Charles, who showed compassion for those who couldn't stand the horrors. Three men who had been due to be hanged in March for cowardice were spared when 'word was brought that the prince had begged all their lives'.[25] For others the violence on the battlefields begat violence in the town. A soldier had been executed recently for the rape and murder of a poor woman, while fights and duels were commonplace. Prince Rupert once had to use a poleaxe to separate two officers who were intent on killing each other. There were dangers of assassination too. It is possible the charged muskets of the guard that lined the street on the queen's arrival had been arranged for the queen's protection. Parliament had many supporters in Oxford. There was also the more pervasive threat of typhus. Here, as in Newark, there was overcrowding, especially in west Oxford where the poorest troops lived cheek by jowl.[26]

A version of court life continued nevertheless. Charles still dined in state, but the aristocrats who served him had moved from their fine pre-war houses 'to lie in a very bad bed'. The masques were finished, 'because Inigo Jones cannot conveniently make such heavens and paradise as he did at Whitehall', the roundheads sneered, 'and because the poets are dead, beggared or run away'.[27] In fact many had turned their hands to new skills, while keeping up as best they could with the old. Inigo Jones designed fortifications – notably for Basing House in Hampshire. The Poet Laureate William Davenant, who came and went from Oxford as the queen's agent and gun runner, also wrote verses for an entertainment that was put on for her that summer.[28] The new favoured court artist was William Dobson, who lived on the High Street and had gained his reputation with a portrait of Sir John Byron, freshly scarred by a cut in the face from a halberd.

The king's Declaration of 30 July gave hope that a peace process could begin. It had dispelled fears amongst parliamentarian MPs that Charles 'meant an utter conquest of them', and strengthened those, like Henry Holland, who were seeking an accommodation. On 2 August Holland set up a new parliamentary committee to prepare peace propositions. Within the week, however, London was rocked by mob violence instigated by the war-party grandees. They also had a delegation in Scotland where their emissaries were soliciting 'their brethren there to aid them in their rebellion'.[29] On 9 August when fresh protests were mounted in London by women allied to the peace party, the protesters found themselves under a hail of bullets. Henrietta Maria wanted Charles to take advantage of the unrest and retake London.

The parliamentarian army under the Earl of Essex was decimated by disease and desertions while the royalists had the opportunity, the men, and increasingly the arms. The capture of Bristol was paying dividends: a ship had just docked 'by the queen's procurement, with great store of arms, especially pistols, grenades and . . . roundshot'.[30] Charles took his army to besiege Gloucester instead. He was backed by Rupert, but Henrietta Maria was reported as weeping with frustration 'that the king wasted his army so before Gloucester and would not rather hasten for London and Kent'.[31] She told Newcastle that the king's decision had given 'dissatisfaction to everybody here' and in her view 'with reason.'[32]

In London many peace-party MPs left the Commons for good, too frightened by the mob violence to return. Six peers defected to the royalists. The Earl of Holland was one, appearing on 15 August at the royalist garrison at Wallingford, thirteen miles south of Oxford. When he 'sent word that if the king now marched towards London the city itself would compel the Parliament to make peace', Henrietta Maria insisted Charles return to Oxford.[33] He did so on 16 August 1643 and spent the next two days deciding how, or if, to receive Holland and another defecting peer, the Earl of Bedford. The queen's former favourite didn't help matters with Charles by offering no apology for his past actions. He wanted what he had always wanted: an old-style Puritan religious settlement, with constitutional liberties enforced. He wasn't going to say sorry for that moderate stand.

Charles listened to his counsellors' advice about the defectors without expressing his own views, 'save that he seemed well pleased with any sharpness expressed towards the Earl of Holland.'[34] Henrietta Maria took a more pragmatic view. Whatever she felt on a personal level about Holland's past betrayals she was keen to be generous in the hope of attracting other defectors. She made this so plain that his old rivals even began to fear his return to influence. Eventually Charles agreed that Holland could return, but he did so only after he had left Oxford for Gloucester. There was to be no fatted calf for the prodigal son. In Oxford other peers took note and gave Holland a cold welcome. Even Henrietta Maria felt obliged not to appear overly enthusiastic at seeing him, 'not out of disinclination or any unwillingness to show any [warmth] but pure compliance with the ill humour of the town, which she detested'.[35]

The parliamentary press was quick to blame the queen for Holland's treatment, but it was surely Henrietta Maria who suggested to her old friend that it would show commitment if he joined the army at Gloucester, as he did a few days later. Charles then began talking to Holland, but the damage had already been done. Other possible defectors backed off, notably Lucy Carlisle's proud brother, the Earl of Northumberland.

The king's decision to ignore his wife's advice concerning Gloucester also proved to be a mistake. While royalist forces were tied up there Parliament had time to reinforce Essex's army. On 5 September Essex and a freshly bolstered army of 15,000 were able to relieve the siege at Gloucester and headed back to London. Charles tried to cut him off at Newbury, but failed. Amongst those who died in the battle was the playboy Earl of Carnarvon whose dragoons had been in the vanguard of the successful assault on Bristol. He was run through with a sword by a roundhead who recognised him after he was returning from a cavalry charge. Three days later Henrietta Maria wrote to the Earl of Newcastle. She tried to be upbeat. Although it had not been a 'total defeat' for the enemy at Newbury, and the royalists had lost 'a great number of honest men', nevertheless 'our people, who I brought with me have not done badly'.[36]

A turning point had, however, been reached. Henrietta Maria had fought hard for Charles to win before the Scots entered the war, and so nearly succeeded. Her wish for her husband to take London and her frustration that her advice had been ignored was a moment she would return to again and again in the years ahead. It would be remembered even in the oration given at her funeral. A sense of defeatism hung over Oxford. 'I am so weary, not of being beaten, but of having heard it spoken of,' Henrietta Maria confessed.[37] The only hope lay in Ireland where a cessation of arms with the rebels was at last agreed on 15 September 1643. Parliament's alliance with the Scots was largely in place and in October an advance guard of three troops of Scottish horse and 600 foot crossed into the English border town of Berwick.

'A DISTRESSED WANDERING PRINCESS'

TROUBLE SEEMED TO BE FOLLOWING WAT AROUND AND HE HAD made some very bad new enemies. Whereas he and Madame de Chevreuse had shared many a plot against Richelieu, they had soon discovered they felt very differently about Mazarin. The court beauty hadn't, at first, realised that Wat's friendship with this cardinal was quite genuine, so she had told him of her plans to engineer Mazarin's fall. As a long-standing favourite of Anne's she had foreseen no difficulties, but when Wat learned of a possible plot by some of the leading figures at court to assassinate Mazarin, he had reported it. 'The Important Ones', as an observer called them, were now 'furious with Montagu'.[1] It seemed an opportune moment to leave France and rejoin Henrietta Maria at Oxford. He could pass unnoticed through England, he believed, if he arrived in the train of the French ambassador, the Count of Harcourt.

On 7 October 1643, when the ambassador and his suite reached Rochester, the roundhead captain of the town guard arrived to inspect the retinue. Wat feared he might be recognised after all and so 'besmutched' his face and 'put on a very great perriwig'.[2] Unfortunately his extravagant wig only attracted attention, and the parliamentarian officer 'well viewing all the ambassador's retinue [and] observing one amongst the rest in a disguised habit . . . was somewhat inquisitive to speak with him'. Wat made a run for it, 'went to take horse and ride away'.[3] He was caught. Letters to Charles and Henrietta Maria were found on him and he was taken to the Tower.

The queen was annoyed that Wat had chosen 'to amuse himself' with his disguise and observed it was 'great misfortune to me' that they would not be reunited.[4] Mazarin was also saddened, begging his ambassador to secure Wat's release: 'He is my special friend.'[5] The war party in Parliament had little incentive to do so. They had discovered the ambassador had brought £20,000 for Henrietta Maria as a gift from Anne. Wat would remain in the Tower for four unhappy years. They took a more personal revenge on Harcourt. After the ambassador had set off for Oxford, armed men broke into his London residence and stole his silver. Parliament issued a reward to catch the thieves, but the wider diplomatic community reported this did not 'affect the belief that it has been done by some secret order, out of resentment for the money taken to the queen'.[6]

At Oxford Harcourt was greeted with a nine-gun salute and lodged at St John's College where king and queen visited him for two hours on 19 October 1643. Henrietta Maria was said to have returned to Merton weeping openly.[7] The following day there were smiles instead of tears at a banquet for Harcourt at Christ Church. Henrietta Maria's emotional displays were a public performance intended to reassure royalists that France was offering them substantial support. The truth was that while Wat had succeeded in fanning Mazarin's fears of a parliamentarian victory, France could not afford to invest heavily in Charles.

The economic demands of fighting the Thirty Years' War continued to exacerbate existing problems in the tax structure of France which fell hardest on the peasants and urban lower classes. Neither Mazarin nor Anne of Austria wished to pile further financial pressures on the system.

Mazarin planned for France to remain officially neutral and avoid offending Parliament, while offering the royalists covert support. Yet he did not want an outright win for Charles. After all, Charles had been to war with France in the 1620s and might go to war with France in the future. What he now sought was a negotiated peace to end the English Civil War that would restore a weakened king. The question was how to reach acceptable terms with Parliament.

The ambassador found Henrietta Maria had 'an intense desire for peace'.[8] She spent many afternoons with Holland in her rooms at Merton. She listened as he spoke 'of the great wisdom and power of Parliament, and what great things they would be able to do'.[9] She had heard similar things in 1641 from Suckling and Davenant. She had proven herself willing to try and encourage the king to make dramatic concessions in the past and would do so again. But would this parliament ever be prepared to make an acceptable peace? Of that she was less sure. To force their hand Charles would need to negotiate from a position of parity or strength. This was the view of the royalist war party, a mixed bag of swordsmen and courtiers, Calvinists and Catholics, of which she was head.

Henrietta Maria's efforts to engage the King of Denmark had failed because of Danish mistrust in Charles's tepid assurances concerning Orkney. She was trying, more in hope than expectation, to broker a marriage treaty in which the Prince of Wales would be betrothed to her niece, Gaston's daughter, the now thirteen-year-old Grande Mademoiselle. Harcourt also made all sorts of assurances of a possible offensive and defensive league with Charles if peace terms were not reached, but she suspected, rightly, that this was hot air. That left only the controversial repatriation of the English army in Ireland. By November, the first contingents of these Protestant royalist troops were being shipped home. But Charles continued to deny Irish Catholics the same religious rights he had granted the Presbyterian Scots, and so the cessation of arms with the Confederate rebels they had been fighting was only a temporary fix.

There was no peace treaty in Ireland, and despite the fears of English Protestants, and the myth of Charles's crypto-Catholicism, very few Irish Catholics wished to fight for a king who was their persecutor. The fact Lord George Digby, who was largely in charge of Irish policy in Oxford, was ready to accept these few nevertheless appalled many of Charles's supporters, including even Prince Rupert, a leading figure in the war party. To Henrietta Maria, who was doing her own bit to support her Protestant husband, this prejudice against Catholic troops was incomprehensible and she worked hard to keep even Holland – who hated the Catholic Irish – within the fold.

The queen understood that to win over moderates, royal forgiveness of past betrayals had to be demonstrated in concrete terms. Holland wanted his former position as Groom of the Stool – the king's closest body servant. He had had assurances he would get it from her favourite Henry Jermyn before he had defected. Unfortunately, 'though the queen was gracious' and 'did in truth heartily desire that he might receive satisfaction in all things', Charles 'was always upon his guard' with Holland and 'did not abate in any of his former rigour or prejudice and continued in his former resolutions'.[10] To her irritation, Charles offered the post to the Marquess of Hertford instead. She tried to persuade Hertford – who had Tudor blood – that carrying the king's turds was beneath him, but on 6 November 1643, Hertford was confirmed as Groom of the Stool.[11] Holland re-defected to Parliament the very next day. Four of Holland's fellow defectors would soon join him in London.

Henrietta Maria had greater success in patching up other quarrels. She reached out to Rupert, with whom she had disagreed over the siege of Gloucester, and, with Jermyn's help, was spectacularly successful in doing so. She also pushed ahead in her efforts to get men and arms from Europe. Lord Goring was in Paris and had sent 20,000 muskets home by January. William Davenant was acquiring further weaponry in Holland – with the roundheads claiming that 'No man . . . hath been a greater enemy to Parliament.'[12] Briefly she entered negotiations for another marriage alliance, this time between Prince Charles and the daughter of the Prince of Orange. Yet she was beginning to feel overwhelmed by the scale of the task ahead.[13]

On 3 January 1644 the House of Lords assigned the articles of impeachment against the 'Lady Henrietta Maria, Queen of England' to committee, taking the process forward. Then, on 19 January, the first units of 21,000 Scots crossed the river Tweed into England. Camp fever was raging through Oxford and Henrietta Maria was not only unwell with a persistent cough, but also pregnant again.

On 22 January 1644 Charles opened a session of the Long Parliament in Oxford. He hoped moderate MPs and peers would make a peace agreement and raise taxes for his armies to oppose the Scottish invasion. Most of the House of Lords and about a third of the Commons came, but they suggested that as a goodwill gesture, Charles should first give up the army plotters of 1641 as traitors. Charles had already sworn he would not give up another servant as he had Strafford, and Henrietta Maria stiffened his resolve. If he sacrificed friends like Henry Percy and Henry Jermyn, no one would stand by him, she warned, and there was no reason why they would not ask for her also.

The parliamentarian press claimed that 'half a dozen of the queen's closet' ensured the king reversed all further efforts to reach an accommodation and that the Speaker of the House of Commons conducted 'the next day's debate according to the wishes of the queen'.

In fact, Henrietta Maria wanted a ceasefire at the very least. As she told the newly made Marquess of Newcastle, 'the truth is, the king's army here needs it'. The trouble was that, with the Scots behind them, the parliamentarian war party had no incentive to offer reasonable terms, 'and are so haughty . . . that they will make no propositions'.[14]

The royalists were already being pushed into retreat. Montrose now had his royal commission to serve as captain general of the king's forces in Scotland, but had yet to achieve anything. The royalist army in Ireland had returned about 10,000 troops to England, but had been defeated in Cheshire and had failed to stop a Covenanter–parliamentarian advance in the north. By the time the Oxford parliament was prorogued on 16 April 1644, the Marquess of Newcastle had been driven back to York and he faced the advance through Lincolnshire of Wat Montagu's brother, the Earl of Manchester, and his Lieutenant General of Horse, Oliver Cromwell. It would not be long before parliamentarian forces would be able to focus on attacking Oxford.

Henrietta Maria, now seven months pregnant, decided it was time to leave England again. She needed to be in Paris if they were to stand any chance of the French intervening militarily in the English Civil War. 'There is no more hope of the treaties of peace, therefore nothing must be thought of but fighting well,' she told Newcastle.[15] Rupert made it clear he was very disappointed at Henrietta Maria's imminent 'remove from Oxford'. It was said 'he willingly receives orders from no one else'.[16] But she had made her decision.

The following day Henrietta Maria said farewell to Charles at Abingdon, eight miles from Oxford. They clung to each other while he reassured her that she had made the right decision; 'who would liberate me from the hands and snares of these ungrateful wretches, and who can procure me aid better than you?' Henrietta Maria told her eldest son she felt so numb after she said goodbye that she had travelled 'ten leagues' before 'I became conscious that I had left him'.[17] Her first stop was the spa town of Bath. She hoped the waters would improve her health, but her 'rheum' only seemed to get worse and there was little time to rest. She left the following day for Bristol and was at Bridgwater on 28 April. By 3 May she was at Exeter. Rumours that the queen had miscarried her baby and had died were rife, and indeed she was seriously unwell.

Henrietta Maria wrote to the Huguenot doctor who had helped deliver Prince Charles fourteen years earlier, asking him to come to her to help deliver her latest child: 'My indisposition does not permit me to write much to beg you to come . . . I will only say this, having always in my recollection the care you have taken of me in my necessities, which makes me believe you will come if you can.'[18] Anne of Austria despatched the midwife Madame Peronne. Childbirth was always dangerous and Henrietta Maria wrote to Charles as she prepared for labour, warning that 'perhaps this will be the last letter you will ever receive from me. The weak state in which I am, caused by the cruel pains I have suffered . . . makes me believe that it is time to think of another world . . . Let it not trouble you I beg. By preparing for the worst we are never taken by surprise, and good fortune appears so much the greater. Adieu, my dear heart. I hope before I leave you to see you once again in the position in which you ought to be.'[19]

On Sunday 16 June the queen delivered 'a fair princess' whom she was to name Henrietta Anne.[20] Five days later the baby was given a Protestant baptism, in accordance with Charles's wishes, in Exeter Cathedral. Henrietta Maria was even weaker now and her doctor did not think she would live long. She described 'a seizure of paralysis in the legs and all over the body', her bowels and stomach felt as if they weighed 'a hundred pounds', and 'so tightly squeezed in the region of the heart that I was suffocating . . . at times I am like a person poisoned. I can scarcely stir and am doubled up. The same weight is also upon my back: one of my arms has no feeling, and my legs and knees are colder than ice. This disease has risen to my head. I cannot see with one eye.'[21]

The queen was also frightened by the possibility of capture: the Earl of Essex was threatening to besiege the city. So determined was Essex to seize his prize that his army had bypassed royalist strongholds and left pockets of resistance to his rear to get to Exeter as quickly as possible. Henrietta Maria begged Essex 'to forbear any acts of hostility towards the town for that she was weak and ill being lately brought to bed there'.[22] Essex replied that if she gave herself up, he would happily escort her to London where 'the air . . . would be . . . more healthy'.[23] Anxious as she was, Henrietta Maria asked Charles not to respond by sending an army to protect her: 'your affairs . . . would be in danger if you came to help me, and I know that your affection would make you risk everything for that'. 'I would rather set out on the road towards Falmouth [in Cornwall], to pass from thence to France . . . nothing is so much in my thoughts as your preservation, and my own life is of very little consequence compared with that.'[24]

Shortly afterwards she left her newborn baby in the care of Lady Dalkeith and fled the city with a small group of servants. 'Was it necessary that you be born in the power of the enemies of your house?' a French priest asked of Henrietta Anne – or Minette as the future Charles II would call her. 'Holy angels range around her and place your invisible squadrons as guards around the cradle of a princess, so great and so forsaken.'[25]

Henrietta Maria felt her powerlessness to protect her newborn acutely.

The parliamentarian general Sir William Waller later recalled that on her way the queen stopped

> at the cottage of a poor woman whom she heard making doleful cries. She sent one of her train to know what is was that occasioned it; the page returned and said the woman was sorrowing grievously, because her daughter had been two days in the straw, and was almost dead from lack of nourishment, she having nothing to give her but water, and not being able for the hardness of the times to get any. On this the queen took a small chain of gold from her neck, which hung an agnus [a lamb representing Christ as the 'lamb of God'], and put it to her bosom, and having the woman called to her, gave her the chain and had her go into the city to a goldsmith, and sell it and keep the money for the [child] in the straw.[26]

Her baby had to be cared for by others: at least she could help this one.

On 3 July a gentleman described seeing Henrietta Maria near Cornwall; 'the woefellest spectacle ever my eyes beheld; the most worn and pitiful creature in the world'.[27] She was too ill to go on and she returned to Exeter. In the Tower Wat Montagu was smuggled a letter which informed him that 'the lady who loved him, had three infirmities, namely vapours, paralysis and depression of spirits'.[28] The Venetian ambassador also heard that her doctor 'cannot promise that she will be out of danger for weeks'.[29] Within a few days, however, he reported 'the queen, though suffering greatly in body, yet with a spirit worthy of the great Henry her father' set off from Exeter again.[30]

Henrietta Maria wrote to Charles from Falmouth as she prepared to set sail on Saturday 13 July 1644: 'Adieu my dear heart, If I die believe you will lose a person who has never been other than entirely yours.'[31] In London it was being said that all her children were to be excluded from the throne as bastards sired by her lovers. Vice Admiral Batten had again been dispatched by Warwick to capture or kill the queen, with no holds barred.[32] The following morning his sailors spotted ten or eleven royalist ships heading out to sea. Henrietta Maria was on the Dutch man-of-war, the *George*. She had a fast galley of sixteen oars on which to make a getaway if her ship was boarded, but she told the captain that if she could not escape, then he should blow the gunpowder in the hold.[33]

A parliamentarian naval officer described their attack on the queen's ship: Batten 'gave [the *George*] twelve guns in his quarter, but he without any reply got out to winward and then made out all his sail. The rest of the ships, being ten in number, followed him and getting the advantage of the wind, avoided all annoyance from our ships.' The fleet had not yet escaped, however, for 'a nimble frigate of ours got into play and made the enemy use their ordnance for their own safety'. The ships continued firing at each other 'to the very borders of France, where they took in at Brest and there landed Her Majesty'.[34] Henrietta Maria's opponents were pleased to see the back of her. 'May the wind never permit her to return the third time into England,' a newssheet prayed, 'may all her designs frustrate, and may that mischief she intends towards this kingdom fall on her own head.'[35]

Henrietta Maria had not in fact landed in Brest, as the sea captain had reported, but twenty-five kilometres away at L'Aber Ildut. There her first task was to persuade the locals her servants were not pirates. Her party included Henry Jermyn, the dwarf Jeffrey Hudson, Susan, the Countess of Denbigh, the Duchess of Richmond, Father Phillip, and

Monsieur and Madame Vantelet, who had been with her since child-hood. They made strange pirates, but the coast was regularly raided and the whole area was in arms, so they carefully raised a staff with a handkerchief on it.[36] Henrietta Maria then explained to the locals that she was Queen of England, while looking, she recalled, more like 'a distressed wandering princess from a romance'.

Messengers were sent post-haste to Paris, local dignitaries swept in and the queen, along with twenty-five of her suite, was accompanied to Brest. There she rested for a couple of days before she set out on a slow and stately progress towards Paris. Every possible honour was heaped on Henrietta Maria as the returning daughter of Henry the Great. The *Gazette de France* described the formal entry at each town: rows of gentlemen and hundreds of armed guards would greet her at the outskirts, speeches were delivered, gifts presented (including velvets embroidered with her arms and basins of pure gold). She was then carried on litters down streets hung with tapestry, processions of infantry before her and cavalry behind. In churches and cathedrals she would hear Mass and the great hymn of thanks, the 'Te Deum' was sung. For Henrietta Maria it must have been a relief to be in a country where her faith was not vilified and attacked. At home Parliament was displaying a painting belonging to Charles that depicted early Christians, but which they had interpreted as an image of Henrietta Maria persuading Charles to offer England to the Pope. A new pamphlet explained that she was able to use her sexual powers 'under the royal curtains' to make it seem that 'darkness' was 'light'.[37]

As her progress continued contingents of the French nobility joined her on the road and huge crowds began following her, 'because of the memory of Henry IV'.[38]

When she reached the village of Sainte-Anne-d'Auray, Henrietta Maria asked to stop to pray at a newly built shrine to St Anne, the mother of the Virgin Mary.[39] She was suffering a cyst in her breast – a reminder that she was a newly delivered mother – and as she prayed she collapsed in pain and with a serious fever. She spent that night in Vannes, on the rue de Chanoine, where her stay is still commemorated: 'Henrietta Maria, daughter of Henri IV of France, wife of Charles I, fleeing the English revolution, rested here'.

Six days later on 13 August she was at Ancenis and, feeling better briefly, she penned a note to Charles. 'I have been everywhere received with such honours and marks of affection by everyone, from the greatest to the least, as could not be imagined. I think you will be very glad of it.'[40] The queen thought her fever might have been caused by the breast abscess. Happily, 'The physicians whom I sent for from Paris have arrived,' she told him.[41] One had served her mother, the other she had known as a child. It was recommended that Henrietta Maria take the waters in the spa town of Bourbon-l'Archambault, rather than heading more directly to Paris. She set off with her train at 5 p.m. the next day. The diarist John Evelyn reported Henrietta Maria reached Tours on 18 August and 'was very nobly received by people and clergy who went to meet her'. Evelyn, who had fought briefly for the royalists, kissed her hand at the archbishop's palace. At Amboise two days later, Hennrietta Maria wrote again to Charles and told him her health continued to improve. Anne of Austria had sent her money and a patent for a pension of 30,000 livres a month as a daughter of France. 'I am so well treated everywhere, that if my lords of London saw it, I think it would make them uneasy.'[42] Her health, however, worsened again and by the time she reached Bourbon-l'Archambault, she was in 'in so weak a state that she could not walk without the support of an attendant on both sides'.[43]

It was from this town's 'ancient and ragged castle' standing 'on a flinty rock overlooking the town' that the Bourbon family took its name. At its heart 'lie some baths of medical waters, some of them excessive hot, but nothing so neatly walled and adorned as ours in Somersetshire', Evelyn reported, 'indeed they are chiefly used to drink of, our queen being lately lodged there for that cause'.[44] After ten days of this treatment, and having her breast lanced, Henrietta Maria assured Charles 'I begin to hope that I shall not die.' Nevertheless, she warned, 'this numbness still continues and a redness like the measles, which has covered my whole body for three months'.[45]

Her spirits were surely buoyed by the arrival of her brother Gaston.[46] He had, surprisingly perhaps, been supportive of the regency, to the disappointment of some of his friends. He was no longer the heir to a king – Louis XIV had a younger brother Philippe who was almost four – and had gained instead a reputation as a courageous and successful military commander who showed compassion for ordinary soldiers. He had just returned from a very successful campaign in Flanders where he had prevented his army from pillaging areas they conquered and protected people whose towns were occupied. He had accepted the surrender of Gravelines from the Spanish on 28 July, and in Paris he was being celebrated as a hero.[47]

If the courtier Madame de Motteville, who was sent to attend on the queen, is to be believed, Gaston would have found his sister 'much changed' from the young girl who had left France: 'her misfortunes had given her such sadness, and her mind was filled with such sorrows, that she wept continually, which shows what the suffering of body and soul can do, for by nature this princess was gay'. Henrietta Maria fretted about her baby, suffering 'violent apprehensions for her infant, abandoned to the fury of those tigers'.[48] Yet there were flashes of gallows humour. She told Madame de Motteville that when she said to her doctor she had felt her mind weakening and feared she might go crazy, he had answered brusquely, she was not to worry, 'for you are that already'.[49] It struck Madame de Motteville that often, 'even if amid her tears, if it occurred to her to say something amusing, she would stop them to divert the company'.[50] Gaston also knew something about loss and humiliation: it must have bound them closer.

As Henrietta Maria grew stronger she began to take stock. She had learned that on 2 July, just before she had left England, 20,000 royalists under Prince Rupert and the former earl, now Marquess of Newcastle, had confronted 30,000 Scots and parliamentarians under Leven and Manchester at Marston Moor in Yorkshire. It was the greatest battle of the Civil War thus far and had ended in a crushing defeat for the royalists. Newcastle's men, known by the undyed cloth of their uniforms as the Whitecoats – and who she well remembered – had fought and died almost to the last man: a mere thirty had survived. Newcastle had sent her a letter to which she now replied. He felt scorned by other royalists. She assured him of her personal support and continued esteem.

If Charles could not now win the war, she still hoped he could achieve an honourable peace. That meant she needed to strengthen his hand. Reports had already reached Oxford of her success in raising money from French convents. When she had collapsed at the shrine to St Anne she had been tended by Carmelites. They were told that Parliament sanctioned the persecution, even the murder, of Catholics – and their pockets had opened.[51] She had missed no other opportunities since to press the king's case. When a delegation of Jesuits presented her with verses praying that the spas would heal her sad heart as well as her health, she told them that while she thought their verses excellent, she hoped for something more substantial from them – she wanted money, not only fine words.

The kindness she had been shown led Henrietta Maria to hope that Anne of Austria might still be persuaded to send military aid. She wrote to the Prince of Orange requesting Dutch ships, which could be used to transport French troops to England at the end of the campaigning season in Europe.[52] She left Bourbon in litters pulled by mules and accompanied by coaches and chariots for her servants, all provided by her nephew Louis XIV. She looked forward to seeing Paris, but before she again saw the city of her birth, her health would collapse once more and she would realise there was more than one price to pay for being a beggar queen.

'THE VIOLENCE OF DESTINY'

PARIS WAS HORRIFIED BY THE SPECTACLE OF THE FALLEN daughter of France. 'Here gentlemen is an image', one Frenchman recalled, 'of the Queen of England . . . constrained to appear to the world, and to be displayed, so to speak . . . at the Louvre, where she had been born with so much glory, for all to see her misery.'[1] Physically there was 'no trace remaining of her past beauty. Her eyes were fine, her complexion admirable, and her nose well-shaped', but she had been 'much disfigured by the severity of her illness and her misfortunes'. The illness had left her so thin 'her figure was even deformed, and her mouth, never handsome naturally, was now, from the thinness of her face, too large'.[2]

Henrietta Maria had been waylaid by illness at Nevers in the Loire and had lost a dear friend as well as a sister during her stay. The first blow had been to learn of the death of Elisabeth in Spain. She had fallen ill on 25 September 1644 with a bacterial skin infection that attacked her throat, and was bled for a week. When that did no good the people of Madrid had prayed and led processions of relics. Elisabeth had refused to allow her fourteen-year-old son or her six-year-old daughter to visit her, frightened that they might catch her illness. Instead she had taken comfort in a fleur-de-lys taken from her crown, which held a splinter of the true cross.

Philip IV had been in Zaragoza overseeing the war against the

Catalan rebels and their French allies. He had kept carriages waiting at points along the route to Madrid so that he could return if he was told she was dying. In the event he had set off too late. Elisabeth Bourbon, Princess of France, Queen of Spain, died aged forty-one on 6 October 1644. By the time Philip reached Madrid three days later, Elisabeth's embalmed body was already in its lead coffin covered in a yellow cloth trimmed with gold. He could see her face through a window cut into it. She had been dressed and veiled in the habit of a Poor Clare.[3]

Philip was grief-struck. After the difficult early years of their marriage, he had come to appreciate her many qualities. She had raised troops for him, money and provisions for his armies. She had attended religious processions and ceremonies to call on divine help, and as Governor of Castile she had 'exercised and practised the highest power like the hand of God'. Her hard work and piety were greatly admired and her funeral exequies celebrated the political role she had played, with Philip using her reputation to rally the Spanish people to the Habsburg cause.[4] How differently were Henrietta Maria's efforts for her husband perceived.

Not only did she have to absorb the death of her sister, she was also to be parted from Jeffrey Hudson, the 'human thumb' who had been in her service since he was a child. He had quarrelled with the brother of William Crofts, a great favourite who was now her Captain of the Guard. Jeffrey had challenged the brother to a duel and 'running his horse in full career, shot his antagonist in the head and left him dead'.[5] Duelling was a capital offence in France, and Jeffrey, whose height was no impediment to his horsemanship, had been fortunate to suffer only dismissal and banishment. Matters went from bad to worse after he was captured by Barbary pirates in the Channel. He would spend the next twenty-five years as a slave. Henrietta Maria would never see her Jeffrey again.

The bereft Queen of England had put on a brave face for a magnificent formal entry to Paris on 5 November 1644. Anne of Austria and Louis

XIV had joined her in a coach giving her the most important seat, in the front on the right side. The streets were decorated in her honour and filled with huge crowds. Leading her to her rooms in the Louvre, Henrietta Maria was given right of way through every door. Her apartment was on the ground floor of the south wing. Inhabited formerly by her mother and then by Anne of Austria, it had been empty for a decade and the French court was now resident at the Palais-Royal, built for Richelieu.

Six rooms had been set aside for Henrietta Maria's personal use and were hung with magnificent tapestries. A further thirty rooms were set aside for her ladies and principal officers. Her childhood home at Saint-Germain-en-Laye was to be lent to her as her country retreat.[6]

Members of the Council of State came to Henrietta Maria's bedchamber to pay their respects. She greeted them dressed in scarlet silk trimmed in silver and blue, by a balustraded bed, hung in red silk embroidered with gold.[7] She had brought the furnishings for such a bed to England in 1625 and had introduced the French tradition of using the bedchamber for ceremonial occasions. At Somerset House she had two such beds. Both furnished in green and white they had a silver balustrade, one was dressed in satin, the other was an angel bed, where the canopy was suspended above by chains, rather than by posts to the floor.[8] Other visitors to Henrietta Maria now brought her presents of musk-scented candles and boxes of preserves. A dinner was given where twenty-five violins were played for her. These entertainments and the greeting of visitors went on for a week. Away from the spectacle, meanwhile, Anne listened to her sister-in-law describe Charles's 'miserable state' and sat patiently as Henrietta Maria spilled out her feelings, 'justly angry and unjustly oppressed'. Henrietta Maria recalled 'She pitied me, wept with me, remembered that she too was a queen, and a mother, and promised me every assistance.'[9]

Promises were cheap and Henrietta Maria found 'the very sun that gladdened me in the morning went down [at night] on my sorrow for the council made difficulties of everything.'[10] France and Spain had been at war since 1635 at huge financial cost, so while 'the great-hearted Henrietta was constrained to plead for help; the great-hearted Anne was unable to give enough.'[11] Henrietta Maria would be honoured as a daughter of France. The fact she was also a refugee Queen of England and of Scots was an embarrassment.

The New Year opened in England with the execution of Archbishop Laud on 10 January 1645. As with Strafford there had been no conviction for treason at trial. He had been condemned by Act of Attainder on the same day that Parliament had abolished the Book of Common Prayer and with it the old Elizabethan and Jacobean liturgy. The parliamentarians were making a decisive shift towards a more radical religious position. The question was only how radical the eventual settlement would be. On the one hand were the Independents: those, like Oliver Cromwell, who favoured freedom of religion for independent Protestant congregations, known as sects, and who were set on the absolute defeat of the king. On the other hand were those who wanted a national Presbyterian Church, similar to the Kirk in Scotland, and who favoured a negotiated peace with Charles. They included the leading generals, Essex and Manchester.

Charles was still dodging the knockout blow his enemies had long sought. He had defeated Essex in Cornwall in September 1644, while Montrose was now winning battles in Scotland. This royalist success prompted a demand for a reform, or remodelling, of the parliamentarian army. The rank and file would be expected to serve anywhere in the three kingdoms and a new focus was placed on a professional officer class with Members of Parliament – with the exception of Cromwell – expected to resign their commissions. In April 1645 Essex was replaced by the Independent's choice: Lord Fairfax's son, Sir Thomas Fairfax. Strikingly his commission omitted the phrase calling for 'the preservation of the king's person', which had been used in 1642.

Charles came very close to being killed on the battlefield two months later, on 14 June 1645, when royal forces met the New Model

Army near the Northamptonshire village of Naseby. If the Earl of Carn-wath hadn't grabbed the reins of Charles's horse as he prepared to gallop at Cromwell's cavalry he would have been in the line of fire. Charles's life was saved that day – but he lost his army. The ensign of the last royalist regiment to resist the roundheads was killed by Thomas Fairfax with his own hand. The baggage train then became the focus of Cromwell's cavalry. Henrietta Maria had been in charge of the baggage train and the women camp followers when she had brought her army south in 1643. Cromwell's cavalry slaughtered and mutilated such women at Naseby. As many as 400 were killed, others had their noses slit and mouths gashed to give them the 'whore's mask'.

The atrocity – which was far worse than anything inflicted on the fleeing soldiers – was celebrated in the parliamentarian press as just desserts for popish 'harlots with golden tresses'. The reality was rather different. There were many respectable ladies in carriages and others of the 'middling sort'.[12] One such was Elizabeth Rumney who had been a member of the royal household since the reign of James I, 'in the office for providing flowers and sweet herbs for the court'. Henrietta Maria had perhaps noticed her garnishing the royal palaces. Two of Elizabeth Rumney's grandsons were also killed, leaving her daughter to raise her remaining 'six small children' without her help and grieve the two who had been killed.[13]

After the bloodbath the wagons were plundered. Charles had trav-elled to many of his battles with his state crown. He had it with him in Exeter the previous year, where he had seen his daughter Henrietta Anne for the first and last time. At the end of the war it was in the Tower, but there is no mention of it being captured. Perhaps this is because at Naseby there was something else 'more valuable than all the wealth and soldiers that we took' and that the parliamentary press wanted to draw attention to: Henrietta Maria's correspondence with Charles. Here was propaganda gold.

Thirty-seven letters were chosen, carefully edited and published with commentary, under the prurient title *The King's Cabinet Opened*.

Cabinets were private spaces from which the public gaze was excluded, until 'now by God's good Providence the traverse curtain is drawn' and the royal couple and all 'they must not disclose, is presented upon the stage'.[14] The secret exposed with lip-smacking relish was that 'the King's Counsels are wholly managed by the Queen, though she be of the weaker sex, born an alien [and] brought up in a contrary religion'. Only six of the letters were hers, but like the rest they were framed to 'prove' and that she was fully deserving of the charges of treason laid against her.

Set out in chronological order, the published letters began with the queen writing from York in 1643, sending out her armies against 'the rebels'. The second from 1644 mentioned the need to make concessions to Irish Catholics. The next letters were from France. She warned him that his 'strictness' against Catholics discouraged them from serving him. The last returns to June 1643, when she joked about being commander of the baggage train as they rode south from Newark: 'you see', the parliamentary commentary noted, 'she marcheth at the head of an army and calls herself the Generalissima!' Now she was 'resident in France, to procure embargoes of our ships, to raise foreign forces against us, and in this she is restless to the neglect of her own health. She vows to die by famine rather than fail the king'.[15]

For weeks afterwards the parliamentarian press dedicated their news-sheets to the letters: 'let us rifle the Cabinet. In the first place a letter from the king to the queen'. It began, the journalist noted, 'Dear Heart', 'and she has so much [of this affection] that there is none left for Great Britain. This is the Dear Heart which hath cost him almost three Kingdoms.' The letter ended 'eternally thine': this meant 'you must never look to see him own his own manhood again for . . . breeches and all are resigned up into her hands for all eternity'.[16] Royalists argued back, remarking that in supporting her husband she had done nothing that did not 'befit a wife', but the mud stuck and it sticks still.

In France, however, Henrietta Maria turned Parliament's claims to her advantage. The queen's long-standing almoner, Jacques du Perron, gave a speech to an assembly of the French clergy on 19 February 1646. He told them that the queen could now admit publicly that there was indeed a secret contract between Charles and Catholics. This was not true, of course, but this was what Parliament had been saying, and while it hurt Charles in England, it helped him in France. To support their fellow Catholics, du Perron told them, they needed not only to give money to the queen, but also to loan it. To further advertise this request du Perron's discourse was printed. It then became a subject of French newsletters that underscored Henrietta Maria's role as a champion of the Catholic Church and as England's queen.[17]

There is a drawing of Henrietta Maria done by Daniel Dumonstier during this period of exile. He had drawn her when she was a girl as a minx in a bob. This new work was of a grown woman with careworn eyes, but her spirit unextinguished, and with it 'that constancy by which, not being able to vanquish the violence of destiny, she nobly upheld the effort!'[18]

Charles gave himself up to the Scots on 5 May 1646, and two weeks later he ordered royalists to lay down their arms. His Scottish captors were anxious to make a peace deal – and their condition remained an old one: he must sign their Covenant. The English Parliament had established Presbyterianism in March, but to the Scots it was the wrong kind of Presbyterianism. Instead of being run by Calvinist councils – the presbyteries that gave their faith its name – it was under the secular control of Parliament where the powerful faction of Independents put it under threat. If Charles signed their Covenant it was possible the Scots would turn against Parliament. 'I think you ought to content the Scots,' Henrietta Maria told him.[19]

When Charles refused to sign the Covenant the queen sent William Davenant to change his mind and to warn that she would retire to a convent if he did not. Charles was horrified by her 'threat', which 'if it fall out, (which God forbid) is so destructive of my affairs I say no more of it, my heart is too big'. The royalist cause needed her – but he would not obey her. Signing the Covenant would mean denying his belief that episcopacy was divinely ordained and he saw it as a pillar of divine-right monarchy. Echoing his father's phrase 'No bishop, no king', he told her 'the absolute establishing of a Presbyterian government would make me but a titulary king'.[20]

How unfortunate, Mazarin exclaimed, that Charles's 'own best interests have not been able to overcome his stubbornness'. Why could Charles not see the need to use compromise as a tactical weapon? Why could he not see that his defence of the bishops was a useless handicap, and that the key issue was military power?[21] On this Henrietta Maria and Mazarin were agreed. As for Charles – she must have wished that she really was 'the true controller of the breeches'.[22]

A constant stream of impoverished royalists arrived in Paris following the king's defeat. Charles's friend, the collector and art patron Endymion Porter, whose teenage son had been killed at Newburn in 1640, complained he was 'in so much necessity that if it was not for my Irish barber, that was once my servant, I might have starved for lack of bread'. He had been lent enough cash to last a fortnight 'and I want clothes for a Court having but that poor riding suit I came out of England in'.[23] Porter hoped the queen would help him. So did many others, but she had little enough money of her own and what she had to spare all went to the king. She had even persuaded Anne to let her employ Madame de Chevreuse in this task, but the duchess had been captured off Dartmouth in 1645. Mazarin wouldn't take back the troublesome duchess, so Parliament had sent her on to the Spanish Netherlands.[24]

Henrietta Maria was now trying to send Cornish tin to the Dutch and borrow against it. She was also continuing to 'search and grope' for cash 'in the dark cells of monasteries and nunneries' in France.[25] Pope Urban had died in July 1644, but Cardinal Barberini was currently in France, having fallen out with Urban's successor Innocent X. He had given Henrietta Maria a number of gifts with which to decorate her rooms and she hoped to pawn many of the best items as soon as he returned to Italy. The strain was immense. She was often in tears and she feared not only for the king but also for her children.

Henrietta Maria lobbied hard for Prince Charles to flee to Jersey, an island the king had commended into her care.[26] He arrived there in time to celebrate his sixteenth birthday on 19 May 1646. Henrietta Maria expressed relief that he was now on 'a small island that is still ours'.[27] She remained concerned, however, about his possible capture and argued he should come on to France. James was taken prisoner only the following month when Oxford surrendered. He was placed under the care of the Earl of Northumberland at St James's Palace with his sister Elizabeth and brother Henry. Baby Minette was also a prisoner: Lady Dalkeith had surrendered her to Parliament in Exeter, albeit on the understanding that she be allowed to care for Minette at Oatlands Palace in Surrey. One of Henrietta Maria's clergy recalled how 'The thoughts of the queen on her arrival in France flew a hundred times a day towards the princess, her daughter, left behind in England; and a hundred times her prayers, mingled with her tears, demanded her of God.'[28]

To her relief on 19 July 1646, Henrietta Maria was reunited with her son Prince Charles at Saint-Germain.[29] She had had to battle with men like Charles's counsellor Edward Hyde who had been anxious to keep the prince in Jersey and away from her popish influence, but she believed he would not only be safer with her, he could achieve more. Meanwhile the loss of her baby was making Henrietta Maria very angry – and not only with God. She had been furious that Lady Dalkeith had not spirited her out of Exeter before it was placed under siege. It was pointed out to the queen that 'the governess could have as easily have beaten Fairfax as prevented being shut up in Exeter.'[30] A mother parted from her baby is not given to being reasonable, but Lady Dalkeith was about to prove to the queen how intrepid she could be.

Lady Dalkeith had been told the princess was going to join her siblings at St James's Palace and she was going to be dismissed, against the promises Parliament had made her. When her negotiations to prevent this failed, Lady Dalkeith plotted escape. On 25 July, six days after prince Charles arrived in Paris, Lady Dalkeith disguised herself as an old peasant woman, stuffing her clothes with rags so she looked hump-backed. She dressed the two-year-old Henrietta as a boy she named Peter – to the rage of the toddler – and fled for the coast. She left behind a letter for the gentlewomen servants begging them to keep her flight secret for as long as they could. They managed to do so for three days, which allowed Lady Dalkeith to get on a boat to France. In Paris Henrietta Maria was ecstatic, she 'embraced, she hugged again and again that precious infant'.[31]

It was the prince, however, who was the more important for the royalist cause, both as heir to the throne – and as a potential bridegroom.

It was not only Henrietta Maria and the royalist exiles who were short of money in France. The burdens of fighting the Thirty Years' War saw around 25,000 French go to jail in 1646 rather than pay their taxes. There were, however, still some very rich individuals, Gaston's nineteen-year-old daughter Mademoiselle de Montpensier being the fattest cat at court. Raised by Mamie St George and known as the Grande Mademoiselle, she had noticed Prince Charles's striking height and his dark complexion. She thought him 'passably agreeable', although the fact he did not speak French was 'a most inconvenient thing'. Henrietta Maria set her son the task of seducing her, and Prince Rupert, who had joined the queen in exile, stepped in as interpreter.

Prince Charles never missed any of the plays Mademoiselle attended at the Palais-Royal and made every effort to stroke her stupendous ego. He 'always sat next me' at the theatre, she recalled, and 'when I went to see the Queen of England he took me in his coach and, whatever the weather he did not put his hat on until he had left me'.[32] Henrietta Maria did her bit, lavishing attention on her proud niece. When the princess was off to a party Henrietta Maria would oversee how her hair was dressed, 'and adorning me herself, came to my house in the evening on purpose, and took every possible trouble over my toilette. The Prince of Wales held a candle to me all the while, to give light.' He even dressed in a manner that co-ordinated with her colour of clothes, 'everything was as the Queen of England had ordained'.[33]

For one reception it took three days to organise the princess's jewellery, which was to include England's crown jewels, for the queen 'still had some left at that time', the princess recalled. They included a huge pale yellow diamond once worn by Henry IV, and which had been bought by King James from the Seigneur de Sancy. The Grande Mademoiselle, who was reasonably attractive, thought she looked pretty good in them: 'many people told me, appropriately enough, that my shapely figure, my good looks, my white skin, and the sheen of my fair hair adorned me no less than all the riches that glittered on my person'.

Prince Charles's wooing lasted all winter, but Mademoiselle considered herself better suited to a greater prize. Henrietta Maria guessed who this was. When she spotted her niece at a party looking at Prince Charles with pity she reproached her, asking if she was thinking about a marriage to the recently widowed Holy Roman Emperor, Ferdinand III.[34] Mademoiselle admitted she was. Gaston told his daughter she would be better off with Prince Charles than with a man old enough to be her father, but she snapped back that she viewed the position as more important than the person. Come the spring of 1647 Prince Charles had had enough and 'forgot' to ask the princess to dance at a ball given for the wife of the Danish ambassador.

The prince hoped perhaps that his father might yet be restored to his throne. When the Scots had realised Charles was not going to sign the Covenant they had sold him for £400,000 to the Presbyterian-dominated English Parliament. He was handed over in February 1647 when their armies returned to Scotland. On Charles's journey to his new prison in the Midlands, crowds came out to cheer him. People remained desperate for peace and hoped for fresh negotiations. He was held at one of Henrietta Maria's former properties – Holdenby House in Northamptonshire – until June when he was snatched by an officer from the New Model Army. He then became a prisoner of Sir Thomas Fairfax and Oliver Cromwell along with their radical Independent allies in the House of Commons. On 3 July 1647, Charles was placed at Lord Craven's house on the Thames at Caversham.

Here was an opportunity to cut out the Scots and the Presbyterians in Parliament who wanted Charles to declare episcopacy an intrinsic evil, something he had said he would never do. Once again Henrietta Maria urged Charles to come to an accommodation. He should, she told him, grant 'whatsoever with a good conscience and honour he may [to the Independents], for the further prevention of the shedding of innocent blood'.[35] The prince, meanwhile, hoped his father's restoration would spare him a marriage to the Grande Mademoiselle.

Whoever held Charles had control of the peace process and members of the Presbyterian faction were soon plotting to get him back in their hands. They included Holland and that 'puritan she saint' Lucy Carlisle. Her friend Pym had died of cancer in December 1643 and her London house had been a hotbed of royalist conspiracy since the following year. A plan was now laid in Lucy's rooms at Whitehall and on 26 July 1647 it was put into operation. A huge mob invaded Parliament and demanded the Speaker put to a vote a demand that Charles be brought to London to conclude a peace treaty. It did no good. On 6 August Fairfax marched his army into London and took back control. Charles was then moved closer to the capital, at Hampton Court.

Henrietta Maria published her advice to Charles, but the king continued to stall, concerned in part that the Independents did not have the legal authority to make a peace. Within the army there were calls for the king now to be put on trial as 'a man of blood'. This was a biblical reference: 'the land cannot be cleansed of the blood that is shed therein, but by the blood of him that shed it'. Charles was told that he might even be murdered. This was the traditional way to dispose of a fallen king and Charles took the threat seriously. His son James recalled him observing 'there is little distance between the prisons and graves of princes'.[36] It had been true for his grandmother, Mary, Queen of Scots, as well as for deposed kings of England like Henry VI.

In November 1647 Charles escaped Hampton Court and headed to the south coast, hoping to get to France. He was captured at Place House in Hampshire and imprisoned in Carisbrooke Castle on the Isle of Wight. Henrietta Maria sent a ship to attempt a rescue. It dropped anchor on 17 December 1647 and Charles, given the news, immediately put on his boots 'and with great joy ran to the window to see how the wind stood'.[37] It was against them. The queen's ship was stuck in the harbour for six days. Thereafter Charles was more carefully watched. Henrietta Maria and the king now laid their hopes on a royalist rising in England and an invasion from his other kingdoms.

Puritan rule in England was proving unpopular. It offended against the moderate conservatism of the majority who wanted a return to the old ways of a king ruling with his Parliament. Nor did most people like Parliament's bossy interference in their lives: the closing of theatres, the banning of sport and dancing on Sunday. At Christmas there were serious riots against Parliament's injunctions forbidding the usual seasonal celebrations as 'popish'.

In Scotland, meanwhile, a moderate group of Covenanters under the Duke of Hamilton had taken control of the Edinburgh Parliament. There was widespread regret that Charles had ended up a prisoner of the Independents. The king's warnings in 1643 that the English rebels posed the real danger to Scotland now seemed prescient. On 26 December 1647 Hamilton and the Scots signed a secret treaty with Charles known as the Engagement. It promised an invasion from Scotland in alliance with a royalist army from Ireland under James, Marquess of Ormond.

A Calvinist and a friend of the late Earl of Strafford, Ormond had led the royalist forces against the Catholic confederates since 1641. He had surrendered Dublin to Parliament in June, but heavy-handed roundhead officials had since united Irish Presbyterians, Episcopalians and

Catholics against them. As the three kingdoms trembled on the brink of a second civil war, Henrietta Maria maintained contact with Charles using ciphered letters smuggled to him by his laundress. Many were intercepted, but her code proved hard to break. The Captain Anthony Mildmay complained that in one such he could only decipher a reference to James, Duke of York, something about the north and prayers for the destruction of the king's enemies.[38]

'THE LAST ACT OF THIS TRAGEDY'

IN JULY 1648 MADAME DE MOTTEVILLE VISITED HENRIETTA MARIA at her favourite Carmelite convent in Paris. The second Civil War – sometimes known as the war of the Engagement – had begun with a mutiny in Wales on 23 March. A royalist rising in the north had soon seen Berwick and Carlisle fall to royalist forces. Then, on 20 April, James, Duke of York had escaped England to his sister Mary, who had become Princess of Orange in March 1647, on the death of her father-in-law. Henrietta Maria had meanwhile been in further contact with her former favourites Henry Holland and Lucy Carlisle. They planned new risings in the south of England. Lucy had sold a pearl necklace for £1,500 for the war effort and successfully encouraged the former Vice Admiral Batten – the man who had tried to kill the queen – to defect. He was a fellow Presbyterian and was alleged to have said that the army intended to execute the king. His fear was that the army radicals would then take power.

Henrietta Maria was sitting 'alone in a little chamber, writing and drawing up despatches, as she told us, of great importance', Madame de Motteville recalled. The war was reaching a crucial stage. On 8 July 1648, the Duke of Hamilton had led 10,000 Scottish infantry and 4,000 horse into England for the king. The following day the eighteen-year-old Prince Charles had set sail from Calais in the *Constant Reformation*, one of several ships that had defected to the royalist cause, along with Batten. The planned risings in the south had, however, been exposed prematurely and Holland was captured the same day. By 10 July all of Wales was back in Parliament's hands and Oliver Cromwell was heading north to confront Hamilton.

Henrietta Maria pointed to the gold cup she was drinking from and told Madame de Motteville it was the only gold she had left. She had tried to pawn an erotic painting by Guido Reni – probably the one originally intended for the ceiling of her bedroom at Queen's House in Greenwich.[1] She had been 'unable to raise even a thousand scudi on it' and was being bombarded with requests of money from her officers – especially the French.[2] Nevertheless, she had matters of more immediate concern to deal with.

Prince Charles had sailed to Holland where James had joined him before their fleet headed to London. Henrietta Maria told Madame de Motteville she hoped the spiritual support of the convent would help 'to soothe the grief she felt at the departure of her son'.[3] She suffered greatly being separated from all her children, 'two of whom [Elizabeth and Henry] are in the hands of rebels', she noted, while Prince Charles and James might be 'killed or taken'.[4]

Troublingly, royalist support in the north had been dampened by their hatred of the Scots but the picture across England remained confused. On 12 July, when the Prince of Wales was blockading the Thames, several royalist prisoners were freed by a mob as they were brought into London. People still wanted to return to the old ways and MPs were under immense pressure from their constituents to come to terms with the king. On 28 July they agreed to hold negotiations with Charles without condition. The New Model Army wanted revenge, however, for this new bloodshed and they were crushing the royalists in the field.

On 17 August Cromwell defeated the Scots. Prince Charles's blockade of the Thames then broke when the wind turned against him and drove his navy back to Holland. By September the only royalist force left was in Ireland, but despite Irish Catholic fears of the Puritan New

Model Army, the Confederates had not yet agreed to fight for the king. The possibility that they might was, nevertheless, one of the few cards Charles had left to play when, on 15 September, negotiations with Parliament for Charles's restoration as king began again.

To encourage Charles to accept Parliament's terms, efforts were made to make him more comfortable at Carisbrooke. He was even permitted visits from a red-haired spy called Jane Whorewood, who had run gold for the royalists and with whom he had a brief sexual relationship. It would, however, take more than the embraces of Jane Whorewood to win the king over to the terms demanded of him. They included the abolition of episcopacy, as well as his power over the militia and court appointments. He was also expected to accept responsibility for the wars.

Charles instead prepared to justify his actions over the past years. A series of papers provisionally entitled 'The King's Plea' or 'The King's Sigh' had been gathered and edited with a view to appealing directly to public opinion, as Parliament had done so often in the past. In Paris, meanwhile, Henrietta Maria laid preparations for the remaining military option. The Marquess of Ormond, who had been with the queen since early March, left for Ireland at the end of September 1648 with £3,000 she had raised. It is unlikely she heard anything about Jane Whorewood. If she had, she might have reflected that Charles had not seen her in four years and might never do so again. Whatever happened between the walls of his prison, she had little reason to doubt he still loved her.

The following month troubling news arrived in Paris from Louis's agents in London. They had learned that the New Model Army was contemplating ending Parliament's negotiations with the king by force and putting Charles on trial as a 'man of blood'. Any MPs likely to oppose them would be purged. 'God knows how the strangest affair which has occurred in this century will finally terminate and what will be the last act of this tragedy,' Mazarin observed.[5] Perhaps he had already guessed.

* * *

The Thirty Years' War had come to an end with the last of a series of treaties between the great powers signed on 24 October. Charles's nephew, Charles Louis, was not restored to the crown of Bohemia, the claim that had triggered the conflict. He was returned only the Lower Palatinate, which had lost 90 per cent of its population to war, famine and disease. Nevertheless, while the Habsburgs had Bohemia, they were forced to recognise the Dutch Republic as a sovereign state and France had gained most of Alsace-Lorraine. Yet the costs for France of their involvement in the Thirty Years' War had also been high, and the rivalry with Spain continued. There would be conflict and proxy wars between them for another ten years.

The need for money to pay for the armies continued to accentuate French social divisions and the parliaments and other sovereign courts of Paris were now attempting to reassert authority they had lost under Richelieu. Following frenzied riots in Paris, Anne agreed to the administrative and fiscal reforms Parliament demanded. Henrietta Maria commented that in the early stages of the rebellion against Charles, feelings had been less heated than they were in Paris.[6] She feared France could now follow the path of what was happening in England where the news concerning her husband grew ever more frightening.

On 30 November the New Model Army seized Charles from Carisbrooke and he was moved from the Isle of Wight to Hurst Castle on the coast. On 6 December the army purged Parliament of any MPs likely to oppose their plans. Amongst those arrested was William Prynne, who had once condemned Henrietta Maria as a whore for talking on stage. He was now perceived as a conservative. On 23 December Charles was moved from Hurst Castle to Windsor. On 4 January the rump of MPs left in Parliament after the purge declared the acts of the House of Commons alone had the force of law. The French ambassador dispatched the news that Charles was to be charged with having 'a wicked design totally to subvert the fundamental laws and liberties of this nation, and, in their place, to introduce an arbitrary and tyrannical government'. These crimes, it was declared, deserved 'exemplary and condign punishment' – in others words, death.

The news stunned the French court, who 'could not wonder enough at the evil influence that seemed to rule over these crowned heads [Charles I and Louis XIV], victims of the two parliaments of France and England'.[7] The ten-year-old Louis was only a victim in the sense he had given up powers his mother was determined to get back. Charles's head was at risk. Still, Mazarin was firmly convinced that there were powerful forces in France who also wished for a republic. The civil wars known as the Fronde, after the slings the poor carried and used to attack the rich, had begun, with mobs roaming Paris.

Fearing the influence of England's example Anne issued a proclamation in the name of her son describing the Puritans as traitors to the world and condemning the English Parliament and the army for their attacks on their sovereign.[8] Louis also addressed an appeal to neighbouring states to unite with France against the English rebels. Anne then made the decision to withdraw the court from Paris to Saint-Germain-en-Laye. Escorted by Gaston they left in secret on the night of 5 January 1649. As their arrival was unexpected the king and his mother had to spend the night sleeping on camp beds, while their courtiers made do with straw. This was not unlike Hampton Court on the night Charles and Henrietta Maria had fled London in 1642 – but Anne had an army led by Gaston and the Prince of Condé and it was soon blockading Paris, where Henrietta Maria had chosen to remain.

Rebel militiamen now garrisoned the Bastille, the Arsenal and Paris's city walls against the royalist army. Disaffected nobles, meanwhile, flooded in to offer support, determined to dismantle the machinery of prerogative rule as the noble-led Junto had once done in England. There was a 'frightening quantity' of anti-government pamphlets being sold. Anne was often the target. One eight-page verse claimed she was having sex with Mazarin, 'People doubt it no longer: it's true that he's fucked her / And through her hole, Jules Mazarin pelts us with shit'.[9]

Meanwhile, edicts were issued that declared Mazarin a disturber of the public peace and an enemy of the king and the state.

Shut up in her apartment in the Louvre Henrietta Maria had no fuel to keep out the cold. 'Posterity will hardly believe that a Queen of England and granddaughter of Henry IV, and her daughter, wanted fire-wood, in this month of January in their house,' a visitor recalled.[10] She sat with Minette in bed to keep her warm and wrote letters to Thomas Fairfax and the Speaker of the House of Commons, begging to be allowed safe conduct 'to give unto ourselves, and our dearest lord the king, the consolation of going to him.'[11] The letters were not even opened.

When Charles's trial began at Westminster Hall on 20 January 1649, no one was certain what the outcome might be. If Charles accepted the legality of the tribunal, he would be accepting that he had no veto over the Commons decisions. He could then be returned to the throne, 'a sword always over his head [and] grown grey in the documents of misfortune'. Executing the king risked provoking a popular rising or foreign reprisals led by his Dutch son-in-law or his French nephew. Even Fairfax was against it. Cromwell reportedly warned, however, that if Charles refused to plead he would leave them no choice: they would have to 'cut off his head with the crown on it'.

Charles, Prince of Wales had so little money that he had been forced to dismiss most of his servants and could no longer support his brother James. The Duke of York duly left Holland for France, stopping en route at Brussels. Henrietta Maria urged him to stay there. The Seine had burst its banks and the flooding, together with the blockade, meant there was very little bread in Paris. Hungry mobs were roaming the streets looking for royalist targets. Madame de Motteville was almost lynched before she took refuge with Henrietta Maria who shared 'with great kindness' the two rooms that she and her whole court were using. James nevertheless arrived in Paris while his father's trial was still underway.

To the English Parliament's disappointment Charles refused to recognise the court, claiming his judges represented 'power without law'. His words echoed the warnings made in Parliament in 1643 when the queen's impeachment had been debated. Treason was defined in law as an act against the king. To claim otherwise was the law of brute force, and one MP had predicted during the debate that if this was permitted it 'would put all to trial by the sword', and anything Parliament did 'must and would be maintained by it'.[12]

The risk of Charles having his head cut off had risen sharply, and the Dutch and Scots ambassadors pleaded for the king's trial to be brought to an end to avoid such an outcome. Shockingly, Mazarin sent no instructions to the French ambassador who consequently did nothing. On 23 January 1649 Charles was convicted of treason and sentenced to death.

Only now was an emissary sent from Paris with letters entreating mercy. He was still in Boulogne when he learned Charles was already dead, executed on 30 January.[13]

During a public execution the victim is utterly powerless. He faces the ultimate violation of the body before a watching crowd. Charles had done all he could to raise his death above mere degradation. He wore two shirts so he wouldn't shiver in the cold and seem afraid. He had prepared a martyr's speech. He died for 'his people', for he represented the law and it was now the rule of law that allowed them true liberty. It was not in having a share in government. A subject and a sovereign 'were clean different things'. He ruled church and state by divine right and as a good Protestant, a member of 'the Church of England as my father left it'. Here was the same man that Henrietta Maria had married in his authoritarian and Protestant beliefs, and his ill fortune. He had lost Breda before they consummated their marriage and been humiliated at Cadiz before he was crowned. His fate had been suggested then, with talk of a prayer last said at the coronation of Henry VI, whose reign had also ended in civil war. Charles now feared a blunt blade would still make a butchery of his beheading. In the end, however, it was a clean kill.

When the news reached Paris it was kept from the queen. Someone told her Charles had been taken to the scaffold only to be rescued by the populace. She repeated the story, weeping, to Madame de Motteville, who guessed it had come from Henry Jermyn. The favourite did not want to be the bearer of bad news. It was later said that he so often was that her face would blanch when he came into a room.

Henrietta Maria sent a dispatch of servants to Louis XIV's court at Saint-Germain to discover further details of Charles's 'escape'.[14] She awaited their return dining in the Louvre, passing the time in innocuous conversation. As time went on with no sign of their return she grew increasingly agitated. Jermyn said that he would surely have come quicker if he had good news. 'What is it then?' she demanded, 'I perceive plainly that you know.' Jermyn broke the truth as gently as he could, but 'the queen, not expecting anything of this kind, was so deeply shocked that for a moment she was quite overwhelmed, without words, without action, without motion, like a statue'.[15]

Henrietta Maria's friends and relations tried to comfort to her, but she did not respond. 'We were obliged to desist, and to remain about her all in profound silence, some weeping, others sighing, all with dejected countenance, sympathising in her extreme grief.' It was already growing dark when her childhood friend the Duchess of Vendôme – wife of Henrietta Maria's illegitimate half-brother – arrived to see her. The duchess's son had spent time with Henrietta Maria and her army in Yorkshire. 'All in tears', the duchess 'took her hand and kissed it very affectionately, and then spoke to her' until eventually Henrietta Maria was roused from her stupor and the taken to her rooms.[16]

Henrietta Maria was amazed, she later told her son Charles, that she ever recovered from the blow. It was her darkest hour. She remained hidden from view until two days later, when she agreed to see Madame de Motteville, who was leaving for Saint-Germain-en-Laye. Henrietta Maria waved to her to kneel by her bed. Weeping she told her to warn Anne of Austria not to anger the people unless she had the means to face them down, that she needed to employ people who would dare speak the truth to her and that she must work hard to discover where the truth lay, for the greatest danger to kings and empires lay in ignorance.

Madame de Motteville left Paris by coach with her sister and footman. Because of the dangers they were forced to take a circuitous route, passing through villages that had suffered 'the most frightful devastation. Houses were burned and pulled down, churches pillaged, and an image of the horrors of war was painted in its actual truth'. She admitted 'the tears of this princess touched me deeply', but she was also struck by her warnings. When Madame de Motteville arrived at Louis's court she was appalled to find Anne surrounded by people joking about the Fronde and refusing to take the rebels seriously. 'I was forced to smile with those who turned into ridicule the most serious matters.'

Anne called for Madame de Motteville that night and asked her what she could tell her about Paris.

She told Anne what she had seen and gave her Henrietta Maria's messages. Henrietta Maria had something to ask: that France recognise her eldest son as Charles II, King of England, and that James now be treated as the Prince of Wales had been: that is, as a king's heir. 'Truly', Anne said, Charles's death was one 'which ought to make all kings tremble'.[17] She took an immediate lesson from it. Although the opposition in France was united in their hatred of Mazarin, Anne would not dismiss him, 'fearing the same thing would happen to her as happened to the King of England [after the execution of Strafford] namely, she herself would be attacked'.[18]

Henrietta Maria was also fearful for her nephew, the ten-year-old Louis XIV, but, she observed, she could not 'forget [my children]' in England.[19] She wanted to have Harry and Elizabeth sent to her, but she was sure the newly declared English republic, the Commonwealth, would not let Harry go – a prince was too valuable an asset. She longed, however, for the thirteen-year-old Elizabeth. 'Oh! If before my death, I could see her out of the hands of the traitors I would die content!' She reserved one of her two remaining significant pieces of jewellery to support Elizabeth financially when she arrived in France.[20]

The new Charles II – proclaimed in Scotland and Ireland but not England – broke down in tears when he had learned the news of his father's death. His aunt, the Winter Queen, and his sister Mary responded differently: with anger. Yet it was not only members of the Stuart family who reeled at Charles's death. On 22 February the Parliament of Paris appointed a committee to offer its condolences to Henrietta Maria. They also publicly voted a pension for her.[21] The city of Hamburg was soon described as one of the Commonwealth's most cordial new enemies. In Russia the English Muscovy Company had its charters cancelled. The Poles were said to have introduced a new tax payable to the Stuart king. The Danes threatened to close the Baltic Sound to English trade.

Sympathy for Henrietta Maria increased exponentially when Charles's defence of his actions, the *Eikon Basilike*, or *Royal Portrait*, reached Europe. The work that had begun as 'The King's Sigh', republished in French, Latin, Dutch, German and Danish, made Charles the tragic hero of the British civil wars. In France the first editions were translated by the Calvinist Huguenots who feared that 'the atrocity of this crime, committed by those most people believe to be the same religion as we, might draw upon our churches a blame that would never erase'.[22] They had reason to be anxious: it was even being speculated that the masked and anonymous executioner had been a Protestant minister.[23]

The Paris Parliament was so anxious to further distance itself from the regicide that peace negotiations with Anne were opened and in March they annulled their edicts against Mazarin. The French public, meanwhile, hungered for more detail: pamphlets offered reports of the trial and of Charles's tearful last meeting with Harry and Elizabeth. Amongst all classes in France the regicide diminished rather than encouraged republican feeling. The delegates to the Paris Parliament pondered the fate of English MPs purged at sword-point by the New

Model Army. Aristocratic rebels considered the execution of the Earl of Holland, who had been well known at the French court and who died outside Westminster Hall on 9 March 1649.[24] Lucy Carlisle, whose late husband had been ambassador in Paris, was languishing in the Tower where she was held 'close prisoner'. Meanwhile the war between royalists and the English Parliament continued.[25]

In the Carmelite convent on the rue Saint-Jacques to which she had again retreated, Henrietta Maria was grateful for 'a most loving letter' from her eldest son. She told Charles II that she felt with his father's death she had lost 'all my happiness in this life'. Henrietta Maria did not blame her French family for their failure to help save the late king. Her brother Louis XIII would have helped him at the outbreak of civil war had it not been for his servants, she told her son. They had remembered 'the ancient enmity with England, and if they had wished to accomplish the ruin of Great Britain, they could not have done it more effectively'.[26]

Richelieu had betrayed the Stuarts – and so had his successor. 'Had I believed Cardinal Mazarin, I should have thought he was putting to sea with the most powerful army that ever left France for the help of our lost kingdoms, and I confess that at first he deceived me,' Henrietta Maria admitted to Charles II. 'I thought that the indelible character of a daughter of the great Henry [IV] would have been the greatest incentive to move the ministers of the crown of France, not only to aid me, but to pledge themselves to redress my fortunes'. She had understood for a while that Mazarin's promises were all hot air: 'you know that I wrote you word . . . that all that he said was only a cheat to quiet me'.[27]

All agreed, however, that greater forces had also been at work, for a king raised by God had not been protected by God. Charles believed that his execution was divine punishment for sacrificing Strafford. Henrietta Maria looked to the sins of someone other than her husband. 'Would it have pleased heaven that Henry VIII . . . had not apostised from God! Then would the kingdom of England not now have committed . . . so execrable a parricide!'[28] It seemed to her that

Henry VIII had made himself head of the Church of England and Charles's role as such divided his people and led to his death.

Henrietta Maria had agreed to have Minette baptised a Protestant – as she had all her children. Now she turned her back definitively on Charles I's wishes. Minette would receive instruction only in the Catholic faith.[29]

Henrietta Maria would also exert far more pressure on her courtiers and other children to convert than she had ever done in the past. Susan, Countess of Denbigh and William Davenant were amongst those who would convert in France. The most important conversion she sought, however, was that of the new king.

'Our misfortunes are many: they would overwhelm hearts greater than ours,' Henrietta Maria told Charles II. She hoped that God would help him back on his throne, 'But, meanwhile, what can your wretched mother advise you?' She reminded him that he had once told her that he wished to declare himself a Catholic one day. She insisted that the time to do so was now, that it was a practical solution to their problems, as well as the moral choice.

There was no immediate prospect of help from any of the European powers. 'The crowns of Scotland and Ireland are doubtless plotting steps to bring you to your entire kingdom of Great Britain, yet, nevertheless, I fear the infidelity of the Scots, who for the price of a few pieces of money, sold the life of the king, your incomparable father, to Parliament.'[30] Ormond had made terms with the Irish Confederates in January, but if Charles II did not now become a Catholic, 'with what affection would Ireland follow you?' There was also another reason to do so. Henrietta Maria had persuaded Gaston and Anne to pressure the Grande Mademoiselle to think again about a marriage. The reluctant bride had claimed that Charles's Protestant religion 'was one thing I could not overlook'.[31] Becoming a Catholic had helped Charles's maternal grandfather become King of France after years of civil war, Henrietta Maria reminded her son: 'Would that . . . the great Henry could rise again to read you a lecture on the manner in which you should govern these kingdoms!'

Henrietta Maria's last request, however, concerned his sister Elizabeth. 'To this, at least, I will exhort you, to employ every force, to use every artifice, to withdraw from London, so dear a part of my own heart, this innocent victim of their fury, your worthy sister.' Henrietta Maria concluded by telling her son she intended to stay in retirement at the convent 'with only two maids, my secretary and confessor . . . and you can be sure that my spirit . . . will ever pray for you and your happy success.'[32] Her retirement did not last long.

Three years earlier Charles had begged Henrietta Maria, 'by thy love for me . . . never retire thyself from my business, so long as I have a child alive, whatsoever becomes of me.'[33] If she read the *Eikon Basilike* she would have had a reminder of this request. Her husband described how he had taken comfort in believing that, although his enemies might kill him, thanks to her, 'I can perish but half.' Their children would ensure that he would 'yet survive the malice of my enemies, although they should be satiated with my blood.'[34] Yet how could she help the Stuarts now?

Henrietta Maria was no longer the wife of a king, merely a poor widow. She needed to cast herself in a better role, one that would project an image with widespread appeal. In 1578, the postmenopausal Elizabeth I took on the sobriquet of the Virgin Queen. Henrietta Maria also looked to Marian imagery to make a virtue of necessity. She returned to the French court dressed in black – as her mother had after the murder of her father – but there were no pearls, no diamonds. She was stripped of all ornament. Henrietta Maria had been born in a room of rosaries celebrating the seven joys of the Virgin. Now she pronounced herself to be '*la reine malheureuse*', the unhappy queen. There was a rosary for that too, used in Lent, the period of fasting leading to Easter.

Henrietta Maria had chosen the iconic role of Our Lady of Sorrows depicted in Catholic iconography with tears on her cheeks and a dagger piercing her heart. It resonated with anyone who had known suffering and promised that all would be well. The king was dead. But a resurrection would follow.

Part Six

PHOENIX QUEEN

'NO OTHER RAINBOW'

CHARLES II WAS NOT TO DECIDE ANYTHING UNTIL THEY HAD met in France, Henrietta Maria told him: not whom he should have on his council, not what he would do. Just how obedient he would be remained to be seen, however, when he left Holland at the end of June 1649 bringing his latest mistress with him: a 'brown, beautiful, bold, but insipid creature' called Lucy Walters.[1]

The teenage lovers had had a son in April, named James and who was later given the title Duke of Monmouth. Henrietta Maria was surely excited to see her first grandchild and would grow very fond of him, but royal marriages were about political alliances on which kingdoms depended. The mistress was bundled out of sight when the couple arrived in France for Henrietta Maria had ensured that the Grande Mademoiselle was there to greet Charles at Saint-Germain.

Mademoiselle had made an extra effort to look appealing, curling her hair ('rare for me', she noted) and she thought Charles had grown 'very good-looking'.[2] With the 'romantic' reunion out of the way, Henrietta and her 'favourite child' spent the next two or three days together in 'tears and lamentations' over the execution of his father.[3] Then the quarrels began.

To Henrietta Maria's frustration, Charles told her he would use his 'own reason and judgement' in all his decisions. She thought him too young for that and felt it was her duty to tell him what she thought was best in robust terms. Posterity has judged her harshly for this. Charles II did not. When she lost her temper with him – as she not infrequently did – he would take himself off 'with some abruptness'.[4] He often found her infuriating, but angry exchanges of views did not mean they loved each other less. She told Christine that she and Charles had the 'greatest friendship possible', and while this served a political purpose – her position looked stronger – there was an element of truth in what she said.[5]

Another reunion followed not long after that with Charles: Henrietta Maria had not seen her beloved Wat Montagu for over six years. He had been freed from the Tower on grounds of ill health the previous year and in August he was given permission to leave England for France.[6] Most of the cavaliers in Paris were going the other way, returning to England in despair. Only diehards remained in Paris and these Wat found split between the so-called 'Louvre' group around Henrietta Maria, who were prepared to cut deals with anyone who could help restore the Stuarts; and those labelled the Old Royalists, who were prepared neither to grant Catholics freedom of religion in Ireland or to accept Presbyterianism in England. Edward Hyde, an Old Royalist, was Charles II's leading counsellor.

The first plan Charles II agreed to was to go to Ireland and he left for the staging post of Jersey shortly after Wat's arrival. He took his brother James, Duke of York with him, to annoy his mother, according to the Venetian ambassador. She was, understandably, concerned to see both king and heir risking their lives. Charles, on the other hand, wanted James under his – rather than their mother's – influence. In the event, no sooner had Charles II returned to Jersey soil than Oliver Cromwell put paid to the Irish plan. In September 1649 the diarist John Evelyn recorded the news arriving in Paris of Cromwell and the New Model Army's sacking of the royalist garrison of Drogheda 'all put to the sword, which made us very sad, forerunning the loss of all Ireland'.[7]

When Charles made the reluctant decision to go to Scotland instead of Ireland, Henrietta Maria helped pay for his new enterprise by

Christine of France, Duchess of Savoy, as Minerva, goddess of wisdom and war, and patroness of the arts. Richelieu condemned her as a woman 'irresolute between her madness and her malice'. She proved annoyingly successful, however, in protecting the interests of an independent Savoy.

Thomas Wentworth, Earl of Strafford, had exchanged full-length portraits with Lucy Carlisle as a mark of their friendship and mutual esteem.

Henrietta Maria's faithless favourite, Lucy, Countess of Carlisle.

Charles I's formal entry into London in November 1641 was planned by Henrietta Maria with his Secretary of State, Sir Edward Nicholas, and was a huge success with the king cheered by large crowds.

Marie de' Medici, the exiled 'mother of three kings', receiving visitors in her bedchamber at St James's Palace in 1638. She remained in England until the summer of 1641.

Henrietta Maria as St Catherine, who used to appear to the warrior saint Joan of Arc and offer her advice.

Sir John Suckling, friend of William Davenant, veteran of the Île de Ré and the Thirty Years' War, and the 'greatest gallant' of his day.

George Goring (right), royalist commander and one of the witty and dashing young men who had surrounded the queen, here with his brother-in-law Mountjoy Blount, Earl of Newport. Strongly anti-Catholic, Newport was the half-brother of Henrietta Maria's favourite, the 'Puritan'-leaning Henry Rich, Earl of Holland.

Henrietta Maria's departure from Scheveningen for England bringing arms and men in 1643. It was said that 'without [the queen's] encouragement and aid the king would never have put himself into a position to resist [his enemies]'.

23. May. 1643. Voted that y Queene Pawning the Iewells of y Crowne in Holland & there with buying Armes to assist the warr agaist y Parliam: & her owne actuall performances with her popish army in the North was high Treason & transmited to the Lord: images, Cruci-fixes papistecall bookes in Somerset and Iameses ware burnt and 5 Capuchin friers sent away

The destruction of Henrietta Maria's chapel at Somerset House in 1643: amongst the works of art destroyed was a Rubens painting of the crucifixion that had once belonged to Buckingham. His Catholic widow had given it to the king, perhaps with the chapel in mind.

5

Henrietta Maria's army rode over Burton bridge before taking the town, which saw scenes of looting and possible rape.

Statue of Henrietta Maria at St John's College Oxford: the town was Charles I's wartime capital and the queen hated its 'fetid' air.

Henrietta Maria in France in 1645. She is older and more careworn than the sparkling girl the artist had depicted twenty years earlier, but remained energetic in raising money and arms for the king.

Anne of Austria in her coronation robes, a style of portrait inspired by a similar painting of her mother-in-law Marie de' Medici. Anne was sympathetic to Henrietta Maria personally but, as regent for her son Louis XIV, she only ever offered very limited support for the royalist cause.

The execution of Charles I caused shockwaves across Europe, and was 'a blow' from which Henrietta Maria thought she would never recover.

Henrietta Maria as Mary Magdalene. She is tearing off her pearls in grief and as an act of penance after the execution of God's anointed. She is not merely an impoverished widow who had to sell her pearls.

The so-called 'Mancini' pearls were a gift to Henrietta Maria from her mother. She sold them to the teenaged Louis XIV who gave them to his mistress, Cardinal Mazarin's niece, Marie Mancini. 'Lofty ideals', Henrietta Maria declared, were more important than 'splendour'.

Charles II dances with his sister Mary in Holland, celebrating his restoration as King of England in 1660. Their brother James can be seen behind Charles's left shoulder, while the youngest sibling, Henry, can be seen over Mary's left shoulder. Mary's son, the future William III, aged ten, is placed centrally, between the two ladies in black.

Henrietta Maria, her nephew and son-in-law Philippe of France, her granddaughter Marie-Louise (the future Queen of Spain) and her 'little edition of myself': her daughter Henrietta of England. Henrietta Maria is depicted as Amphitrite, the personification of the sea – with which the island of Britain was associated.

pawning a set of gold and silver Mortlake tapestries that had been a gift from Barberini.[8] The king arrived in June 1650 having failed to prevent an invasion attempt in Scotland by Montrose, which had ended in the marquess's capture and execution. Although he condemned Montrose's action he was now obliged to alleviate Scottish suspicions by dismissing many of his cavaliers, signing the Covenant and disavowing Ormond's treaty with the Catholic Irish. He also advertised his 'shame' for his father's faults and the idolatry of his mother. Charles said he feared he would never be able to look her in the face again.

With Ireland defeated Cromwell now arrived in Scotland where he crushed the Scottish army at Dunbar on 3 September. The Scottish alliance, meanwhile, had also demanded a personal price from the Stuarts. Henrietta Maria had been pleading for the ten-year-old Harry and fourteen-year-old Elizabeth to be sent to Holland or France. Instead the English Parliament had decided to move them to confinement at Carisbrooke Castle on the Isle of Wight. Elizabeth warned that she was ill and too sick to travel. This was ignored. Parliament feared that, with Charles in Scotland, 'if any insurrections should happen the public peace would be much the more endangered' if the children escaped.[9]

When Henrietta Maria had last seen Elizabeth she had been a very active six-year-old, but the little girl had broken her leg in 1644 while running across a room. Forced to sit for weeks on end Elizabeth had turned to study. She had proved extremely bright. Henrietta Maria would never have the opportunity to get to know the intelligent and sensitive young woman she was becoming. After a fever lasting ten days Elizabeth died at Carisbrooke on 8 September 1650. She had had no medical help, Henrietta Maria told her sister Christine, and she had suffered from imagining her father in the same place. 'I should rejoice to see her out of the hands of those traitors,' she wrote, 'but I can't help but feel [her loss] deeply' for love is 'stronger than reason'.

Elizabeth was buried in a small vault in St Thomas's Church in Newport, her grave marked only by her initials, carved into a wall. Another death in the family followed soon after. On 6 November 1650, Charles

II's most powerful ally in Europe, his brother-in-law William II, also died. Henrietta Maria hoped her daughter Mary could take consolation in the birth of her son on 14 November. She wished she could see the baby, but after the death of Elizabeth her health had taken a turn for the worse. She said she feared she was too ill to ever have the good fortune to do so.[10] Henrietta Maria longed again to retire to a convent.

The queen's visits to the Carmelite convent in Paris were disruptive for the nuns and they had complained about it. If she was able to found a convent of her own, she would, however, be entitled to private apartments. There her creditors could not trouble her, and she could lead a prayerful life, while remaining a part of the secular world, where her children still needed her. After the defeat of Dunbar the Scots had rallied around Charles, who was crowned king on 1 January 1651. He was also gathering support in England from those who had supported the rising of 1648. He hoped a new invasion from Scotland, this one led by himself, would succeed where that of 1648 had failed. As usual Henrietta Maria raised funds for the royalist war effort, but now she also raised money for a religious foundation. Rather than the Carmelites, Henrietta Maria chose the Order of the Visitation whose convents had a vocation to give widows a place of retreat.

Henrietta Maria hoped to buy Catherine de' Medici's former pleasure palace at Chaillot outside Paris, as she liked its pastoral setting and the convenience of its proximity to Paris. She had soon gathered 57,200 livres in donations of the 67,000 required. The remainder was borrowed. There was a final hurdle when the Archbishop of Paris complained that Henrietta Maria would do better to focus on her children. This had less to do with any genuine concern about her maternal role than the fact that the power of female piety was seen as a threat to male clergy.[11] Henrietta Maria went to Anne of Austria for support and the archbishop backed down. The nuns were given the quieter rooms in the new convent away from the river while Henrietta Maria chose those facing Paris. She then began filling what would become an extensive library, bestowing rich vestments and altar hangings for the chapel, and decorating her rooms. There were black and white brocades for her bedroom, walnut furniture for her cabinet and everywhere floral motifs: a 'verdure' or 'garden' tapestry in her parlour, embroidered stools in her bedroom and hangings in her cabinet which depicted pots bursting with flowers.[12]

The convent and its routine provided the kind of all-female community Henrietta Maria had known as a young girl with her mother. The nuns in turn found her to be a kind patron, 'affable to everyone, compassionate about the afflictions of each one, concerning herself with the least of the domestics in order to ease their pains and to keep them content, not being able to suffer injustice anymore than ill-speaking'. Henrietta Maria 'reflected that to be a queen she was not less a human being' and this 'rendered her equal to the most miserable'.[13]

Paris was rocked by violence again that summer of 1651. A new Fronde had begun the previous year and as it continued the nuns at Chaillot briefly had to leave their convent. The last time things had been this bad Henrietta Maria had been fretting about her husband's trial in England and its possible outcome. It was her son she now feared for. 'I have no other rainbow than remembering I am your mother', she told him.[14] In July, Charles II led his army of 12,000 Scots into England, but the war-weary English did not rise up for the king and, on 22 August, Cromwell defeated Charles at the Battle of Worcester. The king fled the battlefield – and vanished. 'Wanted' posters went up across England with a description of Charles II as 'a tall black man, over two yards high'. Henrietta knew what it was like to be hunted. Desperate to protect him, she angrily threatened to dismiss ladies-in-waiting who did not pray for him as Catholics. It was six weeks before Henrietta Maria had news of Charles's escape. He arrived at the Louvre in October still wearing the rough clothes and cropped hair of his English peasant disguise. She greeted him 'with transports of joy'.[15]

To please Henrietta Maria, the Grande Mademoiselle got out of bed, where she had been lying unwell with a swollen face, to go and see Charles later the same day. By then Henrietta Maria was full of the excitement of what she had learned of Charles's adventures on the run.

'You will find my son quite ridiculous because, in order to escape, he cut his hair, and he has an extraordinary outfit,' Henrietta Maria warned Mademoiselle. Charles walked in at that moment, looking 'very handsome, and much better-looking than before his departure, though he had short hair and a full growth of beard', Mademoiselle recalled. Even more remarkably he seemed to have acquired the ability to 'speak French very well'. The new urgency for a marriage to an heiress may have helped Charles's language skills. Where else did he have to turn?

Cromwell had defeated the Irish and the Scots. William II was dead and Mary held no power in Holland. Charles's uncle Philip IV had recognised the government of the English Commonwealth nine months earlier.[16] France was entering a new period of the Fronde, leaving little money to be had from his cousin, Louis XIV, who aged thirteen had now reached his majority. The Grande Mademoiselle was to Charles like a biscuit to a starving dog. He had endured many traumatic experiences in Scotland and England but at their greeting he restricted his conversation to amusing and flirtatious anecdotes. As they walked back to her apartments in the Tuileries he told her that, after Worcester, he had hidden from his pursuers in an oak tree and described how, in Scotland, there had 'not been a single woman and the people were so backward they had thought it a sin to listen to violins, and he had been terribly bored'. He told her he was delighted to be returning to France, 'where he found so much charm in people for whom he had a great liking' and he 'asked if we should not begin dancing soon'.[17]

Charles ignored the hovering Lucy Walters that winter, visiting the Grande Mademoiselle every other day. The princess, who was still suffering from her swollen face, would get out of bed to see him, and they would dance (at which Charles excelled). Henrietta Maria often came, once bringing the Duke of York.[18] Despite the gravity of their situation Henrietta Maria was 'constantly wonderfully merry . . . overjoyed to see the king safe near her'. Charles was 'very sad and sombre for the most part', but put on a good front as he pursued Mademoiselle.[19] The little group played cards 'for small stakes' while Charles 'simpered and smirked as they say lovers do'. She told him she expected him to go to England to get his crown, even if it cost him his head. She also said that she wouldn't marry him unless he become a Catholic. He claimed he would do – if she pledged herself to him.[20] She never did.

The Grande Mademoiselle later admitted that 'having been brought up in the lap of luxury' she was 'alarmed' at the prospect of 'selling my property and risking it to conquer his kingdom' – and there was no further pressure from her father to do so. Henrietta Maria had fallen out with Gaston after trying – and failing – to dissuade her brother from allying with the Frondeurs who had long sought his leadership. Once she was seen emerging from Gaston's palace to find herself being shouted at by a crowd as a 'Mazarine'. The truth was Henrietta Maria had little affection for the hated Mazarin, who had promised Charles I help and never given it. She had much in common with Gaston and they had many shared friends. Ultimately, however, a rebellion against a king was too close to the bone: as the eighteen-year-old James later observed, the Frondeurs were going down a path trodden by all revolutionaries who claimed they were attacking a king's minister and not the king.[21] The ghosts of Buckingham and Strafford haunted them still.

The collapse of order in Paris was soon such that Henrietta Maria was again going hungry and she told Christine she feared there was nowhere to escape the violence. At Chaillot the nuns were forced to leave their convent once more and Henrietta Maria worried that she could be lynched. The scenes of the mobs in London must have replayed often in her mind. It was 'the manner of death . . . not coming when one would like it' that horrified her. 'God wants to humiliate kings and princes. He began with us in England. I pray France is not to follow.'[22]

In April 1652 James rode out of Paris to join Louis's army against the rebels. He proved to a good soldier, liked by his commanders and acting in battle with 'extraordinary gallantry and courage'.[23] Henrietta Maria and Charles played a different role, as mediators. They succeeded in setting up peace negotiations between Louis and the rebels, but when Mazarin insisted on being present they collapsed.

Louis did not prove grateful for his aunt's efforts when, in October, he and Anne returned to Paris victorious over the rebels in the city. Two months later the decision was made that France should recognise the Commonwealth. Henrietta Maria protested in person, to no avail. 'Imagine what it is like for me to have such a horrible spectacle before my eyes,' Henrietta Maria asked Christine : her own nephew acknowledging 'these traitors'.[24] She told James nothing had so upset her since the execution of his father.[25] The last spasms of the Fronde ended in February 1653 and royal authority in France was established more firmly than Henrietta Maria had ever known it: 'people breathed only obedience', one courter recalled.[26] Yet France remained at war with Spain, as they had since the conclusion of the Thirty Years' War, and both Louis and Philip were anxious Cromwell not take their enemy's part.

In March 1653 Henrietta Maria sold Mazarin two magnificent faceted diamonds and a ruby ring, 'for my support'.[27] A Van Dyck portrait of the queen in silks and lace and jewels was also pawned. The image of herself as *la reine malheureuse* was, however, published in a book on eminent people by Pierre Daret: a rebuke to their conscience and a reminder to the princes of Europe of the humiliation of one of their own.[28]

In April 1653 the rump of the purged 'perpetual' parliament was dismissed on Cromwell's orders with the aid of forty musketeers. In December Cromwell took political authority in England as Protector for life. He had done so because, he believed, God willed it. He also took on much of the mantle of kingship. He lived in Charles I's former royal palaces, admiring their works of art, and developed a love of music. Not all his former soldiers and followers were enamoured of this kingly Cromwell. He had denied the hopes of those who wished for a fairer society and a wider electoral franchise.

Henrietta Maria had been reunited with her son Harry in Paris at the same time as the rump was dismissed. The English republic had no wish for a puppet king. Charles, however, was forced to leave France the following year, in July 1654. Cromwell insisted that good relations with Louis could be maintained only if Charles was expelled, so his small and penniless court was obliged to decamp to Cologne, the city where his grandmother Marie de' Medici had died in exile. Henrietta Maria had not seen her youngest son Harry, now fourteen, since he was a toddler, and thought he looked like his father, but with darker colouring. Charles had left orders for Harry to 'obey my mother in all things, religion only being excepted'. They were the same orders, he noted, that his father had given him. Nevertheless, by mid-October 1654 efforts to ensure Harry's conversion were underway.

Having been raised a prisoner of his father's enemies Harry had grown used to hiding his true feelings. This meant that no one was sure what way he would jump. Charles II was aghast at this turn of events. He told his mother that Harry's conversion 'would be the greatest misfortune that ever befell me in all my life' for 'all that I can say or do will never make my Protestant subjects believe but it is done with my consent'. If she persevered, 'I cannot expect Your Majesty does either believe or wish my return to England.'[29] Henrietta Maria has been accused since of acting purely out of 'bigotry', even of losing her mind in persisting with her intentions, but she told Charles she believed it was the only means through which Harry 'might be happy in this world'.[30] The Stuart cause was at its lowest ebb. If he became a Catholic she might find Harry a rich, royal bride, or persuade the Pope to make him a cardinal. Either way, he would gain power and wealth that he had no obvious means of getting from his elder brother.

Henrietta Maria sent Harry to Pontoise under the care of another convert – Wat Montagu. Wat's friendship with Anne of Austria had held good and, having taken priestly vows, he had been made Abbot of Nanteuil and of St Martin's, Pontoise, as well as serving as Henrietta Maria's grand almoner. Henrietta Maria understood Charles's concern about the possible reaction in England, but felt he exaggerated its significance. His English subjects wanted nothing more than a return to the old ways of a Protestant king ruling with his Parliament and some stability of matters of religion. The religion of junior members of the royal family was surely of less importance, she felt. Even the Scots, if their religious rights were guaranteed, would be pleased to see the back of Oliver Cromwell.

Anne of Austria backed Henrietta Maria in insisting that it was her right to educate her youngest son as she wished. Under the terms of her marriage contract, Henrietta Maria had been promised that she could educate her children until they were thirteen. Harry was now fourteen, but, as she pointed out to Charles, she had been denied any access to Harry during his formative years. Her closest Protestant servants – Jermyn amongst them – refused to support her (even if they did not openly dare defy her). The key decision was, however, to be made by young Harry. The boy had no childhood memories of his mother, but his father had been able to see him and play with him during his imprisonment in England in 1646 and 1647. His last memory of his father was on the eve of his execution in 1649. Charles I had sat the eight-year-old on his lap and told him to be loyal to his brother and explained that he was about to die for the Protestant religion.

When Harry told Henrietta Maria he would not convert, she informed him 'she would not more own him as her son, commanded him out of her presence, and forbade him any more to set foot in her lodgings.'[31] She had moved to the Palais-Royal after the Fronde – Anne believed the Louvre was more secure for her son – and here his bed was stripped and her cook was told to deny Harry food. He was given shelter by a generous English courtier until he left France in mid-December 1654. His mother refused to say goodbye. Harry hoped to join his brother in Cologne, but Charles advised him to go to Mary in Holland instead. The city was turning against Charles over his attacks on Harry's possible conversion. It had made a mockery of his efforts to woo the support of Catholic powers by promising he would permit Catholics to practise their religion after his restoration. Nor had Charles's stand helped him in England. The Church of England of the Book of Common Prayer was itself associated with popery in parliamentary propaganda.

Harry tried to reach out to his mother, writing to her from Brussels. She declined to open his letters. For this Henrietta Maria has been condemned as an unloving and cruel mother. Yet she was not the only widowed Stuart queen who expected obedience from her children. Her sister-in-law, Elizabeth the Winter Queen, was estranged from her son Edward and her daughter Louise Hollande, both of whom had converted to Catholicism. In matters of life and death, let alone of heaven and hell, neither Henrietta Maria nor Elizabeth Stuart were prepared to accept adolescent rebellion. Defiant children made them look weak and that reduced their political and diplomatic clout, risking damage to the wider family. Henrietta Maria's children understood this even if posterity has not.

Despite the fury of her quarrel with Charles, their ties of affection remained. 'I will end assuring you in good faith of what . . . can never change,' she wrote to him, 'which is that I am with all my heart, my son, Your most affectionate mother.'[32]

In October 1655 France signed a treaty with Cromwell aimed against Spain. Anne of Austria, knowing Henrietta Maria's love of fashion, sent a bale of silver tissue to mollify her. She never opened it and told her sister Christine that she would not even remain in Paris while the ambassadors of 'that traitor Cromwell', 'this villain', were there. Louis's government was 'killing' the memory of her husband 'which is so dear.'[33]

The Anglo-French treaty meant, however, that there was a good chance Spain might now be persuaded to back the royalist cause. When Charles II heard his sister Mary was planning to go to Paris he tried to dissuade her, fearful it would highlight the Stuarts' strong links to the Bourbons.[34] Mary, however, was determined to go. She was a miserable, powerless widow in Holland and observed that 'All the world' would understand her wish to see her mother, 'which I have not done since I was a child'.[35] Mary arrived in Paris in January 1656 and was received 'righty royally', Henrietta Maria told Christine. Indeed she, Mary and Minette were 'today so overwhelmed with visits that I am half dead with fatigue'.[36]

Mary had brought a lady-in-waiting with her who immediately caught James's eye. Anne Hyde, the daughter of Charles's leading counsellor, Sir Edward Hyde, was no beauty, but bold, attractive, and highly intelligent. James was proving to be an even greater womaniser than Charles, so Henrietta Maria did not take their flirtation very seriously. Instead she took pride in Mary who, she noted, 'had pleased both high and low'.[37] Mother and daughter wore widow's black, but in Mary's case, her sombre dress was adorned with magnificent jewels. Even Mademoiselle de Montpensier was impressed by them. They included 'the most beautiful diamond earrings I ever beheld, very fine pearls clasps, and large diamond bracelets, with splendid rings of the same'. Henrietta Maria knew the importance of magnificence, but excused her own plain clothes as a deliberate choice. She wanted to demonstrate that 'lofty ideals' were more important than 'splendour', she explained.[38]

Not everyone was impressed, however, by mere expressions of lofty ideals. There was, indeed, an unpleasant incident after one party where Minette was seemingly slighted by the Grande Mademoiselle, who had inadvertently walked in front of her. Henrietta Maria complained about the breach of etiquette only to learn that this had prompted Louis XIV's younger brother, Philippe, to ask 'what business do these people, to whom we give bread, have to walk before us? Why don't they go elsewhere?' His cruel words reduced Henrietta Maria to tears.[39] After nine months it was Mary who left France, returning to Holland. Her son, the future William III, was ill briefly from measles and she needed to be with him. It was a sad loss for Henrietta Maria whose jewellery collection continued to diminish: even her mother's pearl earrings were sold.

In 1657 the eighteen-year-old Louis XIV gave the Medici pearls to his mistress, Cardinal Mazarin's seventeen-year-old niece Marie Mancini. Henrietta Maria's pearls have been known as the Mancini pearls ever since. There were, however, some acts of generosity. Anne of Austria had given Henrietta Maria the money to buy the small château of Colombes near her childhood home of Saint-Germain-en-Laye. It had gardens running down to the Seine and a large park with a lake full of aquatic birds. By the summer of 1658 Henrietta Maria was preparing to spend the rest of her life in France while her children lived out their own in different parts of Europe. Louis XIV remained allied to Oliver Cromwell and Henrietta Maria's particular concern was her younger sons, James and Harry, who were fighting for Spain.

Charles had several royalist British regiments assisting the Habsburgs in defending Flanders against an Anglo-French invasion. On 14 June James and Harry took part in the Battle of the Dunes at Dunkirk. Their forces were defeated and Dunkirk fell to the French a few days later, leaving Henrietta Maria 'in the greatest possible apprehension' for her sons. Happily they had survived. 'I only wish we were able to meet altogether,' she told Charles, 'I hope that the good God will at length put an end to our misfortunes and will re-establish us in spite of all the world.'[40]

'THE PHOENIX OF OUR TIMES'

CROMWELL HAD ESCAPED ASSASSINATION ATTEMPTS AT THE hands of radicals and royalists – even a gunpowder plot – to die in his bed on 3 September 1658. According to reports he had suffered from malarial fever and kidney disease. Charles II was in Brussels playing tennis with a number of Spanish grandees when he learned the news. They broke off their game to discuss what this meant for his future. His mother wondered the same. Her friends rejoiced at the news of the 'abominable' Cromwell's end, but she confessed she felt no joy over the death 'of that wretch'. She wasn't sure if her grief still ran so deep that she was incapable of feeling happy, or if it was because 'I do not as yet perceive any good advantage set to accrue from it.'[1]

It was diplomatic protocol for the French court to wear black to mark the passing of an ally such as Cromwell was. It was only the fact they were already in mourning following the death of the baby son of the Prince of Conti that they were 'spared . . . the shame of going into mourning for the death of the great destroyer of the English monarchy'. The Grande Mademoiselle was not alone in being relieved, noting 'I should not have worn it without an express order from the king.'[2] The fact remained, however, that the English republic remained France's ally and, as Henrietta Maria had noted, it was uncertain that anything much had changed. With Cromwell buried his son Richard had inherited his role. 'We must await opportunities to avail ourselves of them,' Henrietta Maria reminded Charles, 'I assure you, I will let none slip.'[3]

Meanwhile Henrietta Maria was using her diplomatic leverage to support her daughter Mary. The princess was in conflict with Dutch anti-royalists who wished to deny William III his father's office as stadtholder. She was also keen to arrange a marriage for Minette with Louis XIV. Her youngest daughter was now fourteen, and for Henrietta Maria, a 'little edition of myself'.[4] Christine, who hoped to marry her own daughter Marguerite to Louis, had reported rumours that Minette remained a Protestant. This infuriated Henrietta Maria, who was not going to allow this untruth to spike her daughter's chances. She is 'a good Catholic' she told her sister, firmly, and was well educated by the nuns in matters of religion.

Minette was also a very a popular figure at court. She was pretty, 'her hair of a bright, chestnut hue, and her complexion rivals that of the gayest flowers' one courtier reported, 'Her eyes blue and brilliant, her lips ruddy, her throat beautiful, her arms and hands well made.'[5] She enjoyed reading and poetry, she sang well, played the harpsichord and the guitar, was a graceful dancer and shared her mother's and grandmother's love of masques and ballets, in which she had performed to great acclaim. What made her stand out most, however, was her character. 'You could see by her very perfections that she had been trained in the school of misfortune,' it was said.[6] In contrast to other princesses, she wasn't spoilt, 'She had the mind, the voice, the beauty of an angel,' another recalled.[7]

To Henrietta Maria's disappointment her plans to marry Minette to Louis came to nothing. Like his father, Louis was to marry a Spanish infanta. The long war between the Habsburgs and the Bourbons was at last coming to an end. Richard Cromwell was proving to be a poor leader of a bitterly divided England. Mazarin feared they now had a greatly weakened ally and so, in May 1659, France opened peace negotiations with Spain. A treaty was signed in November ending a war that had continued since 1635. At the same time the marriage alliance was arranged between Louis and the Infanta Maria Theresa, daughter of Henrietta Maria's late sister Elisabeth of Spain. Marie de' Medici would have been delighted. By this time Richard's Protectorate had failed and there was a power vacuum in England. Opportunities of which the Stuarts might yet avail themselves had become a real possibility.

That winter, a courtier recalled, 'there was a greater resort to the Palais-Royal than to the French Court, the good humour and wit of the Queen Mother of England and the beauty of the Princess [Minette] her daughter, giving greater invitation than the particular humour of the French Queen'.[8] To the surprise of Louis's courtiers Henrietta Maria showed 'a great affection for England, notwithstanding the severe usage she and hers had received from it. Her discourse was much with the great men and ladies of France in praise of the people and of their country; of their courage, generosity, good nature; and would excuse all their miscarriages in relation to unfortunate effects of the late war, as if it were a convulsion of some desperate and infatuated persons rather than from the genius and temper of the kingdom.'[9]

Charles had travelled to Spain in November hoping to get French or Spanish support for his restoration. Neither looked forthcoming, but on his return journey to Holland he took the opportunity to visit his mother at Colombes and became very close to Minette, who he found all grown up. It was the first time he had seen Henrietta Maria since their quarrels about her attempts to convert Harry, but since she had repeatedly pledged her support. She told him now she would try and borrow money from Christine to aid his cause. Charles left France just before Christmas, begging Minette 'to continue your kindness to a brother that loves you more than he can express'. She duly sent him a scapular – a piece of cloth, worn by Catholics, as a devotional item. He promised to wear it, asking her not to address him 'with so much ceremony or so many Your Majesties, for between us there is only affection'.[10]

Henrietta Maria was distracted by the death in February 1660 of her brother Gaston. It had taken years for Gaston to emerge from the disgrace of his association with the Fronde. Ironically it may have been his entertaining that winter (Charles was amongst those who had been to his court at Blois) that had proved fatal for his weakened constitution. Yet as the past fell away a brighter future beckoned. In March 1660 the process of the election of a new English Parliament began and the House of Lords, abolished in 1649, was to be restored. The most powerful man in England, the parliamentarian general George Monck – a former member of the royalist Irish army of 1644 – was involved in a secret negotiation with Charles on the terms of his restoration as King of England. On 4 April Charles arrived in the city of Breda in the southern Netherlands and issued a declaration that committed him to Monck's demands for arrears of army pay, indemnities, toleration of the Protestant sects that lay outside the Church of England, and confirmation of purchases of royal and Church land. The new parliament was assembled on 25 April and Charles was proclaimed king. It was, Henrietta Maria declared, 'a miracle', and 'God's doing alone, to have changed the hearts of the English people in an instant, from hate to love'.[11]

A deputation was sent from Parliament to The Hague to request Charles, officially, to return to England as king. The diarist Samuel Pepys was amongst them and shocked to see 'what a sad poor condition for clothes and money the king was, and all his attendants . . . their clothes not being worth 40sh the best of them'.[12] How different from the clothes his father's favourite, the Duke of Buckingham, had worn in Paris in 1625. One suit alone had been valued at fourscore – that is, £80,000. On 23 May Charles prepared to sail for England from Scheveningen, the small port his mother had left in 1643 to fight the civil war. James, restored to his position as England's Lord High Admiral, which his father had given him aged five, had renamed the English ships that were to escort the king home. The *Naseby* – where the massacre of the royalist baggage train had occurred – became the *Royal Charles*, the *Richard* became the *James*, while the *Speaker* was renamed the *Mary*.

As Charles sailed away his siblings Mary, James and Harry took part in celebrations in Breda and The Hague, along with Mary's son William. Over the following weeks they were officially received and entertained in several Dutch cities, while in Amsterdam twenty pageants were staged telling the story of the restoration of the Stuarts. Mary took the opportunity of this boost to her status to once again ask the Dutch states to consider reinstating her son in his father's dignities. While still awaiting an answer Mary planned to return to England. Staying in the Netherlands was, she told Charles, 'the greatest punishment of this world'.[13] Henrietta Maria also took advantage of their new situation to arrange a royal marriage for Minette. After Louis, the greatest prize in France was his brother and heir, Philippe, who now claimed to be in love with Minette.

It was not so very long ago that Philippe had complained about mother and daughter begging bread and suggesting that they be shipped out of France. Although the match was agreed and Philippe continued to express his delight, there were few indications it would be a happy union. Aged nineteen, Philippe was 'handsome, but with a stature and type of beauty more suited to a princess'. He enjoyed cross-dressing at court masques and regularly wore rouge and beauty spots, while 'His vanity, it seemed, made him incapable of affection, save for himself.'[14] Henrietta Maria must have hoped that his obvious faults were merely youthful arrogance. Troublingly, Minette began to lose weight. Henrietta Maria nevertheless pressed forward and prepared to travel to England to negotiate a good dowry for Minette, as well as a marriage for Charles.

Henrietta Maria told Christine how much she was looking forward to returning home and seeing her 'family together', after they had so long been 'vagabonds'.[15] It would have been a moment of great joy. Tragically, however, Harry, who had been in England since May, caught smallpox and died aged twenty on 13 September 1660, shortly before Mary's arrival. He had begun to charm everyone with his natural cheerfulness and his whole family were devastated. Christine understood the depths of his mother's grief and Henrietta Maria wrote to thank her for all she had done 'in my sorrow'. It was 'a blow' that had struck 'close to home'. She felt that God did not want her ever to have complete happiness. Her grief was compounded by the fact a row with another son was brewing. Henrietta Maria had learned that James had married in England without the permission 'of the king my son', and to a commoner 'who was pregnant before their marriage'.[16]

James's bride was Anne Hyde, daughter of Charles's counsellor Sir Edward Hyde and Mary's former lady-in-waiting. 'A girl who will give herself to a prince will do so with anyone,' Henrietta Maria sniffed. This view was shared by Mary and several courtiers told Charles II that they had also slept with her. One even offered to give the baby his surname. Henrietta Maria's concern was that James was wasting diplomatic opportunities for England by marrying a nobody. Anne Hyde's baby was born on 22 October. It was a boy, named Charles. 'I am going to England tomorrow to marry the king my son and to try and unmarry the other one,' Henrietta Maria declared, nonetheless.[17]

On 29 October 1660 Henrietta Maria was at Calais, preparing to sail for Dover in an English ship, accompanied by Wat Montagu, Minette, and the Winter Queen's Catholic son, Prince Edward of the Palatinate. James, as Lord Admiral, had done his best to please his angry mother. The navy was arrayed to greet her, 'in such a manner that their masts appeared like large trees in a spacious wood'. The guns began to thunder their salute, 'in turn and order, one after another they kept up a noise marvellously loud and delightful, which lasted for a good half-hour'. He remained in England, however, possibly to avoid being left alone with her and being given a piece of her mind on his marriage.

The journey across the Channel proved peaceful – almost too peaceful. There was no wind, and the sea was described as like glass. A day passed at sea and a night: time for those aboard to reflect on what lay ahead. Wat had sent a letter to his brother, the former parliamentarian general, the Earl of Manchester, whom Charles I had hoped to arrest along with the five members in 1641. Wat told him that 'though my stay will be very little yet I confess to my great satisfaction in seeing once again my friends, and especially you whom I love with all the tenderness of nature'. Where once he had goaded his father about his conversion, now he worried about how Manchester would respond to seeing him dressed as a priest, 'since it is incumbent to my duty to the queen I presume my appearance in my own profession cannot be offensive'.[18] Wat was also concerned about the reception that Henrietta Maria might face.

The scandalous propaganda of *The King's Cabinet Opened*, with its description of a power-mad queen, had been hugely successful. Wat had, however, published a reply under the title *The Queen's Closet Opened*. His book offered other 'incomparable secrets', but this time they were more innocent: recipes for the kitchen and the medicine cabinet suggested by great court ladies or which had been used in the royal kitchens since the reign of Queen Elizabeth.[19] Henrietta Maria was portrayed not as a warrior and leader of men but in the role of a domestic goddess at the heart of a native British elite. It was proving a massive bestseller. Yet there remained a frisson of danger in the queen's reputation. Her return was heralded by one Englishman as that of 'the phoenix of our times', while others spoke of her 'perfumed rising', describing a martyr of the civil wars, and of her 'Amazonian courage'.[20] For all Wat's efforts it was not going to be for her cakes and preserves that Henrietta Maria was remembered.

On 30 October Henrietta Maria spent her first night in England at Dover Castle, as she had when she arrived in 1625. Charles II came with Mary, James and their cousin, Prince Rupert, to celebrate. Charles's Protestant chaplain and her Catholic priest both said grace at dinner. Some witnesses were, reportedly, 'inflamed' by the sight of a priest making the sign of the cross. In contrast to the past, however, there were no quarrels between the clergymen over who should begin first, with Charles II making it clear he was quite happy to have both men say their prayers. Henrietta Maria returned to London quietly, arriving after dinner on 2 November. The river was packed with sightseers, who stood in boats and on the stairs to the shore. They were disappointed, however, for she had taken a 'very private' way, meeting her sons and Prince Edward at Lambeth, before crossing the Thames and entering Whitehall by the privy stairs. No bells were rung and Pepys counted only three bonfires.

Charles had decorated apartments for his mother and had scarlet silk taffetas and velvets delivered to her from the Great Wardrobe.[21] Her household was restored in full with all its senior officers and ladies of the bedchamber, councils and clerks. There would be a retinue of guards dressed in black velvet cassocks and gold embroidered badges, liveried watermen and coachmen. Many of them – even the watermen – were the same people, or from the same families, who had served her before the war. Some French names went back to before her marriage.[22] Over the next few days, Henrietta Maria accepted visits from many of her old friends and allies.[23]

Lucy Carlisle, who had been released from the Tower in 1651, hoped to see the queen on 5 November, but had a stroke and died as she prepared her toilette 'without ever speaking one word'.[24] Perhaps she feared what kind of greeting she would have been given by the queen she had betrayed in 1642. Yet she needn't have worried. Henrietta Maria never pressed for any retributions and was 'dear and kind' to the parliamentarian son of Susan, Countess of Denbigh, who had died in 1652.[25] Charles wished to limit punishment to the regicides alone. On 20 November Henrietta Maria and Charles attended the Cockpit theatre that Charles I had built at Whitehall, and which had been closed to plays since 1649. The prologue, written by William Davenant, observed that 'They that would have no king, would have no play / The laurel and the Crown together went / Had the same foes and the same banishment'.[26] What followed was a comedy: Ben Jonson's *The Silent Woman*.

The king caused something of a stir by stopping the lutanist John Singleton and asking for the French musicians to play instead.[27] It was an early example of Charles's cultural Francophilia. French food, French dance and the art of conversation were all returning with the half-French king. The Marquess of Halifax referred with disgust to 'this unbounded liberty of talking'.[28] The diarist John Evelyn admired it, however, as 'a politer way of living' while even the Earl of Sandwich admitted that night that the French musicians 'outdo all ours'. The evening at the Cockpit was a happy one, yet Henrietta Maria was still weighed down by the loss of Harry and her quarrel with James.

Two days later, when Pepys got to see the queen, he pronounced her 'a very little plain old woman and nothing more in her presence or garb than any ordinary woman'.[29] There were bitter reminders too of the war for the returning queen. Her former palace, Somerset House, was a sad shell of what it had been. The gardens were 'utterly spoiled and defaced, and many great dunghills made there, by the three regiments that lately have quartered there'.[30] Orders had been made demanding the return of artworks sold by the Commonwealth, but only a few had come home. One such was a 'brazen statue' that Cromwell had taken to Whitehall but then sold for £50 after a 'zealous Quaker' had tried to destroy it.[31] She had just begun work to restore her ruined chapel when Mary fell ill with smallpox.

She sent her own doctor, but on Christmas Eve it became evident her daughter was dying. Asked several times what she wanted for her son, William, Mary replied that she trusted her brother Charles, and her mother. Her death that night at Whitehall aged twenty-nine 'altered the face and gallantry of the whole court'.[32] Mary's body was laid out at Somerset House and at 9 p.m. on 29 December 1660 was taken in a torchlit procession to Westminster Abbey. There she was buried with Harry, as she had asked.[33] Henrietta Maria 'feels the loss severely, after all the misfortunes experienced for so many years and the recent death of her son', the Venetian ambassador reported. Her resolve against James's marriage crumbled. The quarrel no longer seemed so important.

Three days after the burial, on 1 January, she gave a supper for her family in which she gave Anne Hyde and James her blessing. Mary's death also prompted her to make another decision. 'Unable to find consolation in her stay here she has decided to leave for France, overcoming the severity of the weather and caring nothing that the roads have been rendered impassable by the quantity of rain that has fallen these last days.'[34] Charles had restored the income from her jointure estates and provided a generous pension. Now Henrietta Maria wished to see Minette's marriage settled.[35] As their ship set out to sea, it became evident, however, that Minette was ill – perhaps with smallpox, which had just killed Harry and Mary.[36] The ship returned to Portsmouth and for fifteen days Henrietta Maria fretted for her last surviving daughter.

Henrietta Maria was spared further grief. Minette recovered, and they set off again for France.[37] It must have been a relief to reach Pontoise where Wat had organised a welcome at his house. While Henrietta Maria was shown Wat's 'rich pictures . . . jewellery [and] porcelain', the sound of drums and trumpets heralded the arrival of Louis XIV, Anne of Austria, and Minette's groom-to-be, Philippe. There was gossip that Mazarin had hoped to marry the king's brother to one of his nieces, but the cardinal was dying – and before Easter Minette would be Duchess of Orleans. As Louis, Anne and Philippe returned to Paris, Henrietta Maria, Wat and Minette celebrated their good fortunes over a supper of the most 'delicious wines' and 'delicate viandes' that Wat could find.[38] After all that the three had been through together, the feast Wat provided must have tasted all the sweeter.

THE LAST CONSPIRACY

MINETTE'S WEDDING NIGHT ON 31 MARCH 1661 WAS SCARCELY less grim than that of Louis XIII and Anne of Austria over four decades earlier. She was visited by 'the cardinal', she told her brother Charles – a euphemism for menstruation. Philippe proved unable to consummate the marriage, but for a couple of weeks they managed to keep on good terms. This may have been because Minette was still living with her mother. They had almost never been apart since she had arrived in France and when they at last separated the 'sighs, tears, sobs of madam and the queen made some weep, melted the hearts of others and pained all'.[1]

Minette spent that May at Philippe's beautiful palace of Saint-Cloud, about five kilometres west of Paris. Louis wrote to her telling her he wanted to visit, 'not because of its grottos or the freshness of its foliage . . . but the company which is there now is so good that I find myself furiously tempted'.[2] He was bored by his wife, who resembled their grandmother, Marie de' Medici, in her robust appearance, but was a much smaller personality. Soon Louis was spending so much time with Minette there were rumours they were having an affair. Henrietta Maria was anxious her daughter be more discreet and Philippe became extremely jealous. Minette was enjoying star status at court and took pleasure in provoking her husband, even developing a close friendship with one of his previous male lovers.

Despite their mutual antipathy Minette and Philippe managed to produce a daughter on 26 March 1662 – Marie Louise, a future Queen of Spain. With Minette settled, Henrietta Maria prepared to return to England. While she had not succeeded in arranging a marriage for Charles when she was last in England, as she had hoped, she was pleased with the choice he had made over the previous few months: the twenty-three-year-old Portuguese princess, Catherine of Braganza. Portugal was a useful ally for Britain against Spain – and so the marriage was backed by France – and the Portuguese empire offered Britain new trading opportunities. She was also a Catholic. Despite the problems his father had encountered in marrying a 'popish brat', Charles was going out of his way to be sensitive to his wife's religious convictions. He had guaranteed the protection and perpetuation of Roman Catholicism in Tangier and other Portuguese territories. The marriage treaty also stipulated that Catherine should enjoy the same privileges in chapels and clergy as had been granted to Henrietta Maria, though there was less pressure for him to do so.[3]

Most strikingly Charles married Catherine in Portsmouth on 21 May 1662 in a secret Catholic ceremony conducted in Catherine's bedroom.[4] The priest was Henrietta Maria's almoner, Ludovic Stuart, Lord d'Aubigny, whose sister-in-law, the Duchess of Richmond, was also Henrietta Maria's long-standing lady-in-waiting.[5] This ceremony was only then followed by a public Anglican marriage. Henry Jermyn – now Earl of St Albans – wrote to Henrietta Maria describing Catherine as small, dark, and very gentle. Charles told his mother he was quite satisfied with his choice, but it did not seem she would pose much threat to Charles's current mistress, the beautiful black haired, blue eyed Barbara Villiers, who was heavily pregnant with their son.

Henrietta Maria prepared to travel with Lucy Walter's son, the thirteen-year-old Duke of Monmouth. The boy had lived an itinerant life with his mother and her lovers, never even learning to read, write or count. In 1658 Charles had had him kidnapped and taken to Paris. Lucy had died not long afterwards and Monmouth had been living ever since with Henrietta Maria's former Captain of the Guard, William, Lord Crofts, whose brother had been killed by her dwarf, Jeffrey Hudson. In July 1662 Minette accompanied her mother and bastard nephew through France as far as Beauvais. Henrietta Maria had announced that she intended to stay in England for 'the rest of her life'.[6] This was terrible news for Minette and at their parting both shed an 'abundance of tears' for 'love like a weight . . . kept the heart of the queen pressed to that of her daughter, who could not bear that kingdoms and seas should part them'.[7]

Henrietta Maria believed, however, that she had a great deal to achieve in England. Although Parliament had thus far blocked Charles's attempts to offer freedom of religion to both Catholics and Protestants who worshipped outside the Church of England, she believed the persecution could still be ended. The mission she had sworn to in 1624 in her letter to the Pope was not yet complete. Still aged only fifty-two, she remained a forceful character. She had had seals made depicting her sitting under a canopy of state holding a sceptre mounted with a fleur-de-lys, and an orb: attributes of royal power. She intended to use it.[8]

In October 1662 Henrietta Maria told Christine she was the 'happiest person in the world'. Her son held more power, it seemed to her, than his father ever had. Henrietta Maria thought her daughter-in-law, Catherine, was 'the best person'. As a demonstration of her affection she gave Catherine an exquisite headdress of diamonds and emeralds with a watch dial to match. John Evelyn, who had seen Henrietta Maria half dead in Tours in 1644, rejoiced now to see her stay up late at parties, and regale people with dramatic or amusing stories, 'of her escapes during the rebellion and war in England'.[9] Pepys too, noted Henrietta Maria's court was developing a reputation for being 'the greatest court nowadays' with the most 'laughing and . . . mirth'.[10] He also saw her at Somerset House that autumn with Catherine and 'the king's bastard' young Monmouth. The boy was 'a most pretty spark' to whom the queens were both reputed to be 'mighty kind'.[11] Catherine had 'a good, modest and innocent look which is pleasing'. Barbara Villiers was also there, along with the king, James and his wife Anne.

Pepys was amazed to see the royal family all together, plus mistress and bastard son, staying until dark, 'with so much ease and leisure'. Charles was teasing Catherine that he was sure she was pregnant, to which the 'young queen answered, "you lie"'. These were the first words he had heard her speak in English and Charles tried to teach her more, 'Confess!', he said.[12] A month later Henrietta Maria began to hope that Catherine really might be pregnant, as Anne was.[13] Sadly, however, Catherine would never bear children. There were ludicrous accusations that Anne's father had deliberately encouraged Charles to marry Catherine knowing she was barren, so a grandchild of his might one day inherit the throne. Yet Henrietta Maria, so fecund as a young woman, never said a word against her daughter-in-law. Instead she helped smooth the quarrels that arose over Charles's determination to have Barbara Villiers in his wife's household, and not just an occasional companion. She knew that without a son Catherine was in a weak position, and it was better to have the gratitude of the king, and chose other, more significant battles. Barbara Villiers duly joined Catherine's household on 1 June 1663.

As Henrietta Maria's court grew in reputation as 'the greatest of them all' she remained in close contact with Christine.[14] They often shared remedies for their health – Henrietta Maria once recommended tea, 'a leaf which comes from the Indies', which she had newly discovered. In November 1663 she was concerned to have learned Christine had been unwell, but was 'so happy' to have discovered at the same instance that she was now better. Sadly, Christine's health worsened again and on 27 December 1663, she died. Her sister's death felt like a pain from 'hell', Henrietta Maria observed. Only God was capable of easing such 'a great blow'.[15] Like Henrietta Maria, Christine had faced great trials, but she had embodied the spirit of the duchy to which she had come to belong as consort. She left it in a strong position and Christine's grandson achieved the title King of Sardinia, confirming the royal status she had sought. Henrietta Maria's New Year was spent in mourning, but she was comforted by her loyal friends and old servants.

Envy and spite prompted rumours that Henry Jermyn was more than a friend – that he was her lover. It was even said she was his wife and that they had a daughter in France, or that Barbara Villiers was, in fact, their child.[16] The truth was more mundane. She was fond of Barbara Villiers, who had just become a Catholic following a serious illness, and she would even leave her a large amount of money in her will, but Henrietta Maria spent more time with her ladies-in-waiting than she ever did with Jermyn: companions like Susan Denbigh's daughter Elizabeth Boyle, Countess of Guilford, who had taken on her mother's role as Mistress of the Wardrobe and Groom of the Stool. [17]

The spring of 1664 brought better times. The theatre Henrietta Maria so loved was enjoying a vigorous renaissance. Davenant put on over fifty productions in five years: comedies and tragicomedies, farces and burleseques, with women reappearing on the stage. The royal patent issued to him in 1662 made their role official, 'so long as their recreations may by such reformation be esteemed not only harmless delight but useful and instructive to representations of human life'. Davenant even introduced opera. Henrietta Maria, meanwhile, was now spending three times what she had in the 1630s. Some went to charitable causes – in particular, she liked to buy poor debtors out of prison, remembering, perhaps, her own troubles.[18] But she still enjoyed buying beautiful and fashionable clothes and retained her passion for building and planting.

The new lodgings for her household at Somerset House was the largest-scale architectural commission of the first nine years of the Restoration. When Pepys visited in February 1664 he declared it both 'magnificent and costly'.[19] A new suite of state rooms overlooking the Thames was also built, and her private apartments were 'most nobly stately and nobly furnished'.[20] Henrietta Maria introduced parquet floors – almost unknown in England – and hung the set of gold and silver Mortlake tapestries depicting Hero and Leander which she had pawned in February 1650. The first sash windows were built and gardens were planted with contributions to the design by Le Nôtre.

More significant, however, was the restoration of the queen's chapel. Even Protestants like Pepys thought it 'very fine'.[21] She acquired plate that had once belonged to Richelieu, and 'it was a ravishing sight to the eyes, a subject of high admiration to the mind, and a strong incitement to devotion of heart!'

The quality of the sermons given by the Capuchins once again attracted attention. Her almoner's sermons on the Real Presence of Christ in the Eucharist were later published in France. They may even have prompted Charles II to make some injudicious comments to the Anglican Bishop Burnet, in which he appeared to accept the Roman Catholic doctrine of transubstantiation.[22] Henrietta Maria revived the Confraternity of the Rosary and was delighted that people were again soon flooding to hear Mass in her chapel. Pepys noted it was 'ten times more crowded than [Catherine of Braganza's] chapel at St James's, which I did wonder at'.[23] She advertised conversions, making a Chinese boy who had arrived on a trading boat from the East Indies her godson, the Mass for his confirmation performed before 'a great concourse of the people [with] many Protestants mingled amongst them'.[24]

Henrietta Maria also followed up work she had begun in 1660 in commissioning English translations of religious books and by establishing a printing press. A number of Anglican clergy who had become Catholics published works arguing for a reunification of the churches, a subject that had been close to the heart of her late husband and father-in-law.[25] Provincial Catholics were drafted into court positions and once again there were concerns that those at Somerset House 'carried on the government . . . and that popery was coming in'.[26] Placards appeared at Somerset House, but those who came to her chapel were not physically attacked as they had been before the civil wars.

Henrietta Maria's health, however, remained poor.[27] In June 1665, Pepys was at Somerset House where he saw her goods being packed up, as she had 'a consumption' and was about to leave to take the waters in France.

The queen mother's packages included a dozen pictures from the restored royal collection. Amongst them were two Van Dycks, one of her three eldest children and a portrait of the eight-year-old Charles II when Prince of Wales. From the Queen's House she took Orazio Gentileschi's *Joseph and Potiphar's Wife* – a subject that had attracted his artist daughter Artemisia who had been employed by the queen on the eve of the Civil War. She also kept a portrait of Charles's brother Prince Henry. It may have reminded her of her husband – and she took a new acquisition: Tintoretto's *Portrait of Marco Grimani*.[28] The scientist and architect Christopher Wren was to travel with her, to see the works that Louis XIV wished to carry out at the Louvre, and to study other palaces in France. Charles II, whose bedchamber at Whitehall closely resembled that of Louis XIV at the Louvre, was as anxious to rebuild Whitehall as his father before him.

An outbreak of plague was hastening her departure, so Henrietta Maria left money for the sick and spoke to her Capuchins before she left. 'As God had endowed her with a shrewd and ready understanding and great fluency of speech, she made us immediately a fine address,' one recalled. They were sorry to see her go. As one of the Capuchins observed, she was 'the *primum mobile* that impelled the whole machine; nothing was done but under her authority and protection'.[29] She hoped not to be away long and she assured them that the chapel would remain open while she was away.[30] It was estimated she would be back in twelve months, but the plague was to be worse than anyone imagined.

As thousands died Henrietta Maria sent a message back from France asking for her chapel to be shut, 'that this contagious disease not be spread further by the intermixture and communication of healthy and infected persons'. The friars dissuaded her, and two of the eight Capuchins subsequently succumbed to the disease, as did over a quarter of the population of London in eighteen months.

Henrietta Maria had escaped London's plague, but not what ailed her. Although she went regularly to the spa town of Bourbon-l'Archambault to take the waters, there were fainting fits and bouts of sleeplessness.[31] Henrietta Maria liked to say 'complaints in illness were useless' and so she did not. Madame de Motteville remembered the queen during these years as 'lively, pleasant, penetrating, free and gay'.[32] On holy days Henrietta Maria would retreat to her convent and enjoy quiet and contemplation in an exclusively female space. Otherwise she divided her time between winter at the magnificent Hôtel de la Bazinière, which Louis XIV had given her as her Paris residence, and summer at Colombes.[33]

Louis granted permission for a weekly market and a twice-yearly fair to be held in the grounds of Colombes. This ensured it was an important fixture in the community and, modest as it was in scale, the two-storey château was an exquisite setting for important visitors. Henrietta Maria had paid her gardener a large pension to ensure the gardens at Colombes were developed while she was away and the public rooms were hung with her pictures and tapestries. A trumpeter was employed to announce her presence and houses were rented nearby for her ladies-in-waiting and other staff.[34] Yet her past suffering was not erased, 'which, to my mind, made her more solid, more serious, more estimable than she might have been had she always been happy', Madam de Motteville remarked.[35]

Every day Henrietta Maria read a chapter from Thomas à Kempis's fifteenth-century spiritual handbook *The Imitation of Christ*, so that she might live her life better. One characteristic, noted throughout her life, had become more noticeable. This was Henrietta Maria's thoughtfulness towards her lowly domestic servants. While she herself was 'quick', she went out of her way to be patient with those who were slow, and 'took great care of them'.[36] She was still employing the same cobbler she had in the 1620s. She had herself survived longer than she had ever expected. Indeed, she outlived Anne of Austria, who died in January 1666, attended during her last months by Wat Montagu.

Louis XIV, who had adored his mother and missed her, turned to his aunt that year for her help and advice, 'more than once'. In particular, he asked Henrietta Maria to help promote peace between England and France (who had been allied with the Dutch against England), finding her, so it was reported, 'very competent and helpful'.[37] During the complex negotiations in 1667 the château at Colombes was even suggested as the ideal place for the peace conference to take place.[38] It was grinding work for a woman in poor health, and the following year, 1668, when Charles had joined the Dutch in a Triple alliance with Sweden against France, Minette began to take on the burden. Henrietta Maria's 'little edition of myself', also had a dramatic proposal to make. Minette suggested Charles should ally with Louis against the Dutch and agree to convert to Catholicism at some future date. In return he would get a pension from Louis large enough to free him from parliamentary constraints, and the promise of French troops if his conversion triggered a rebellion.

Charles II, at this stage in his reign, was deep in debt, his prestige had been damaged by a failed war against the Dutch, and there were attacks also on his personal morality. He had fathered at least nine illegitimate children. In March 1668, when crowds attacked several of London's brothels, people observed that they were doing a poor job, ripping down the little bawdy houses, and leaving 'the great bawdy house at Whitehall'.[39] There were warnings that revolution could return as easily as simmering water brought back to the boil.

Minette's assurances to Charles that a French alliance, and French money, could be 'the veritable foundation of your own greatness' were attractive if any promises to convert were kept from his Protestant subjects. It seems quite possible, however, that Henrietta Maria knew something of what became known as the secret Treaty of Dover.

The elements in the treaty negotiations concerning religion were handled by British figures associated with Somerset House and with Henrietta Maria's court in exile. It was her Master of the Horse, Lord Arundell of Wardour, who brought over a draft of the secret treaty to France early in 1669. It was her old friend Wat Montagu who translated correspondence sent to Minette by other Englishmen involved in the secret negotiations.[40] As these negotiations continued, however, her health continued to fail. On 23 August 1669, Henrietta Maria came to visit her daughter at Saint-Cloud, where Minette was due to have a second baby. Minette's daughter, Marie Louise, was staying at Colombes, as was James's daughter, the future Queen Anne, who was being treated for a problem with her eyes. James's first son had died, but he had another living, Edgar – the current third in line to the Stuart throne – who was almost a year old. Minette was hoping desperately that she would now have a son, a possible future king of France. Four days later she had another daughter and there was no opportunity to see her mother for consolation.

Henrietta Maria was in pain, not sleeping, and was talking about retiring to the convent at Chaillot to die. Minette persuaded her instead to see a panel of the best doctors in Paris – including her own and that of Louis. The king's doctor, Monsieur Vallot, duly reassured Henrietta Maria that she was 'without danger of death' and suggested that she have three grains of opium to help her sleep. She replied that her own doctor had warned her against opiates, but Vallot reassured her that the 'grains he proposed were of a particular composition, and that he would not have been so ill advised as to propose them, had he not known to a certainty that they would be conducive to her health'. Minette's doctor chipped in that he was sure Vallot knew best.

After they had gone, Henrietta Maria had her supper. Her best dining chair had been brought over from Somerset House. Covered in black velvet and with a gold trim it had two footstools to match. She liked soup in the evening made from meat stock flavoured with a little lemon.[41] She laughed and enjoyed herself. She then went to bed and slept for a time, but woke at around 11 p.m. The lady-in-waiting who was sleeping in her chamber gave her the grains of opium mixed with raw egg. To the woman's horror Henrietta Maria immediately became insensible. She shook the queen, and shouted, in a failed attempt to wake her. Then she called for the priests. They performed the last rites while she was still breathing, but she died on 10 September 1669 unaware of their prayers.[42] The priests were angry that a final confession and Communion had been denied her. The grains had been a tiny quantity but they blamed Louis's doctor for giving her a 'murderous dose'. Henrietta Maria was, in any case, beyond the anger and arguments of the world, even if her body and her story were not.

THE LESSONS OF FAILURE

CHARLES II HEARD THE NEWS OF HIS MOTHER'S DEATH ON 10 September 1669 'with infinite grief' and was 'unable to hold back his tears'.[1] He broke off from his hunting and retired with Catherine of Braganza to Hampton Court. He stayed there for two weeks as the formal period of court mourning was prepared. Even a week later it was evident that it had affected him to 'an extraordinary extent'. The whole of Whitehall was hung with black, and his 'inner grief' matched 'these outward shows'.[2] Charles's siblings were also deeply saddened.

For James, the news had come at a significant juncture: he and his wife Anne Hyde were soon to convert to Catholicism. The hatred of 'popery' in England had come to seem absurd to James in exile in Europe where he was surrounded by Catholics. He was also dismayed by the inter-Protestant quarrels that had played such a key role in his father's fate. Unsure what to do, he recalled 'a nun's advice that he pray every day that, if he were not in the right way, God would set him straight'.[3] It was surely, however, Anne Hyde, who converted first, who had most encouraged James.

In France Minette took charge of her mother's funeral arrangements. Henrietta Maria's body had been laid out on a bed of state in her chamber for one night. It was then embalmed and now lay in the hall at Colombes. She was to be buried with her royal ancestors at the Basilica of Saint-Denis on 21 November. The Bishop of Amiens was to officiate. It was in Amiens in 1625 that she had been given the Golden Rose from the Pope along with a text exhorting her to be 'a flower' amongst the thorns of heresy, reseeding the Catholic faith in England.[4] She had done her best to do so – both in supporting British Catholics who were forbidden the Mass and by advertising the best of her faith. A further requiem would be held at Notre Dame on 28 November. Meanwhile Henrietta Maria's heart and entrails were placed in a silver casket resembling a reliquary and, a few days after her death, taken in a mourning coach to the nuns at Chaillot.

The gates at the convent were draped in black and the casket was received by Wat Montagu in a formal ceremony. Forty-four years earlier Wat had been at Amiens. He was then a young man with a baby face, a Calvinist with a taste for amusing and intelligent female company and a great favourite of Henrietta Maria's enemy, the Duke of Buckingham. He now struck a very different figure, in his black clerical robes, standing at the door of the cloister, a man Edward Hyde, Earl of Clarendon described as 'wholly restrained from the vanity and levity of his former life'. The nuns took the casket, and 'conducted it in double file, singing the Miserere as far as the choir'.[5] This was hung with black, while the altar where her heart was to be placed was dressed in black velvet embroidered with the arms of the queen. Her remains were placed on a credenza and Wat led the prayers, before addressing the abbess, Anne-Marie Bollain – an echo of another controversial French-educated consort to an English king.

Henrietta Maria was, Wat believed, a 'martyr for the faith' in what she had suffered and all Henrietta Maria's 'temporal greatness' was 'not equal to the virtues of her spirit'. The abbess replied, describing the honour to the convent of being granted 'a heart all penetrated with sorrow' and of a 'great queen', praying that their order 'would always display the great and heroic virtues which we saw her practise'.[6] The funeral service at Chaillot was due on 16 November. This was still weeks away and, in the meantime, Henrietta Maria's financial affairs had to be settled. It transpired that Henrietta Maria had not left a will.

She was said to have called for one on the night she died and, having reread it, announced she didn't like it, and so tore it, saying she would arrange for another to be written the following day.

Philippe Orleans laid a claim to all her goods, as did William of Orange. Minette declined to be involved in this unseemly scramble, and, happily, Charles, rather than push his own claims, came to an amicable agreement with Louis. Colombes and its fixtures and fittings would go to Minette, while anything moveable would return to England. Charles II's commissioners for surveying the queen's property arrived in Paris at the end of October.[7] Several of them were simultaneously involved in negotiating the secret Treaty of Dover.

The commissioners found over seventy paintings at Colombes. Most were family portraits, especially of Henrietta Maria's children and grandchildren. There was a picture of Charles II as a boy in the vestibule, and one of James in her bedroom. In her cabinet she kept a miniature of Charles I as Prince of Wales. It was placed in a little Indian box with two wedding rings. She had left a picture by the Dutch artist Duo, called 'the Tooth Drawer' to Minette – this may have been a joke reference to the suffering she had endured from her bad teeth since 1642 when she wrote complaining about them to Charles. Otherwise, anything that could be moved was taken – including a Guido Reni that was fixed to the wall but found nevertheless to be removable. Persian carpets, an Indian screen that she had had in her dressing room at Somerset House, sets of tapestries, all were packed up. One of the religious pictures was given to Catherine of Braganza.[8]

Minette had chosen her own spiritual director, Bishop Jacques-Bénigne Bossuet, to give the major funeral oration for her mother at Chaillot on 16 November. He did not know Henrietta Maria well, and at Minette's suggestion he turned to Madame de Motteville, who wrote a short biography of the queen's life for the bishop. It was one of the first royal memoirs written by a woman in French and Bossuet, considered to be one of the finest orators of all time, used it as the basis of what would be one of his greatest funeral orations.

Bossuet detailed the story of Henrietta Maria's marriage, of her struggles for persecuted Catholics, of the dangers she had faced during the Civil War, of her successes and, more importantly, her failures. Henrietta Maria had told Madame de Motteville that she had become grateful that she had known sorrow. Bossuet explained why. 'Failure is the only lesson that can successfully call us back [to God] and wrench from us the avowal that we have sinned, which costs so much to our pride. So when misery opens our eyes, we reconsider with bitterness up all our false steps; we find ourselves equally guilty for what we have done and what we have failed to do.' It taught her acceptance without despair, the examination of conscience and the importance of getting to the truth, the heart of things. 'Let us no more complain of her disgrace,' he observed; 'If she had been more fortunate, her history would have been more pompous, but her works would have been less full and with these superb titles she might, perhaps, have appeared empty-handed before God.' In the end, small acts of kindness matter more than great victories.

Yet Bossuet hoped that Henrietta Maria's sacrifices would help to save the House of Stuart from further afflictions and that Minette would follow her mother in working 'ceaselessly for the union of the two kings you are so close to, so that their power and virtue may create the destiny of all Europe'.[9] Work on the secret Treaty of Dover was reaching a crucial stage.

Minette was physically frail. It is possible that, like her mother, she had tuberculosis. Philippe was also exercising what we would now recognise as attempts at coercive control. Minette was dismissed, abused, separated from her friends, not just by her husband but also by his lover, the Chevalier de Lorraine. Philippe tried to prevent her travelling to England, where she was to help complete the treaty, but after Charles complained, she arrived in England to celebrate his fortieth birthday on 29 May 1670. The boat races, banquets, ballets and expeditions provided cover for celebrating the treaty, which had been signed on 22 May.

When Minette returned she left a beautiful French woman behind in England, Louise de Kérouaille, who was intended to be her eyes and ears. Louise would duly become Charles's mistress – but Minette would not even outlive her mother by a year.

On 29 June 1670, Minette complained of a sudden pain in her side after drinking a glass of iced chicory water. It is now believed she had a duodenal ulcer. She died at Saint-Cloud the next day and was buried at Saint-Denis on 21 August. The secret treaty was effectively buried with Minette and not unearthed until the papers were printed by the English Catholic historian John Lingard in 1830.[10] Wat Montagu retreated from court after officiating at Minette's funeral. He gave up his abbey and retired to the Hospital of the Incurables, where he died in 1677. He left much of his art collection to Queen Catherine.[11] What of other old friends? The Duchess of Richmond had travelled to Paris in 1667 to serve as Henrietta Maria's Groom of the Stool, and was now serving Catherine of Braganza, as were many others of her household.

Jeffrey Hudson, the dwarf Henrietta Maria had raised since he was five years old and had been captured into slavery in 1644, had returned to England. His freedom had been bought along with that of other English slaves in Africa. Perhaps Henrietta Maria had learned of it – he was in England in May 1669 when he had written a letter about a small pension he was receiving from George, Duke of Buckingham – the son of the man who had gifted him to the queen. The letter was composed in Rutland, where he had been born. He was probably living with his brother Samuel, but in 1677 a year after Samuel died, Jeffrey decided to return to court.

The London Jeffrey found looked quite different from the one he had left. The Great Fire of 1666 had consumed the Cathedral of St Paul's as well as many other churches and houses. The foundation stone of Wren's new cathedral had been laid in 1676 and thousands of new houses had been built. But there was still Somerset House, and an inn on Newgate Street had a sign on which a figure was engraved of himself alongside Henrietta Maria's giant porter William Evans. Old as he was, he must have felt some sense of excitement at his return – but there was also danger. The fire had been blamed on Catholics, giving a fresh impetus to English anti-popery. A psychopath called Titus Oates had used this to fuel accusations of a Catholic conspiracy against Charles II. Jeffrey Hudson was briefly imprisoned and was fortunate it ended there – around thirty-five innocent men were executed.[12]

Catherine of Braganza claimed that Charles II had been tormented by having allowed the execution of these men and that he took the last rites of the Catholic Church on his deathbed in 1685. According to James they were given at the hands of a Father Huddlestone, whom Charles had met while on the run for Worcester. We cannot know whether or not this is true. Charles had said during his exile that he hoped to tolerate Catholics, but that neither political expediency nor his conscience, would permit his acceptance of the Roman Catholic faith.[13] It is possible this had changed over time. One contemporary believed that when he returned to England in 1660, 'he was certainly a Roman Catholic, as that he was a man of pleasure, both very consistent by visible experience'.[14] Many others agreed, 'though he hid his popery until the last'.

If Charles had not been prepared to risk his crown to publicly declare what he may (or may not) have believed in his heart, he was willing for James to reign as a Catholic monarch. So were others, who preferred accepting a Catholic king to risking another civil war. When in 1688 James's second wife Catherine of Modena had a son, James Francis Edward, the prospect of a line of Catholic kings changed the calculation. James II and his son were overthrown and barred in favour of his Protestant daughter Mary II and her husband, William III of Orange. The following year James visited the convent of Chaillot where he went to pray for his mother. He hoped to return home, but never would. Instead, every September, while he lived in exile at Saint-Germain-en-Laye, he attended a requiem said for Henrietta Maria's soul on the anniversary of her death. When he died his heart was buried alongside hers. Henrietta Maria's story exemplifies one of life's bitter truths: you may win your battles, but you cannot win the battles of those you love.

The last Stuart monarch was to be James's second daughter, Anne, the little girl with poor eyesight who had been staying with Henrietta Maria at Colombes in the queen mother's last days. When Queen Anne died, the throne passed to her nearest Protestant heir, a junior descendant of Charles I's sister, the Winter Queen. The bloodline of Henrietta Maria and Charles I will, however, be restored in our future king, Prince William. He is descended from Charles II, through Barbara Villiers – once said to have been Henrietta Maria's bastard daughter – and Louise de Kérouaille, the French beauty Minette brought to England and whom he loved to the last.

HENRIETTA MARIA JOKED TO CHARLES IN 1642 THAT SHE would pray for the man who had married 'the popish brat of France, as the preacher said in London.'[1] She knew she was seen as an agent of the papal Antichrist, seducing Charles into his evil and tyrannical ways. In popular legend she remains very much the preacher's queen: one who was only going to become more popish and brattish in the years ahead. What happens, however, if we look at the events of her marriage and widowhood from Henrietta Maria's point of view?

Aged fifteen in 1625, Henrietta Maria saw the match with Charles as in the tradition of her father's alliances with Protestants against the Catholic Habsburgs. She was willing to show him love from the moment they met, running into the arms of her new husband at Dover. That night, when she was asked if she could 'stand' a Huguenot she observed that her father had been one. When Henrietta Maria reached London, she accepted a blessing of her marriage at the hands of a Protestant bishop.

Yet it was immediately clear that there were many in England who could not 'stand' a Catholic. Her husband was breaking the terms of the marriage treaty, denying her suitable chapels for her worship. In Parliament her religious rights were under further attack and MPs were threatening to take children away from any Catholic parent.

The Pope had only agreed to permit the marriage in return for a commitment from Henrietta Maria that she would raise her children as Catholic, act as a protector of her co-religionists and work for the conversion of the British kingdoms. Henrietta Maria had been advised by her mother to achieve these conversions by example. From an early age Henrietta Maria had been taught that women had an important role to play in making the world a better place, containing male violence and inspiring a more refined way of living. She applied these lessons to her religious duties.

Henrietta Maria set an example by demonstrating a strong commitment to her religion and in projecting her values through her artistic and cultural endeavours. As for converting Charles: she had not been told to manipulate him. She had been assured that the fact that his grandmother, Mary, Queen of Scots, had died virtually a Catholic martyr would be enough to bring him to the Catholic fold. When, in 1625, Charles renewed and increased the persecution of Catholics (thus breaking his promises to the Pope and to Louis), Henrietta Maria did not respond with attempts at seduction, but with anger.

After she lost her French household in 1626, Henrietta Maria felt very alone and became ill and depressed. Who now was more likely to convert? Henrietta Maria was a child, far from home, in a country of millions of Protestants who hated her religion. The denial of papal authority in religious as well as secular matters was part and parcel of Charles I's belief in 'divine right' kingship, and, as he was demonstrating, he expected all his subjects to worship as he did.

Marie de' Medici had always feared that her daughter might succumb to the pressure she would be placed under in England to become a Protestant. This is why she told Henrietta Maria at the farewell ceremony in Amiens that she must be prepared to accept martyrdom rather than give up her religion, and had warned that if she did turn apostate, then her maternal blessing would turn to a curse.

In the event neither Charles nor Henrietta Maria would ever abandon their birth religion. The association today of Charles with Roman Catholicism is a hangover from seventeenth-century Puritans defining

'Arminian' Protestantism as 'popish' – and Charles was an 'Arminian' before he ever set eyes on his wife. Indeed, far from converting Charles, Henrietta's influence on him in matters of faith would only ever mitigate his persecution of Catholics. She never convinced Charles to end it. Nor was she able to have her children baptised as Catholic, whatever her promises to the Pope.

The 1630s, when her elder children were born, were, however, the happiest period of Henrietta Maria's life. Van Dyck's portraits of the queen in silk and lace, and the myth of a dressing-up-box culture of masques and romances, have associated her with the image of a Marie Antoinette on the eve of a revolution. What some would remember as 'halcyon days' of peace and gaiety others would later label the 'eleven-years tyranny', since they coincided with Charles decision in 1629 to rule without Parliament. In what way, however, had Henrietta Maria been responsible for the collapse in Charles's relationship with Parliament? And were the 1630s really a period of unrelenting frivolity for the queen?

The king's quarrels with his MPs in the 1620s had been rooted in their dislike of the Duke of Buckingham (whom she had detested), in his Arminian religious reforms (in which she had no interest), and in his willingness to raise money from his subjects without parliamentary approval, most notably the forced loans, which he had raised to fund a war with France that she had strongly opposed. Far from expressing antipathy to Parliament as an institution, the queen's subsequent support during the early 1630s for an aggressive anti-Spanish foreign policy associated her with court supporters of the parliamentary cause. Charles could not afford such a war without calling a parliament.

When Henrietta Maria welcomed Panzani, the first of the papal envoys to arrive in England, her closest friends were from Calvinist families: Wat Montagu and Henry Holland amongst them. Holland was infamous for his love of fine clothes, and Wat Montagu was well known for his amusing conversation, but these were also serious men who had been involved with the queen in conspiring against Richelieu, the architect of French absolutism, and in pushing their anti-Spanish agenda. The arrival of Panzani, and still more of George Conn, did mark a shift, however, and the opening of the queen's chapel at Somerset House demonstrated her growing confidence in asserting her faith. She wanted a British version of the Edict of Nantes, that would give Catholics the rights Protestants had enjoyed in France during her childhood. She also hoped to see the same successes the Catholic missionary efforts had enjoyed in her homeland. Conn, in particular, emboldened Henrietta Maria to multiply her efforts to push her agenda, even to build a devot party at court. In retrospect this was unwise, but before the Bishops' Wars even the king's most powerful enemies assumed he was far more secure on his throne than he turned out to be.

Contrary to Puritan propaganda it wasn't Henrietta Maria's influence that saw Charles impose a new Arminian-style prayer book on the Scots, but when the Scots rose up against it, she did seek to support her husband.

Like her sister Elisabeth in Spain (working in support of Philip IV), Henrietta Maria turned to her court ladies, asking them to sell their jewels to pay for the king's army against rebels. Like her sister she also took a lead in advocating regular prayers and fasts to call on God to aid her husband's cause. The difference was that she did so as a member of a minority religion, one that still had no right to practise its faith. Henrietta Maria was persuaded by Conn that proofs of Catholic loyalty, especially in raising money for the king's armies, could change that, and so she saw to it that they did so. Belief in a deep state popish conspiracy put paid to her hopes.

Instead of erasing memories of the Gunpowder Plot, it was assumed that Catholics were active in raising money because they had manipulated and created this inter-Protestant war – and Charles failed to win it. In 1640 Henrietta Maria was extremely fearful about what MPs in the new parliament might do to Catholics in return for raising taxes to aid the king in a second war with the Scottish rebels. In the event no taxes were raised and the parliament was to be short. Henrietta Maria was glad to see the back of it. If Charles had won the second Bishops' War he would have been able to face down his enemies and prevent a possible pogrom against her co-religionists – but he lost and the queen found herself and her fellow Catholics under physical as well as verbal attack.

The Henrietta Maria of the 1630s was described as a woman who put her trust entirely in the king. This was not to be the Henrietta Maria of the 1640s, but that does not mean that she dominated her husband, or that her advice was childish and extremist as it had so often been characterised. In 1640 Henrietta Maria wanted Charles to take control of the narrative, to give up powers willingly rather than have them forced from him, to focus on regaining the love of his people. He either would not or could not show the necessary flexibility. Nor did Charles prove able to match the ruthlessness of opponents who arrested – and would execute – his leading servants.

Henrietta Maria supported a fight back in the arrest of five Members of Parliament in 1642 for being in treasonous collusion with the Scottish rebels. She was frustrated at the king's inability to have his orders carried out. It does not follow that Henrietta Maria supported Charles's spur-of-the-moment decision to go to Parliament in person to arrest the MPs. That was his choice alone, one that failed in its objective and precipitated the loss of London.

From 1642 Henrietta Maria would do whatever it took to save a king who had only ever known defeat in war dating back to the loss of his army at Breda in 1625. Even the king's enemies believed it was only Henrietta Maria's advice and support over the following years that allowed him to fight as long as he did. As the Venetian ambassador noted, 'without [the queen's] encouragement and aid the king would never have put himself into a position to resist'.[2] She was able to work with such diverse figures as Lucy Carlisle and Henry Holland, who had betrayed her in 1642, and Rupert of the Rhine, with whom she quarrelled over military strategy and yet he deeply regretted her departure from the Civil War capital in Oxford in 1644.

What is better remembered than her successes is Henrietta Maria's wish to see Catholic troops in Charles's armies, and that is seen as a gross misjudgement. Certainly, it was not a popular call, but Charles needed men, especially after he had ignored her advice to try and take London in 1643. Catholic France was helping German Protestants against the Habsburgs in the Thirty Years' War. The parliamentarian Prince Palatine, Charles Louis, would never have been able to return to his homeland in 1648 without French Catholic help. Whether or not Catholics troops would have helped Charles, we know that when the Scots joined the war for Parliament in 1644 a tipping point was reached. He couldn't match their numbers.

Fighting against the odds, Henrietta Maria continued to give Charles material support from France until his defeat and imprisonment in 1646. Henrietta Maria then tried to persuade Charles to come to an accommodation with his various captors. First the Scots, then with Parliament and finally with the New Model Army. When all these efforts failed she helped supply and support a second civil war in 1648. That too was lost and Charles's trial and execution the following year saw him announce his willingness to die for the Church of England and express his unswerving belief in 'divine right' kingship. This was the same king, holding the same beliefs, that Henrietta Maria had first met in Dover in 1625. She had neither turned him Catholic nor formed his authoritarianism.

Yet Henrietta Maria saw her husband's death as a consequence of her mistakes, as well as his own, and her tearful words to Madame de Motteville the day after she learned of his execution are revealing. She warned Anne of Austria that she needed to employ people who would dare speak the truth to her and that she must work hard to discover where the truth lay, for the greatest danger to kings and empires lay in ignorance. She had taken too much on trust.

Henrietta Maria also believed, however, that what had happened to her husband and his ruined kingdoms was divinely ordained, and she blamed the sins of Henry VIII. Protestant division, as she saw it, had caused the English to cut the head off their own king. Where in the past she had hoped to encourage conversions by example, she now began to take a much more aggressive stand and not least with her own children. There were, however, practical as well as religious reasons for Henrietta Maria's infamous attempts to convert Harry. She wished to spare him the penury and powerlessness that appeared to be Charles II's lot.

Henrietta Maria's estrangement from Henry when he disobeyed her was also a political act. She could not afford to be seen as weak while Charles II remained an impoverished exile and needed what help she could give him through her influence in France. The tragedy was that she was looking forward to her family being reunited after the Restoration in 1660, and Harry died before that could happen. Henrietta Maria did, though, emerge from her period of grief and mourning as a still powerful and dynamic figure, truly the 'phoenix queen' she was hailed as on her return in 1660.

Was Henrietta Maria the great queen prophesied at her birth and hailed as at her funeral? In her lifetime she had become a symbol of division, and she has never come to embody a national myth that we can take pride in and share. If she is not to be remembered as a great queen, she was surely, however, one of our most remarkable. Of those queen consorts we have seen since the union of the crowns, she was perhaps the most remarkable of them all.

ACKNOWLEDGEMENTS

THERE ARE A NUMBER OF IMPORTANT HISTORIANS WHO HAVE been working on Henrietta Maria, bringing new aspects of her life to public attention: Caroline Hibbard, Malcolm Smuts, Diana Barnes, Karen Ruth Britland, Stephanie Marie Seery-Murphy, Erica Veevers, Sara J. Wolfson, Michelle Anne White and many others. I wish this biography could have been twice as long, for their work shows just how much more there is to say. I am particularly grateful to Erin Griffey who read my first draft and supplied me with articles she had written on a number of areas, often before they had gone to press. It was – is – incredibly generous of her.

I enjoyed very much rereading the biographies by Katie Whitaker (crammed with wonderful detail) and that of my witty friend Dominic Pearce. I am also grateful for conversations and email contacts I have had with my friend the historian Sarah Poynting and for her sharing her research and PhD on Wat Montagu. Thank you to the editor and screenwriter Lorren Boniface for her help transcribing the Louvre Manuscript on the character of Henrietta Maria, and to Camilla Anderson who helped with translations. The staff at the British Library and London Library are always extremely helpful, and I would particularly like to mention those at the London Library's Country Orders Department who post me books or email me scanned pages and make a huge difference to my working life. I would further like to thank my very supportive editors Becky Hardie and David Milner, and my dearest friend and agent, Georgina Capel.

I have dedicated this book to my beautiful granddaughter Cosima, but I would also like to add a word about my daughter-in-law, Daisy. Thank you Daisy for being you, and for all the joy you bring to our family.

Abbreviations and Commonly Cited Sources:

AAE	Archives des Affaires Étrangères Paris
Barb. Lat.	Biblioteca Apostolica Vaticana
Belvoir MSS	Manuscripts held at Belvoir Castle, private collection.
BL	British Library
BNF	Bibliothèque nationale de France
CSPD	Calendar of State Papers, Domestic
CSPV	Calendar of State Papers, Venetian
Hastings MSS	Huntingdon Library
HL	Parliamentary Archives, House of Lords, Record Office
HMC	Historical Manuscripts Commission
Louvre BNF	Bibliothèque nationale de France
ODNB	*Oxford Dictionary of National Biography*
PRO	Public Record Office
TNA	The National Archives

Clarendon, Edward Hyde, Earl of (1609-1674), *Calendar of the Clarendon state papers, preserved in the Bodleian Library*, 5 volumes.

Chapter 1: A Carpenter's Workshop

1. Louise Bourgeois, *Midwife to the Queen of France: Diverse Observations*, ed. Alison Klairmont Lingo, trans. Stephanie O'Hara (2017), p. 244. Marie de' Medici described her appearance, and see also her portrait p. 91. This chapter is drawn largely from Louise's memoirs.
2. Ibid., p. 242.
3. Dominic Pearce, *Henrietta Maria* (2018), p. 17.
4. Henry insisted no one else should touch a hair of his wife's head. Fernand Hayem, *Le Marechal D'Ancre and Leonora Galigai* (1910), p. 29.
5. Bourgeois, p. 243.
6. Ibid., pp. 244, 245.
7. Marie's achievement was celebrated with a flood of heroic maternal imagery in portraits and commemorative medals: she was Juno to Henry's Jupiter and Minerva to his Mars.
8. William Goodell, 'A sketch of the life and writings of Louise Bourgeois, midwife to Marie de' Medici, the queen of Henry IV of France. The annual address of the Retiring President before the Philadelphia County Medical Society' (July 2015), p. 36.
9. Bourgeois, p. 264, n. 349.
10. It seems strange that Marie had kept a workshop so close to her private suite of rooms. Was the carpenter Leonora's old father?
11. Quoted in Katherine Crawford, 'Perilous Performances: Gender and Regency in Early Modern France', *Harvard Historical Studies* (November 2004), p. 65.
12. Remarkably there is a surviving medieval image of her in the church at Stoke Dry, Rutland. She was a very popular saint in England before the Reformation.
13. Jean Héroard (1551–1628), quoted in Carola Oman, *Henrietta Maria* (1939), p. 8.
14. The name Henrietta Maria was being used in England at least from the early 1630s. A ship was named the *Henrietta Maria* in January 1633 (*The Autobiography of Phineas Pett*, ed. W. G. Perrin

(1918), p. 149); also she is referred to as such in Calendar of State Papers, Colonial America and West Indies, Vol. I, 1637 (54).

15. Marie replied smartly, 'that would come to pass when you are a great Pope', on which the future Urban VIII's comments are not recorded; *The Memoirs of Gregorio Panzani: Giving An Account of His Agency In England, in the Years 1634–36*, trans. Joseph Berington (1793), p. 216.

Chapter 2: The Wrong Religion

1. George Smeeton, *The Life and Death of Henrietta Maria de Bourbon: Queen to That Blessed King and Martyr, Charles I, Mother to His Late Glorious Majesty and Most Gracious Sovereign, James II* (1685), p. 4.

2. The Pope was a secular ruler of extensive territories in central Italy, as well as a religious leader.

3. Henrietta Maria and her sisters were depicted in the sixth station as the celestial graces, who would conquer vice, also with love. It was a woman's superpower.

4. Roland Mousnier, *The Assassination of Henry IV* (1973), p. 23.

5. Who could forget the story of Richard III of England, and his nephews, the so-called Princes in the Tower, who disappeared after their uncle seized the throne? Certainly not the French, who, in 1485, provided Richard's nemesis, Henry Tudor, with much of his invasion force: so one dynasty ended and another had begun.

6. Katherine Crawford, 'Perilous Performances: Gender and Regency in Early Modern France', *Harvard Historical Studies* (November 2004), pp. 70–1.

7. Amongst the instruments used was 'the boot', which would twist and crush your leg.

8. His career as a lawyer had broken down when he began to have what he thought were religious visions. He had tried to join the Jesuits, but they had told him he was suffering from hallucinations, 'a result of the mental confusion clearly visible in his face'.

He had been advised to go home, eat well, and meditate to calm his thoughts. Ravaillac had instead become increasingly paranoid as he listened to the extremists who claimed that Henry was a tyrant and heretic. His visions had assured him that in killing the king he was set on God's work. Mousnier, p. 35.

9. Ravaillac's right arm – the arm that had committed the assassination – was plunged into burning sulphur. Then his body was torn and plucked by hot pincers, the wounds filled with molten lead, and boiling oil. After that came the horses.

10. Smeeton, p. 4.

11. His heart was to be buried separately at the Jesuit college at La Flèche, according to his last wishes.

12. Smeeton, p. 4.

13. Héroard, quoted in Elizabeth Marvick, *Louis XIII, the Making of a King* (1986), p. 108.

14. Quoted in Elizabeth Hamilton, *Henrietta Maria* (1976), p. 10.

15. Jonathan Spangler, *Monsieur: Second Sons in the Monarchy of France 1550–1800* (2021), p. 53.

16. Crawford, pp. 85, 86.

17. Richelieu, *The Political Testament of Cardinal Richelieu*, trans. Henry Bertram Hill (1961), p. 40.

18. Hamilton, p. 12.

19. Spangler, p. 52.

20. Harry Friedenwald, 'Montalto: A Jewish Physician at the Court of Marie de' Medici and Louis XIII', *Bulletin of the Institute of the History of Medicine*, Vol. 3, No. 2 (February 1935), p. 14; this treatment was not unlike what the Jesuits had suggested to the mentally 'confused' Ravaillac.

21. Ibid., p. 131.

22. Ibid., pp. 129–58.

23. K. A. Patmore, *The Court of Louis XIII* (1909), p. 36.

24. Historians sometimes project descriptions of the celebrations into the reign of Louis XIV as an example of the magnificence of

the court of the Sun King, but he was merely following in his grandmother's footsteps; Patmore, pp. 39–41.

25. Marie understood this process of transformation, having been through it herself. When she was in Italy, Henry had sent her dolls dressed in French fashions for her to imitate. She began to do so after Louis was born; Laura Oliván Santaliestra, 'Isabel of Borbón's Sartorial Politics: From French Princess to Habsburg Regent', in Anne J. Cruz and Maria Galli Stampino (eds), *Early Modern Habsburg Women: Transnational Contexts, Cultural Conflicts, Dynastic Continuities* (2014), pp. 225–43.

26. Louise Olga Fradenburg, *City, Marriage, Tournament: Arts of Rule in Late Medieval Scotland* (1991), pp. 76–80.

Chapter 3: The Witch's Spell

1. *Letters of Queen Henrietta Maria*, ed. Mary Anne Everett Green (2009), p. 4.
2. Louvre BNF MSS Fr. 3818, Letter 5, f. 6.
3. One such was the convent of the Ursulines, which began offering first communion classes to little girls, followed by a service where all the young communicants dressed in white. Her mother also kept an apartment in the Carmelite convent in the Faubourg Saint-Jacques. Here Henrietta Maria was introduced to the leading Carmelite prioress of the seventeenth century, Mother Madeleine de Saint-Joseph; Barbara B. Diefendorf, *From Penitence to Charity: Pious Women and the Catholic Reformation in Paris* (2004), pp. 12, 130.
4. The most frightening event Henrietta Maria experienced was when Elisabeth suffered a bout of smallpox en route; A. Lloyd Moote, *Louis XIII, the Just* (1991), pp. 82–3.
5. Louis had been taught what the sex act looked like by the time he was three and would use cushions to demonstrate what he had learned. When Louis was four Henry had drawn attention to the differences in Elisabeth's anatomy asking Louis, 'My son, where is the infanta's package?' Louis had pointed to his sister's genitalia

and observed 'It has no bone in it!'; Elizabeth Marvick, *Louis XIII, the Making of a King* (1986), p. 27.

6. *Memoirs of Madame de Motteville on Anne of Austria and Her Court. With An Introduction By C.-A. Sainte-Beuve*, trans. Katharine P. Wormeley (2015), Vol. 1, pp. 28–9.

7. Ibid., p. 117.

8. Louvre BNF MSS Fr. 3818, Letter 13, f. 14.

9. Moote, p. 192.

10. Marie de' Medici was grateful for all the care the doctor had given her children and had ordered his body be embalmed and escorted to the Jewish cemetery in Amsterdam. Leonora meanwhile had laden his children and widow with gifts for their sad journey. The Ouderkirk cemetery where he is buried still exists and it is possible to visit his tomb and those of many other famous Jews, including Menasseh ben Israel, the rabbi who convinced Oliver Cromwell to accept the return of practising Jews to England.

11. Moote, p. 201.

12. Dominic Pearce, *Henrietta Maria* (2018), p. 36. In England King James, who had written a treatise on witchcraft, had once asked a courtier why he thought witches were most commonly old women. The reply had been 'a scurvy jest' that it was said in the Bible 'that the Devil walks in dry places'. This reference to the atrophied vagina of the menopausal woman was apt because behind the face of Eve, the beautiful seductress, who proffers Adam the forbidden fruit, lies evil and her body is now aging into that of a hag.

13. It was here that Marie Antoinette would be held during the Terror.

14. Moote, p. 212; Henrietta Maria's later husband, Charles I, would say much the same thing about attacks on her, commenting that her supposed faults really amounted to one thing – that she was his wife.

15. In Italy Leonora's son always spoke well of Louis. He died there of plague in 1631.

16. Pearce, p. 42.

17. She would have her first baby only two years later, a little boy, stillborn.
18. Héroard, quoted in Moote, p. 145.
19. Brian Sandberg, *A Good Mother and a Loyal Subject: Positioning and Identification in Maria de' Medici's Correspondence* (2008), p. 405.
20. Christine was not to leave for Italy for another year.
21. Louvre BNF MSS Fr. 3818, Letter 28, f. 33; Henrietta Maria was forced to sell them to Louis XIV in 1657 to raise money while she was living in exile. He gave them to his mistress Marie Mancini. They were sold in 1979 at Christie's in New York for $253,000.

Chapter 4: A Prince Errant

1. Louvre BNF MSS Fr. 3818, ff. 2, 3.
2. The edicts were reissued in 1610, 1612, 1614 and twice in 1615; A. Lloyd Moote, *Louis XIII, the Just* (1991), p. 46.
3. Letters from Louis to Henriette Marie in Louvre BNF MSS Fr. 3818, ff. 1, 4.
4. Philip III had died in 1621.
5. This second son would die in 1628. There was a princess Ludovica Cristina, b.1629, two princes b.1632 and 1634, and two further princesses b.1635 and 1636.
6. George Smeeton, *The Life and Death of Henrietta Maria de Bourbon: Queen to That Blessed King and Martyr, Charles I, Mother to His Late Glorious Majesty and Most Gracious Sovereign, James II* (1685), p. 5; Louvre Letters BNF MSS Fr. 3818, Letters 13 and 18.
7. The French referred to Britain's three crowns meaning England, Scotland and Ireland. In fact the three crowns were England (which included Ireland as a colony), Scotland – and France. The English had not yet accepted the loss of the Hundred Years' War in the fifteenth century, or of Calais (England's last French possession) in the sixteenth.
8. Courtiers, walking with Charles, struggled to keep up with his fast gait, and he performed well 'In all corporeal exercises'; 'excels at

tilting and indulges in every kind of horsemanship'; CSPV 1621–3 (450–3).

9. *Letters of Charles I*, ed. Sir Charles Petrie (1935), p. 8.

10. James Shirley (1596–1666), quoted in Robert Wilcher, *The Discontented Cavalier* (1984), p. 52.

11. CSPV 1621–3 (450–3).

12. *Letters of Charles I*, p. 8.

13. Ibid., p. 9, and thank you to Sarah Poynting for showing me her more accurate transcription.

14. John Colin Dunlop, *Memoirs of Spain during the Reigns of Philip IV and Charles II, from 1621 to 1700: Volume 1* (1834, reprint 2002), p. 24.

15. She said that, if necessary, to save national embarrassment she would instead join an order of barefoot nuns, CSPV 1623 (833).

16. One begged for the blue stockings as a gift, another sent him several of the simple starched white collars Philip wore, and asked him, as an honour, to wear one that day, CSPV 1623 (863).

17. Quoted in Laura Oliván Santaliestra, 'Isabel of Borbón's Sartorial Politics: From French Princess to Habsburg Regent', in Anne J. Cruz and Maria Galli Stampino (eds), *Early Modern Habsburg Women: Transnational Contexts, Cultural Conflicts, Dynastic Continuities* (2014), p. 232.

18. Henrietta Maria later recalled Charles describing how Elisabeth had alluded to the assassination, warning him not to speak to her in French in case their conversation was misconstrued, 'for it was the custom in Spain to poison all gentlemen suspected of gallantry towards the queen consort'.

19. CSPV 1625–6 (600).

20. Henry Rich – Lord Kensington at this time – would be made Earl of Holland in September.

21. English kings also had a track record of rejecting French brides in favour of local beauties. In the fifteenth century Prince Charles's ancestor, the young Edward IV, had rejected a marriage with a French princess in favour of marrying Elizabeth Woodville. In the

sixteenth century Henry VIII had done the same, preferring Anne
Boleyn to a French princess Wolsey had hoped he might marry.

22. *Memoirs of Madame de Motteville on Anne of Austria and Her Court.
With An Introduction By C.-A. Sainte-Beuve,* trans. Katharine
P. Wormeley (2015), Vol. 1, p. 31.

23. She came from another princely family, the Rohans, who claimed
descent from the former sovereigns of Brittany.

24. Smeeton, p. 6.

25. It was a sign of the importance of Marie de' Medici in any future
negotiations towards a marriage. Melinda J. Gough, 'A Newly Discovered Performance by Henrietta Maria', *Huntington Library
Quarterly,* Vol. 65, No. 3/4 (2002), pp. 435–47. The material concerning the ballet is drawn from this fascinating article.

26. Ibid., p. 440; Elizabeth Hamilton, *Henrietta Maria* (1976), p. 35.

27. Buckingham, who had brought back a portrait of the infanta from
Spain, gave it to his to sister the Countess of Denbigh, after the
betrothal to Charles was ended. The family kept this now lost portrait until the twentieth century, and hung it alongside a portrait
of Charles – with Henrietta Maria on his other side.

28. *Calendar of the Clarendon state papers preserved in the Bodleian
Library; Clarendon, Edward Hyde, Earl of, 1609–1674; Coxe, Henry
Octavius, 1811–1881,* Vol. 1, Appendix 2, pp. 9–11.

29. BL Harley MSS 1581, f. 31.

30. *Calendar of the Clarendon state papers,* Vol. 1, Appendix 2, pp.
9–11.

31. See Leanda de Lisle, *White King* (2018), p. 14.

32. Montagu to the Earl of Carlisle, British Library, Egerton MS
2596, f. 49, from Sarah Poynting, *A Critical Edition of Walter Montagu's The Shepherds' Paradise, Acts 1–3,* DPhil thesis, University
of Oxford (2 vols, 2000), Vol. I, p. 3. (NB page refs are to the
document Sarah Poynting kindly shared with me and may not be
the same as that supplied by Oxford.)

33. Ibid.

34. Michael Questier, *Stuart Dynastic Policy and Religious Politics, 1621–1625: Volume 34* (Camden Fifth Series, Vol. 34, 2009), p. 83, n. 380.
35. Questier, p. 83.
36. *The Chamberlain Letters*, ed. Elizabeth Thomson (1965), December 1624, p. 318.
37. It would take place on England's May Day: a day that celebrated fertility. Under the Gregorian calendar used in France it would be 11 May.
38. The Savoyards had been very helpful in Rome in support of the dispensation for the marriage and in Paris their ambassador was on intimate terms with the English ambassadors.
39. Olivares had to calm down a very irate French ambassador. Isabel had turned out to be more formidable than he had supposed. Laura Oliván Santaliestra, 'Isabel de Borbón, "Paloma Medianera De La Paz": Políticas Y Culturas De Pacificación De Una Reina Consorte En El Siglo XVI', Departamento de Historia Moderna de la Universidad de Granada, p. 13.

Chapter 5: 'The game and play of favourites'

1. In the French calendar.
2. Anonymous, 'L'ordre des Ceremonies', in Erin Griffey, *On Display: Henrietta Maria and the Materials of Magnificence at the Stuart Court* (2016), p. 35.
3. Suzanne Lussier, '*Habillement de la Dite Dame Reine': An Analysis of the Gowns and Accessories in Queen Henrietta Maria's Trousseau* (2018), p. 31. She was to wear one for a grand entry to Amiens on her journey to the coast and the green one on her arrival in London.
4. CSPV 16 May (67). Soissons was absent, nursing his resentment.
5. Charles Cotolendi, *La Vie de très-haute et très-puissante princesse, Henriette-Marie de France, reyne de la Grande-Bretagne* (1690), pp. 10ff; Gesa Stedman, *Cultural Exchange in Seventeenth-Century France and England* (2013), p. 30 and note.

6. Tallemant de Reaux (1619–1692), quoted in Jonathan Spangler, *Monsieur: Second Sons in the Monarchy of France 1550–1800* (2021), p. 175.

7. Griffey, p. 36; *A True Discourse of all the Royal Passages, Tryumphs and Ceremonies, obserued at the Contract and Marriage of the High and Mighty Charles, King of Great Britaine, and the most excellentest of Ladies, the Lady Henrietta Maria of Burbon, sister to the most Christian King of France* (1625), p. 13.

8. Griffey, p. 36.

9. Sara Galletti, 'Architecture and Ceremonial in Early Modern France: the Court of Maria de' Medici', in Giulia Calvi and Isabelle Chabot (eds), *Moving Elites: Women and Cultural Transfers in the European Court System* (2010), p. 90.

10. Griffey, p. 37.

11. CSPV 16 May (61).

12. *The Chamberlain Letters*, ed. Elizabeth Thomson (1965), p. 350.

13. Marie de' Medici had set an example to her daughter in commissioning great art for chapels: she commissioned Philippe de Champaigne (to whom she was close enough to have given him a self-portrait she had done in Florence aged fourteen) to produce work for the Carmelites of the rue Saint-Jacques and she also gave an altarpiece by Guido Reni of the Annunciation. It was the first great picture by Reni to arrive in France. Benoit Wells, 'Complementarity and Competition: Marie de Medici and Cardinal Richelieu as Patrons and Collectors of Art', available online.

14. CSPV 9 May 1625 (46).

15. CSPV 1625 (99).

16. Clare Jackson, *Devil-Land: England Under Siege 1588–1688* (2021), p. 183.

17. Richard Weston, quoted in ibid., p. 194.

18. CSPV 25 May 1625 (80).

19. Galletti, p. 81. Sara Galetti also mentions the foot injury.

20. K. A. Patmore, *The Court of Louis XIII* (1909), pp. 223–4.

21. Pierre de la Porte, quoted in Leanda de Lisle, *White King* (2018), p. 30.

22. Richelieu tried to replace Rubens as the painter of the cycle with Orazio Gentileschi (who later went to work for Charles and Henrietta Maria in England), who did produce a fresco for the Luxembourg, and also Guido Reni (whose works would be collected by Charles and Henrietta Maria).

23. Letter from Rubens, 13 May 1625, quoted in Galletti, p. 90; Marie de' Medici wanted to commission a matching cycle depicting the life of Henry IV.

24. CSPV 1625–6 (120) (127).

25. Christine and the House of Savoy supported the British. The ambassador for Savoy (himself a cleric) had also visited the legate and had insisted to him that Spanish aggression presented a greater threat to Europe than the heretical Huguenots.

26. CSPV 1625–6 (117).

27. Karen Ruth Britland, 'Neoplatonic Identities; Literary Representation and the Politics of Henrietta Maria's Court Circle', PhD thesis, University of Leeds (2000), p. 43.

28. These were held in place by a piece of metal clamped between their teeth – a fact that helped disguise their voices just as the masks did their faces.

29. *Memoirs of Madame de Motteville on Anne of Austria and Her Court. With An Introduction By C.-A. Sainte-Beuve*, trans. Katharine P. Wormeley (2015), Vol. 1, p. 36. Marie de' Medici had done little to help Anne in her relationship with Louis. She had no wish to encourage a rival influence over her son.

30. *Memoirs of Madame de Motteville*, Vol. 1, p. 37.

31. CSPV 1625–6 (153).

32. Chaulnes was the brother of Madame de Chevreuse's first husband, Luynes.

33. Griffey, p. 40.
34. Stephanie Marie Seery-Murphy, 'Hazarding the Queen: Henrietta Maria, Religious Controversy and the Construction of a Rhetorical Figure', PhD thesis, Claremont Graduate University (2008), p. 150.
35. *Memoires inedits de Louis Henri de Lomenie Comte de Brienne*, Vol. 1 (1828), pp. 331, 332.
36. *Memoirs of Madame de Motteville*, Vol. 1, p. 32.
37. *Archaelogica*, Vol. XII (1796), p. 124; he hadn't been to Canterbury since 1623, when he was on his way to Spain to woo the infanta. His disguise then, as an ordinary gentleman, had been so effective that he and Buckingham had been arrested as suspicious characters and brought before the mayor. There was still a sense of lingering embarrassment amongst the city's officials as he moped in the city.
38. Seery-Murphy, p. 133.
39. Ibid. Seery-Murphy also recalled the execution of Mary, Queen of Scots, p. 10.
40. CSPV 1625–6 (114).
41. *Memoirs of Madame de Motteville*, Vol. 1, pp. 32, 33.

Chapter 6: 'What she will think, and say, or do'
1. CSPD 9 June 1625.
2. Buckingham took this last opportunity to dash back to Amiens for another farewell to Anne. According to Henrietta Maria's later account he went to her bedchamber and sobbed over the bedclothes, making such declarations than even Anne became quite alarmed.
3. CSPV 1625–6 (81).
4. *The Chamberlain Letters*, ed. Elizabeth Thomson (1965), p. 350.
5. *The Autobiography of Phineas Pett*, ed. W. G. Perrin (1918), pp. 135, 149.

6. Katie Whitaker, *A Royal Passion: The Turbulent Marriage of Charles I and Henrietta Maria* (2010), p. 51.

7. *Autobiography of Phineas Pett*, p. 135.

8. Finet, quoted in Margaret Toynbee, 'The Wedding Journey of Charles I', *Archaeologia Cantiana*, Vol. 69 (1955), p. 80. The type of bridge is illustrated in the Rubens picture of Marie de' Medici's *Disembarkation at Marseilles*.

9. Thomas Birch, *The Court and Times of Charles I* (2 vols, 1848), Vol. 1, pp. 30, 31.

10. Quoted in Margaret Shewring, 'Divergent Discourses', in Marie-Claude Canova-Green and Sara Wolfson (eds), *The Wedding of Charles I and Henrietta Maria, 1625: Celebrations and Controversy* (2020), p. 170.

11. Birch, Vol. 1, pp. 30, 31.

12. *Letters of Charles I*, ed. Sir Charles Petrie (1935), pp. 42, 43.

13. *Epistolae Ho-elianae: The Familiar Letters of James Howell, Historiographer Royal to Charles II*, ed. Joseph Jacobs (1890), p. 238.

14. John Heneage Jesse, *Memoirs of the Court of England During the Reign of the Stuarts, Volume 2* (1840), p. 217.

15. CSPV 19 1625–6 (600).

16. BL King's MSS 136, f. 337, v; Sara Wolfson, 'The Welcoming Journey', in Canova-Green and Wolfson (eds), p. 106.

17. Birch, Vol. 1, p. 31.

18. 'A Character of the Queen of Great Britain, composed during the exile of Marie de' Medici and before the death of Van Dyck, composed by a leading Catholic', Louvre, Manuscripts Dept, Côté Anglais, 57.

19. Birch, Vol. 1, p. 31.

20. Ibid., and also see Helen King, *The Disease of Virgins: Green Sickness, Chlorosis and the Problems of Puberty* (2014).

21. Michael Questier, *Stuart Dynastic Policy and Religious Politics, 1621–1625: Volume 34* (Camden Fifth Series, Vol. 34, 2009), p. 373.

22. Gervas Huxley, *Endymion Porter: The Life of a Courtier 1587–1649* (1959), p. 128; CSPD 1625/6 p. 45

23. Patricia Ranum, 'Audible Rhetoric and Mute Rhetoric: The 17th-Century French Sarabande', *Early Music*, Vol. 14, No. 1 (February 1986), pp. 22–30, 32–36, 39.

24. 'A Character of the Queen of Great Britain', 57.

25. Birch, Vol. 1, p. 30.

26. Ibid.

27. CSPV 1625–6 (600).

28. Simon Thurley, *Palaces of Revolution: Life, Death and Art at the Stuart Court* (2021), p. 169.

29. Birch, Vol. 1, p. 33. King James had already issued instructions to prevent his subjects concerning embassy chapels. It was impossible to arrest English Catholics on what was technically 'foreign' ground, so he had declared that 'the Lord Mayor and Mr Recorder of London may take them as they come from thence, and make some of them examples'; A. E. Adair, *The Extra-territoriality of Ambassadors in the Sixteenth and Seventeenth Centuries* (1929), p. 192.

30. Questier, p. 116.

31. Quoted in Karen Britland, 'A Ring of Roses', in Canova-Green and Wolfson (eds), p. 91.

32. Stephanie Marie Seery-Murphy, 'Hazarding the Queen: Henrietta Maria, Religious Controversy and the Construction of a Rhetorical Figure', PhD thesis, Claremont Graduate University (2008), pp. 123–4.

33. 'A Character of the Queen of Great Britain', 57.

Chapter 7: Rows

1. Stephanie Marie Seery-Murphy, 'Hazarding the Queen: Henrietta Maria, Religious Controversy and the Construction of a Rhetorical Figure', PhD thesis, Claremont Graduate University (2008), p. 142.

2. John Heneage Jesse, *Memoirs of the Court of England During the Reign of the Stuarts, Volume 2* (1840), pp. 217–18.

3. Thomas Birch, *The Court and Times of Charles I* (2 vols., 1848), Vol. 1, p. 40.

4. Hastings MSS 1931, 21 July 1625.

5. Birch, Vol. 1, p. 33.

6. *Letters of Charles I*, ed. Sir Charles Petrie (1935), p. 43.

7. CSPV 1625–6 Appendix I.

8. CSPV 1625–6 (600).

9. Dorothy de Brissac Campbell, *The Intriguing Duchess: Marie de Rohan, Duchesse de Chevreuse* (1933), p. 83.

10. Mark S. R. Jenner, 'Plague on a Page: *Lord Have Mercy Upon Us* in Early Modern London', *The Seventeenth Century*, 27:3 (2012), p. 255, DOI: 10.7227/TSC.27.3.2.

11. Charles's excuse for reneging on the terms of the marriage treaty was that Catholics had been hearing Mass publicly, rather than privately, and so he considered his promises to Louis void.

12. Birch, Vol. 1, p. 50.

13. Ibid., pp. 50, 51, 52.

14. *Letters of Charles I*, p. 43.

15. Ibid., p. 44.

16. Ibid.

17. CSPV 1625–6 (296).

18. *Letters of Charles I*, p. 42.

19. Karen Britland, *Drama at the Courts of Queen Henrietta Maria* (2006), p. 194.

20. Birch, Vol. 1, p. 68.

21. Karen Britland, 'A Ring of Roses', in Marie-Claude Canova-Green and Sara Wolfson (eds), *The Wedding of Charles I and Henrietta Maria, 1625: Celebrations and Controversy* (2020), p. 96.

22. CSPV 1626 (454).

23. CSPV 20 February 1626 (473).

24. Peter Helwyn, *Life of William, Lord Archbishop of Canterbury* (1671) p. 138. The warning was supposed to have been issued by the Earl of Pembroke.

25. Karen Ruth Britland, 'Neoplatonic Identities; Literary Representation and the Politics of Henrietta Maria's Court Circle', PhD thesis, University of Leeds (2000), p. 56.

26. Birch, Vol. 1, p. 80.

27. Edward Hyde, Early of Clarendon (from 1661), quoted in David Nichol Smith, *Characters from the Histories and Memoirs of the Seventeenth Century* (1918), p. 161.

28. Britland, 'Neoplatonic Identities', p. 61.

29. Ibid., p. 38; in France women were seen as arbiters of taste and a civilising influence on men.

30. For a thorough examination of this pastoral see Britland's fascinating and illuminating *Drama at the Courts of Queen Henrietta Maria*.

31. Britland, *Drama*, p. 37.

32. Ibid.

33. Quoted in Sophie Tomlinson, 'She That Plays the King: Henrietta Maria and the Threat of the Actress in Caroline Culture', in Gordon McMullan and Jonathan Hope (eds), *The Politics of Tragicomedy: Shakespeare and After* (1992), p. xxx.

34. The cut-purse Mary Frith had a play written about her called *The Roaring Girl*. She had performed it on stage herself, dressed as a man, bantering with the audience. Later she had taken to working as a fence and pimp, not only for female prostitutes, but also procuring male lovers for bored wives. Despite all this there was something about her character – or type – that had encouraged a fashion for slightly masculine clothing at court.

35. A. Lloyd Moote, *Louis XIII, the Just* (1991), p. 182.

36. Katharine Dorothea Ewart Vernon, *Italy from 1494 to 1790* (1909), p. 219.

37. CSPV 1625–6 Appendix I.

38. Birch, Vol. 1, p. 121.

Chapter 8: Winning the King

1. Jean François Paul de Gondi (1613–1679), quoted in *Secret History of the French Court under Richelieu and Mazarin; or, Life and times of Madame de Chevreuse*, trans. Mary L. Booth (1859), pp. 9–10; A. Lloyd Moote, *Louis XIII, the Just* (1991), p. 193.
2. Michael Prawdin, *Marie de Rohan, Duchesse de Chevreuse* (1971), p. 43.
3. Thomas Birch, *The Court and Times of Charles I* (2 vols, 1848), Vol. 1, p. 120.
4. Ibid.
5. CSPV 1625–6 Appendix I.
6. Ibid.
7. For a very interesting assessment of this incident see Karen Britland, 'A Ring of Roses', in Marie-Claude Canova-Green and Sara Wolfson (eds), *The Wedding of Charles I and Henrietta Maria, 1625: Celebrations and Controversy* (2020), p. 99.
8. Birch, Vol. 1, p. 121; CSPV 1625–6 (705).
9. Garnet was so hated, a book condemning his actions had been bound in his skin. The book and its original carrying box came up for sale at Wilkinson's auctioneers in Doncaster in 2007 with an estimate of £3,000 to £5,000. He had, in fact, been executed at St Paul's Churchyard and not Tyburn.
10. Roy E. Schreiber, 'The First Carlisle: Sir James Hay, First Earl of Carlisle as Courtier, Diplomat and Entrepreneur, 1580–1636', *Transactions of the American Philosophical Society* (1984), p. 98.
11. 5 June 1626, BL Egerton MS 2597, f. 13r.
12. Vincent de Voiture, *The Works of the Celebrated Monsieur Voiture* (1731), p. 219.
13. Erin Griffey, 'Restoring Henrietta Maria's English Household in the 1660s: Continuity, Kinship and Clientage', *Court Historian*, published online 6 September 2021.
14. Canova-Green and Wolfson (eds), p. 317. Madame Garnier was the nurse, and her dresser was Madame Vantelet.

15. Belvoir MSS QZ/6/12.
16. Le Comte de Baillon, *Henriette-Marie de France, Reine d'Angleterre* (1877, reprint 2018), pp. 347–50.
17. *Letters of Charles I*, ed. Sir Charles Petrie (1935), p. 41.
18. CSPV 1625–6 (707).
19. *Letters of Queen Henrietta Maria*, ed. Mary Anne Everett Green (2009), p. 4.
20. CSPV 1625–6 (742).
21. Quoted in Karen Britland, *Drama at the Courts of Queen Henrietta Maria* (2006), p. 54.
22. *Memoirs of Richelieu, Vol. III*, ed. Leon Valle (1903), p. 64.
23. Ibid, p. 105.
24. Ruth Kleinman, *Anne of Austria* (1985), p. 70.
25. Moote, p. 193.
26. K. A. Patmore, *The Court of Louis XIII* (1909), p. 91.
27. CSPV 25 September 1626; the agent then rode on to Savoy.
28. CSPV 5 April 1630 (386).
29. For dates and a great deal of fascinating detail see Erin Griffey, 'Multum in parvo: Portraits of Jeffrey Hudson, Court Dwarf to Henrietta Maria', *British Art Journal*, Vol. 4, No. 3 (Autumn 2003), pp. 39–53.
30. CSPV 5 April 1630 (386).
31. Henrietta Maria described this to Madame de Motteville. See also Roger Coke (fl. 1696), 'A detection of the court and state of England during the four last reigns and the inter-regnum consisting of private memoirs, &c., with observations and reflections, and an appendix, discovering the present state of the nation: wherein are many secrets never before made publick: as also, a more impartiall account of the civil wars in England, than has yet been given: in two volumes', p. 194: 'When Buckingham came out of France with the Queen of England, he left, or soon after sent Sir Balthazar Gerbier to hold secret Correspondence between the Queen and himself; and tho Richlieu watch'd Gerbier narrowly, yet he brought the Queen's Garter, and an exceeding rich Jewel to Buckingham

from her. Upon the breaking out of the Feuds in the Queen's Family, which began almost as soon, if not before it was settled, Buckingham prevails with the King to be sent into France to compose them, which was granted. But Nani says, the true Motive of Buckingham's Journey being ascribed to Love, contracted in that Court, Richlieu perswaded the King to refuse him Entrance into the Kingdom. The Rage hereupon of the other was inflamed to extremity, and sware, since he was forbidden to enter in a peaceable manner into France, he would make his Passage with an Army.'

32. *Les papiers de Richelieu, Section politique intérieure correspondance et papiers d'État: Tome I* (Monumenta Europae Historica) (1982), No. 203, pp. 458–9, and No. 234, p. 478; Schreiber, p. 99.
33. Britland, p. 63.
34. Ibid., p. 60.
35. As described by the doctor who stitched it in 1643; David Lasoki, *A Biographical Dictionary of English Court Musicians, 1485–1714, Volume I* (2018), p. 470.
36. The woman in question was called Lady Anne Hay.
37. Canova-Green and Wolfson (eds), p. 317.
38. Britland, p. 63.
39. 'A Character of the Queen of Great Britain, composed during the exile of Marie de' Medici and before the death of Van Dyck, composed by a leading Catholic', Louvre, Manuscripts Dept, Côté Anglais, 57.
40. Thomas, Lord Cromwell, CSPD 5 October 1634; Raymond A. Anselment, 'The Countess of Carlisle and Caroline Praise: Convention and Reality', *Studies in Philology*, Vol. 82, No. 2 (Spring 1985), p. 215.
41. Marc Antonio Pavadin, quoted in Clare Jackson, *Devil-Land: England Under Seige 1588–1688* (2021), p. 201.
42. The Countess of Buckingham to the Duke of Buckingham, 26 August 1627, TNA SP 16/75, f. 22.

43. Leanda de Lisle, *White King* (2018), p. 59.
44. *Letters of Charles I*, p. 52.
45. TNA SP 16/81, f. 49r.
46. Laurence Spring, *The First British Army, 1624–1628: The Army of the Duke of Buckingham* (2016), p. 176.
47. Ibid., p. 194; BL Add. MSS 26, 51.
48. Quoted in Jackson, p. 202.

Chapter 9: Becoming a Leader

1. Sarah Poynting, *A Critical Edition of Walter Montagu's The Shepherds' Paradise, Acts 1–3*, DPhil thesis, University of Oxford (2 vols, 2000).
2. Laurence Spring, *The First British Army, 1624–1628: The Army of the Duke of Buckingham* (2016), p. 206.
3. Thomas Birch, *The Court and Times of Charles I* (2 vols, 1848), Vol. 1, pp. 364–5; 'John Lambe', *ODNB*.
4. Birch, Vol. 1, p. 367.
5. Poynting, Vol. 1, p. 11.
6. Their names were Edmund Arrow and Richard Herst.
7. He was buried in La Rochelle. A memorial stone was set up on his family estate of Houdancourt at the church of Sacy Le Petit and recalled the care he had given to the lonely young queen amidst 'the false British'.
8. Quoted in Clare Jackson, *Devil-Land: England Under Seige 1588–1688* (2021), p. 201.
9. Unbound letter, Belvoir, transcribed in Leanda de Lisle, *White King* (2018), p. 321.
10. Helena Kazárová, 'The Time of the Dancing Kings', in Andrea Rousová (ed.) *Dances and Festivities of the 16th–18th Centuries* (2008), pp. 3, 11, 69–79.
11. Letter from Viscount Dorchester to the queen, 23 August 1628, in Henry Ellis, *Original Letters Illustrative of English History, Volume 3* (1827), pp. 256–9.

12. Birch, Vol. 1, p. 388.
13. Unbound letter, Belvoir, transcribed in de Lisle, p. 321.
14. Letter from Viscount Dorchester to the queen, 23 August 1628, in Ellis, pp. 256–9.
15. Lord Percy, CSPD 3 September 1628; Erin Griffey, 'Express Yourself? Henrietta Maria and the Political Value of Emotional Display at the Stuart Court', *The Seventeenth Century*, Vol. 35, Issue 2 (2020), pp. 187–212.
16. A small revenge for the time Isabel snubbed the wife of the French ambassador to show her disapproval of Henrietta Maria's marriage to Charles. Birch, Vol. 1, p. 417.
17. CSPV 1626–8 (448); Poynting, Vol. 1, p. 7; PRO 31/3/67 f 2; Poynting, Vol. 1, p. 16. A diplomat in Turin had once observed how he was amazed that 'one so young and beardless' could have been employed in the sensitive diplomatic missions Charles and Buckingham had sent him on, but, 'I found him so wise prudent and well informed, that my astonishment was converted into amazement at his abilities'.
18. Birch, Vol. 1, p. 417. If she was pregnant this was in the very early stages.
19. CSPD 11 April 1629.
20. Birch, Vol. 2, p. 13.
21. Ibid.
22. CSPD 13 May 1629.
23. Ibid.
24. CSPV 25 May 1629.
25. CSPD 13 May 1629.
26. For this letter see de Lisle, p. 75 and note.
27. *Letters of Queen Henrietta Maria*, ed. Mary Anne Everett Green (2009), p. 14; *Lettres de Henriette-Marie de France, reine d'Angleterre à sa soeur Christine, Duchesse de Savoie*, ed. Hermann Ferrero (1881), Letter IV.

28. *ODNB*. Charles had sent him to Paris in 1625 when HM had been feeling 'indisposed' with messages 'to wish her good health with compliments of love'.

Chapter 10: Foreign Affairs

1. TNA SP 16/529, f. 36v.
2. TNA SP 16/101, f. 93.
3. Raymond A. Anselment, 'The Countess of Carlisle and Caroline Praise: Convention and Reality', *Studies in Philology*, Vol. 82, No. 2 (Spring 1985), p. 218.
4. Toby Osborne, *Dynasty and Diplomacy in the Court of Savoy: Political Culture and the Thirty Years War* (2002), p. 126.
5. John Adamson, 'Policy and Pomegranates: Art, Iconography, and Counsel in Rubens' Anglo-Spanish Diplomacy of 1629–30', in Luc Duerloo and Malcolm Smuts (eds), *The Age of Rubens: Diplomacy, Dynastic Politics and the Visual Arts in Seventeenth-Century Europe* (2016), p. 57.
6. CSPV 1630 (366).
7. The infanta died in 1633 and the Spanish Netherlands returned to the crown of Spain under Philip IV.
8. *ODNB*. He would also deliver her last child.
9. Michael Prawdin, *Marie de Rohan, Duchesse de Chevreuse* (1971), p. 54.
10. A. Lloyd Moote, *Louis XIII, the Just* (1991), p. 218.
11. Prawdin, p. 61.
12. Osborne, pp. 196, 200, 205–6.
13. Dudley Carleton, Viscount of Dorchester to Sir Balthazar Gerbier, 8 December 1631, SP 77/20, ff. 323–5A. With thanks to Sarah Poynting.
14. 'A Character of the Queen of Great Britain, composed during the exile of Marie de' Medici and before the death of Van Dyck,

composed by a leading Catholic', Louvre, Manuscripts Dept, Côté Anglais, 57.

15. CSPV 1629–32 (685).

16. Ibid.

17. See Michelle Dobbie, 'Henrietta Maria, Court Intrigue and Early Modern Diplomacy', *Lives and Letters*, Vol. 2 , No. 1 (Summer 2010), accessed online http://www.xmera.co.uk/journalarchive/dobbie.pdf; Weston was created Earl of Portland on 17 February 1633.

18. 'A Character of the Queen of Great Britain', 57.

19. TNA SP78/89, f. 380; TNA SP 78/90, f. 27; Dobbie, p. 10.

20. *Ceremonies of Charles I: The Notebooks of John Finet 1628–1641*, ed. Albert Loomie (1987), p. 106.

21. Benoit Wells, 'Complementarity and Competition: Marie de' Medici and Cardinal de Richelieu as Patrons and Collectors of Art', available online.

22. Erin Griffey, *On Display: Henrietta Maria and the Materials of Magnificence at the Stuart Court* (2016), pp. 111, 112.

23. Letter from Viscount Dorchester to the queen, 23 August 1628, in Henry Ellis, *Original Letters Illustrative of English History, Volume 3* (1827), p. 279.

24. Lucy Carlisle, who was back in favour now that the issue of peace with Spain was settled, was godmother, along with the late Duke of Buckingham's sister, the Countess of Denbigh. The king's memory of Buckingham was not merely neutralised it was co-opted by the queen, who treated the Villiers women almost like family.

25. Melinda Gough, 'Courtly Comediantes', in P. A. Brown and P. Parolin (eds.), *Women Players in England 1500–1660* (2005), pp. 209–10.

26. H. Noel Williams, *A Fair Conspirator: Marie de Rohan, Duchesse de Chevreuse* (1913), p. 108.

27. Dobbie, p. 14.

28. Ellis, p. 274.

29. Bonham's sale 19386, 29 March 2011, lot 457.

30. Quoted in Sarah Poynting, *A Critical Edition of Walter Montagu's The Shepherds' Paradise, Acts 1–3*, DPhil thesis, University of Oxford (2 vols, 2000), Vol. 1, p. 19

31. Michael Leapman, *Inigo: The Troubled Life of Inigo Jones, Architect of the English Renaissance* (2004), p. 298. Inigo Jones wrote of one example in which Henrietta Maria appeared as Divine Beauty, floating above the stage 'in a chariot of goldsmith's work all adorned with precious gems'. There were stars over her head, lighting the chariot which then flew to the ground, where stood a chorus of fifty men and women, all 'richly attired', 'showing the magnificence of the court of England'.

32. John Finet, quoted in Rebecca A. Bailey, *Staging the Old Faith: Queen Henrietta Maria and the Theatre of Caroline England, 1625–1642* (2009), p. 134.

33. Prynne, quoted in Sophie Tomlinson, 'She That Plays the King: Henrietta Maria and the Threat of the Actress in Caroline Culture', in Gordon McMullan and Jonathan Hope (eds), *The Politics of Tragicomedy: Shakespeare and After* (1992), p. 194.

34. Ibid., p. 202.

Chapter 11: The Road to Rome

1. Carnarvon *ODNB*.

2. Sarah Poynting, *A Critical Edition of Walter Montagu's The Shepherds' Paradise, Acts 1–3*, DPhil thesis, University of Oxford (2 vols, 2000), Vol. 1, p. 19.

3. Anthony Hamilton, *Memoirs of Count Grammont* (reprint, 2010), p. 25.

4. Georges Dethan, 'Mazarin, un homme de paix à l'âge baroque: 1602–1661', in *Le Quatrième de la Collection Personnages* (1981), p. 167.

5. Rebecca A. Bailey, *Staging the Old Faith: Queen Henrietta Maria and the Theatre of Caroline England, 1625–1642* (2009), p. 139.

6. Quoted in Georges Dethan, *The Young Mazarin* (1977), p. 128.

7. Quoted in ibid., p. 129.

8. Quoted in ibid.

9. Robert Oresko, 'The House of Savoy in search for a royal crown in the seventeenth century', in Robert Oresko, G. C. Gibbs and H. M. Scott (eds), *Royal and Republican Sovereignty in Early Modern Europe: Essays in Memory of Ragnhild Hatton* (1997), p. 308. Richelieu later instructed that the Prince of Orange's wife Amalia, who had not even been born a princess, should be accorded the royal title of Highness at the French court, while denying this to Christine – Louis XIII's own sister.

10. Montagu visited churches to admire their beauty and listened to Monteverdi conduct his own music. He met up regularly with friends at a fashionable inn. Once they carried a whole barrel of wine to a friend's apartment, and drank it with little snacks and sweets, laughing and joking. He also witnessed an execution. Poynting, Vol. 1, p. 21.

11. Mancini, quoted in Dethan, *Young Mazarin*, p. 12.

12. Ibid.

13. *Newsletters from the Archpresbyterate of George Birkhead*, ed. M. C. Questier (Camden Fifth Series, Vol. 12, 1999), p. 246.

14. 'A Character of the Queen of Great Britain, composed during the exile of Marie de' Medici and before the death of Van Dyck, composed by a leading Catholic', Louvre, Manuscripts Dept, Côté Anglais, 57.

15. Thomas Birch, *The Court and Times of Charles I* (2 vols, 1848), Vol. 2, p. 308.

16. Ibid.; Bailey, p. 90.

17. Birch, Vol. 2, pp. 309–10.

18. Ibid.

19. See for one example: CSPD 1633–4 (349).

20. Bailey, p. 142.

21. Simon Thurley, *Palaces of Revolution: Life, Death and Art at the Stuart Court* (2021), p. 174.

22. Henri Hymans, 'Les Derniers Années de Van Dyck', *Gazette de Beaux Arts*, 36 (1887), p. 434.

23. Poynting, Vol. 1, pp. 19–22.

24. Gordon Albion, *Charles I and the Court of Rome: A Study in 17th-Century Diplomacy* (1935), p. 152.

25. 'William Cavendish, Duke of Newcastle', *ODNB*.

26. 'A Character of the Queen of Great Britain', 57.

27. CSPV May 1636 (668).

28. 'A Character of the Queen of Great Britain', 57.

29. Martina, who was beheaded in 226. Her body had been rediscovered in October 1634 and the Pope had personally written hymns to be sung at her office.

30. *The Memoirs of Gregorio Panzani: Giving An Account of His Agency In England, in the Years 1634–36*, trans. Joseph Berington (1793), pp. 137–8.

31. *The Earl of Strafforde's Letters and Dispatches: With An Essay Towards His Life by Sir George Radcliffe* (reprint 2018), Vol. 1, p. 373; Poynting, Vol. 1, p. 22.

32. Edward, Earl of Clarendon, *History of the Rebellion and the Civil Wars in England begun in the year 1641*, ed. W. Dunn Macray (1888), Vol. 6, p. 481; M. V. Hay, *The Blairs Papers (1603–1660)* (1929), p. 248.

33. Albion, p. 152.

34. R. Smuts, 'The Puritan followers of Henrietta Maria in the 1630s', *English Historical Review* (1978), p 33.

35. Maquis de Saint Chamond (1586–1649) to Richelieu, 15 June 1632, PRO 31/3/67, f. 49.

36. Caroline M. Hibbard, *Charles I and the Popish Plot* (2017), p. 22.

37. *Memoirs of Gregorio Panzani*, p. 194.

38. Ibid., p. 157.

39. S. R. Gardiner, *History of England from the Accession of James I to the Outbreak of Civil War* (1884), Vol. 8, p. 150; Tabby cats were so called because their coats resembled the watered silk known as tabby. Tabby silk was in turn named after the city of

Baghdad, where this form of silk may have first been made. Laud's tabby cats were supposedly the first to be introduced to England and came from Cyprus. They were so popular that by later in the century they had become more common than the traditional English cat, which was white with blue-grey patches.

40. Bailey, p. 148 (March 1636).
41. *Memoirs of Gregorio Panzani,* p. 194.
42. Stephanie Marie Seery-Murphy, 'Hazarding the Queen: Henrietta Maria, Religious Controversy and the Construction of a Rhetorical Figure', PhD thesis, Claremont Graduate University (2008), p. 265.
43. 'A Character of the Queen of Great Britain', 57.
44. Poynting, Vol. 1, pp. 24, 25; George Garrard to Thomas Wentworth, December 1635, *Earl of Strafforde's Letters,* Vol. 1, p. 480.
45. *Letters of Queen Henrietta Maria,* ed. Mary Anne Everett Green (2009), p. 32.

Chapter 12: The Golden Rose

1. The date is pinpointed by a letter from the Catholic George Leyburn to Bishop Richard Smith, 9 December 1635, Westminster Cathedral Archives A series, XXVEI, item 54, pp. 195–6.
2. Thomas Birch, *The Court and Times of Charles I* (2 vols, 1848), Vol. 2, p. 313.
3. For more on this see Andrew Horn, 'Andrea Pozzo and the Jesuit "Theatres" of the Seventeenth Century', *Journal of Jesuit Studies,* Vol. 6, Issue 2 (2019), pp. 213–48.
4. It came from the late Duke of Buckingham's estate. His widow was a Catholic and may have been gifted it by the king with the intention that it be used in the chapel; Erin Griffey, *On Display: Henrietta Maria and the Materials of Magnificence at the Stuart Court* (2016), p. 103.
5. Birch, Vol. 2, p. 314. Henrietta Maria's role is indicated in letters from Cardinal Barberini to Gregorio Panzani and George Conn

(Barb. Lat. 8634; Barb. Lat. 8640, f. 261); see n. 317 p. 188, and n. 349 p. 211, Stephanie Marie Seery-Murphy, 'Hazarding the Queen: Henrietta Maria, Religious Controversy and the Construction of a Rhetorical Figure', PhD thesis, Claremont Graduate University (2008).

6. Birch, Vol. 2, p. 313; Rebecca A. Bailey, *Staging the Old Faith: Queen Henrietta Maria and the Theatre of Caroline England, 1625–1642* (2009), p. 138; Perspective tableaux were very fashionable in Rome where artists like Bernini, and leading clerics like Cardinal Barberini, competed to create the most lavish and striking examples.

7. CSPV 1633–6 (590).

8. CSPV 1632–6 (327). She met this ambassador again when she was in exile in The Hague, and reminded Charles of the incident with Hudson in a letter.

9. Kevin Sharpe, *The Personal Rule of Charles I* (1992), p. 185.

10. Georges Dethan, *The Young Mazarin* (1977), p. 136.

11. Gordon Albion, *Charles I and the Court of Rome: A Study in 17th-Century Diplomacy* (1935), p. 152.

12. *The Memoirs of Gregorio Panzani: Giving An Account of His Agency In England, in the Years 1634–36*, trans. Joseph Berington (1793), p. 342.

13. Apethorpe was a favourite palace of King James, who had met the young George Villiers there twenty years earlier, and also with Charles who had stayed several times. The Earl of Westmorland had built new suites of rooms to entertain the Stuart kings, but he must have found this visit hard. His wife had died in childbirth less than a month earlier, on 29 June; Siobhan Keenan, *The Progresses, Processions and Royal Entries of Charles I 1625–1642* (2020), p. 127.

14. Albion, p. 162.

15. Neither brother could remember their homeland. Charles Louis had lived in exile since he was three and Rupert had almost been left behind in Prague when his mother had fled the Habsburg

army, being thrown into the bottom of her carriage at the very last moment.

16. Caroline M. Hibbard, *Charles I and the Popish Plot* (2017), pp. 33–5.
17. John Adamson, 'Policy and Pomegranates: Art, Iconography, and Counsel in Rubens' Anglo-Spanish Diplomacy of 1629–30', in Luc Duerloo and Malcolm Smuts (eds), *The Age of Rubens: Diplomacy, Dynastic Politics and the Visual Arts in Seventeenth-Century Europe* (2016), p. 18.
18. Francis Cheynell, quoted in Keenan, p. 148. The same had been true at Charles's coronation, where in the end, the congregation had to be led to acclaim him king; Leanda de Lisle, *White King* (2018), p. 50.
19. S. R. Gardiner, *History of England from the Accession of James I to the Outbreak of Civil War* (1884), Vol. 8, p. 152.
20. Matthew Wilson, quoted in Bailey, p. 154; Sir Philip Warwick, quoted in David Nichol Smith, *Characters from the Histories and Memoirs of the Seventeenth Century* (1918), p. 56.
21. Bailey, p. 153.
22. Keenan, pp. 154, 156–8.
23. 'A Character of the Queen of Great Britain, composed during the exile of Marie de' Medici and before the death of Van Dyck, composed by a leading Catholic', Louvre, Manuscripts Dept, Côté Anglais, 57.
24. Quoted in Seery-Murphy, p. 206.
25. Dethan, p. 136.
26. Ibid., p. 137.
27. Ibid.
28. Sharpe, p. 762; Griffey, p. 120.
29. Gardiner, Vol. 8, p. 237, n. 1.
30. David Baldwin, 'The Politico-Religious Usage of the Queen's Chapel, 1623–1688', MA thesis, Durham University (1999), p. 37; Bailey, p. 141. There was also a successful drive to convert the Huguenots who attended their own chapel in the precincts of the Savoy Palace next door to Somerset House.

31. Conn to Barberini 1637, quoted in Albion, p. 163.
32. Calendar of State Papers Colonial, America and West Indies, May 1637 (54).
33. William Montgomerie Lamont, *Marginal Prynne, 1600–1669, With a Portrait* (1963), p. 2.
34. John Aubrey, *Aubrey's Brief Lives: Omnibus Edition*, ed. Simon Webb (2017), p. 250; Lamont, p. 1.
35. PRO C 115/N4/8615, 17 May 1637; Sharpe, p. 760.
36. Sharpe, p. 762.
37. Ibid., p. 763.
38. Albion, p. 224.
39. Dethan, p. 138.

Chapter 13: Last of the Halcyon Days

1. John Aubrey, *Aubrey's Brief Lives: Omnibus Edition*, ed. Simon Webb (2017), p. 287.
2. Ibid.
3. Ibid.
4. Ibid.
5. HMC de L'Isle and Dudley MSS, VI, pp. 67, 94
6. Simon Thurley, *Palaces of Revolution: Life, Death and Art at the Stuart Court* (2021), p. 171; Nadine Akkerman, 'A Triptych of Dorothy Percy Sidney (1598–1659), Countess of Leicester, Lucy Percy Hay (1599–1660), Countess of Carlisle, and Dorothy Sidney Spencer (1617–1684), Countess of Sunderland', in Margaret P. Hannay, Michael G. Brennan and Mary Ellen Lamb (eds), *The Ashgate Research Companion to The Sidneys, 1500–1700: Volume 1: Lives* (2015), pp. 139, 146.
7. A. H. Nethercot, *Sir William Davenant* (1938), p. 151; Robert Wilcher, *The Discontented Cavalier* (1984), p. 112.
8. Aubrey, p. 180. Davenant was buried at Westminster Abbey thirty-one years later, 'O Rare Sir William Davenant'.
9. Ibid., pp. 289, 290.

10. Wilcher, pp. 159–60.

11. He was anxious not to see Dunkirk fall into French hands and the French were making difficult demands on, for example, that perennial problem between England and France – fishing rights.

12. Zahira Véliz, 'Signs of Identity in *Lady with a Fan* by Diego Velázquez: Costume and Likeness Reconsidered', *Art Bulletin*, Vol. 86, No. 1 (March 2004), p. 76.

13. Quoted in ibid., p. 76.

14. Georges Dethan, *The Young Mazarin* (1977), p. 139.

15. Ibid., p. 138.

16. Cardinal Richelieu to M. de Bellièvre, 6 October and 13 November 1638, *Lettres, Instructions Diplomatiques et Papiers d'état du cardinal de Richelieu*, ed. M. Avenel (8 vols., 1853–77), Vol. VI, pp. 211–13.

17. *Ceremonies of Charles I: The Notebooks of John Finet 1628–1641*, ed. Albert Loomie (1987), p. 245.

18. The comments were made by the courtier Leon Pinelo.

19. Véliz, p. 79.

20. AAE, CP, Espagne, vol. 19, ff. 7r–8v, Le roy d'Espagne au Cardenal-Infante, 13 February 1638.

21. Dorothy de Brissac Campbell, *The Intriguing Duchess: Marie de Rohan, Duchesse de Chevreuse* (1933), p. 203. Famously she once went swimming in the Thames, causing no little excitement on the banks of the river. 'The humble willows on the shore grew proud', a poet punned of the watching men, 'To see her in their shade her body shroud'.

22. *The Earl of Strafforde's Letters and Dispatches: With An Essay Towards His Life by Sir George Radcliffe* (reprint 2018), Vol. 2, p. 194.

23. This was Panzani's observation.

24. It had been shown in February 1638.

25. CSPV v 24, p. 264.

26. His secretary of state Sir Francis Windebank, quoted in H. Noel Williams, A *Fair Conspirator: Marie de Rohan, Duchesse de Chevreuse* (1913), p. 141.

Chapter 14: The Bishops' War

1. Jean Puget de la Serre, *Histoire de l'entrée de la reine mère du roi très-chrétien dans la Grande Bretagne* (1639).
2. TNA PRO 31/3/70 f. 83; CSPV 1636–9 (528).
3. David Cressy, *Charles I and the People of England* (2015), pp. 15–16.
4. *Ceremonies of Charles I: The Notebooks of John Finet 1628–1641*, ed. Albert Loomie (1987), pp. 254ff.
5. *Letters of the Lady Brilliana Harley, Wife of Sir Robert Harley, of Brampton Bryan, Knight of the Bath*, with an introduction by Thomas Taylor Lewis (2007), p. 10; Rebecca A. Bailey, *Staging the Old Faith: Queen Henrietta Maria and the Theatre of Caroline England, 1625–1642* (2009), p. 179.
6. CSPV 1636–9 (534); *Lettres de Henriette-Marie de France, reine d'Angleterre à sa soeur Christine, Duchesse de Savoie*, ed. Hermann Ferrero (1881), Letter XXX.
7. The statue had once belonged to no less a figure than Philip II's daughter, the Infanta Isabella; Cordula Van Wyhe, 'Reformulating the Cult of Our Lady of Scherpenheuvel: Marie de' Medici and the Regina Pacis Statue in Cologne (1635–1645)', *The Seventeenth Century*, 22:1 (2007), pp. 47–8.
8. *Lettres de Henriette-Marie de France*, Letters XXIX, XXX.
9. In a letter to Scaglia; Toby Osborne, *Dynasty and Diplomacy in the Court of Savoy: Political Culture and the Thirty Years War* (2002), p. 263. Henrietta Maria, who had once hosted a performance of Shakespeare's *Richard III* for Charles, could easily guess the danger her nephew's rule faced from royal uncles.
10. Osborne, p. 260, n. 66; Georges Dethan, *The Young Mazarin* (1977), p. 130.
11. Bailey, p. 185.
12. CSPV 1636–9 (273).
13. Caroline M. Hibbard, *Charles I and the Popish Plot* (2017), p. 109.
14. Nearly 13,700 Scots and Ulster Scots had joined the Dutch service before 1629 alone, and by 1631 there were another 12,000

serving in the Swedish armies. Dozens had been made governors of fortified cities and garrisons; Hibbard, pp. 105–6.

15. Ibid.
16. Robert Wilcher, *The Discontented Cavalier* (1984), p. 259.
17. John Aubrey, *Aubrey's Brief Lives: Omnibus Edition*, ed. Simon Webb (2017), p. 285.
18. Michael C. Questier, *Catholicism and Community in Early Modern England: Politics, Aristocratic Patronage and Religion, c.1550–1640* (2006), p. 503.
19. Erin Griffey, *On Display: Henrietta Maria and the Materials of Magnificence at the Stuart Court* (2016), p. 115.
20. Erin Griffey has written extensively on this.
21. Michael S. Kimmel, *Absolutism and Its Discontents: State and Society in Seventeenth Century* (1988), p. 56.
22. CSPV 1636–9, 29 March 1639 (612).
23. Osborne, p. 265.
24. It was co-signed by Wat Montagu and another Catholic convert called Sir Kenelm Digby, son of the Gunpowder Plotter Everard Digby. Suckling had gained some notoriety for a quarrel over a woman he had had with Kenelm Digby's strapping brother John. He had paid a group of toughs to help him jump them outside the Blackfriars theatre, but John had beaten the slightly built Suckling roundly, while Kenelm had fatally injured one of the paid thugs.
25. Gordon Albion, *Charles I and the Court of Rome: A Study in 17th-Century Diplomacy* (1935), p. 335, n. 2.
26. Davenant was serving under Holland's half-brother, the Earl of Newport.
27. Mary Chambers, *The Life of Mary Ward*, Vol. 2 (1882), p. 459.
28. Hibbard, p. 108.
29. Giuliano Ferretti, 'La politique italienne de la France et le duché de Savoie au temps de Richelieu', *Dix-septième siècle* (2014), 1, p. 262.
30. Ibid.

31. Dethan, p. 131.
32. Ibid. He would not be released until after Richelieu's death.
33. J. H. Elliott, 'The Year of the Three Ambassadors', in Hugh Lloyd Jones, Valerie Pearl and Blair Worden (eds), *History and Imagination* (1981), p. 171.
34. Clarendon, quoted in David Nichol Smith, *Characters from the Histories and Memoirs of the Seventeenth Century* (1918), p. 62.
35. *The Earl of Strafforde's Letters and Dispatches: With An Essay Towards His Life by Sir George Radcliffe* (reprint 2018), Vol. 2, p. 120.
36. HMC de L'Isle and Dudley MSS, VI, p. 157.
37. *Memoirs of Madame de Motteville on Anne of Austria and Her Court. With An Introduction By C.-A. Sainte-Beuve*, trans. Katharine P. Wormeley (2015), Vol. 1, p. 25.
38. Bailey, p. 197.
39. Ibid., pp. 201–2.

Chapter 15: To Rebel Without Fear

1. J. H. Elliott, 'The Year of the Three Ambassadors', in Hugh Lloyd Jones, Valerie Pearl and Blair Worden (eds), *History and Imagination* (1981), p. 174.
2. *Ceremonies of Charles I: The Notebooks of John Finet, 1628–1641*, ed. Albert Loomie (1987), p. 280.
3. Ibid., p. 278.
4. R. Smuts, 'The Puritan followers of Henrietta Maria in the 1630s', *English Historical Review* (1978), p. 42.
5. John Adamson, *The Noble Revolt: The Overthrow of Charles I* (2009), p. 18.
6. Centre for Kentish Studies, de L'Isle MSS. U1475/C129/8.
7. Gordon Albion, *Charles I and the Court of Rome: A Study in 17th-Century Diplomacy* (1935), p. 337.
8. Ibid., p. 339.
9. Gervas Huxley, *Endymion Porter: The Life of a Courtier 1587–1649* (1959), p. 250.

10. CSPV 1640–2 (126).
11. Laura Lunger Knoppers, *Politicizing Domesticity from Henrietta Maria to Milton's Eve* (2011), p. 37.
12. Rebecca A. Bailey, *Staging the Old Faith: Queen Henrietta Maria and the Theatre of Caroline England, 1625–1642* (2009), p. 221.
13. CSPV 1640–2 (127).
14. Generally Charles 'saw and observed men long before he received them about his person, and did not love strangers or very confident men'. Clarendon, quoted in David Nichol Smith, *Characters from the Histories and Memoirs of the Seventeenth Century* (1918), p. 50.
15. BL Harley MSS, 165, f. 8.
16. *The Diary and Correspondence of John Evelyn*, ed. William Bray (1859), Vol. 1, p. 14.
17. CSPV 1640–2 (79).
18. CSPV 1640–2 (93).
19. Albion, p. 342.
20. Bailey, p. 220.
21. Albion, p. 346
22. CSPV 1640–2 (150, 152).
23. CSPV 1640–2 (140).
24. CSPV 1640–2 (150, 152, 168).
25. CSPV 1640–2 (150, 152).
26. Katie Whitaker, *A Royal Passion: The Turbulent Marriage of Charles I and Henrietta Maria* (2010), p. 185.
27. HMC de L'Isle and Dudley MSS, VI, p. 346.
28. Adamson, p. 153; Brian Manning, *The English People and the English Revolution* (1976), p. 48.
29. Richard Cust, *Charles I and the Aristocracy, 1625–1642* (2017), pp. 52, 53, 54.
30. *Clarendon's Four Portraits*, ed. Richard Ollard (1989), pp. 125, 126.
31. Cust, p. 52.

32. HMC de L'Isle and Dudley MSS, VI, p. 360; Clarendon, quoted in Cust, p. 49.
33. Albion, p. 349.

Chapter 16: The Army Plots

1. John Adamson, *The Noble Revolt: The Overthrow of Charles I* (2009), pp. 178, 192.
2. HMC de L'Isle and Dudley MSS, VI, p. 374.
3. Caroline M. Hibbard, *Charles I and the Popish Plot* (2017), pp. 186, 191.
4. Adamson, pp. 165–7, 169.
5. Re-establishing an Elizabethan-style monarchy and Church might suit the landed classes who dominated Church patronage, access to Parliament, the county commissions and militias. For ordinary Londoners it was a different matter.
6. CSPV 1640–2 (138).
7. Belvoir: QZ/22/1 La Reine d'Angleterre Feur. 1641 Léon Bouthillier, Comte de Chavigny.
8. CSPV 1640–42 (165) (168) (172).
9. Conrad Russell, 'The First Army Plot of 1641', *Transactions of the Royal Historical Society*, Vol. 38 (1988), p. 89.
10. Ibid.
11. She had rushed to his bedside in the past, staying at Richmond until he was better; CSPV 1632–6 (536) and undated letter, *Letters of Queen Henrietta Maria*, ed. Mary Anne Everett Green (2009), p. 28.
12. *Letters of Queen Henrietta Maria*, p. 38.
13. Georges Dethan, *The Young Mazarin* (1977), p. 141. Charles opposed Wat Montagu's candidature in favour of the youngest brother of the Duke of Lennox.
14. HMC de L'Isle and Dudley MSS, VI, p. 360.
15. Newport was the uncle of the dead Charles Porter, who was Goring's brother-in-law.

16. Clarendon, quoted in David Nichol Smith, *Characters from the Histories and Memoirs of the Seventeenth Century* (1918), p. 50.

17. Quoted in John Callow, *The Making of King James II: The Formative Years of a Fallen King* (2000), p. 33.

18. *Ceremonies of Charles I: The Notebooks of John Finet 1628–1641*, ed. Albert Loomie (1987), p. 109.

19. For this and other comments see Brian Manning, *The English People and the English Revolution* (1976), pp. 91–2.

20. *Memoirs of Madame de Motteville on Anne of Austria and Her Court. With An Introduction By C.-A. Sainte-Beuve*, trans. Katharine P. Wormeley (2015), Vol. 1, pp. 196, 197.

21. Leanda de Lisle, *White King* (2018), p. 126.

22. Adamson, *The Noble Revolt*, p. 272.

23. Russell, pp. 85–106.

24. *Notebooks of John Finet*, p. 112.

25. Ibid.

26. Agnes Strickland, *Stuart Princesses* (1872), p. 14.

27. BL Harley MSS 163, f. 175. They arrived at Portsmouth with Carnarvon on 7 May.

28. CSPV 1640–2 (188).

29. CSPV 1640–2 (190).

30. Gordon Albion, *Charles I and the Court of Rome: A Study in 17th-Century Diplomacy* (1935), pp. 364–5.

31. *Journal of the House of Lords*, Vol. 2, 11 May 1641.

32. CSPV 1640–2 (190).

33. *The Correspondence of Elizabeth Stuart, Queen of Bohemia, Volume 2: 1632–1642* (2011), ed. Nadine Akkerman, p. 957.

34. *Journal of the House of Lords*, Vol. 2, 11 May 1641.

35. C. V. Wedgwood, *Strafford* (1953), p. 386.

36. *Correspondence of Elizabeth Stuart*, p. 957.

37. HMC de L'Isle and Dudley MSS, VI, p. 403.

38. John Aubrey, *Aubrey's Brief Lives: Omnibus Edition*, ed. Simon Webb (2017), p. 289.

Chapter 17: The Struggle for London

1. *Lettres de Henriette-Marie de France, reine d'Angleterre à sa soeur Christine, Duchesse de Savoie,* ed. Hermann Ferrero (1881), pp. 57–9.
2. Ibid.
3. Ibid.
4. Agnes Strickland, *Stuart Princesses* (1872), p. 16.
5. *Journal of the House of Commons,* Vol. 2, 15 July 1641.
6. *Letters of Queen Henrietta Maria,* ed. Mary Anne Everett Green (2009), p. 40; *Lettres de Henriette-Marie de France,* p. 58.
7. CSPV 26 July 1641 (228).
8. *The Diary and Correspondence of John Evelyn,* ed. William Bray (1859), Vol. 1, p. 14.
9. *Lettres de Henriette-Marie de France,* pp. 57–9.
10. CSPV 1640–42 (127).
11. Trevor Royale, *Civil War: The War of the Three Kingdoms 1638–1660* (2005), p. 134; the rebellion broke out on 23 October.
12. CSPV 1640–2 (279).
13. Ibid.
14. Ibid. A Spanish connection to the rebellion was also suspected. Spain had, in the past, looked to Ireland as a possible entry point to an invasion of England. It was a view the French ambassador encouraged.
15. Clarendon, quoted in David Nichol Smith, *Characters from the Histories and Memoirs of the Seventeenth Century* (1918), p. 162.
16. See Newport, *ODNB.*
17. David Baldwin, 'The Politico-Religious Usage of the Queen's Chapel, 1623–1688', MA thesis, Durham University (1999), p. 104.
18. Siobhan Keenan, *The Progresses, Processions and Royal Entries of Charles I 1625–1642* (2020), p. 182; LMA Corporation of London, *Common Council Journal,* 14, COL/CC/01/01/041 f. 8.
19. *Diary and Correspondence of John Evelyn,* Vol. 4, p. 102.

20. Georges Dethan, *The Young Mazarin* (1977), pp. 142, 183; 'Van Dyck', *ODNB*.

21. Sharon Achinstein, 'Plagues and Publication: Ballads and the Representation of Disease in the English Renaissance', *Criticism*, Vol. 34, No. 1 (Winter 1992), p. 37.

22. Keenan, pp. 184–5.

23. CSPV 1640–1 (296).

24. Keenan, p. 185.

25. John Milton, *The Life and Reign of King Charles* (1651), p. 78.

26. John Adamson, *The Noble Revolt: The Overthrow of Charles I* (2009), p. 445 and notes.

27. Keenan, p. 194.

28. CSPD 3 December 1641 (64).

29. Brian Manning, *The English People and the English Revolution* (1976), p. 79.

30. CSPD 3 December 1641 (99).

31. CSPD 3 December 1641 (103) (110).

32. Ibid.

33. CSPV 27 January 1641.

34. *Lettres de Henriette-Marie de France*, p. 60.

35. Tobie Matthew, quoted in Nadine Akkerman, 'A Triptych of Dorothy Percy Sidney (1598–1659), Countess of Leicester, Lucy Percy Hay (1599–1660), Countess of Carlisle, and Dorothy Sidney Spencer (1617–1684), Countess of Sunderland', in Margaret P. Hannay, Michael G. Brennan and Mary Ellen Lamb (eds), *The Ashgate Research Companion to The Sidneys, 1500–1700: Volume 1: Lives* (2015).

36. Manning, p. 96.

37. CSPV 7–17 January 1642 (323).

38. Ibid.

39. Bulstrode Whitelocke, in Michelle Anne White, *Henrietta Maria and the English Civil Wars* (2017), p. 54.

40. CSPV 7–17 January 1642 (323).

Chapter 18: Saving the King

1. John Adamson, *The Noble Revolt: The Overthrow of Charles I* (2009), p. 499.
2. Glamorgan Record Office, Stradling MSS. D/D.TD.8, Charles I to Captain Stradling, 8 January 1642; Glamorgan Record Office, Stradling MSS. D/D.TD.9, Charles I to Captain Stradling, 27 January 1642.
3. To have ordered Charles to remain would be to announce he was their prisoner. It had not yet come to that.
4. CSPD 1641–3 (254).
5. 'Proceedings, Principally in the County of Kent, in Connections with the Parliament Called in 1640', *Camden Society*, 80 (1862), pp. 67–8.
6. London Metropolitan Archives COL/CC/01/01/039, f. 206.
7. Gervas Huxley, *Endymion Porter: The Life of a Courtier 1587–1649* (1959), p. 270.
8. CSPD 1641–3 (256).
9. Glamorgan Record Office, Stradling MSS. D/D.TD.8, Charles I to Captain Stradling, 8 January 1642; Glamorgan Record Office, Stradling MSS D/D.TD.9, Charles I to Captain Stradling, 27 January 1642.
10. CSPD 1641–3 (274).
11. CSPD 1641–3 (283).
12. Philip A. Knachel, *England and the Fronde: The Impact of the English Civil War and Revolution in France* (1967), pp. 565–7.
13. *Letters of Queen Henrietta Maria*, ed. Mary Anne Everett Green (2009), p. 69. Anne of Austria and Mazarin later acted in a similar manner. They accepted reforms presented by sovereign courts in 1648, intending to repudiate this later on the grounds action was forced on them in order to keep the peace.
14. Michelle Anne White, *Henrietta Maria and the English Civil Wars* (2017), pp. 55–6.
15. Simon Thurley, *Palaces of Revolution: Life, Death and Art at the Stuart Court* (2021), p. 162.

16. *Letters of Queen Henrietta Maria*, pp. 118–19.
17. CSPV 1642–3 (8); Thomas Birch, *The Court and Times of Charles I* (2 vols, 1848), Vol. 2, p. 349.
18. Birch, Vol. 2, p. 349.
19. Cecilia Mary Clifford Feilding Denbigh, *Royalist Father and Roundhead Son; Being the Memoirs of the First and Second Earls of Denbigh, 1600–1675* (1915), p. 177; Arundel and Goring had also lost money and possessions and the maids their clothes.
20. CSPV March 1642 (12). There is a story that the relic miraculously survived and one of the Capuchin gave it to the Bishop of Mans who placed it in the convent of the Visitadines in his city. There is a remote possibility of some nugget of truth in this legend which appears in Marie-Ange Duvignacq-Glessgen, *L'ordre de la Visitation à Paris* (1994), p. 228. It wasn't unknown for people to steal relics. It may however be a myth linked to another story dating to the French Revolution. A priest from the diocese of Angers was going back to his parish when he stopped in Le Mans, where the conflict between the republican and royalist armies was very violent. While he was praying in the cathedral, someone gave him several relics of local saints and a relic of the true cross to keep safe. He took them back to his parish, and died in Champtoceau in 1831. The relics stayed there until around 2018 when the saints' relics were given back to the diocese of Le Mans. They are now kept in the cathedral. They do not include any relics of the true cross, which appear to have stayed in the diocese of Angers. Are they still in the parish of Champtoceau? I would love to hear from anyone who finds out! https://docplayer.fr/132441487–Le-petit-rapporteur-bulletin-municipal-de-champtoceaux-n-453–juillet-2018.html.
21. *Letters of Queen Henrietta Maria*, p. 72.
22. Nancy Goldstone, *Daughters of the Winter Queen: Four Remarkable Sisters, the Crown of Bohemia and the Enduring Legacy of Mary, Queen of Scots* (2019), p. 190.

23. Ibid., pp. 190, 191.

24. *Lettres de Henriette-Marie de France, reine d'Angleterre à sa soeur Christine, Duchesse de Savoie*, ed. Hermann Ferrero (1881), p. 59.

25. *Letters of Queen Henrietta Maria*, p. 52.

26. The northern Netherlands had declared their independence in 1581.

27. *Letters of Queen Henrietta Maria*, p. 72.

28. HMS *Providence* and HMS *Entrance* had been destined for Ireland as escorts for vessels carrying troops and supplies to fight the rebels, but the coming conflict in England took priority. For the Junto too Ireland was only the pretext for their arms-gathering; 'The Navy in the English Civil War', Michael James Lea-O'Mahoney, PhD thesis, University of Exeter (2011), p. 33.

29. Mary Edmond, *Rare Sir William Davenant: Poet Laureate, Playwright, Civil War General, Restoration Theatre Manager* (1987), p. 89. Davenant had returned to his London home at St-Martin-in-the-Fields where his daughter had been baptised a week after Charles's attempted arrest of the five members.

30. *Journal of the House of Commons*, Vol. 2, 619.

31. *Letters of Queen Henrietta Maria*, p. 51.

32. BL Harley MSS 7379, f. 86; *Letters of Queen Henrietta Maria*, p. 64.

33. *Journal of the House of Commons*, Vol. 2, 11 June 1642.

34. Some of the crown jewels were also left with 'certain Jews of Amsterdam'. https://www.researchgate.net/publication/272781983_To_Sell_England's_Jewels_Queen_Henrietta_Maria's_visits_to_the_Continent_1642_and_1644.

35. *Letters of Queen Henrietta Maria*, p. 98.

36. Ibid., pp. 55–6.

37. Ibid., pp. 59–63.

38. Ibid., pp. 68–9.

39. Quoted in John Callow, *The Making of King James II: The Formative Years of a Fallen King* (2000), p. 33.

40. *Letters of Queen Henrietta Maria*, p. 130.

41. Ibid., pp. 70–1.

42. Denbigh, p. 178.

43. *Letters of Queen Henrietta Maria*, p. 97.

44. Lea-O'Mahoney, p. 60.

45. *Letters of Queen Henrietta Maria*, p. 103.

46. Erin Griffey, *On Display: Henrietta Maria and the Materials of Magnificence at the Stuart Court* (2016), p. 157.

47. Cordula Van Wyhe, 'Reformulating the Cult of Our Lady of Scherpenheuvel: Marie de' Medici and the Regina Pacis Statue in Cologne (1635–1645)', *The Seventeenth Century*, 22:1 (2007), pp. 42–75.

48. Ibid. The Virgin resembled the sixth-century Maria Antigua from the Forum Romanum, the prototype of almost all representations of the Virgin as Maria Regina, or Queen of Heaven.

49. The statue Marie had brought to England and bequeathed to the Carmelites in Cologne became almost immediately the centre of a major cult, reproduced in mass printed images, and offered public veneration in sumptuous ceremonies. A new convent was built within months, to house Our Lady of Peace. There, every 2 July, for over three centuries, Marie de' Medici's bequest would be commemorated with a requiem Mass for her soul. This ended only at the close of the Second World War when, in 1945, Our Lady of Peace and the convent were destroyed in an Allied bombing raid.

50. Benoit Wells, 'Complementarity and Competition: Marie de' Medici and Cardinal Richelieu as Patrons and Collectors of Art', available online.

Chapter 19: To Kill a Queen

1. CSPV 1642–3 (142).

2. Ibid.

3. 'My God! What a world we live in' he had said on the scaffold – a sentiment with which Louis must have concurred. Georges Dethan, *The Young Mazarin* (1977), p. 143.

4. Belvoir QZ/22/30 The Queen of England La Hage 8 September 1642.

5. Ibid., 26 October 1642.

6. *Letters of Queen Henrietta Maria*, ed. Mary Anne Everett Green (2009), p. 126.

7. Ibid.

8. Ibid.

9. D. R. Guttery, *The Great Civil War in Midland Parishes* (1950), p. 32.

10. Leanda de Lisle, *White King* (2018), p. 168.

11. Bernard Stuart, p. 41.

12. Cecilia Mary Clifford Feilding Denbigh, *Royalist Father and Roundhead Son; Being the Memoirs of the First and Second Earls of Denbigh, 1600–1675* (1915), pp. 178–9, 182.

13. *Letters of Queen Henrietta Maria*, p. 147.

14. Gilbert Burnet, *The Memoirs of the Lives and Actions of James and William, Dukes of Hamilton and Castleherald* (1677), letter dated 2 December 1642, p. 293.

15. *Letters of Queen Henrietta Maria*, p 136.

16. He was pleased to get the parrot, although he couldn't resist taking one of her fine tapestries as well. Jean-François Dubost, *Marie de' Medici* (2009), p. 856.

17. *Letters of Queen Henrietta Maria*, p. 147.

18. CSPV 1642–3 (142).

19. J. R. Powell and E. K. Timings (eds), *Documents Relating to the Civil War: 1642–1648* (1963), p. 62.

20. CSPV 1643 (221); Madame de Motteville, quoted in Stephanie Marie Seery-Murphy, 'Hazarding the Queen: Henrietta Maria, Religious Controversy and the Construction of a Rhetorical Figure', PhD thesis, Claremont Graduate University (2008), p. 271.

21. Thomas Birch, *The Court and Times of Charles I* (2 vols, 1848), Vol. 2, p. 363. She describes this in a letter to the Bishop of Lyon in 1644. Madame Acarie – the founder of the Carmelite order in

France – had been taken to the Shrine of Our Lady of Liesse as a child and dedicated to her. This connection was undoubtedly important to Henrietta Maria.

22. Powell and Timings (eds), p. 63.
23. Ibid., p. 62.
24. *Letters of Queen Henrietta Maria*, p. 162.
25. Birch, Vol. 2, p. 363.
26. John Barratt, *Cavaliers: The Royalist Army at War 1642–1646* (2004), p. 155.
27. *Letters of Queen Henrietta Maria*, pp. 164–5.
28. Ibid., p. 163.
29. Powell and Timings (eds), pp. 64, 65.
30. CSPV 1642–3 (232).
31. Powell and Timings (eds), p. 69; CSPV 1642–3 (232).
32. Powell and Timings (eds), p. 65.
33. *Letters of Queen Henrietta Maria*, pp. 166–8; Powell and Timings (eds), p. 66.
34. *Lettres de Henriette-Marie de France, reine d'Angleterre à sa soeur Christine, Duchesse de Savoie*, ed. Hermann Ferrero (1881), p. 63.
35. Clarendon, quoted in David Nichol Smith, *Characters from the Histories and Memoirs of the Seventeenth Century* (1918), p. 119.
36. *Letters of Queen Henrietta Maria*, pp. 166–8. It was a Friday.
37. Ibid.
38. Powell and Timings (eds), p. 66.
39. Once exposed Goring had been unable to save Portsmouth for the royalist cause and had fled to Henrietta Maria's little court in Holland, returning to England in December with a consignment of arms. Clarendon, vol. 2, p. 997.
40. Charles Carlton, *Going to the Wars: The Experience of the British Civil Wars 1638–1651* (1994), p. 53.
41. Denbigh, p. 185.
42. CSPV 1642–3 (244).

43. In the clothing towns of the north royalist plundering had triggered a furious response from townsfolk, yeomen and the poor. Hotham's fellow commander, Lord Fairfax's son, Sir Thomas Fairfax, had recruited amongst these so called 'clubmen', triggering fears amongst the gentry that the poorer sort would eventually set their sights against the entire landed class. It was a view encouraged by Newcastle who described how 'the Badges and Monuments of ancient Gentry in Windows and pedigrees have been by them defaced; Old Evidences, the Records of private Families, the Pledges of Possessions, the boundaries of Properties have been by them burned, torn in pieces, and the Seals trampled under their feet.' Hotham's son John observed of the clubmen that, 'whosoever they pretend for at first, within a while they will set up for themselves, to the utter ruin of all the nobility and gentry of the kingdom'; Andrew James Hopper, ' "Fitted for Desperation": Honour and Treachery in Parliament's Yorkshire Command, 1642–1643', *History*, Vol. 86, No. 282 (April 2001), pp. 152–3.

44. The terms included Charles giving up his friends to trial and probable death. How well that had served him in the past was illustrated by what had happened after the execution of Strafford; David Scott, *Politics and War in the Three Stuart Kingdoms, 1637–49* (2017), p. 47.

45. Account of Sir William Fairfax, 27 February 1643, Belvoir QZ 23, f. 13, 16A.

46. The letter was published on 14 March.

47. He was married to Buckingham's widow.

48. *Sir Robert Poyntz to the Marquess of Ormond: A Collection Of Original Letters and Papers, Concerning the Affairs of England: From the Year 1641 to 1660: Found Among the Duke of Ormond's Papers, Volume 1*, ed. Thomas Carte (1739), p. 19.

49. Mark Napier, *The Life and Times of Montrose: Illustrated from Original Manuscripts* (1840), p. 229.

50. Sir Robert Poyntz to the Marquess of Ormond, 1 June 1643, quoted in ibid., p. 199.

Chapter 20: Her Popish Army

1. *The Memoirs and Memorials of Sir Hugh Cholmley*, ed. Jack Binns (1893), p. 143.

2. He would gain nothing at court, Hotham had told him, as 'the women rule all'. Andrew James Hopper, ' "Fitted for Desperation": Honour and Treachery in Parliament's Yorkshire Command, 1642–1643', *History*, Vol. 86, No. 282 (April 2001), p. 143.

3. *Letters of Queen Henrietta Maria*, ed. Mary Anne Everett Green (2009), p. 205.

4. Ibid.

5. *Memoirs and Memorials of Sir Hugh Cholmley*, p. 143.

6. J. R. Powell and E. K. Timings (eds), *Documents Relating to the Civil War: 1642–1648* (1963), p. 68.

7. It was, Fairfax recalled, 'one of the greatest losses we ever received'.

8. *Letters of Queen Henrietta Maria*, p. 182.

9. Ibid., p. 177.

10. John Aubrey, *Aubrey's Brief Lives: Omnibus Edition*, ed. Simon Webb (2017), p. 194.

11. CSPV 1642–3 (257).

12. Thomas Birch, *The Court and Times of Charles I* (2 vols, 1848), Vol. 2, p. 353.

13. Albert Loomie, 'The Destruction of Ruben's Crucifixion', *Burlington Magazine*, Vol. 140, No. 1147 (1998), pp. 680–1.

14. Ibid.

15. CSPV 1642–3 (264) (266).

16. Michelle Anne White, *Henrietta Maria and the English Civil Wars* (2017), pp. 98, 99.

17. Nithisdale to Antrim, 8 May 1643, in Mark Napier, *The Life and Times of Montrose: Illustrated from Original Manuscripts* (1840), p. 210.

18. *Memoirs and Memorials of Sir Hugh Cholmley*, p. 84.

19. *Letters of Queen Henrietta Maria*, p. 217.

20. David Stevenson, *The Scottish Revolution 1637–44* (2011), pp. 264–5.

21. Napier, p. 193.

22. Sir Robert Poyntz to the Marquess of Ormond, 1 June 1643, in Napier, p. 199.

23. Goring had been ill for days and was in bed when the attack took place – though it would later be claimed that the heavy-drinking cavalier had simply been hungover.

24. *Letters of Queen Henrietta Maria*, p. 209.

25. Ruth Kleinman, *Anne of Austria* (1985), p. 131.

26. Georges Dethan, *The Young Mazarin* (1977), p. 143.

27. *Letters of Queen Henrietta Maria*, pp. 215, 216. She left it to an emissary to describe to Mazarin her 'affliction' on the news of Louis's demise.

28. Ibid., pp. 198–9.

29. Ibid., p. 209.

30. CSPV 1642–3 (259).

31. 'A Copie of a Letter from a Gentleman in the House of Commons Concerning the Proceedings of that House against the Queen's Majestie', in John Somers (ed.), *A Third Collection of Scarce and Valuable Tracts* (4 vols, 1751), I, pp. 317–19.

32. Ibid.

33. Ibid.

34. *Letters of Queen Henrietta Maria*, 214.

35. Somers (ed.), I, pp. 317–19.

36. CSPV 1642–3 (268) .

37. White, p. 100.

38. David Scott, *Politics and War in the Three Stuart Kingdoms, 1637–49* (2017), p. 60.

39. *Letters of Queen Henrietta Maria*, p. 217.

40. Ibid., p. 212.

41. Sir Henry Slingsby, quoted in David Cooke, *The Civil War in Yorkshire: Fairfax Versus Newcastle (Battlefield Britain)* (2004), p. 63.

42. It belonged to a Lady Leake.
43. Le Comte de Baillon, *Henriette-Marie de France, Reine d'Angleterre* (1877, reprint 2018), p. 480.
44. *Letters of Queen Henrietta Maria*, p. 219.
45. 'A Perfect diurnall of some passages in Parliament, and daily proceedings of the army under his excellency Sir Thomas Fairfax', No. 23 (1643), p. 4. Amongst other supposed deaths they reported was that of Henriette Maria's nephew, the Duke de Beaufort, son of her illegitimate half-brother César, Duke of Vendôme. He had been with her but had returned to France after the death of Richelieu and Louis and was spending now 'whole days' with Anne of Austria and 'entertaining her gaily'.
46. Now in St Mary Magdalene Church with the following inscription: 'Here lies the remains of 31 persons, formerly buried in the crypt beneath the altar of Newark Church and removed thence to this spot in 1883. Among them rest the bodies of Baron Dhona, Commander of Queen Henrietta Maria's forces, Sir John Girlington, Sir Gervase Eyre and other loyal officers killed in action during the sieges and gallant defence of Newark 1643–46'.
47. Richard Baxter, quoted in David Nichol Smith, *Characters from the Histories and Memoirs of the Seventeenth Century* (1918), pp. 143, 144.
48. 'A Continuation of certaine speciall and remarkable passages from both houses of Parliament, and other parts of the kingdom' (1642–3), 29 June–6 July 1643, pp. 2–3. 'John Hotham', *ODNB*, Indeed it was said that they were 'ready to cut each others throats'; Hopper, p. 144.
49. If Captain Hotham had been able to fulfil his promise and turncoat the royalists might have won the war that summer, for it would have added momentum to a remarkable run of royalist victories that began the next day, 30 June 1643, with Newcastle's victory over Fairfax at Adwalton Moor outside Bradford. They were both executed later that year. Hopper, p. 151.

50. A Perfect diurnall', No. 24 (1643), p. 5; she told Charles she would be leaving Newark on 'Friday or Saturday' that is, 30, 31 July; *Letters of Queen Henrietta Maria*, p. 222.

51. *Letters of Queen Henrietta Maria*, p. 222. 'She was fonder [of Cavendish] than it was right for a virtuous woman to show herself', one critic later observed. Eliot Warburton, *Memoirs of Prince Rupert and the Cavaliers* (1849).

52. 'A commemoration sermon preached at Derby, Feb. 18, 1674, for the Honourable Colonel Charles Cavendish, slain in the service of King Charles the First, before Gainsborough in the year 1643', p. 17.

53. *Letters of Queen Henrietta Maria*, p. 222.

54. White, p. 99.

55. Philip Tennant, *The Civil War in Stratford-upon-Avon: Conflict and Community in South Warwickshire, 1642–46* (1996), pp. 70, 71.

56. *Letters of Queen Henrietta Maria*, p. 222.

Chapter 21: Oxford

1. *Mercurius Aulicus*, 18 July 1643.

2. 'Certain Informations from Several Parts of the Kingdom and from other Places Beyond the Seas, for the Better Satisfaction of all such who Desire to be truly informed of every weeks passage', No. 27 (1643), p. 211.

3. Ibid., p. 212.

4. *Mercurius Aulicus*, 18 July 1643.

5. *Journal of Sir Samuel Luke* (1950), p. 117.

6. Ibid.; *Mercurius Aulicus*, 18 July 1643.

7. *Mercurius Aulicus*, 18 July 1643.

8. Ibid.

9. HL/PO/JO/10/1/183 Letter 6, 8/9 July 1643, from Walsall.

10. Ibid.

11. Eliot Warburton, *Memoirs of Prince Rupert and the Cavaliers* (1849), Vol. 2, p. 41.

12. The queen is reputed to have stayed at what is now the Saracens Head on the green, while the army was camped by the river Rea in an area still called the Camp and Camp Lane; Philip Tennant, *The Civil War in Stratford-upon-Avon: Conflict and Community in South Warwickshire, 1642–46* (1996), p. 74.

13. Ibid., p. 64.

14. Ibid., p. 74.

15. Ibid., pp. 72–3.

16. Ibid.

17. *Mercurius Aulicus*, 12 July 1643.

18. *Letters of Queen Henrietta Maria*, ed. Mary Anne Everett Green (2009), p. 222.

19. Tennant, p. 74.

20. William Hamper (ed.), *Two copies of Verses on the Meeting of King Charles I & His Queen Henrietta Maria* (2010).

21. *Mercurius Aulicus*, 14 July 1643.

22. *Mercurius Aulicus*, 15 July 1643.

23. Following the Battle of Lansdowne near Bath on 5 July 1643.

24. Charles Carlton, *Going to the Wars: The Experience of the British Civil Wars 1638–1651* (1994), p. 222.

25. Quoted in John Barratt, *Cavalier Capital: Oxford in the English Civil War 1642–1646* (2021), p. 70.

26. *Memoirs of Lady Fanshawe* (2019), p. 56.

27. Mary Edmond, *Rare Sir William Davenant: Poet Laureate, Playwright, Civil War General, Restoration Theatre Manager* (1987), p. 93.

28. Ibid. In London, meanwhile, Parliament was to tear down the Globe theatre in 1644 to make way for housing.

29. *Mercurius Aulicus*, 30 July 1643. They arrived on 7 August – the same day as the first mob attack on Parliament.

30. Ralph Hopton to Prince Rupert, 15 August 1643, Warburton, p. 57.

31. *Mercurius Britanicus*, No. 2, 29 August–5 September 1643.
32. *Letters of Queen Henrietta Maria*, p. 225.
33. Clarendon, III, pp. 166, 167.
34. Ibid., p. 151.
35. Ibid., p. 156.
36. *Letters of Queen Henrietta Maria*, pp. 227–8.
37. Ibid.

Chapter 22: 'A distressed wandering princess'

1. Quoted in Georges Dethan, *The Young Mazarin* (1977), p. 144.
2. 'The Perfect diurnal', 2–9 October 1643, in *Letters of Queen Henrietta Maria*, ed. Mary Anne Everett Green (2009), pp. 228–9.
3. Ibid.
4. Ibid., p. 230. She was cross with Newcastle too: 'It is so long since I have heard tidings from you I fancy you believe we are all dead here.'
5. Dethan, p. 145.
6. CSPV 20 November 1643 (42).
7. *Journal of Sir Samuel Luke* (1950), p. 173; DS RN p. 153.
8. CSPV 20 November 1643 (42).
9. Clarendon, III, p. 196; Digby agreed that kings of England 'out of parliament have a limited, a circumscribed jurisdiction. But waited on by his parliament no monarch of the east is so absolute'; Leanda de Lisle, *White King* (2018), p. 41.
10. Clarendon, III, pp. 195, 196.
11. Ibid., pp. 184, 195, 196, 246.
12. Mary Edmond, *Rare Sir William Davenant: Poet Laureate, Playwright, Civil War General, Restoration Theatre Manager* (1987), p. 96.
13. *Journal of Sir Samuel Luke*, p. 222.
14. *Letters of Queen Henrietta Maria*, p. 235. Newcastle was made a marquess in October 1643.
15. Ibid., p. 238.

16. BL Add. MSS 18981, ff. 86–7, v; Marcus Trevor to Ormond, Shrewsbury, 13 April 1644.

17. *Letters of Charles I*, ed. Sir Charles Petrie (1935), p. 43.

18. *Letters of Queen Henrietta Maria*, p. 243.

19. Ibid., pp. 244, 245.

20. *Mercurius Aulicus*, 22 June 1644.

21. *Letters of Queen Henrietta Maria*, p. 248.

22. *Whitelocke Memorials* (1682) p. 88; Vernon F. Snow, *Essex the Rebel: Life of Robert Devereux, Third Earl of Essex, 1591–1646* (1970), p. 439.

23. CSPV 15 July 1644 (125).

24. *Letters of Queen Henrietta Maria*, p. 248.

25. Jacques-Bénigne Bossuet, 'Funeral Oration For Henriette-Marie of France, Queen of Great Britain', translated and introduced by Christopher Olaf Blum, Christendom Media (2004), https://media.christendom.edu/2004/12/funeral-oration-for-henriette-marie-of-france-queen-of-great-britain/.

26. *The Poetry of Anna Matilda* (1788), p. 122, quoting Waller's memoirs of 1657. Thanks to Mark Turnbull for drawing my attention to this anecdote.

27. *Letters of Queen Henrietta Maria*, p. 250.

28. CSPV 1644 (134).

29. Ibid.

30. CSPV 1644 (136).

31. *Letters of Queen Henrietta Maria*, p. 249.

32. CSPD 1644 (342); Earl of Warwick to Committee of Both Kingdoms, 11 July 1644.

33. J. R. Powell and E. K. Timings (eds), *Documents Relating to the Civil War: 1642–1648* (1963), p. 163.

34. Ibid.

35. Michelle Anne White, *Henrietta Maria and the English Civil Wars* (2017), p. 152.

36. *Gazette de France*, No. 103, 31 August 1644, available online.

37. White, pp. 142–4.

38. *Memoirs of Madame de Motteville on Anne of Austria and Her Court. With An Introduction By C.-A. Sainte-Beuve*, trans. Katharine P. Wormeley (2015), Vol. 1.

39. *Gazette de France*, No. 103, 31 August 1644; it was said that St Anne had appeared to a villager in March 1625 – just weeks before Henrietta Maria had left France. The figure had lit a candle on the site of a lost sixth-century shrine to Anne and asked for another to be built. In 1996 John Paul II said Mass for 160,000 people at this spot.

40. *Letters of Queen Henrietta Maria*, p. 252.

41. Ibid.

42. Ibid., p. 253.

43. Ibid.

44. *Diary of John Evelyn*, ed. E. S. de Beer (2006), p. 84.

45. *Letters of Queen Henrietta Maria*, p. 255.

46. Le Comte de Baillon, *Henriette-Marie de France, Reine d'Angleterre* (1877, reprint 2018), p. 219.

47. Jonathan Spangler, *Monsieur: Second Sons in the Monarchy of France 1550–1800* (2021), p. 188.

48. Thomas Birch, *The Court and Times of Charles I* (2 vols, 1848), Vol. 2, p. 359.

49. *Memoirs of Madame de Motteville*, Vol. 1, p. 118.

50. Ibid., p. 122.

51. Warwick had issued orders to the navy in May 1644 for the summary execution of any soldiers captured coming from Ireland (although six out of seven were English-born), and on 24 October Parliament gave legal sanction to the cold-blooded killing of any Catholic Irish. This was used as a pretext for killing anyone of any ethnicity suspected of being 'Catholic'. Many Lancastrians were, for example, Catholic.

52. CSPD 1644 (401–3).

Chapter 23: 'The violence of destiny'

1. Jacques-Bénigne Bossuet, 'Funeral Oration For Henriette-Marie of France, Queen of Great Britain', translated and introduced by Christopher Olaf Blum, Christendom Media (2004), https://media.christendom.edu/2004/12/funeral-oration-for-henriette-marie-of-france-queen-of-great-britain/.

2. *Memoirs of Madame de Motteville on Anne of Austria and Her Court. With An Introduction By C.-A. Sainte-Beuve*, trans. Katharine P. Wormeley (2015), Vol. 1, p. 122.

3. Steven Orso, 'Praising the Queen, The Decorations at the Royal Exequies for Isabela de Bourbon', *Art Bulletin*, Vol. 72, No. 1 (March 1990), p. 52.

4. Ibid., pp. 63, 64.

5. *Letters of Queen Henrietta Maria*, ed. Mary Anne Everett Green (2009), p. 260

6. Karen Britland, 'Exile or Homecoming', in P. Mansel and T. Riotte (eds), *Monarchy and Exile: The Politics of Legitimacy from Marie de' Medici to Wilhelm II* (2011), p. 124; Erin Griffey, *On Display: Henrietta Maria and the Materials of Magnificence at the Stuart Court* (2016), p. 166.

7. Griffey, pp. 164, 165, 166.

8. Simon Thurley, *Palaces of Revolution* (2021), pp. 169–70.

9. *Letters of Queen Henrietta Maria*, p. 353.

10. Ibid.

11. Bossuet, 'Funeral Oration'.

12. Glenn Foard, *Naseby: The Decisive Campaign* (2004), p. 289.

13. https://www.civilwarpetitions.ac.uk/blog/echoes-of-a-massacre-the-petition-of-bridget-rumney/.

14. Laura Lunger Knoppers, *Politicizing Domesticity from Henrietta Maria to Milton's Eve* (2011), p. 45.

15. Ibid., pp. 51–5.

16. Ibid., p. 63.

17. Britland, p. 126.

18. Bossuet, 'Funeral Oration'.
19. *Letters of Queen Henrietta Maria*, p. 328.
20. Mary Edmond, *Rare Sir William Davenant: Poet Laureate, Playwright, Civil War General, Restoration Theatre Manager* (1987), pp. 99, 100.
21. Philip A. Knachel, *England and the Fronde: The Impact of the English Civil War and Revolution in France* (1967), p. 30.
22. Knoppers, p. 63.
23. Edmond, p. 97.
24. CSPD 22 April 1645.
25. Michelle Anne White, *Henrietta Maria and the English Civil Wars* (2017), p. 155.
26. Britland, p. 125.
27. *Lettres de Henriette-Marie de France, reine d'Angleterre à sa soeur Christine, Duchesse de Savoie*, ed. Hermann Ferrero (1881), p. 67.
28. Thomas Birch, *The Court and Times of Charles I* (2 vols, 1848), Vol. 2, p. 409.
29. Linda Porter, *Royal Renegades: The Children of Charles I and the English Civil Wars* (2016), p. 141.
30. Edward Hyde, Earl of Clarendon (from 1661), quoted in Agnes Strickland, *Lives of the Tudor and Stuart Princesses* (1888), p. 384.
31. Birch, Vol. 2, p. 409.
32. *Memoirs of Mademoiselle de Montpensier (La Grande Mademoiselle)*, trans. P. J. Yarrow and William Brooks (2010), p. 18.
33. Ibid., p. 19.
34. His wife (Charles's almost-bride the Infanta Maria) had died in May 1646.
35. White, p. 185.
36. James II, *His Majesty's letter to the Lords and Others of his Privy Council* (1689); Clare Jackson, *Devil-Land: England Under Seige 1588–1688* (2021), p. 489.
37. John Ashburnham, *A Narrative* (1830), Vol. 2, p. 120.
38. *Letters of Queen Henrietta Maria*, p. 345.

Chapter 24: 'The last act of this tragedy'

1. It had been a gift from Cardinal Barberini, who had returned to Rome in February.
2. *Memoirs of Madame de Motteville on Anne of Austria and Her Court. With An Introduction By C.-A. Sainte-Beuve*, trans. Katharine P. Wormeley (2015), Vol. 1, p. 286; Erin Griffey, *On Display: Henrietta Maria and the Materials of Magnificence at the Stuart Court* (2016), p. 168. Barberini was in Paris from 1646 until February 1648.
3. *Memoirs of Madame de Motteville*, Vol. 1, p. 286.
4. *Lettres de Henriette-Marie de France, reine d'Angleterre à sa soeur Christine, Duchesse de Savoie*, ed. Hermann Ferrero (1881), p. 68.
5. Philip A. Knachel, *England and the Fronde: The Impact of the English Civil War and Revolution in France* (1967), p. 35.
6. Ibid., p. 39.
7. *Memoirs of Madame de Motteville*, Vol. 1, p. 286.
8. Knachel, p. 117.
9. Geoffrey Parker, *Global Crisis: War, Climate Change and Catastrophe in the Seventeenth Century* (2014), p. 310.
10. *My Dearest Minette: Letters Between Charles II and His Sister Henrietta, Duchesse d'Orleans*, ed. Ruth Norrington (1996), p. 25.
11. *Letters of Queen Henrietta Maria*, ed. Mary Anne Everett Green (2009), p. 348.
12. Leanda de Lisle, *White King* (2018), p. 253.
13. Knachel, pp. 117–18.
14. 19 February in the French calendar.
15. Thomas Birch, *The Court and Times of Charles I* (2 vols, 1848), Vol. 2, p. 382.
16. Ibid.
17. *Memoirs of Madame de Motteville*, Vol. 2, p. 90.
18. Ibid. The fifteen-year-old James, who had been with his father for much of the Civil War, never spoke publicly about his father's death, but he would often remind Charles II what happened after their father agreed to the execution of Strafford.

19. *Letters of Queen Henrietta Maria*, p. 357.
20. Ibid., pp. 357–8.
21. Henrietta Maria politely declined the pensions, despite her dire circumstances. Knachel, p. 222.
22. Ibid., p. 107.
23. Birch, Vol. 2, p. 380.
24. For further details see de Lisle, pp. 283–4.
25. Jason McElligott and David L. Smith (eds), *Royalists and Royalism during the English Civil Wars* (2011), p. 215.
26. *Letters of Queen Henrietta Maria*, pp. 351–8.
27. Ibid.
28. Ibid.
29. It was recorded that she intended to wait for Charles's consent – which she would never have got – and that instruction began when 'the sparks of reason began to glimmer'. Seven is the age of reason. Henrietta Anne turned five in 1649. Birch, Vol. 2, pp. 410–11.
30. *Letters of Queen Henrietta Maria*, pp. 351–8.
31. *Memoirs of Mademoiselle de Montpensier (La Grande Mademoiselle)*, trans. P. J. Yarrow and William Brooks (2010), p. 33.
32. *Letters of Queen Henrietta Maria*, pp. 351–8.
33. *Charles I in 1646: Letters of King Charles the First to Queen Henrietta Maria* (2015), p. 68.
34. *The Eikon Basilike; The Pourtraecture of His Sacred Majestie in His Solitudes and Sufferings*, ed. John Gauden (2016), pp. 25–6.

Chapter 25: 'No other rainbow'

1. *The Diary of John Evelyn*, ed. E. S. de Beer (1959), p. 249.
2. *Memoirs of Mademoiselle de Montpensier (La Grande Mademoiselle)*, trans. P. J. Yarrow and William Brooks (2010), p. 34.
3. Clarendon, V, p. 50.
4. Ibid.
5. *Lettres de Henriette-Marie de France, reine d'Angleterre à sa sœur Christine, Duchesse de Savoie*, ed. Hermann Ferrero (1881), p. 74.

6. Sarah Poynting, *A Critical Edition of Walter Montagu's The Shepherds' Paradise, Acts 1–3*, DPhil thesis, University of Oxford (2 vols, 2000), Vol. 1, p. 41.

7. *Diary of John Evelyn*, p. 250. Three thousand were killed. Cromwell insisted they merited it as Catholic rebels. The truth was that these were Ormond's men – Protestants for the most part – and the officers largely English. The surrendered commander, Sir Arthur Aston, who hailed from Cheshire, was, however, a Catholic and suffered a particularly gruesome death – his brains were beaten out with his wooden leg. A similar vindictiveness was shown to Catholic clergy, who were hunted down and killed in cold blood. Cromwell had form in this regard, in the murder of priests caught at the siege of Basing House in the summer of 1645.

8. They were pawned in February 1650 and described as Francis Clein's 'masterpiece'. Erin Griffey, *On Display: Henrietta Maria and the Materials of Magnificence at the Stuart Court* (2016), p. 168.

9. The man appointed as the children's guardian, Anthony Mildmay, had been their father's jailor at Carisbrooke and had detested the king. He was currently involved in drawing up inventories of royal goods for sale. These would later include a jewel that Elizabeth had given to Lucy Carlisle's sister, Lady Leicester.

10. *Lettres de Henriette-Marie de France*, pp. 93–4.

11. Especially when supercharged by royalty: the leading example of this in France was set by Henrietta Maria's legitimised half-sister, Mother John the Baptist de Bourbon, who was abbess of the double convent and monastery of Fontevrault and wielded an autonomy not far removed from that of a bishop. Monks would occasionally rebel against Mother John the Baptist's rule. Once two ran away to the Benedictines, but Mother John the Baptist soon them brought back to heel. Even on her deathbed she remained determined that men remembered their place, correcting the priest who called her 'sister' while giving her the last sacraments: 'Say "mother", the rule commands you to,' the dying

nun admonished him; Stephanie Marie Seery-Murphy, 'Hazarding the Queen: Henrietta Maria, Religious Controversy and the Construction of a Rhetorical Figure', PhD thesis, Claremont Graduate University (2008), pp. 267–8.

12. Ibid., p. 247.
13. Ibid., p. 260.
14. *Letters of Queen Henrietta Maria*, ed. Mary Anne Everett Green (2009), p. 356.
15. Thomas Birch, *The Court and Times of Charles I* (2 vols, 1848), Vol. 2, p. 394.
16. In January 1651.
17. *Memoirs of Mademoiselle de Montpensier*, pp. 39–40.
18. She hoped to marry James to a daughter of the Duke of Longueville, but Louis XIV's government had no desire to see her father's arrogance inflated by a marriage to the heir to the English throne, while some of the royalist exiles didn't think her rich enough, so it was destined to founder.
19. *Letters of Queen Henrietta Maria*, p. 373.
20. *Memoirs of Mademoiselle de Montpensier*, pp. 40–1.
21. *The Memoirs of James II*, trans. A. Lytton Sells (1962), p. 69.
22. *Lettres de Henriette-Marie de France*, pp. 90, 100.
23. Edward Hyde, Earl of Clarendon (from 1661), quoted in 'James II & VII', *ODNB*.
24. *Lettres de Henriette-Marie de France*, p. 103.
25. Le Comte de Baillon, *Henriette-Marie de France, Reine d'Angleterre* (1877, reprint 2018), p. 561; trade agreements were made between the Protectorate and the United Provinces, Sweden and Denmark–Norway in 1654.
26. *Journal de Jean Vallier, Vol. 4: Maître d'Hôtel du Roi (1648–1657); 1 Août 1652–31 Décembre 1653* (2019), pp. 399–400.
27. Griffey, p. 168.
28. It described her as a virtuous princess whose sorrows had prompted her to found the convent at Chaillot; Griffey, pp. 173–5.

29. Nicole Greenspan, 'Public Scandal, Political Controversy, and Familial Conflict in the Stuart Courts in Exile: The Struggle to Convert the Duke of Gloucester in 1654', *Albion: A Quarterly Journal Concerned with British Studies*, Vol. 35, No. 3 (Autumn 2003), pp. 420, 421.

30. Ibid., p. 407.

31. Ibid., p. 408.

32. *Letters of Queen Henrietta Maria*, p. 378.

33. Griffey, p. 171; *Lettres de Henriette-Marie de France*, p. 112.

34. In March 1656 Charles held talks in Brussels with King Philip IV's viceroy in the Spanish Netherlands. On 2 April they agreed an offensive and defensive alliance in which Charles promised to restore Jamaica, help to recover Portugal, suspend laws against Catholics, and implement Ormond's 1649 treaty with the Irish, all in return for 6,000 troops for the invasion of England.

35. Linda Porter, *Royal Renegades: The Children of Charles I and the English Civil Wars* (2016), p. 279.

36. Agnes Strickland, *Lives of the Tudor and Stuart Princesses* (1888), p. 308.

37. Ibid.

38. Henrietta Maria did not forget to advertise her hope of converting her Protestant daughter, taking her to visit her favourite convents – an experience that Mary described as leaving her 'a little weary'. Strickland, p. 312; *Memoirs of Mademoiselle de Montpensier*, pp. 88, 113, 114.

39. Ibid.

40. *Letters of Queen Henrietta Maria*, p. 388.

Chapter 26: 'The phoenix of our times'

1. *Letters of Queen Henrietta Maria*, ed. Mary Anne Everett Green (2009), p. 388; *Lettres de Henriette-Marie de France, reine d'Angleterre à sa soeur Christine, Duchesse de Savoie*, ed. Hermann Ferrero (1881), p. 112.

2. *Memoirs of Mademoiselle de Montpensier (La Grande Mademoiselle)*, trans. P. J. Yarrow and William Brooks (2010), p. 123.

3. *Letters of Queen Henrietta Maria*, p. 389.

4. Ibid., p. 409.

5. *My Dearest Minette: Letters Between Charles II and His Sister Henrietta, Duchesse d'Orleans*, ed. Ruth Norrington (1996), p. 31.

6. Ibid., p. 29.

7. Ibid., p. 30.

8. Karen Britland, 'Exile or Homecoming', in P. Mansel and T. Riotte (eds), *Monarchy and Exile: The Politics of Legitimacy from Marie de' Medici to Wilhelm II* (2011), p. 137.

9. *The Memoirs of Sir John Reresby, Written By Himself*, ed. J. J. Cartwright (2015), p. 45.

10. *My Dearest Minette*, pp. 34, 35.

11. *Lettres de Henriette-Marie de France*, p. 121.

12. *The Diary of Samuel Pepys: Volume 1, 1660*, eds. Robert Latham and William Matthews (1971), p. 143.

13. *Letters of Queen Henrietta Maria*, p. 403.

14. Marie-Madeleine Pioche de La Vergne, Comtesse de La Fayette (1634–1693), quoted in *My Dearest Minette*, p. 39.

15. *Lettres de Henriette-Marie de France*, p. 121.

16. Ibid., p. 124.

17. Ibid.

18. 23 October 1660, HMC Eighth Report, Appendix II, p. 657; Sarah Poynting, *A Critical Edition of Walter Montagu's The Shepherds' Paradise, Acts 1–3*, DPhil thesis, University of Oxford (2 vols, 2000), Vol. 1, p. 49.

19. There was nothing to suggest which recipes she preferred: that would have to wait for a later book by one of the contributors, Kenelm Digby. He reported she liked suppers of mutton, beef and veal broth, flavoured with orange or lemon citrus. This sounds a lot nicer than some of the recipes suggested by the court ladies in

Wat's book, especially those with ingredients that included crab eyes and ground white dog turd.

20. John Dauncey, *The History of the Thrice Illustrious Princess Henrietta Maria de Bourbon, Queen of England* (1660).

21. Erin Griffey, *On Display: Henrietta Maria and the Materials of Magnificence at the Stuart Court* (2016), p. 186.

22. Erin Griffey, 'Restoring Henrietta Maria's English Household in the 1660s: Continuity, Kinship and Clientage', *Court Historian*, published online 6 September 2021.

23. Amongst them was the French Huguenot, Charlotte, Countess of Derby whom she had never got on with before the Civil War. Charlotte had disapproved of Henrietta Maria's religion and the tone of the court, but had proved to be a loyal and passionate supporter of the royalist cause. It was she who had led the defence of the family seat, Lathom House, and what she had lacked in military experience, she made up for in determination and charisma, skilfully motivating her troops. The countess had been labelled a popish whore, despite her Calvinism, and much like Henrietta Maria was condemned as a generalissima, 'an admirable expert in sallying against men as well as dallying'. B. L. Thomason, *Tracts, E44 (18), The Spie.*

24. HMC de L'Isle and Dudley MSS, VI, p. 623.

25. Susan's bowels were surely never buried with her brother, the murdered George Villiers, Duke of Buckingham, as she had hoped, and as is claimed on the inscription on his tomb (since she died in France), but she would have been pleased that the family were fully reconciled with the Stuarts. Cecilia Mary Clifford Feilding Denbigh, *Royalist Father and Roundhead Son; Being the Memoirs of the First and Second Earls of Denbigh, 1600–1675* (1915), p. 296.

26. Mary Edmond, *Rare Sir William Davenant: Poet Laureate, Playwright, Civil War General, Restoration Theatre Manager* (1987), p. 147.

27. *Diary of Samuel Pepys: Volume 1, 1660*, p. 298.

28. Gesa Stedman, *Cultural Exchange in Seventeenth-Century France and England* (2013), p. 66.

29. *Diary of Samuel Pepys: Volume 1, 1660*, p. 299.

30. Jerry Brotton, 'The Art of Restoration: King Charles II and the Restitution of the English Royal Art Collection', *Court Historian*, 10:2 (2005), p. 124.

31. Ibid., pp. 118–19.

32. *The Diary of John Evelyn*, ed. E. S. de Beer (1959), p. 378.

33. What Mary may not have known was that Oliver Cromwell was also buried there, in the wall of what remained of the damaged Henry VII Chapel. Later that month Parliament resolved to disinter his corpse and perform a posthumous execution for treason.

34. CSPV 7 January 1661 (261).

35. *Letters of Queen Henrietta Maria*, p. 409.

36. CSPV 28 January 1661 (274).

37. For the other passengers the stopover had been 'extremely dull'. A Frenchman complained Portsmouth had 'nothing agreeable about it save a fine harbour'. Thomas Birch, *The Court and Times of Charles I* (2 vols, 1848), Vol. 2, p. 421. The young Duke of Buckingham, whose father had been murdered in the town in 1629, had spent his time gambling with the Earl of Sandwich, who was captain of the flotilla, but now refused to pay Sandwich his winnings. At Le Havre Henrietta Maria and Wat had to intervene personally to prevent a duel, 'waylaying them in their lodgings till the difference was made up'. *The Diary of Samuel Pepys: Volume 2, 1661*, eds. Robert Latham and William Matthews (1971), p. 33.

38. Birch, Vol. 2, p. 422.

Chapter 27: The Last Conspiracy

1. Thomas Birch, *The Court and Times of Charles I* (2 vols, 1848), Vol. 2, p. 424.

2. Linda Porter, *Royal Renegades: The Children of Charles I and the English Civil Wars* (2016), p. 351.

3. It states she 'shall enjoy the free exercise of the Roman Catholic religion, and to that purpose shall have a Chapel, or some other place set apart for the exercise thereof, in all the Royal Palaces where she shall at any time reside, in as full a manner, to all intents and purposes, *as the Queen Mother now living enjoyed the same*, and shall have such Chaplains and Ecclesiastical Persons in number and quality about her, *as the said Queen Mother hath had*, with the same privileges and immunities [my italics]. And the King of Great Britain promiseth not to disquiet or disturb, the said lady Infanta his Wife, in anything appertaining to religion or conscience.' David Baldwin, 'The Politico-Religious Usage of the Queen's Chapel, 1623–1688', MA thesis, Durham University (1999), p. 83.

4. Registered as 22 May in accordance with maritime law: in the seventeenth century mariners recorded the events of the twenty-four-hour day from midday to midday, since the day was defined by reference to the sun. Each of the twenty-four-hour periods was assigned a date twelve hours in advance of the ordinary calendar date. 22 May is the date entered in the Register of the Cathedral Church of St Thomas of Canterbury, because the ceremony took place in the Governor's Lodging, adjacent to the garrison's Domus Dei church, overlooking the quayside. In maritime law the Governor's Lodging had the status of a ship. Baldwin, p. 84.

5. Gilbert Burnet, *Bishop Burnet's History of His Own Time from the Restoration of King Charles*, Vol. 1 (1818), pp. 85, 192.

6. CSPV 1661–4 (242).

7. Birch, Vol. 2, p. 428.

8. Marie de' Medici had been depicted the same way in an engraving celebrating her entry into London. Erin Griffey, *On Display: Henrietta Maria and the Materials of Magnificence at the Stuart Court* (2016), p. 197.

9. *The Diary of John Evelyn*, ed. E. S. de Beer (1959), 22 October 1662, p. 405.

10. *The Diary of Samuel Pepys: Volume 3, 1662*, eds. Robert Latham and William Matthews (1971), pp. 191, 299.

11. Ibid., p. 191.

12. Ibid, pp. 191, 299.

13. *Lettres de Henriette-Marie de France, reine d'Angleterre à sa soeur Christine, Duchesse de Savoie*, ed. Hermann Ferrero (1881), pp. 126, 127.

14. *The Diary of Samuel Pepys: Volume 4, 1663*, eds. Robert Latham and William Matthews (1971), p. 48.

15. *Lettres de Henriette-Marie de France*, p. 135.

16. These rumours about Jermyn – repeated by Pepys amongst others – are still accepted in some quarters so it is worth pointing out a few reasons why this is ridiculous. A marriage to a Protestant would have required a papal dispensation. None was asked for. Henrietta Maria was far less tolerant of having Protestants serving her after Charles I's death. Marrying one was unthinkable. What kind of example would that have set to future converts? Nor would a queen who set such store on her dignity as Charles I's widow, and on being Henry IV's daughter, have wished to be the wife of a stout, red-faced commoner. He had been a loyal servant, that was all. *Diary of Samuel Pepys: Volume 3, 1662*, p. 303.

17. Erin Griffey, 'Restoring Henrietta Maria's English Household in the 1660s: Continuity, Kinship and Clientage', *Court Historian*, published online 6 September 2021.

18. George Smeeton, *The Life and Death of Henrietta Maria de Bourbon: Queen to That Blessed King and Martyr, Charles I, Mother to His Late Glorious Majesty and Most Gracious Sovereign, James II* (1685), p. 14.

19. *The Diary of Samuel Pepys: Volume 5, 1664*, eds Robert Latham and William Matthews (1971), p. 63.

20. Ibid., p. 300.

21. Ibid., p. 63.

22. Baldwin, p. 96. 'Some of the Church of England loved to magnify the sacrament in an extraordinary manner, affirming the real presence, only blaming the Church of Rome for defining the manner of it; saying Christ was present in the most unconceivable manner. This was so much the mode, that the King and all the Court went into it: so the king upon some raillery about transubstantiation, asked Sir Elisha if he believed it. He answered he could not well tell; but he was sure the Church of England believed it. And when the King seemed amazed at that, he replied, do not you believe that Christ is present in the most unconceivable manner? Which the King granted; then said he, that is just transubstantiation – the most unconceivable thing that was ever yet invented . . .' Transubstantiation: at the moment of consecration Christ is present in every element of the blood and wine, and the very moment of his crucifixion is relived.

23. *Diary of Samuel Pepys: Volume 5, 1664*, p. 63.

24. This 'little Chinese lad' was aged fourteen or fifteen when he arrived in London on an English boat from the East Indies, and was described as 'of a gentle disposition, well made and of good figure'. She incorporated him into her household and had him given instruction. The boy was given the Christian name Peter at his baptism, with d'Aubigny as co-godparent. 'Thus,' one witness recalled, 'the young Chinese so far distant from his country, deprived of his own father and mother, had on earth for his spiritual father, one of the most illustrious gentlemen of England, and for a mother a mighty queen'. Birch, Vol. 2, pp. 439–40. Charles was lobbying the Pope for d'Aubigny to be made a cardinal. He died in France in 1665, but the almoner to Catherine of Braganza, Philip Howard, was made a cardinal in 1673.

25. The Franciscan Christopher Davenport, who had pleased Charles I with such arguments in the 1630s, was still associated with

Somerset House and he was joined by another Franciscan, Vincent Canes, who described himself as 'a friend to men of all religions'.

26. Quoted in Griffey, *On Display*, p. 203.
27. She had told her sister in 1663 that she hoped to go to Bourbon-l'Archambault for her health, but the Catholics under her protection begged her not to leave.
28. Jerry Brotton, 'The Art of Restoration: King Charles II and the Restitution of the English Royal Art Collection', *Court Historian*, 10:2 (2005), pp. 132, 133.
29. Birch, Vol. 2, p. 453.
30. Ibid., p. 456.
31. Ibid., p. 465; a reception had been given for her at the palace of Versailles on her return.
32. *Memoirs of Madame de Motteville on Anne of Austria and Her Court. With An Introduction By C.-A. Sainte-Beuve*, trans. Katharine P. Wormeley (2015), Vol. 1, p. 122.
33. Birch, Vol. 2, p. 455.
34. Griffey, *On Display*, p. 221.
35. *Memoirs of Madame de Motteville*, Vol. 1, p. 122.
36. It was a side of her that had been observed in the 1630s, when it was noted 'that she is both very careful and nobly kind to those Servants, who are near her person'; 'A Character of the Queen of Great Britain, composed during the exile of Marie de' Medici and before the death of Van Dyck, composed by a leading Catholic', Louvre, Manuscripts Dept, Côté Anglais, 57.
37. CSPV 1666–8 (63).
38. Griffey, *On Display*, p. 224.
39. Clare Jackson, *Charles II* (2016), pp. 28–9.
40. BL Add. MSS 65, 138, ff. 83–4. Paper by Clifford concerning possible English engagement in war with the Dutch endorsed by him 'sent to Madame Jan. 24 1669/70 to be translated by Mr Montagu and deliver [to Louis XIV]'.

41. As described by Kenelm Digby.
42. Birch, Vol. 2, pp. 467–8. After Henry IV's murder a witness saw priests dutifully, but belatedly, carrying out the Catholic Church's last rites, offered to the dying. It seems possible that Henrietta Maria was also already dead.

Chapter 28: The Lessons of Failure

1. CSPV 20 September 1669 (113).
2. CSPV 27 September 1669 (118).
3. Quoted in David Womersley, *James II: The Last Catholic King* (2019), p. 29.
4. Erin Griffey, *On Display: Henrietta Maria and the Materials of Magnificence at the Stuart Court* (2016), p. 40.
5. Stephanie Marie Seery-Murphy, 'Hazarding the Queen: Henrietta Maria, Religious Controversy and the Construction of a Rhetorical Figure', PhD thesis, Claremont Graduate University (2008), p. 252.
6. Ibid., pp. 251, 253, 254.
7. Wat Montagu, who as her almoner was in charge of her chapel, was also involved.
8. Erin Griffey, 'Picturing Confessional Politics at the Stuart Court', *Journal of Religious History*, Issue 4 (2020), p. 474.
9. Jacques-Bénigne Bossuet, quoted in Griffey, *On Display*, p. 225.
10. Catholics continued to be barred from the office of Lord Chancellor until 1974.
11. Griffey, 'Picturing Confessional Politics', p. 476.
12. Another man who narrowly missed the noose was Henrietta Maria's Master of the Horse, Lord Arundell of Wardour, who pointed out that it didn't make much sense for Catholics to plot to kill a king who was considered sympathetic to them.
13. Ronald Hutton, *Charles the Second, King of England, Scotland and Ireland* (1989), p. 93.

14. George Savile, Marquess of Halifax, quoted in Gesa Stedman, *Cultural Exchange in Seventeenth-Century France and England* (2013), p. 66.

Postscript

1. *Letters of Queen Henrietta Maria*, ed. Mary Anne Everett Green (2009), p. 130.
2. CSPV, 1642–3 (259).

INDEX